Ancestral Maya Economies in Archaeological Perspective

The decipherment of Maya hieroglyphs has enabled scholars to better understand Classic society, but many aspects of this ancestral civilization remain shrouded in mystery, particularly forms of economic integration. How were farmers, artisans, and rulers integrated? How did a tropical forest ecology coexist for more than a thousand years with the construction of monumental shrines and palaces? In this study, Patricia A. McAnany suggests that economic integration can best be understood by foregrounding the ritual and social practices of ancestral Maya societies and following the threads of entanglement through the realms of landscape, identity, gender, religion, and power.

The first comprehensive treatment of ancestral Maya economies, this book brings an array of evidence – archaeological, epigraphic, ethnohistorical, and ethnographic – to bear on the question of economic integration. In the process, McAnany demonstrates interconnectivity between ritual practice and indigenous ecologies, gendered labor, and the construction of colossal architecture. Examining Maya royalty as a kind of social speciation, the author shows the fundamentality of social difference in ancestral Maya societies. The pervasiveness of artisan production is understood in terms of identity – both personal and community-wide. Her analysis of royal iconography and hieroglyphic texts provides evidence of a political economy dominated by tribute extraction, thus lifting the veil of opacity over the financing of palace economies. Written in an engaging and accessible style, this book interprets Maya economies in reference to contemporary theories of social practice, gender, actor networks, inalienable goods, materiality, hierarchy, indigenous ecologies, and strategies of state finance.

Patricia A. McAnany is Kenan Eminent Professor in the Department of Anthropology at the University of North Carolina, Chapel Hill, and past President of the Society for Economic Anthropology. She has received fellowships from the National Endowment for the Humanities, Dumbarton Oaks, and the Radcliffe Institute for Advanced Study at Harvard University. Dr. McAnany is the principal investigator of the Maya Area Cultural Heritage Initiative and also of the Xibun Archaeological Research Project (the latter field site in Belize, Central America). She is the author of *Living with the Ancestors: Kinship and Kingship in Ancient Maya Society* and editor of *K'axob: Ritual Work and Family in an Ancient Maya Village* and *Sacred Landscape and Settlement in the Sibun River Valley.*

Ancestral Maya Economies in Archaeological Perspective

PATRICIA A. McANANY
University of North Carolina, Chapel Hill

CAMBRIDGE
UNIVERSITY PRESS

CAMBRIDGE UNIVERSITY PRESS
Cambridge, New York, Melbourne, Madrid, Cape Town, Singapore,
São Paulo, Delhi, Dubai, Tokyo

Cambridge University Press
32 Avenue of the Americas, New York, NY 10013-2473, USA

www.cambridge.org
Information on this title: www.cambridge.org/9780521895187

First published 2010

Printed in the United States of America

A catalog record for this publication is available from the British Library.

Library of Congress Cataloging in Publication data
McAnany, Patricia Ann.
Ancestral Maya economies in archaeological perspective / Patricia McAnany.
p. cm.
Includes bibliographical references and index.
ISBN 978-0-521-89518-7 (hbk.)
1. Mayas – Economic conditions. 2. Mayas – Antiquities.
3. Mexico – Antiquities. 4. Central America – Antiquities.
5. Mexico – Economic conditions. 6. Central America – Economic
conditions. 7. Economic history – To 500. I. Title.
F1435.3.E27M395 2009
972.81'016–dc22 2009011870

ISBN 978-0-521-89518-7 Hardback

For my mother, Adele, who gave unconditional love to her six children and taught us to strive for perfection wrought from sustained focus

Contents

List of Figures

Preface and Acknowledgments

Sometimes it takes several attempts before a book takes shape and begins to write itself. In this instance, the gestation period has been seventeen years. My dissertation topic, stone tool acquisition and use (McAnany 1986), whetted my appetite for understanding economic process, and I longed to synthesize what I had learned from excavations in dwellings around Pulltrouser Swamp with the larger story of Maya economic practice. I had the opportunity to do that in 1991–1992, as a resident Fellow at Dumbarton Oaks. At that time and as a result of distinctive mortuary deposits that we had excavated at K'axob in Belize, I became deeply engrossed in the topic of ancestor veneration. Elizabeth Boone, then director of Pre-Columbian Studies, consented to my changing the topic of my project. *Living with the Ancestors* (McAnany 1995, second edition to be published by Cambridge University Press) resulted from that period of research. In retrospect, the shifting of gears was more than fortuitous. In 1991, I lacked a perspective that would have resonated with Maya economic practice; I had planned a book similar to the tomes of Old World civilizations such as Diakonoff (1969) or Oppenheim (1964) on ancient Mesopotamia or, more recently, Greene (1986) on the Roman economy. Such studies tended to isolate an economic sector from other parts of society, often relying on a corpus of ancient texts conjoined to various degrees with archaeological information.

While researching *Living with the Ancestors,* I learned of the central role of mortuary ritual in many traditional societies and how ritual practice provides a matrix through which people cooperate and struggle through stressful and uncertain, as well as celebratory, times. It became more and more obvious that even fundamental economic processes – such as weaving, gardening, or making stone tools – were entangled with ritual practice that not only stabilized production and reproduction but also provided space for radical transformation. It was the sociality of ritual practice that imbued production with profound meaning and contoured the social identity of those undertaking production activities. I realized that in order to understand Maya economic processes, I would need to embrace the entanglement of social and ritual practices with production rather than artificially carve out an economic sector as is often done in studies of archaic states that are inspired by the "cultural logic" of Western-style capitalism. With this integrated perspective in place, there remained another thorny issue that needed to be resolved.

Students of social theory have grappled with the issue of "class" and its instrumentality in analytical perspective. I place class in quotation marks because it is far from an unproblematic term. But it suffices here to characterize a society in which there were hierarchically structured sectors inhabited by people with different interests, degrees of influence, power to effect agency, and resources at their disposal. Archaeologists often characterize study of this type of situation as "top down" (focusing on elites and power brokers) or "bottom up" (framed on primary producers and their negotiations with those in power). A real understanding can be achieved only by synthesizing the two perspectives and by moving away from a simplistic "dominator/dominated" approach to archaic states to a study of the "diversity of responses to situational and institutional inequality" (Lohse and Gonlin 2007:xxxiv). Practice and structuration approaches pioneered by Bourdieu (1977, 1990) and Giddens (1984) provide a framework with which to tear down the divide and focus on the dialogue, the negotiations, the practices of both the powerful and the not-so-powerful. Differential archaeological visibility can frustrate the desire to include all agents in a study of the Maya past, but with a perspective in place to do so, efforts hopefully will yield a closer approximation of life as it was lived in the Maya lowlands in the two millennia before and after the start of the Common Era. Another perspective, that of *thing* theory or materiality (Latour 2005; Miller 2005, among others) provides a powerful way to conceptualize bidirectional relations between people and their material "record"; I employ this perspective throughout this study.

In December 2004, I was awarded a National Endowment for the Humanities fellowship, which provided a second opportunity to write a book on ancestral Maya economies – one that focused on the threads of entanglement that knit together social and ritual practice with considerations of power, identity, and materiality. The NEH fellowship was conjoined with a sabbatical from Boston University; with both, I was able to spend calendar year 2005 away from the classroom and committee assignments. I cannot express sufficient gratitude to NEH for providing me with the luxury of time to develop my ideas and commit them to print.

For nearly twenty years, the Department of Archaeology at Boston University served as my home base and provided the intellectual and physical space for the maturation of my research and ideas about ancestral Maya societies. Although the seat of much struggle and contestation over university policies and faculty valuation, my colleagues within the Department of Archaeology were without parallel. Boston University also attracted many talented and dedicated students of archaeology at both the graduate and undergraduate levels. These students worked closely with me in field and laboratory research, and I will be forever grateful for their enthusiasm and keen insights. Since 2008, the University of North Carolina at Chapel Hill has been my academic home. My fellow faculty members at Chapel Hill have been exceptionally collegial and supportive of my human frailties. By arranging time away from teaching, Anthropology Chair Paul Leslie indulged my single-minded desire to complete final revisions of this book before the end of the current Maya calendrical cycle. Many Maya colleagues provided valuable published and unpublished data and images that helped to form and shape my ideas, notably Miguel Aguilera, George Bey, Mark Brenner, Jason Curtis, Tomás Gallareta Negrón, Elizabeth Graham, David Hodell, Allan Maca, Simon Martin, Marilyn Masson, Robert Rosenswig, and David Stuart. I wish to thank Stephen D. Houston for innumerable suggestions and incomparable insights on Maya epigraphy. A seminar on ritual economy held in March 2005, sponsored by the Cotsen Institute at UCLA, provided a venue for important feedback on this book, particularly on the topics of "feeding" a hungry landscape (Chapter 3) and the naturalized authority of the royal court (Chapter 6). For his support of the conference, I wish to thank the director of the Cotsen, Charles Stanish – *maestro* of economic anthropology and source of great ideas – and Julia Sanchez, then assistant director of the Cotsen Institute. I benefited greatly from the free exchange of ideas with my co-organizer – E. Christian Wells – and the session participants: E. Paul Durrenberger, Rhoda Halperin, Susan Kus, Walter Little, John Monaghan, Jerry Sabloff, Alan Sandstrom, Katherine Spielmann, and our unofficial but honored participants, Cathy Costin, Colin Renfrew, and Lothar Von Falkenhausen. Thanks to Ian Hodder for urging me to finish this book while also serving as a reminder that one cannot sacrifice the richness of contextual detail when writing a synthetic narrative. I have worked to balance the two.

Many persons and institutions were generous and provided help with the time-consuming process of securing images and permission to reproduce images; they include Sheldon Annis, Tomas Barrientos (Edwin Shook Archive), Oswaldo Chinchilla, Barbara Fash (Harvard Peabody Museum), Thomas W. Killion, Walter E. Little, Matthew Looper, Michael Love, Sandra Noble (FAMSI), Jorge Perez de Lara, Ruben Reina and Robert Hill, and Dennis Tedlock. Along with the intellectual nurturing that I received from colleagues, the following institutions provided financial support: National Endowment for the Humanities, National Science Foundation (by way of several research grants), Boston University Division of International Programs for support of field research, and the Ahau Foundation (Peter D. and Alexandra Harrison). Josh Feola, Satoru Murata, and Pablo Robles provided assistance with the preparation of graphics. Many thanks to Adam Kaeding for compiling the index. Shoshaunna Parks, along with members of the Maya Area Cultural Heritage Initiative (www.machiproject.org) that works to provide descendent Maya people with access to information about their deep history, directed field operations ably even when I could not give full attention to MACHI. To my partner, Peter D. Joyce, I will be forever grateful for the loving care and feeding that he provided and his endless tolerance for scholars who write books that inevitably contain a colon in the title.

This book is dedicated to my mother, Adèle M. Waser McAnany (1924–2007), who reared me as an orthodox Catholic and provided me with an intimate lived experience of the profound manner in which ritual practice is entangled with economic process.

1

The Materiality of Practice in Ancestral Maya Economies

Economies are strange beasts; in the idiom of The Market, they are said to perform, to be bullish or bearlike. Although few living in the twenty-first century conceive of the market in true animistic terms, the power, the prevalence, the fundamentality of market capitalism within our society imbue it with a vitality that is conducive to animistic tropes. Economies are foundational: humans cannot live by bread alone, but, without bread (or tortillas), humans would starve. Economies are about more than the manner by which humans go about feeding, clothing, and housing themselves; economies also are fundamentally social entities; there is nothing "natural" about economic practice (although some rational choice economist might disagree). From a perspective that is so abstract as to be practically meaningless, we can assert that all economies are organized around production, exchange, and consumption, but radical differences become readily apparent as one drills down and begins to examine economic practice on a human scale – the ethos and social relations of production, the means and motivations behind the circulation of goods, and the tempo and logic that undergird the consumption and replacement of goods. When one moves around the space–time continuum beyond market capitalism, as we do in this study, the extent to which sectors of this tripartite scheme differ from capitalism becomes so great as to render them easily misinterpreted (as often has been the case in the Maya region). With such profound variability to embrace, studies of "cultural economies" (Halperin 1994:1) or the "social structures of the economy" (Bourdieu 2005) have come into their own and provide us with guideposts as we move into a terrain in which the logic of capitalism may be irrelevant.

Geertz (1973:5) used an arachnid trope for culture, referring to it as a "web of significance," a totalizing yet permeable membrane that envelopes and is created and modified by individual agents and the societies they constitute. Even though this metaphor provides a vivid, visual image of this pervasive yet elusive thing called culture, here I would like to stress a more abstract quality of culture – its logical properties. By the term "logical properties," I am not referring solely or even mostly to the rules and norms of culture (although they do exist) but rather to the way in which everyday experience is lived in reference to a socially and culturally constructed realm – a "figured world" to borrow a term from Dorothy Holland and colleagues (1998:52). In no way is cultural logic divorced from daily economic practice; in fact, cultural logic and economic practice are irrevocably married with scant chance of separation (see Fischer 2001). In an astute analysis of postmodernism, Jameson (1991:6) attempts to capture the logic of late capitalism by characterizing it as "a dominant cultural logic or hegemonic norm ... the force field in which very different kinds of cultural impulses ... must make their way." Whether you prefer to think of culture as a sticky spider web or an inescapable force field, it is clear that cultural modes of reasoning undergird action and cannot be separated from economic practice. Moreover, we can expect that variations in cultural logic within and among societies will produce highly variable economic practices in both a fundamental and a situational sense. I do not want to stress the notion of cultural logic to the point of inviting the specter of an essentialism that is divorced from history and creative action, but it is worth considering the manner in which foundational armatures and economic process entangle and result in distinctive social and ritual practices. The oft-noted "embedded" nature of economies owes much to the cultural logic of daily practice; understanding the fabric of the mesh will do much to improve interpretive narratives.

In the case of postmodernism, Jameson (1991) considers the extent to which late capitalism foregrounds commodification and has absorbed into the economic sector many arenas of material production such as art and architecture that previously had existed in a non- or semicommodified state, but are now shrink-wrapped and packaged for convenient sale. In effect, the black hole of capitalism has proven capable of absorbing any element of culture that can be deformed to conform to supply-and-demand market principles – even religion, judging from the economic success of televangelists and the more secular crusade for "creative capitalism" by philanthropist Bill Gates (2008). There is no denying the power (and allure to many living within less growth-oriented economic forms) of the cultural logic of capitalism, especially its ability to deliver goods and a comfortable livelihood to a middle class. Framed in this way, one can see how ridiculous it would be to study twenty-first-century U.S. society without dealing with its dominant form of economic integration. If we carry this point forward (or more accurately backward in time) to the Maya region, then we are somewhat perplexed by the absence of a consideration of economic practice in studies of politics and cosmology. But this analogy lacks elasticity. The vortex and hegemonic quality of twenty-first-century market capitalism must be considered a unique and recent phenomenon that likely would astound even Adam Smith. In archaeological terms, the many-headed hydra of late capitalism that dominates all other sectors of society has scarcely reached puberty.

In noncapitalist societies, on the other hand, economic practice tends not to rule the day but to be entangled with political, social, and cosmological frames – a point to which I return throughout this book. The cultural logic entailed in this entanglement (the term is used here in a way that varies a bit from Thomas 1991, 1996) is more complex and generally not reducible to the forces of supply and demand. Halperin (1994:165) describes a pertinent example from rural Kentucky where householders, with only one foot in the capitalist world, engage in a self-referential, diversified economic practice called the Kentucky Way: "there is a wisdom here, a rationality that has a logic of its own, a steadfastness and a doggedness that has tremendous resiliency precisely because it is multifaceted and flexible."

When economic practice occupies a nuanced position within society, fleshing out the daily workings of economic processes can be very challenging for archaeologists, particularly in the absence of relevant documentary materials. But even when present, documentary materials tend to provide evidence of the dominant cultural logic or hegemonic norm, and problems of sampling bias can lead archaeologists to misread the evidence. Recall how our understanding of land transactions in Sumerian society was skewed toward hegemonic temple-state control by an overreliance on cuneiform tablets relating to temple transactions (for review of this issue, see Foster 1981 and Yoffee 1995). Most scholars of Mesopotamia now embrace a more heterarchical notion of economic power and land rights, particularly for the Old Babylonian period for which there is considerable detail on economic action at the family level from sites such as Nippur (Stone 1987:127). A comparable source of economic data to lead (or mislead) archaeologists working in the Maya lowlands has not been found, and this fact leads us to "go to ground" and synthesize multiple threads of information to arrive at a comparable level of interpretation. In this regard, assertions of elite hegemony over economic spheres tend to say more about the perspective (or cultural logic) of an archaeologist than about the sufficiency of archaeological data. Due to the highly visible archaeological remains referable to Classic Maya royalty – monumental architecture, hieroglyphic texts, portraiture, and beautifully crafted items of personal adornment – there is a tendency to focus on the "lives of the rich and famous" and to impute more hegemonic control to their agency than actually may have existed. In this work, I strive for a balanced perspective and attempt to tease out of the array of available sources some semblance of understanding of the agency of commoners as well as those who were markedly dominant or, as aptly expressed in a Tzotzil Maya "true, ancient narrative," those who were fortunate enough to have been born accompanied by a powerful jaguar coessence (Gossen 1993:428–429).

PRACTICE-BASED APPROACH TO ECONOMIES

The action-oriented nature of economic process suggests that a practice perspective (Bourdieu 2005:213) may serve us well in a study of the social actions that produced and reproduced the material basis of ancestral Maya society. With classic inscrutability, Bourdieu (2005:13) states that "the true object of a real economics of practices is nothing other, in the last analysis, than the economy of the conditions of production and reproduction of the agents and institutions of economic, cultural, and social production and reproduction." The role of agents vis à vis institutions and the bidirectionality of forces of both change and stability have been at the fulcrum of social theories espoused not only by Bourdieu (1977, 1990) but also by Giddens (1979, 1981) and others. Theorists have called for a more profound grounding of social theory in human action and daily practice – the *habitus* or "generative principle of regulated improvisations" (Bourdieu 1977:78) without ignoring the fact that there are larger structures of society that both constrain and enable (Giddens 1979:69). These larger structures – so conspicuous in ancient Maya society – traditionally have received the lion's share of attention and causal reference. Giddens (1979:53, 66), in particular, has taken great pains to emphasize that "the notions of action and structure *presuppose one another* [emphasis in original]" and to define structure as the "rules and resources, organized as properties of social systems." Unlike synchronic theories of earlier structural-functionalists, however, Giddens (1979:66, 69) is actively concerned with the conditions under which society is reproduced (either as continuity or transformation) – a thing that he terms "structuration" – and claims that it proceeds via the "mutual dependence" of agency and structure (duality of structure), which acts as both the "medium and the outcome of the practices that constitute those systems." This interest in long-term change and stability among practice theorists carries resonance for archaeologists as does the priority accorded to the "fundamentally recursive character of social life" (Giddens 1979:69), a notion that harkens back to a goal of 1960s archaeology: to re-create past lifeways. But practice theory represents a sea-change shift in analytical focus with more emphasis placed on what and how and less on why (see Pauketat 2001:76). This shift in research priorities has filtered into archaeology via a critique of master (explanatory) narratives by several groups: postprocessualists who lament the exclusion of ritual action, feminists who decry the exclusion of females, and indigenous people who tend to be less concerned with why their ancestors switched to food production and more concerned with how archaeological information can be used to bolster claims of long-term sovereignty over land.

Practice theory has become so prevalent that, as Kelly and Kaplan (1990:141) note, "practice" has usurped "structure" as the reigning image of the real in anthropology. Theories of social practice and agency, however, are not unproblematic. In the final analysis, one must deal with the basis of motivation and nature of intentionality that sparks agents to effect social practice. Ortner (1994:395, 2006:143), Gero (2000), and others have critiqued the emphasis on aggressive, competitive action – based on the theory of self-interest – that pervades studies of agency. We return shortly to theories of self-interest and methodological individualism, but here it is pertinent to mention the vintage invocation of strain theory by Geertz (1973) as an alternative means of "priming the pump" of agentive action. For Geertz (1973:201), self-interest and strain theories are two primary approaches to the study of the motivational factors that underlie agency (and ideology): "In the one, men pursue power; in the other, they flee anxiety." Although the realm of intentionality is beyond the scope of this essentially archaeological study, it is apparent that practice theory cannot be taken at face value because modeling the how and what of intentionality can be based upon dramatically different theories of human motivation. Reynolds and Tanner (1995), for example, apply strain theory to the social ecology of religion and propose (following Ortner 1994:395) that actors experience the complexity of their situations and attempt to solve problems posed by those situations via religious practice that ironically both creates and alleviates the binds and burdens placed on actors.

The concept of *habitus* (Bourdieu 1977:78) provides a less muscular (some would say overly reflexive) concept for thinking about action that is habitual and deeply seated within cultural DNA – such as the notion of *costumbre* in traditional Maya societies (see Chapter 7). In an effort to link *habitus* to intermediate-scale societal forces, Bourdieu (2005:196–199) – in a manner that is evocative of Goffman's frame analysis (1974; see also Branaman 1997:lxxiv–lxxx) – applied the concept of "field," particularly in his analysis of the Parisian real estate market (see Bourdieu 1993:162–163 for seminal discussion). The field plays a powerful role in determining the "conditions in which agents come to decide (or negotiate) purchase prices ... and selling prices." More in line with strain theory than self-interest theory, Bourdieu (2005:199) describes the field of forces as a field of struggles. For Bourdieu (2005:193), understanding *habitus,* field, and structure constitute the true goal of economic anthropology: "we must ... attempt to construct a realist definition of economic reason as an encounter between dispositions which are socially constituted (in relation to a field) and the structures, themselves socially constituted, of that field." As Holland et al. (1998:58–59) note, field is a kind of "structure-in-practice" and holds two advantages: (1) composed of interacting persons, field does not stand apart from persons in the way that structure – due to its abstractedness – can; and (2) dynamic relations of power and privilege – problematic within agency theory – can be traced somewhat more realistically through a field of interacting persons. In summary, Bourdieu's definition of economic reason as an encounter between dispositions and structures – mediated by fields of interaction – highlights the entangled skeins that must be unraveled in order to understand economic practice.

How would an economy of practice take shape within archaeology? Within Mississippian archaeology, Pauketat (2001:87) urges a consideration of "the historical processes of *how* cultural orthodoxies [or logics] were created and resisted, or how a communal ethos or a corporate organization was co-opted or perpetuated through transformations of identity and scales of negotiation [emphasis in original]." This emphasis on power and its potential defeaters is a strong characteristic of practice studies, which Ortner (1994:390) maintains exhibit a "palpable Marxist influence," a point to which I return shortly. Additional archaeological studies that explicitly employ a practice or agency approach – with varying degrees of success – are increasingly in evidence, beginning with Dobres and Robb (2000). Dobres (2000) singly has attempted to recast the archaeological study of technology in terms of agency theory, while Robb (1999:33) asserts that agency can provide the "theoretical linkage between cultural ideas and economic behavior."

Throughout archaeology, there is renewed attention to putting a human face on narratives of the past. In Maya archaeology, our understanding of the agency of certain actors within Classic society has grown with the decipherment of hieroglyphic texts and the ability to put a name to the face of royalty. Decidedly more historical than the Maya archaeology of old, practitioners are still struggling to register the well-documented ritual practices and martial activities of the über-elites with the dimly focused activities of the very large remaining sector of ancestral Maya society. Was this latter sector coopted, composed of well-informed collaborators, or both? To what extent can knowledge of the royal segment be used to interpret archaeological materials from nonroyal contexts in a kind of intradisciplinary cross-fertilization or were the royals living a world apart, playing by completely different rules? As with much of practice theory, in posing specific questions about what and how, we often surrender the ability to answer these questions in an unambiguous fashion. The cultural logic of authority in ancestral Maya society (explored extensively in Chapter 6) suggests that even though royal power was imputed to have been absolute, it was neither uncontested nor totally foreign. This circumspect approach to the power of "natural lords" carried into the Colonial period when Spaniards quickly learned that many Yucatec Maya people intended to take full advantage of the Spanish judicial system to press their land claims and redress grievances against abusive Colonial practices (see Roys 1939; Restall 1997).

For Bourdieu, the economies of practice cannot be separated from cultural production and reproduction. In this regard, Maya societies of Colonial and more contemporary times are remarkable for their resiliency and ability to reproduce culturally (and biologically) in the face of a harsh Colonial regime and, during more recent times, through tragic epochs of genocide. What is the stuff of culture that results in this suprahuman feat of survival? Economies of practice have played a large role in the Colonial and Postcolonial survival of Maya people: the crafting of a culture that came to be seen as distinctive in dress, cuisine, religious practices, farming, and living in general. This distinctiveness marked Maya people as different and therefore vulnerable, but it also provided a way of being – a socially constituted economy of practice – that promoted intragroup solidarity and cultural survival. It is this characteristic of structure – both enabling and constraining as per Giddens (1984:169–179) – that occupies our thoughts through a good portion of this book.

GHOSTS OF PAST ECONOMIC ANALYSES

Economic anthropology has more than its share of skeletons in the closet. With a contentious past, economic anthropologists have long been divided over what constitutes an anthropologically grounded economic analysis (see Isaac 2005:20; , also Ensminger 2002). Central to this issue has been the question as to whether or not it is a good thing to huddle with economists who produce elegant models of economic "behavior" based on simplistic and unrealistic assumptions. Much abused for their assumption of methodological individualism (otherwise known as *Homo oeconomicus* or rational choice theory), economists have been treated roughly by social theorists as the following quotes indicate. Bourdieu (2005:209) weighs in with the thought that "*homo oeconomicus*, as conceived (tacitly or explicitly) by economic orthodoxy, is a kind of anthropological monster: this theoretically minded man of practice is the most extreme personification of the scholastic fallacy." Not one to hold back, Bourdieu (2005:221) delights in citing a quote from the venerable economist Thorstein Veblen who describes *Homo oeconomicus* as construed by classical economists "as a self-contained globule of desire." Elsewhere, Bourdieu (2005:10) indicts economists in general as being guilty of seeing like a state and colluding with state-sponsored policy makers.

Sahlins (1994:440) is more circumspect in his critique of the central tenets of capitalism and attempts to place rational choice theory within an historical perspective: "by the time of Adam Smith, every person's permanent misery – that is, scarcity and need – had become the premise of economic wisdom and the source of national welfare. The social and moral sublimation of temporal desires had indeed been dissolved by an ongoing capitalism." This, he calls a new rationality, and, indeed, much of the early modern Colonial epoch can be explained by reference to the collision between the cultural logic of early mercantile capitalism and that of kin and tributary modes of production as examined by Wolf (1982).

Halperin (1994:1, 14) bestows upon methodological individualism the mantle of ethnocentrism "especially when it has imposed a utilitarian, 'choice-making' under conditions of scarcity form of rationality upon actors." That economists are culturally tone deaf may come as no surprise to many anthropologists, but there is still much to be reckoned with as archaeologists – embodied with the logic of Late Capitalism – attempt to write narratives of the past that fill in the dots between material remains and social practice.

Decrying the units of analysis and the theory of motivation by means of self-interest, Geertz (1973:202) suggests that

> the main defects of the interest theory are that its psychology is too anemic and its sociology too muscular. Lacking a developed analysis of motivation,

> it [interest theory] has been constantly forced to oscillate between a narrow and superficial utilitarianism that sees men as impelled by rational calculation of their consciously recognized personal advantage and a broader, but no less superficial, historicism.

To be fair, many schools of economic studies – such as New Institutional Economics – have moved away from methodological individualism and self-interest theory to focus on societal institutions and organizational arrangements (see Menard and Shirley 2005:1–18). Still, one has only to glance at the popular 2005 book *Freakonomics* written by University of Chicago economist Steven Levitt and Stephen Dubner to grasp the fact that methodological individualism remains a touchstone – to some a truism – that explains the economics of practice within capitalism. The dust jacket reads, to wit: "economics is, at root, the study of incentives – how people get what they want, or need, especially when other people want or need the same thing." Described as a "rogue" approach to economics, in fact, the study reiterates the basic tents of classic economic theory: self-interest as the underlying motivation with scarcity as an external driving force.

Setting aside the colorful indictments handed down by anthropological theorists cited earlier, a rapprochement between anthropology and economics is complicated by the embrace of diverse forms of cultural economies by the former and a deafness to cultural diversity by the latter fanned by the flames of rational choice theory, which likely is a model that is too simplistic even for explaining economies of practice within full-blown capitalism. Within anthropology, the plot thickened after 1950 when economic anthropologists brought out of the closet the social thinker whose influential ideas about economies and their transformations have reverberated through the nineteenth and twentieth centuries: Karl Marx. With him came several others – including Max Weber, Karl Polanyi, and A. V. Chayanov. Examining the impact of these thinkers would require a volume in and of itself – and many already have been written – so I focus here on how practice and agency theorists have deployed the ideas of seminal Marxists thinkers. Sherry Ortner (1994:391) expressed the influence of these first materialists best:

> As Weber put the actor at the center of his model, so these writers [agency and practice theorists] emphasize issues of human praxis in Marx. As Weber

> subsumed the economic within the political, so these writers encompass economic exploitation within political domination. And as Weber was centrally concerned with ethos and consciousness, so these writers stress similar issues within Marx's work.

So, we can trace the origin of notions such as daily praxis, the exploitation of the masses by political elites, and ethos/consciousness as a kind of cultural logic that informs, shapes, and is shaped by economic practice. Although not accepted uncritically, these notions underlay the chapters of this book in which we examine daily ritual practice and the cultural logic of landscape cognition (Chapter 3), schemes of power generated by monumental architecture (Chapter 5), the naturalization of power and the forcible extraction of tribute goods (Chapters 6 and 9), and the ethos of artisan production (Chapter 7).

Polanyi (1957:250, 254), an economic historian, conceptualized the economy as instituted process and provided the first formulation of different forms of economic integration (namely, reciprocity, redistribution, exchange [price-setting market], and householding). Although the banner of Karl Polanyi is carried by economic anthropologists such as Rhoda Halperin (2007), some archaeologists profess to have been straitjacketed by the limited range of economic forms identified by Polanyi and the poor fit between Polanyi's framework and the early appearance in many civilizations of profit-oriented (or commercial) marketplace exchange (Smith 2004:75; Trigger 2003:60). Halperin (2007) counters that Polanyi's concept of equivalencies provides an umbrella large enough to cover most ancient marketplaces. Polanyi was constrained by the limited archaeological data available during the 1950s. But there is no denying that the concept of power was not well integrated into Polanyi's constructs, nor into those of neoevolutionists such as Elman Service (1975:8) who painted a Pollyanna picture of the economies of archaic states: "The system was redistributive, allocative, not acquisitive: Personal wealth was not required to gain personal political power. And these first governments seem clearly to have reinforced their structure by doing their economic and religious jobs well – by providing benefits – rather than by using physical force." More recent characterizations of archaic states depart dramatically from this description and incorporate the notion of power and inequality into discussions of the financing, legitimacy, and wealth of early states (see Baines and Yoffee 1988; Chapman

2003; Feinman and Marcus 1998; Richards and van Buren 2000; A. Smith 2003; M. Smith and Schreiber 2005, 2006; Yoffee 2005, among others).

The Russian economist, A. V. Chayanov (1966:24–25) raised early objections to the application of modern economic theory to the operation and vitality of early twentieth-century peasant farms – an application that he maintained only served to create "fictions and clouds." Displaying a cultural sensitivity that is/was rare among formalist economists (as Wilk 1996 has noted), Chayanov (1966:28) maintained that "the future of economic theory lies not in constructing a single universal theory of economic life but in conceiving a number of theoretical systems that would be adequate to the range of present or past economic orders and would disclose the forms of their coexistence and evolution." This study follows the spirit of Chayanov in conceiving of ancestral Maya economies as one variant on the economies of archaic states (and as such can be perceived as a "theoretical system"), although here we give more space to the contingencies of history as well as social and ritual practice.

FOLLOWING THE THREADS OF ENTANGLEMENT

As Ortner (1994:392) has noted, practice theorists show more willingness to follow the threads and less need for tidy analytical divisions in which a "system" is broken into artificial chunks. For archaeologists, the sacrifice in analytical precision is compensated by the enhanced realism of narratives that follow the thread of entangled social and ritual practice. Douglas and Isherwood (1996:13) maintain that there is a necessary circularity in "following the thread[s]" of the entanglement of economy with politics and ritual. In a seminal work on the theory of goods, they situate goods as the medium, "less objects of desire than threads of a veil that disguises the social relations under it" (Douglas and Isherwood 1996:152). Attention is directed to the flow of exchanges, the goods only marking out the pattern. But the materiality of goods coupled with their larger social significance is the very thing that allows archaeologists to hope that we can interpret the past based on a theory of goods (Miller 2005). Here, we begin the work of following the threads by considering the entangled nature of a few of the major topics under consideration: ritual practice; power and the question of hegemony over economic agency; production, reproduction, and crafting.

Ritual Practice – Enabling and Constraining Agency

In this book, I suggest that ritual activities provided a kind of armature of cultural meaning that guided and was transformed by daily practice. Not precisely coterminous with the routinized dispositions of Bourdieu's (1977) *habitus*, ritual practice may be more accurately conceived as a many-headed hydra with tendrils wrapped around every conceivable activity, be it oriented toward production, power, or identity. The explicit marriage of economic process to ritual practice not only provides gains in the reality of our narratives of ancestral Maya life but also allows us to reconsider Durkheimian notions of ritual practice as constraining and channeling agency. The strong action orientation of economic process, specifically, interrogates the notion of ritual practice as enforcer of cultural norms. Ortner (1994:398) has noted how the influence of Durkheim in England generated a perspective on ritual as the means by which actors came to be "wedded to the norms and values of their culture." In reference to agency, Kelly and Kaplan (1990:140) discuss the manner in which ritual practice accentuates agency by placing limits on it: "The special power in ritual acts ... lies in the lack of independence asserted by a ritual participant, even while he or she makes assertions about authority. ... Ritual is a crucial part of practice, then precisely because the limit on agency in ritual presentations make the larger claims possible." Others see ritual as both rooted in and enabling societal transformation (Comaroff 1985:194–199) or as occasion for contesting, subverting, and inverting social order (Bakhtin 1984; Davis 1975:103, 131; Dirks 1991:220; Turner 1969:166–203). These latter approaches definitively focus on the manner in which agency is enabled, rather than constrained, by ritual practice. So, ritual may not always be constitutive of social order.

Of the linkage between ritual and economic practice, Durkheim (1961[1915]:466) himself noted that "only one form of social activity has not yet been expressly attached to religion: that is economic activity." More often than not, religion or ideology is sequestered into a realm that Earle (1986:167) describes as an "artificial artifice" distilled from the larger context of "beliefs about the nature of the world as a unitary whole containing spiritual and material aspects." Some archaeological approaches emphasize that religion and ideology are powerful mechanisms of cultural expression and transformation (e.g., Demarest and Conrad 1992), but the ways in which religious beliefs (and expressive ritual practice) were socially entangled was not necessarily a goal of this approach. Bradley (1998:13) has bemoaned the polarization of Neolithic studies into "either ideology or economy, and the relationship between these two subjects is blurred in the course of academic debate." Over the years, concepts have emerged within anthropology that conjoin ritual with economic process and, in doing so, generally augment the agentive nature of ritual process and its ties to larger frames of political economy (McAnany and Wells 2008; Wells 2006). Rappaport (1968:410; see also Spielmann 2002, 2008) offers the "ritual mode of production"; Wells and Davis-Salazar (2007) as well as Wells and McAnany (2008) propose the notion of "ritual economy," and, much earlier, Wolf (1966:7) coined the term "ceremonial fund" to describe production by households for the express purpose of ritual practice: "If men are to participate in social relations, therefore, they must also work to establish a fund against which these expenditures may be charged. We shall call this the ceremonial *fund*." Elsewhere, Douglas and Isherwood (1996:43) propose a theory of consumption as a ritual process in which goods serve as "ritual adjuncts." All of these constructs share a common purpose of entangling ritual with economy – a *modus operandi* that is followed throughout this study.

One of the conspicuous aspects of Maya economic process is the manner in which actions were embedded within a social matrix and not separable, that is, not able to be isolated into an "economic sector" as is common in studies of capitalism. In the words of Polanyi (1957) and more recently, Halperin (1994:1), economic processes were embedded. Even in our postmodern capitalist society, "market forces" do not operate within a cultural void, although the commoditization of labor and food certainly has desocialized and deritualized many of our economic activities. Resulting feelings of alienation and anomie are truly the stepchild of capitalism as is the unprecedented degree of personal freedom and individualism.

If Maya economic processes were embedded within a larger social matrix, why single out for special attention their entanglement with ritual process? Ritual practices are all-encompassing and represent the enactment of core beliefs that are transmitted (often in a transformed state) intergenerationally. As such, ritual practice can be perceived as a kind of fulcrum onto which other types of practices are hinged. As someone who was reared in the Catholic faith and spent over 2,500 hours attending Latin- and English-language orthodox Mass ceremonies before the age of 14, I can attest to the all-encompassing nature of ritual practice. Catholicism pervaded every aspect of my childhood existence from play (enacting the role of a nun), education (attending Catholic schools where nuns inculcated students with Christian values), to the social definition of "other" in reference to children who did not attend a Catholic but rather public school (dubbed "publicans" by Catholic school guards). Sizable portions of family income were transferred to the Catholic church for the purpose of education as well as building maintenance, and the social network of the parish church included preferential consumer spending at commercial places owned by those participating in that network. To be reared within such a totalizing orthodoxy and closed social field provides one with a strong sense of identity and cultural endurance as long as societal transformations do not expose fault lines within the ideological framework such as occurred within the Catholic church following the Vatican II Council and the death of Pope John Paul XXXIII. Although we must always exercise caution in analogic reasoning, this anecdote provides an appropriate example of "total immersion" or the manner in which religious beliefs and ritual practice can expand, in amoeba fashion, into any and all domains of culture, particularly economic domains.

Power and the Question of Hegemony over Economic Agency

As mentioned previously, many of the seminal constructs of economic forms employed by anthropologists did not deal well or realistically with the notion of power and the manner in which political forces are threaded through, shaped by, and shape economic practice. Beyond the Marxist concept of power as economic domination or Gramsci's (1971) notion of totalizing hegemonic forces that saturate all social process, a strong correlation has been noted between social hierarchy and economic inequality. Perhaps Maurice Bloch (1989:18) expresses this view the best:

> the amount of social structure, of the past in the present, of ritual communication, is correlated with the amount of *institutionalized* hierarchy and *that is what it is about*. Some inequality is often manifested as unadorned oppression, but, as Weber pointed out, it is then highly unstable, and only becomes stable when its origins are hidden and when it transforms itself into hierarchy: a legitimate order of inequality in an imaginary world which we call social structure [emphasis in original].

In effect, Bloch models hierarchy as an enabler or a tool for the promotion and maintenance of inequality. Hierarchy makes inequality possible and stabilizes it as part of the social order. Logically, the more pronounced the hierarchy, the greater the inequality and thus the more compromised the economic agency of those who are/were not situated near the bottom of the hierarchy. This chain of logic has guided many archaeological interpretations of the past – particularly of archaic states – however, the linkages remain untested and the ontogeny of hierarchy poorly understood.

A. T. Smith (2003:90) offers a formulation of this chain of logic in four prevailing notions of the archaic state: "(1) radical social stratification preserved through (2) centralized institutions of governmental administration that (3) restrict access to and apportionment of resources through (4) the consistent threat of legitimate force." As Smith (2003:25) notes, scant attention has been paid to "how political practices produced and reproduced authority." And really, the key is authority – how it is naturalized and perpetuated. This topic is revisited in Chapters 5 and 6, which dwell at some length on the synergism between monumental constructions and generative schemes of power and also on the manner in which authority was naturalized in attributes of the body, clothing, food, and products of gendered labor within Classic Maya royal courts. Foremost on the agenda within Chapters 5 and 6 is the question of how power was constituted and how threats to defeat hierarchy overwhelmed.

As our understanding of early archaic states matures, it is clear that Durkheim was on the right path when he linked ritual practice to the religious validation of hierarchy. Weiner (1992:4) used the term "cosmological authentication" to describe "how material resources and social practices link individuals and groups with an authority that transcends present social and political action." For Weiner, this transcendence is not an abstract concept; it is materialized in the production and curation of goods so valuable that they are deemed inalienable (Weiner 1992). The notion of cosmological authentication can be seen as related to what Bourdieu (1990:112–121) terms "symbolic capital" – those forms of power that are not strictly economic but stem from often nontangible qualities such as access to restricted realms of knowledge (like hieroglyphic writing), status through genealogy, and so forth. Once again, the materiality of social practice looms large.

Understanding generative schemes of power assists comprehension of early statecraft – and perhaps also of schemes of state finance – but it does not bring us any closer hermeneutically to answering the question of hegemony over economic practice in early states, such as Preclassic and Classic Maya societies. Ortner (1994:397) notes that practice theorists generally argue that "hegemony is always more fragile than it appears," which leads us to suspect that there may be space for economic agency among all participants. In a similar vein, Geertz (1973:202) has questioned "the view that social action is fundamentally an unending struggle for power." Finally, Ortner (1994:401) has suggested that the examination of domination be balanced by studies of cooperation, reciprocity, and solidarity. All of these theorists question monolithic conceptions of power and exhort us to construct more nuanced and balanced narratives. As the chapters to come indicate, Maya political and social landscapes provided a mosaic of opportunities for agentive action – strong in some areas and weak in others. The intimate relationship between livelihood and landscape was mediated by the agency of ritual practice that likely existed in all sectors of Maya society – including commoners (Chapter 3). Concomitantly, household, garden, orchard, and field were socially constituted by gender-defined labor (Chapter 4). Finally, artisan production – the ultimate materiality of identity – provided generous space for human agency among both elites and non-elites. The thorny question of where control of artisan production resided is a complex issue that can only be dealt with contextually as is done in Chapters 7 and 9.

Production, Reproduction, and Crafting

John Monaghan (1998:50) has suggested that ritual practice should be more properly conceived as a type of production in which labor and resources are marshaled to achieve the materialization of a desired end – be it a dedicatory cache placed under the floor of a new house, the raising of a 30-meter-tall pyramid, or the weeding of a prized field of maize. In Western culture, the production arena – where the work of construction, crafting, cultivation, and processing takes place – largely has been denuded of ritual practice due to the commodification of labor and the hegemonic influence of the hourly wage. This transformation is particularly acute among traditional societies that are caught between the ritually entangled production of work feasts and wage labor (Dietler and Herbich 2001). Such differing approaches to the social practice of production highlight the manner in which the cultural logic of capitalism has created a distinctive kind of *habitus*. Consequently, recurrent themes in the archaeological study of religion and ritual include the following: recognition of the social distinctiveness of both a capitalist *habitus* and the sacred–profane dichotomy of Western structuralists, and the futility and inaccuracy of projecting the presence of separate spheres into the past (Bradley 2005; Fogelin 2007; Insoll 2004).

The topic of ritually entangled production is particularly pertinent to the origins of monumental architecture, and many archaeologists and ancient historians have raised the question as to how and why the large labor force necessary for the construction of such monumental constructions were "hoodwinked" into providing labor. Here, the notion of "ritual work" proposed by Feeley-Harnik (1985) is particularly appropriate as is the conception of early Mesoamerican pyramids as religious structures rather than extensions of the strategies of male entrepreneurial aggrandizers (see Clark and Blake 1994 on the latter). This discussion is further developed in Chapter 5 in which the origins of pyramid construction provide a very concrete example of how the materiality of religious expression (in monumental terms) can engender or reify relations of inequality in a manner not originally foreseen.

Although attention to forces of production and reproduction within ancestral Maya society is most often focused on the hypermaterialized elite structures of domination, we would do well by casting a broader net. As Weiner (1992:4) suggests, "When we acknowledge that so-called secondary domestic values such as biological reproduction and nurturance as well as the 'magical' values of cosmologies and gods underwrite economic and political actions, then the traditional public/domestic boundaries break down." In this way, we can observe social reproduction in many different contexts and also come closer to understanding change as failed reproduction (Sahlins 1981). Vitally intertwined with the notion of reproduction is that of crafting – the materialization of identity through a type of artisan activity that carries a strong notion of *costumbre* – a customary way of doing and being. As such, knowledge of crafting techniques – the *habitus* of crafting – can be passed down through many generations with remarkable replication. This type of agency – in which social practices are reproduced by agents with scant modification – is not terribly popular given the recent emphasis on intentionality and transformative agentive action; however, we cannot lose sight of the "degree to which actors really do simply enact norms because 'that was the way of our ancestors'" (Ortner 1994:394). In Chapter 7, this issue is revisited in depth.

MATERIALITY OF THE *LONGUE DURÉE*

The manner in which archaeologists configure and present studies of the past is greatly influenced, to adapt a term from Peacock (2001), by the long lens and soft focus of the so-called archaeological record: hundreds, often thousands, of years of lived existence compressed into a sedimented sequence of artifacts and structural remains that provide a vivid material reminder of the resilience of humanity. Such materiality of the *longue durée*, a cumulative long-term record with characteristics of both palimpsest and Pompeii-like "fossilization," alludes to the passage of time and importance of place as few other metaphors can do (for more on stratigraphy, see McAnany and Hodder 2009). This fact has not been lost among social theorists such as Michel Foucault and Anthony Giddens who have dipped into the well of archaeological imagery for tropes that convey deep history. Giddens (1979:54) has adopted two frames of archaeological reference – space and time – as key fields within and across which agency operates: "social theory *must acknowledge, as it has not done previously, time–space intersections as essentially involved in all social existence* [emphasis in original]." Further on, the concept of sedimented time–space relations is invoked to create an image of the *longue durée*: "an understanding of institutional forms can only be achieved insofar as it is shown how, as regularized social practices, institutions are constituted and reconstituted in the tie between the *durée* of the passing moment, and the *longue durée* of deeply sedimented time–space relations" (Giddens 1979:110). Elsewhere, Holland et al. (1998:18) note that "[O]ne's history-in-person is the *sediment* from past experiences upon which one improvises, using the cultural resources available, in response to the subject positions afforded one in the present [emphasis added]."

The growing tendency among American archaeologists to adopt a historicist approach to the past – while not without problems – signals a turning away from biological evolutionary constructs and the adoption of a British and European approach to the past that is more particularistic but also more actively peopled (Hodder and Hutson 2003:125–155; Pauketat 2001:73). This trend, among a group that we might call postprocessual or increasingly practice–theory archaeologists, schools well with Maya archaeology. Given the historicity of hieroglyphic texts and the particularism of its praxis, Maya archaeology was preadapted for postprocessualism. Nearly 50 years ago, Clyde Kluckholn (1962) disparaged Maya archaeology for its lack of engagement with general anthropological theory of the 1950s (see McAnany 2007a for further discussion).

Since our primary information about the past lies in the material realm, archaeologists inherently are concerned with the materiality of practice (Brumfiel 2003; Meskell 2005; Miller 2005). As DeMarrais et al. (1996) have suggested, we fervently hope that material remains signal identities, social practices, power relationships, and cooperative alliances that once existed. Subconsciously, this hope is encouraged by the hyper-materiality of contemporary existence, which is problematized in actor-network theory (Latour 2005) as well as ethnographic engagement with materiality (see Henare et al. 2007b among others). For instance, Holland et al. (1998:60–61) state that "[f]igured worlds rely upon artifacts. ... They are the means by which figured worlds are evoked, collectively developed, individually learned, and made socially and personally powerful." But how can we gauge the kind of figured world that existed in the past? How can we check whether our interpretations of the past come anywhere near the texture of past lived experiences? The methodological bind of archaeological interpretation is not easy to circumvent (some would say impossible). This study approaches the past as something that is perceivable and not as totally strange as some may think (cf. Lowenthal 1985). Rather than search for the one true interpretation of ancestral Maya economies, the approach advocated here searches for avenues of understanding or practices and processes that appear to resonate with meaning when placed in contraposition to archaeological materiality. Practices that seem congruent with materials revealed by archaeological research are likely to hold real insight to the past. Knowledge of these congruent practices may emerge in any number of ways, but the important caution that we must exercise in terms of archaeological interpretation is that we provide space for archaeological materials to "talk back" and resist interpretations that lack resonance (Shanks 2001:292). If we do not provide for this space, then we do violence to the past by exerting a kind of hegemonic influence. The materiality of the past, in the same manner, supplements and shifts the perspective of historical documents (Brumfiel 2003:205). The best way that we can feel confident about an interpretation is to find several different kinds of archaeological information that lend themselves to the same interpretation without exerting undue torque, to search, in an idiom used by Hodder (1999:33–45), following many mathematicians, for "the best fit." It is this kind of hermeneutical process that produced the notion investigated throughout this study: namely, that Maya economic processes can best be understood by foregrounding the ritual and social practices of ancestral Maya societies and following the threads of entanglement through the realms of landscape, identity, gender, religion, and power.

GOING TO GROUND

A current trend among archaeologists studying urbanism is to bemoan the excessive reification of "urban types," which has left little space for investigating how things actually worked in specific cases of urbanism (Cowgill 2004:536; A. Smith 2003:25). Indeed, all social researchers walk that tightrope between the work of theory formulation and the analytical need for grouped cases. In researching and writing this topical book on ancestral Maya economies, I have embarked upon a tightrope performance and you, the reader, will judge whether I have maintained a balance or strayed too far in one direction or another. I attempt to tease out some of the central ideas that I believe structured and were structured by Maya economic processes while, at the same time, maintaining a sensitivity to anomalous evidence, thus providing space for archaeological remains to "talk back." This book does not pretend to cover all topics and all primary data relevant to understanding this vast and critically undersynthesized aspect of ancestral Maya life. The last several decades have been witness to a rapidly increasing number of researchers conducting field projects in the Maya lowlands. Attracted by the naturalistic representation (both painted and in stone) of Maya people from the past and a script that is the most detailed in pre-sixteenth-century Americas, archaeologists and art historians have generated a huge amount of primary data, only a small fraction of which has been published. I cannot pretend to synthesize all relevant material within the pages of this book.

The intent of this study really is quite simple: to shed light on the means, methods, and motivating factors by which ancestral peoples of the Maya lowlands went about the business of growing and processing food, hunting for game, creating a built environment on both a domestic and monumental scale, crafting objects for immediate use as well as for trade in marketplaces, practicing a statecraft that included tributary arrangements with client polities, and supplying royal courts with luxury foods such as cacao. The materiality of these actions created a complex entity that we refer to as "Ancient Maya Civilization," but, in fact, such a thing never existed as a monolithic whole but rather emerged in the mind of archaeologists from the material remains of past fields of interaction, negotiation, and contestation. This "performance of culture" as per Schechner and Appel (1989) and the material remains that were produced by such recursive and purposeful action provide grist for the archaeological mill of interpretation. Mulled over, dissected, and published as interpretive narratives, the materiality and meaning of ancient Maya cultures has become a cottage industry for archaeologists, art historians, tour guides, and doomsday theorists such as Jared Diamond (2005).

In structuring this study, I examined the presentation format of ambitious works, such as Bruce Trigger's *Understanding Early Civilizations* (2003) where I found the chapter on "Economy" to be subdivided into the topics of "Food Production," "Land Ownership," "Trade and Craft Specialization," "Appropriation of Wealth," and "Economic Constants and Variables." Given the broad reach of his tome, this structure is understandable but not desirable for the study at hand in which we are more interested in the cross-threading of social and ritual practices with economic process. The resulting structure of this work is more organic. We begin (in Chapter 2) by situating Maya societies in space and time and exploring the continuum that Anthony Giddens found to be so critical to understanding social existence. Interpretive material presented within Chapter 2 provides a framework for later chapters, particularly for those readers who are not familiar with Maya archaeology. The performative basis of Maya religion and ritual practice is introduced in Chapter 3, and the implications of this fact for a cosmology of landscape are explored in great detail. The "debt" relationship between humans and supernaturals – a strong component of traditional Mesoamerican religions – sets in place a series of obligations that can be detected by archaeologists as the materiality of ritual practice. The focus of Chapter 4 is the socially constructed space of house, garden, orchard, and field and the manner in which this built environment was peopled by men, women, and children whose productive efforts and gendered labor produced value for the household. The monumental "ritual works" that so define the Maya world – even today – provide the focus of Chapter 5 in which the factors underlying the transformation of that which was novel into natural are explored in depth. As colossal inalienable goods, these constructions cemented the social memory of hierarchy and effectively thwarted attempts to defeat amplifying social difference. Social difference is the topic of Chapter 6 in which the naturalized authority of the royal court is examined. The smell, look, and diet of royal bodies – those with jaguar coessences – are found to differ significantly from those of commoners and are argued to have supported the notion of "stranger kings and queens." The regal-built environment also was diacritically marked – employing great investments in wealth – as distinctive and different from that of commoners although within the parameters of time-established genres. In Chapter 7, the social identity and daily practice of artisan production is examined across all sectors of Maya society with a critical eye to explanatory constructs of craft specialization. The ethos of crafting according to the time-honored tradition of *costumbre* is found to differ from the palace ethos of crafting labor-intensive sumptuary goods that employed rapidly changing styles and technologies as well as the trope of deity impersonation. Place and practices of commerce provide the grist for Chapter 8 in which particular attention is given to the question of marketplaces. State finance is the topic of Chapter 9 in which the production and transport of tribute goods – especially cacao, cotton *mantas*, jadeite, *Spondylus* spp., and quetzal feathers – between royal courts is considered. Given hieroglyphic and epigraphic evidence, a case is made for the presence of tributary ransom as a finance technique of Classic Maya rulers. Finally, in Chapter 10, I attempt to skein the entangled threads of the previous eight chapters and revisit the topics introduced therein with special consideration for the profound human engagement with the material basis of life.

2

Situating Maya Societies in Space and Time

While looking for the "spice islands" of the East Indies, Christopher Columbus – on his fourth voyage to the Americas in 1502 – found the eastern Caribbean limits of the Maya world. As he sailed into the Bay of Honduras (Figure 2.1), his crew spotted and boarded a large cargo canoe transporting – among many other goods – sacks of cacao, described as "*muchas almendras de cacao*" or many almond-sized chocolate seeds (Casas 1877, Book 2, Chapter 20:274). This was the first European encounter with a people who would come to be called Maya and a foodstuff that would become a premier luxury and comfort food the world over. Subsequent sixteenth-century explorers, such as Juan de Grijalva, encountered the low limestone peninsula of the Maya lowlands farther north, near Tulum, and then sailed north and west along the northern edge of the Yucatán Peninsula into the Gulf of Mexico (Figure 2.1). The infamous voyage of 1519, that of Hernán Cortes, followed a similar tack, stopping briefly at the island of Cozumel, and then continuing around the top of the peninsula ultimately to set ashore well to the west of the Maya region in Veracruz. From this point, Cortes and his *conquistadores* made their assault on the highland Mexican imperial capital of Tenochtitlán, home of the Mexica or Aztecs. Within two years, Cortes laid waste to Tenochtitlán and set his sights on an overland trek to the east that would take him across the large drainages framing the western side of the Maya region (the Grijalva and the Usumacinta) through the hills and *bajos* of the southern Maya lowlands (Petén and

FIGURE 2.1 Maya region with modern political divisions, geographic place names, and Mayan ethnolinguistic groups (indicated with capital letters; map prepared by Josh Feola).

Guatamala) and along the southern side of the Maya Mountains to reach the Caribbean shores. Around the same time, one of Cortes's henchman – Pedro Alvarado – accompanied by a band of *conquistadores* and drafted Mexican warriors, ascended the active volcanic region of the Sierra Madre Mountains to the south of the Petén (Figure 2.1) and carried out a bloody military campaign against the K'iché- and Kaqchikel-speaking peoples inhabiting these areas. Throughout the Colonial period that followed, Spanish incursions penetrated every landscape and community of the Maya region, including the Chiapas highlands, which frames the western side and is home to speakers of Tzotzil, Tzeltal, and several other Maya languages. Spanish incursions or *entradas* also took place in the piedmont slopes of the Pacific Coast where rich alluvial soils supported lucrative cacao orchards; the metamorphic Maya Mountains of southern Belize where Manché Chol Maya speakers once resided; and the drier, northern part of the Peninsula where Yucatec Maya speakers – very populous at the time of Spanish arrival – were organized into multiple, competitive states. Lastly, and not until 1697, Spaniards laid waste to the capital of the last independent Maya kingdom – that of the Itzá – situated in a remote, interior location that had been inaccessible to Spaniards, namely, an island in the middle of Laguna Petén Itzá (Figure 2.1). In the eyes of Spanish *conquistadores*, the Maya region held few riches. There were no deposits of gold or silver, few artifacts of gold, and – in the lowlands – a hot and humid climate that challenged the comfort level of Spaniards and their cattle. Nevertheless, colonization proceeded, albeit in fits and starts, and a sixteenth-century landscape that had been a manicured mosaic of fields, orchards, forests, wetlands, small communities, and large seats of power – set amidst monumental and partially maintained ancestral constructions – was transformed into a landscape of poverty, despair, and death.

In describing the Maya region at the time of Spanish incursions, I begin the work of situating this study in reference to the tragic and pivotal events of the sixteenth through twentieth centuries that forever altered Maya societies and also led to a fierce and successful struggle for survival seated within routinized daily practice. While the spatial limits of what is recognized as the region of contemporary Mayan language speakers and of their ancestral constructions may be outlined in the body of a paragraph, this sketch hardly does justice to the tremendous variation that existed(s) across the Maya area. Expressions such as "The Ancient Maya" and references to *the* Maya people of today mask profound linguistic, social, and economic distinctions; such assertions of homogeneity are not supported by empirical evidence. Temporally, 3,000-plus years of occupation of a landscape – most recently under the extreme duress of colonialism – have created a complex palimpsest of material remains. Here, I can only begin to introduce some of the well-known places of the ancestral Maya world (Figure 2.2). I unfold the space–time continuum of the Maya region in reference to the Gregorian calendar, although I realize that this Western convention does not drill to the heart of indigenous Maya conceptions of time. Time – its calculation and documentation in reference to human and astronomical events – occupies(ed) the thoughts of Maya scribes and calendar-keepers for nearly three thousand years. Of the civilizations of the Americas, Maya societies – particularly the royal segment – invested most heavily in documenting the passage of time, both abstractly and in reference to astronomical cycles.

In the pages to follow, distinct political trends and research topics are entwined around the monumental time frame of Maya *longue durée.* To prepare the reader for the chapters to come, this introduction to Maya studies incorporates a broad spectrum of information. Given the volume of material, I have tried to keep in-text references to a minimum, to cite review articles where more in-depth treatment of a topic can be found, or to refer to chapters to follow in which a topic is taken up. For the period preceding Spanish incursions and colonialism, information is derived from archaeology and epigraphy. After the sixteenth century, however, historical documentary sources that deal with the social, political, and economic milieu of Maya studies are incorporated. We start in the dim recesses of 12,000 B.C.E. (years before Common Era), a time called the Paleoindian period, and work our way back to the present.

Paleoindian, Archaic, and Early Preclassic Periods (12,000–1000 B.C.E.)

Eleven thousand years compressed into a single subheading may seem excessive, but the sheer paucity of information for this long

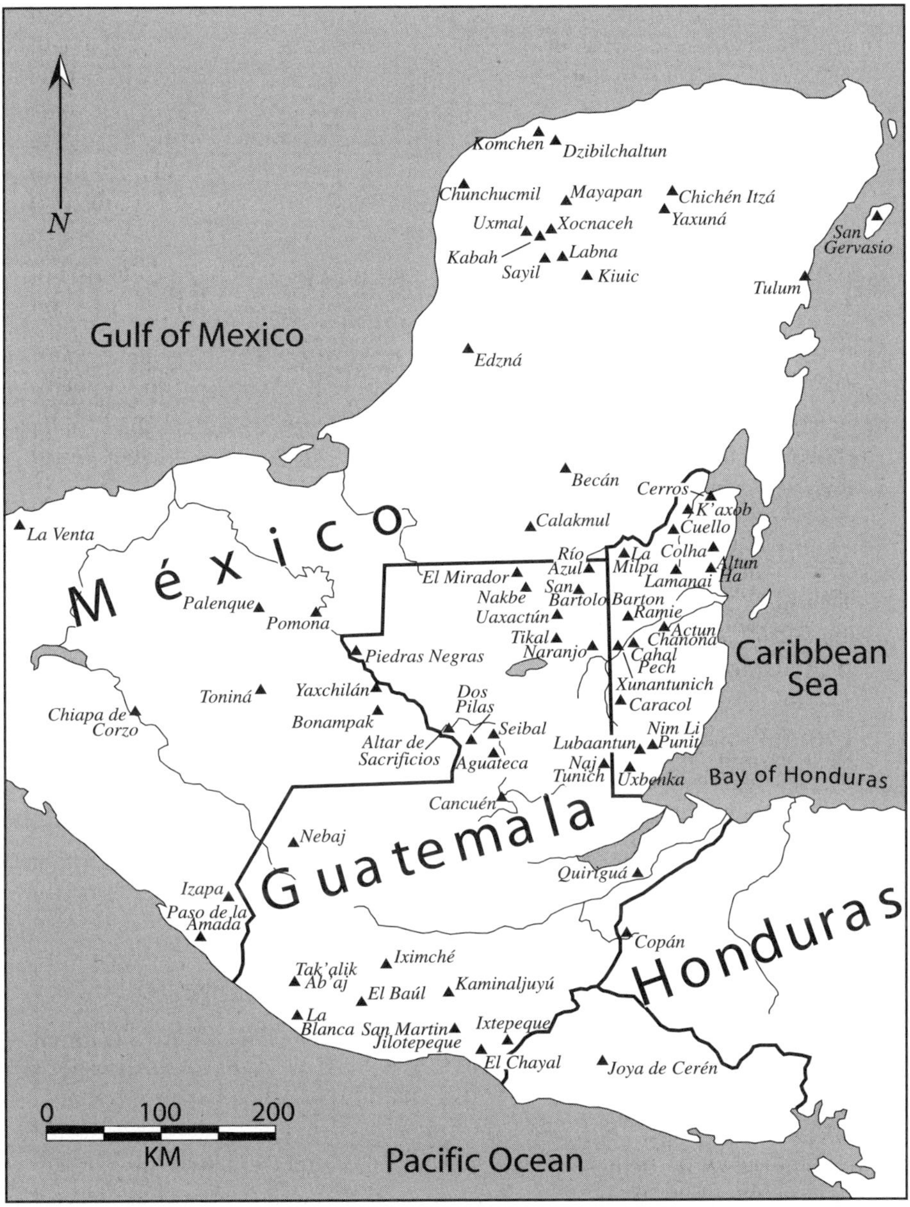

FIGURE 2.2 Ancestral Maya places and contemporary nation-states (map prepared by Josh Feola).

duration necessitates brevity in its treatment. Only a handful of sites and artifacts are known from the Paleoindian and Archaic periods in the Maya region. In Belize, where favorable conditions exist for site visibility, seven Paleoindian projectile points (likely dating to 12,000–3400 B.C.E.) have been recovered: three fluted points and four fishtail points (Lohse et al. 2006). As Lohse and colleagues (2006) point out, the presence of both fluted points, which are more common in North America, and fishtail points, found primarily in South America, suggests that Central America was somewhat of a crossroads during this very earliest time of known human landscape inhabitation.

Regarding the subsequent Archaic period, Lohse and colleagues (2006) provide an insightful review of known finds from this period (see also Clark and Cheetham 2002). The Archaic period can be divided into an early facet (3400–1900 B.C.E.) of a preceramic time that is followed by a later facet (1900–1000/900 B.C.E.) that, in other parts of Mesoamerica, is called the Early Preclassic period. Of Archaic times (3400–900 B.C.E.), little is known, and the artifacts that do exist point to hunting practices. Projectile points, such as Lowe (Figure 2.3) and Sawmill, have been found primarily in surface contexts from a range of landscape types (including mountain slopes and mangrove margins). These projectiles conjure images of highly mobile people skilled in gaining a livelihood from the dispersed small game, fruits, and greens of a landscape that may have been significantly different from the tropical forests and savannahs of today. The people of early Archaic and even earlier Paleoindian times had minimal investment in the kind of materiality that anchors so much of the later Maya sequence. Regardless of lack of investment in material goods such as pottery, there is mounting evidence that Archaic people had a significant impact on their landscape, and they appear to have been horticulturalists as well as hunters after 2500 B.C.E. Information from deep pollen cores (Jones 1994; Pohl et al. 1996) calibrated to the second millennium B.C.E. suggests the following: (1) cultigens such a maize and manioc were present; (2) forest clearance – indicated by heightened levels of wood charcoal – was underway; and (3) the landscape differed from that known historically in terms of forest composition and a greater contrast between the wet and the dry.

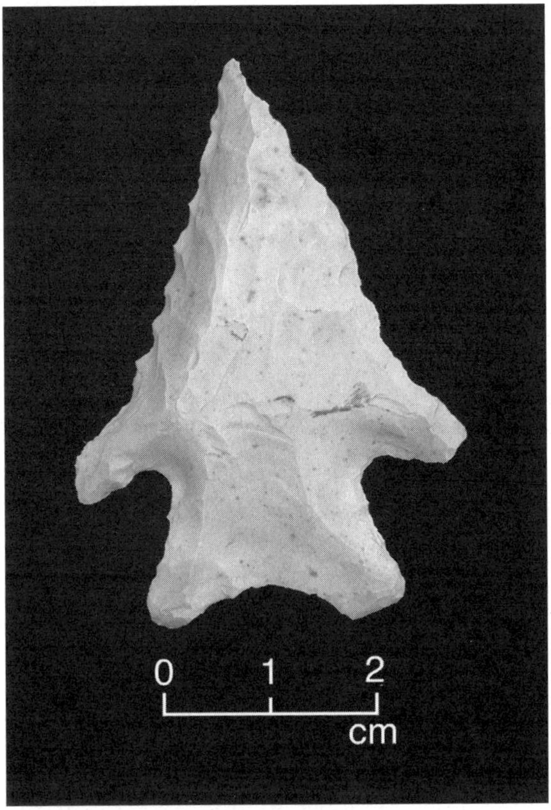

FIGURE 2.3 Archaic-period Lowe projectile point from St. Thomas, Belize (photo courtesy of Xibun Archaeological Research Project).

During late Archaic times, dated deposits from Colha in northern Belize indicate the production of constricted unifaces (thought to have been a tool of forest clearance and perhaps hoeing) as well as oval bifaces and macroblades (Iceland 1997, 2005, among others). Iceland suggests that the technological continuity in lithic production practices provides a bridge between this preceramic time and the subsequent Middle Preclassic period and that there was continuity in population across a dramatic change in lifestyle.

MIDDLE PRECLASSIC SOCIETIES (1000/900–400 B.C.E.)

The centuries surrounding 1000 B.C.E. represent another poorly understood time in the lowlands during which a presumably preceramic occupation of mixed horticulturalist and hunters gave way to settled village agriculturalists who came to be called "Maya" by archaeologists (see McAnany 2006). In other parts of Mesoamerica – such as the Gulf Coast Olmec region – there is a clearly stratified sequence of Early Preclassic remains from the period of 2000–1000 B.C.E. that often underlie Middle Preclassic materials. At La Blanca – on the Pacific Coast – monumental construction was underway by 1000 B.C.E. In the Maya lowlands, however, Middle Preclassic monumental architecture enjoys a patchy distribution and an Early to Middle Preclassic sequence rarely has been found, leading some to suspect that there was a significant migration to the lowlands from the west or south in the centuries before 1000 B.C.E. Conceptualized in terms that are akin to the Neolithic expansion across Europe, the hypothesized Maya Middle Preclassic expansion carries with it the same interpretive caveats that Zvelebil (2004) has discussed in reference to the European Neolithic. Regardless of whether Middle Preclassic Maya societies represent an admixture, a replacement, or an autochthonous emergence from horticultural roots, a very decisive change in daily subsistence practice, ritual practice, and power relations occurred around 1000 B.C.E. As Hodder (2006:233–258) has written in reference to the European Neolithic, it was a time during which there was a "massive increase in the amount of enduring materiality that came to surround people." The lowland Maya Middle Preclassic does not start softly and built to a crescendo, but rather appears writ large on the landscape from its very inception. Well-built residences, redware and bichrome pottery crafted in technologically intricate ways (Figure 2.4), circular nonresidential platforms, and even pyramidal structures are present during this time. Only a very few parts of the lowlands were not touched by Middle Preclassic societies who exhibited a keen interest in wetlands as well as higher dry lands (Berry and McAnany 2007). The ethos of artisanship – explored in further detail in Chapter 7 – was present in Middle Preclassic societies and thus likely was rooted in an even earlier time and place. A fuller understanding of this period of time and that preceding it will require additional data and in-depth critical analysis in the style to which Zvelebil (2002a, 2002b, 2004) has interrogated the Mesolithic-Neolithic transition in Europe.

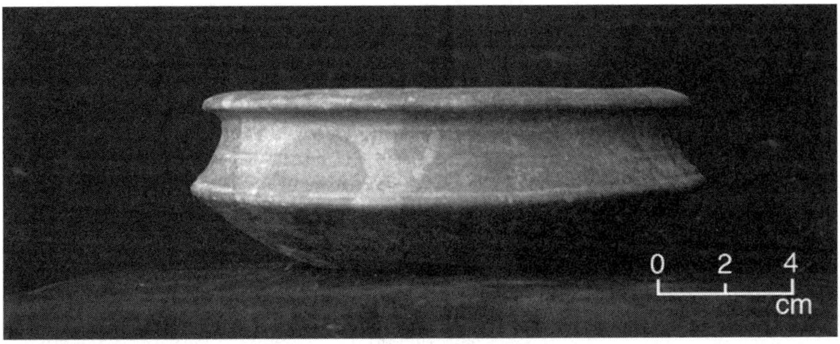

FIGURE 2.4 Middle Preclassic Timax incised bowl decorated with a resist technique (photo courtesy of K'axob Archaeological Project).

LATE-TERMINAL PRECLASSIC SOCIETIES (400 B.C.E.–250 C.E.)

During this excessively long chunk of time, there existed a remarkably large sphere within which monochrome red-slipped pottery was crafted into similar vessel forms (Figure 2.5). The sphere extended from the Caribbean shores west to the Grijalva Basin and from the tip of the Yucatán Peninsula south to the base of the Alta Verapaz. The widespread distribution of this Chicanel pottery complex (generally the Sierra Red type), coupled with the unprecedented construction of massive monumental architecture, led Clark and colleagues (2000) to dub this time period that of the Chicanel kingdoms. Some of the largest pyramids ever built in the Maya lowlands were raised at this time, particularly in the Mirador Basin of the northern Petén, at Lamanai on the fresh-water lagoon of the New River of Belize, and at the recently documented Xocnaceh in the Sierra Puuc of the Yucatán. As discussed in detail in Chapter 5, these constructions do not seem to have been funerary pyramids but rather shrines to the gods. As Taube (1998:446–454) has indicated, however, the elaborate stucco masks that adorn the face of these colossal structures are redolent of kingship and probably represent the burgeoning entanglement of rulership with notions of divinity. The construction of such colossal structures surely was coordinated by rulers, but their residences are not as easy to detect and not as differentiated as are the palatial royal courts of later times. At the Petén site of San Bartolo where an

FIGURE 2.5 Sierra Red shallow bowl from the Early K'atabchek'ax ceramic complex (a local variant of the Chicanel ceramic complex) of K'axob (photo courtesy of K'axob Archaeological Project).

extraordinary mural program has been revealed dating to the Late Preclassic period (Saturno et al. 2005), a palace structure has been identified, and more are sure to be found in the Mirador Basin where the site of Wakna also contains mural paintings.

While the Late Preclassic period was a time of extraordinary construction within the lowlands, the corpus of known long-count dates and hieroglyphic texts associated with these structures is limited. Rather, Pacific Coast sites – such as El Baúl and Tak'alik Ab'aj – feature monuments with the earliest long-count dates that generally occur on stelae depicting a ruler or a mythological scene, such as the well-known Stela 1 from El Baúl (Figure 2.6). From the Late Preclassic Pacific Coast site of Izapa comes a wealth of stelae, some carved with scenes that are highly evocative of the narrative of the *Popol Vuh*, the Colonial-period epic of the hero twins, Hunahpu and Xbalanque. The massive earthen constructions that are associated with these carved stones enjoy a deep history on the Pacific Coast where colossal structures at sites such as La Blanca were built during the earlier Middle Preclassic period.

FIGURE 2.6 Stela 1, El Baúl, featuring a seventh *bak'tun* long-count date of 7.19.15.7.12 (36 C.E.) in association with a ruler (photo courtesy of Oswaldo Chinchilla, Cotzumalguapa Archaeological Project).

Across all parts of the Maya region, the Late Preclassic was a time of population expansion and active modification of the landscape. Timothy Beach and colleagues (2002, 2006), in fact, have suggested that this earlier time, rather than the Late Classic, was the period during which the environmental impact of expansive and intensive farming practices is most perceptible and paved the way for Classic-period agrarian reform that stressed a conservation ethic. Likewise, the generous use of plaster and stucco – both produced by slaking or burning lime – was an environmentally expensive proposition that likely took its toll on the ambient tropical forest (Hansen et al. 2002). Quarrying activities also were required to secure building material for the large pyramids and for basal platforms built to house residential complexes. At K'axob, Belize, large *aguadas* (shallow, seasonal ponds) were created by excavating into the soft, marl bedrock for construction material at this time. Some of these platforms continued to be occupied for up to 600 years and inevitably served as the repository for generations of deceased family members who were interred within the platform, creating an earth-bound genealogy. The stone-tool-producing center of Colha, Belize, ramped up production during the time in order to provide an expanding population in northern and central Belize with tools for a wide range of activities from farming to fighting. The heavy imprint of society on landscape is clearly detectable during the Late Preclassic and also can be traced back to the earlier Middle Preclassic period.

EARLY CLASSIC MAYA SOCIETIES (250–600 C.E.)

In comparison to the heavy and ubiquitous signature left by Late Preclassic lowland populations, the Early Classic period remains somewhat enigmatic and only partially understood. Lowland societies of this time were sandwiched between two extremely populous periods during which both "housing starts" and temple construction skyrocketed; such ironclad indicators of people modifying their landscape into a built environment are patchily distributed across the lowlands during the Early Classic period. The Petén represents a core region within which both indicators are present along with a new, distinctive kind of polychrome pottery (as opposed to the monochromes and bichromes of earlier eras). Polychrome calligraphic/figural painting on a cylindrical form was initiated during the Early Classic and generally is thought to have been patterned on a highland Mexican shape – the Teotihuacan cylindrical vessel with slab-feet supports. Other forms that appear during the Early Classic, such as the basal-flange bowl (Figure 2.7), seem to be lowland innovations. In general, the iconographic program painted on Early Classic vessels tends toward abstract concepts or zoomorphic figures, such as the image of the K'an cross and jaguar in Figure 2.7. As Reents-Budet (1998:72) has discussed, few Early Classic vessels contain court scenes or detailed hieroglyphic texts, and none bears the name of the artist who painted the vessel. A noteworthy exception to this pattern is the stirrup-handled polychrome jar from Early Classic Tomb 19 at

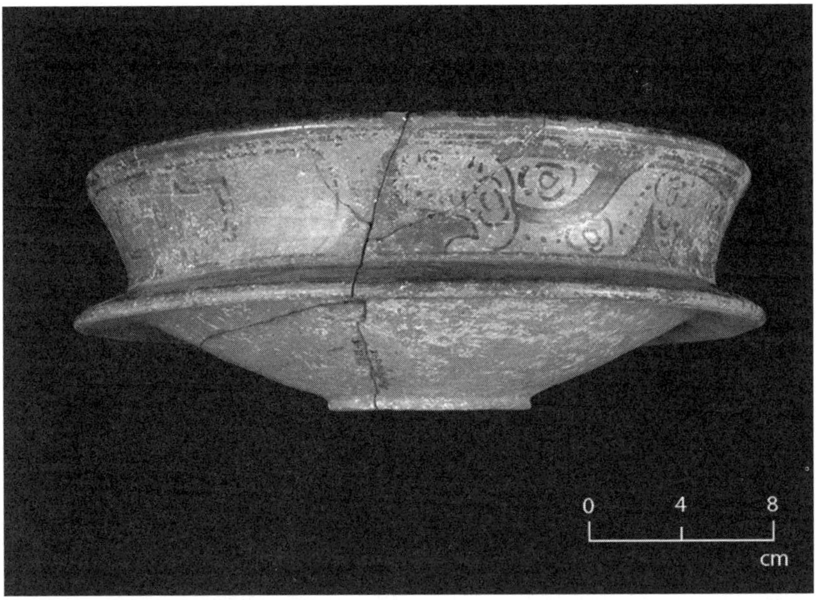

FIGURE 2.7 Early Classic basal-flange polychrome bowl with a naturalistic jaguar on right and a K'an cross faintly discernible on the left (photo courtesy of K'axob Archaeological Project).

Río Azul that contains a rudimentary form of the dedicatory texts so common on Late Classic vessels (see Chapter 9 for more on vessel inscriptions). One of the earliest known examples of the hieroglyphic compound for cacao (Figure 2.8) occurs on this vessel, which features an unusual screw-top lid and the preserved chemical residue of cacao within its interior (Adams 1999; Hall et al. 1990; Stuart 1988).

The example from Río Azul points to the fact that royal tombs were present during the Early Classic and that select persons were interred within monumental architecture, indicating pronounced social differentiation that also was apparent in the presence of palace construction at Río Azul (Adams 1999:42). A comparable pattern exists at many other sites in the Petén of Guatemala – most famously Tikal – and also in southern México at Calakmul as well as at the far-flung capital of Copán in the southeastern zone, which is thought to have been established by a royal dynasty of Tikal (Andrews and Fash 2005; Sharer 2003).

Long-count dates, so integral to marking "monumental time" (Ricoeur 1985:110) created by dynastic rule, appear on carved stelae at this time and often are paired with images of rulers, such as on Tikal

FIGURE 2.8 Hieroglyphic compound for cacao from the Río Azul vessel that contained chemical residue of cacao (redrawn by Josh Feola after Stuart 1988:Figure 2).

Stela 29, which bears a long-count date of 8 *bak'tun*, 12 *k'atun*, 14 *tun*, 1 *winal*, and 15 *k'in* or 292 C.E. These spans of time equal approximately 400 years, 20 years, a solar year, a lunar month, and a day. Tikal Stela 29 contains the earliest such complete date from the Maya lowlands (but earlier long-count dates occur at the highland site of Kaminaljuyu and on the Pacific Coast as mentioned earlier). On Tikal Stela 29, the back of the monument contained the long-count date, while the front featured an image of a ruler. Earliest of the 12 rulers known from the venerable old capital of Tikal, this person (referred to as "Foliated Jaguar") is surrounded by accoutrements of office, including an ancestral "guardian" in his sky, a sceptor, and a belt assemblage that contains the main element (a tied bundle) that forms part of the Tikal emblem glyph for the next 600 years. This example indicates that many of the essential elements of rulership and seats of power were well established by the Early Classic period. Certainly, the Late Classic ushered in a more crowded and presumably more competitive landscape.

Although a distinctive and elite-focused archaeological signature of the Early Classic is not difficult to detect at places that clearly were seats of emerging dynastic power during this time, the Early Classic is more elusive at places that sat lower on the site hierarchy. At secondary, tertiary, and quaternary centers, settlement evidence indicates that there was a drawdown of population from the earlier Late Preclassic when construction activity reached a zenith barely surpassed during the Late Classic period. Excavations at the site of K'axob in northern Belize – where large Late Preclassic basal platforms were constructed to accommodate expanded residential size – revealed the presence of Early Classic ancestors placed within pits intruded into Late Preclassic platforms. The presence of diagnostic Early Classic pottery such as the polychrome bowl of Figure 2.7 provide the only indicator that this person – a young male in this case (Storey 2004:131) – lived and died at the cusp of Terminal Preclassic–Early Classic times. Beyond the rising dynastic centers, amplification of the built environment appears to have slowed in many places during the Early Classic. Perhaps population growth leveled off or the tremendous amount of construction, particularly residential housing that took place during the preceding period, meant that old platforms could simply be refurbished for continued occupation. Regardless, Early Classic societies appear to have been a work in progress – not as diacritically differentiated as during the later Classic period but clearly embracing many of the material characteristics of royalty and rulership so emphatically displayed in the material record of the Late Classic period.

LATE-TERMINAL CLASSIC MAYA SOCIETIES (600–909 C.E.)

Victor Montejo describes Classic Maya society as "finely wrought" (2005:106), and this epithet perhaps best describes this 300-year slice of time generally considered to have been the apogee of Maya civilization. This notion stems largely from the fact that the bulk of hieroglyphic texts carved in stone and painted on pottery or wall murals date to this period, which can be more finely calibrated due to the presence of so many long-count dates chiseled into stone (Figure 2.9). Although most texts are explicitly dedicatory, there is much historical and genealogical information embedded within this hieroglyphic corpus so that patterns of marriage and martial conflicts between dynasties can be gleaned as can biographical knowledge of members of royal dynasties. This material constitutes a written history and brings into question the accuracy of the term "prehistoric" as applied

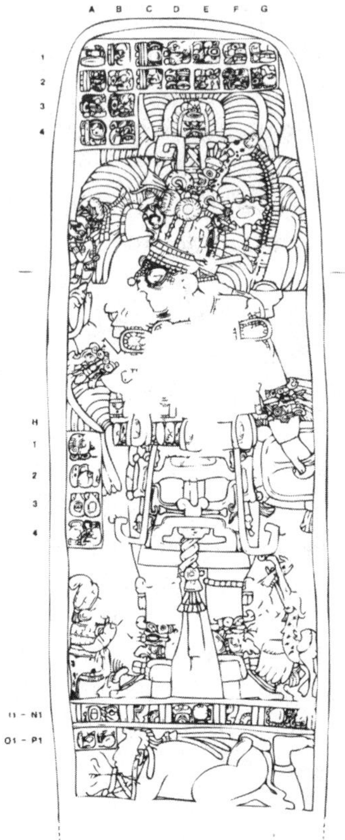

FIGURE 2.9 (*left*) Dos Pilas Stela 14 with a Maya long-count date of 9.14.0.0.0 6 Ajaw 13 Muan (December 1, 711 C.E.) shown at A1–B4. The Dos Pilas emblem glyph appears at F1 and G1. The stela commemorates a military victory of a Dos Pilas ruler, possibly named Itzamnaaj K'awiil, who is shown masked and holding a God K sceptor of office (redrawn by Josh Feola after Houston 1993:91). FIGURE 2.10 (*right*) Naturalistic fired clay figurine of a Classic Maya royal woman (after Schele 1997:Plate 7, Museo Nacional de Antropología, México, D.F., photo courtesy of Jorge Perez de Lara).

to this American civilization. The manner in which the royal component of Late Classic Maya society diacritically defined itself is examined in detail in Chapter 6, but here it is important to note that much of the allure of Maya archaeology can be attributed to the immense output of naturalistic figural painting, sculpture, wood carving, and figurine modeling that occurred during this period (Figure 2.10).

Giving us a glimpse of face, body, gestures, and the proxemics of courtly life, these representations not only were rendered in the well-known Jaina figurines but also were painted on cylindrical pottery vessels and wall murals, carved into freestanding stone panels (stelae and altars) or part of stone or wooden architectural elements (such as lintels, jambs, and stair risers), and molded in stucco over a stone frame as with the high-flying roof combs that soar above the temples of central Tikal. The social context and political message of this tremendous investment in naturalistic representation is discussed in detail in Chapters 6 and 9.

Although some have interpreted references to martial conflict within Late Classic texts as evidence of an escalating spiral of inter-site violence that ultimately led to the collapse of Classic Maya society, there is no basis for comparing the frequency of hieroglyphic statements of martial conflict with previous or subsequent periods; there are far fewer texts from the Early Classic or Postclassic periods. One could just as readily point out that the incidence of marriage statements escalated during the Late Classic period and infer that marital discord led to societal collapse (see McAnany and Gallareta Negrón 2009 for expanded discussion).

An important glyph compound of the Classic period is the so-called emblem glyph (see Figure 2.9) that includes the name and title of a ruler (generally *k'uhul ajaw* or "divine ruler") and a reference to a place name (Stuart and Houston 1994). Found primarily at large Maya sites in southern México, the Petén, and the southeasten zone, this glyph compound is thought to indicate some measure of political autonomy although not complete independence from overlordship (see Martin and Grube 2008[2000] for in-depth analysis of hierarchy, alliance, and conflict among Classic Maya kingdoms and Rice 2004 for a calendrically based interpretation of Classic-period power dynamics). Looming large and among the most influential of Late Classic kingdoms are Tikal and Calakmul (Figure 2.2), which vied for control of the entire lowlands via marriage and diplomatic alliance as well as martial conflict. Both Tikal and Calakmul are located along the central north–south spine of the Maya lowlands and exhibit a pronounced 1,000-plus-year depth of occupation – they are truly venerable old places and hearths of civilization. Other sites with substantial textual records occur around the edges of the

Maya world: Palenque, situated in the lower Usumacinta watershed along the access route to the cacao orchards of Tabasco; Cancuen, to the south at the base of the Alta Verapaz, which is the home of the resplendent quetzal bird; Copán and Quirigua on the southeastern edge near the sole known source of jadeite; Caracol on the western flank of the Maya Mountains controlling access to the mineral and mountain resources; and Naranjo situated near the headwaters of Belize Valley with a direct pipeline to the marine resources and cacao orchards of the Caribbean seaboard (Figure 2.2). The richness of the textual records from these sites provides direct evidence of alliance structures and indirect indicators of complex networks of resource extraction and the centripetal transport of these resources toward the central spine of the lowlands. Another band of ancient capitals with expansive textual records exists along the main course and tributaries of the Usumacinta River that forms partially the boundary between Guatemala and México. At these western sites – Yaxchilán, Piedras Negras, and further upriver, Altar de Sacrificios, Seibal, Dos Pilas, and Aguateca – royal females are more commonly represented on monuments than in capitals farther to the east (more on this pattern in Chapters 6 and 9).

Throughout the course of the Late-Terminal Classic period, there is a clear shift in power from the south to the north where a large Classic-period population – building unparalleled monumental structures – persisted until at least 1000 C.E., if not longer. Paramount among these sites is Chichén Itzá, which seems to have exerted more influence in the south than is generally acknowledged. In the Puuc Hills to the west of the centrally located Chichén Itzá, there likewise was a Late Classic expansion of monumental architecture at places such as Uxmal, Kabah, Sayil, and Labna, to name just a few of the northern capitals. Excepting Chichén Itzá, the hieroglyphic record of the northern sites is somewhat abbreviated, which makes it more difficult to calibrate temporally the emergence of these northern seats of power with the dissolution of power in the south.

Taking into consideration both the north and the south, there exists two to three dozen known sites with abundant textual records and/or emblem glyphs, but these represent only the most visible and prominent material expression of Late Classic Maya societies. Many more sites displaying a substantial core of monumental architecture but a more limited hieroglyphic corpus exist alongside an even larger group of sites with sizable pyramid complexes and no hieroglyphic texts, and finally there is an even larger array of sites composed solely or primarily of the remains of house mounds (platforms for residences built of stone, adobe, wattle-and-daub, thatch, or a combination of materials). The site hierarchy was deep, and although there was a clear break between royal and nonroyal architecture (massive pyramids and royal courts as opposed to smaller pyramids and elite housing), many material characteristics of Maya society exhibit a clinal, rather than a discrete distribution. For instance, obsidian blades that were needed for sharp cutting tasks are more plentiful in royal contexts but are not lacking from elite and commoner contexts. This type of material signature suggests that even though the concept of divine rulership was operative in Classic Maya society and royalty lived a world apart from commoners, ruling dynasties did not wield absolute power over the distribution of material goods. As Smith and Schreiber (2005:204–206) note, the issue of class structure and inequalities among/between classes is under-theorized in the Maya region in which sources of wealth and status were more heterogeneous than simple categorical schemes have been able to accommodate. Here, Chapters 4, 6, and 7 discuss wealth, status, and artisanship and how they fused together to form identity within a very hierarchical social frame.

The monumental architecture of the Late Classic period indeed was finely wrought. Tall, steep-sided pyramids were built alongside long, multiroomed stone structures colloquially called palaces. Late Classic pyramids often were built as funerary shrines (e.g., Temple of the Inscriptions at Palenque), and many contain the remains of members of ruling families who were sent on their journey through the afterlife adorned with their finest jadeite jewelry and sufficient food and drink – particularly chocolate – to satisfy a royal appetite. This pattern of Classic funerary pyramids contrasts with the earlier Preclassic period during which pyramids seem to have been built as shrines to deities rather than dedicated to dead dynasts (see Chapter 5 for extended presentation of this topic).

The Late-Terminal Classic is perhaps the most populous period in the deep history of Maya society. Evidence of both large and small Late-Terminal Classic house mounds as well as ground-level structures are found throughout the Maya region, and the overall population numbered in the millions. Households at the lower end of the spectrum of size and architectural elaboration, however, are noticeably more spartan in terms of material wealth, particularly those located on the fringes of the many large, political capitals of the southern Petén. Following a mortuary tradition started in earlier times, important deceased members of a household might be interred under the floor of the main dwelling or within a shrine that constituted part of the residential complex. Unlike earlier times when the sex and age of subfloor burials was highly variable, Late Classic subfloor burials often were adult males. This pattern suggests greater gender-based power within households than had existed during earlier times.

POSTCLASSIC MAYA SOCIETIES (909–1524 C.E.)

My colleague Marilyn Masson brought to my attention this telling quote from Harry Pollock who offered it as a summary statement on the Carnegie project at the Late Postclassic inland capital of Mayapan (located on the northern Yucatecan plain, see Figure 2.2): "Looking at the results of the work as a whole, I think it has been worthwhile, even though we are dealing with a degenerate civilization, devoid of great art, that to all intents and purposes reached a dead end in the Spanish conquest" (Pollock 1962:17). Published over 40 years ago, this statement conveys a decidedly prejudicial view of Postclassic society that has not completely disappeared from archaeological narratives. True, compared to the monumental constructions of the previous Classic period, Postclassic construction is more modest in scale. As Sabloff and Rathje (1975 and more recently Sabloff 2007:17) note, labor clearly was being funneled elsewhere. And yet, more recent attention to the capital of Mayapan – more or less abandoned before Spanish incursions – indicates that considerable labor and skill was involved in its construction, particularly the elaborate stucco figures adorning the main pyramid (Milbrath and Peraza L. 2003). As Milbrath and Peraza Lope (2003:40), Smith and Berdan (2003a:3), and others have argued, the Late Postclassic was a time of vibrant mercantilism and long-distance trading across the Mesoamerican world. It also represented a period during which the most powerful, pre-Hispanic imperial force recognized within Mesoamerica emerged in the Mexican Highlands at the Mexica capital of Tenochtitlán. During the Late Postclassic period, it appears that Maya lowland societies, somewhat balkanized in relation to the Late Classic period, were positioned at the edge of Mexica imperial tentacles. Lives, identities, and the manner in which power was materialized iconographically were profoundly affected by this powerful and expansive imperial power, despite the distance. Ethnohistorical information provides a glimpse of the participation of Postclassic Maya royalty in the movement of goods along the Caribbean seaboard via large cargo canoes. Specifically, when Mayapan was sacked as a result of what appears to have been an internal conflict between the powerful Xiu and Cocom royal houses, a member of the ruling Cocom family escaped death because, according to informants of Bishop Diego de Landa, he was absent (Tozzer 1941:37) and reputed to have been on a trading voyage in the Gulf of Honduras.

During the Postclassic period, site locations often contrast with those of the earlier Classic period with a decided interest in strategic locales, such as lacustrine island-"fortresses" and coastlines (Tulum being a well-known example of the latter). By and large, archaeologists have interpreted this positional change as an indicator of an increase in both the need for defensive security in a balkanized landscape and a preference for coastal trading activities at the expense of older, inland porter routes. Less often recognized, however, is the veneer of Postclassic artifacts – poorly preserved due to their proximity to the surface – that covers much of the lowlands, which often are characterized, perhaps inaccurately, as depopulated during this time (see Rice and Rice 2005:140 on the continued population of the Petén Lakes districts through the Postclassic period). An extremely important distinction needs to be made between evidence of occupation and evidence of construction. Maya archaeologists recognize the latter with great facility – because it leaves such a heavy footprint – but traditionally have not concerned themselves with detecting more nuanced patterns of landscape inhabitation. Any truly definitive statement regarding the extent of the drawdown in population levels between the Classic and Postclassic periods must grapple with this problem.

A remarkable contrast between Classic and Postclassic residential artifact assemblages exists in the increased frequency of spindle whorls at Postclassic sites. As discussed in Chapters 6 and 9, textiles were a significant materialization of wealth and status and their production appears to have been female-gendered labor. During the Classic period, spindle whorls were far more common in elite contexts but there seems to have transpired a "democratization" in textile production during the Postclassic at which time spindle whorls occur in residences of all size and degrees of elaboration. This change represents a fundamental transformation in the daily practice of females and may have occurred in response to tribute demands linked to the heightened importance of bulk, long-distance trading via cargo canoe (see Masson 2000:165 for an expanded treatment of this topic).

K'iché, Kaqchiquel, and other polities of the Guatemalan highlands – those later ravaged by the *conquistador* Pedro Alvarado – interacted more closely politically and socially with the Mexica who struggled to control the nearby Soconusco Coast – the gold coast of cacao production. In Guatemalan Highland capitals, both ritual practice and personal identities were formulated in reference to the powerful Mexica.

Despite the widespread and seemingly democratic distribution of spindle whorls, there are ample indications that Postclassic societies were as socially complex and stratified as in preceding periods. Although the ethos of divine rulership was reformulated during the Postclassic period, these late polities were governed by hereditary members of royal cadres; there was no impoverishment of principles of political rulership, only changes in the manner in which it was materialized. But changes in materialization are telling, particularly in reference to Maya hieroglyphic writing and calendrics. Monuments carved with elaborate hieroglyphic texts and long-count dates that employed a calculation of *bak'tun, k'atun, tun, winal,* and *k'in* that evoke so powerfully the profound investment of Classic royalty in the calculation of time and the sacred script – not to mention the financial support of scribes and sculptors – were not crafted during Postclassic times. The year 909 C.E. is used here as the hinge point between Classic and Postclassic periods precisely because it is the last known long-count date, carved on Monument 101 at the western site of Tonina (10th *bak'tun*, 4th *k'atun*, 0 *tun*, 0 *winal*, and 0 *k'in* or January 15, 909). During the Postclassic period, a shorter, *k'atun*-based calendar came into use: cycles of 20 *tun* (or one *k'atun*) were intercalculated with a cycle of 20 day names prefaced by a number from 1 to 13. The day name Ajaw (ruler) and its numerical coefficient provided the name for each new *k'atun* cycle. Likewise, Postclassic pottery shows a decided lack of hieroglyphic script as well as figural painting that was so characteristic of the Late Classic, the latter discussed in Chapter 9. On the other hand, sacred hieroglyphic writing in fan-fold codices made of bark paper retained tremendous significance through the Postclassic period. Informants of Bishop Diego de Landa state that upon the sacking of Mayapan, "The most important possession that the nobles who abandoned Mayapan took away to their own country was the books of their sciences" (Tozzer 1941:39). The four extant Maya fan-fold codices were painted during the Postclassic (and probably copied from earlier manuscripts). The Dresden, Madrid, Paris, and Grolier codices deal primarily with astronomy, prognostication, and ritual practice; none is overtly political or genealogical as can be said of Classic-period stone-chiseled texts. Combining pictorial imagery with script (Figure 2.11), the codices follow an established Classic tradition of mixing media (see Houston 2008 for further discussion of Classic–Postclassic changes in Maya hieroglyphic script).

COLONIAL INCURSIONS AND THEIR AFTERMATH (1524–1839)

Victor Montejo (2005:108) places the beginning of the Colonial period at 1524 – the year that the cruel *conquistador* Pedro Alvarado laid waste to the highland K'iché capital of Q'umarkaj and killed many indigenous leaders including the culture hero, Tecun Uman. Over the next 175 years, this event would be repeated again and again throughout the Maya region and would come to signal the loss of Maya political autonomy; the cumulative stripping of the rights, privileges, and power of Maya rulers and leaders; and the practical enslavement of the remaining population who did not die from introduced diseases or escape detection by fleeing to forested, sparsely populated interior regions. Virtually every account of a Spanish *entrada* (military campaign into an "unpacified" region) relates the destruction of Maya codices, indicating the zeal with which Spaniards worked to extirpate the materiality of Maya spirituality, particularly that dealing

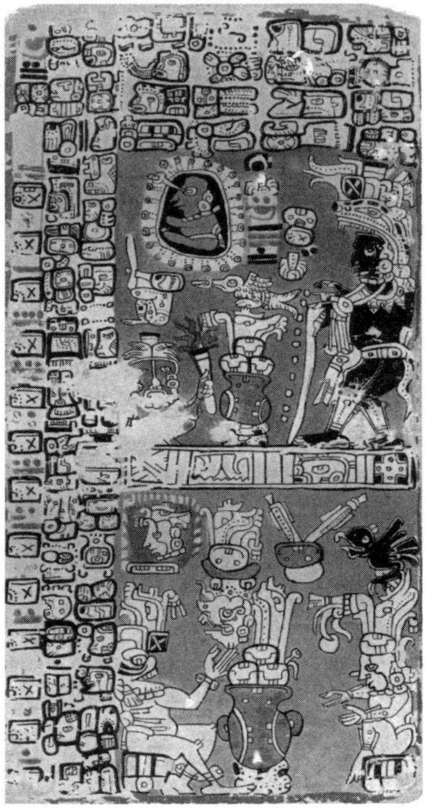

FIGURE 2.11 Codex Madrid, Folio 34, Cauac Yearbearer, showing the juxtapositioning of Postclassic hieroglyphic text and pictorial imagery (reprinted courtesy of Foundation for the Advancement of Mesoamerican Studies, FAMSI).

with sacred scripts and religion. The savagery of the Colonial period cannot be underestimated; in a very real sense, Spanish incursions can be viewed, in the words of Comaroff (1985:5), as a "fracture of a precolonial cosmos." Using Colonial legal documents (particularly wills), Restall (1992) documents the 200 year dissolution of the power and wealth of indigenous Yucatec Maya *hidalgo* (lesser nobility). Jones (1989, 1998) has focused attention on the strategies of resistance (mobility and prophecy) employed by Maya living along the edges of Colonial hegemony as they struggled to maintain some measure of control over their lives, livelihoods, and the well-being of their families. The high mobility of this population undergoing colonization, the conflict with Spaniards over the control of fertile lands, and the decreasing power of elites resulted in the fracturing of many important components of Maya agricultural practices – such as orchard holdings – and helped to give rise to the "myth of the milpa" (Hammond 1978; Harrison and Turner 1978) as the sole component of Maya cultivation strategies.

The repression and turbulence of the Colonial period worked to sever the connection between Maya people – who struggled for survival – and the material remains of their distant ancestors (Parks and McAnany 2007). Although many Classic-period monumental sites remained sacred places of pilgrimage, the Spanish Crown followed by the five emergent nation-states of the Maya area began to lay claim to "the ruins" by sponsoring exploration, early on as part of a burgeoning European interest in antiquarianism and later as part of a larger management and tourism-promotion effort (see Yaeger and Borgstede 2004:262 for expanded discussion).

During the Colonial period, Spanish colonists devised several different techniques for sequestering labor and wealth from Maya people: *encomienda*, *repartimiento*, and *reducción* being three particularly repressive policies (see Farriss 1983; Gasco 2005; Jones 1989 for detailed treatments). Outright labor drafts of able-bodied males were common, and, as will be discussed further in Chapter 4, Spanish colonialists demanded tribute of finely woven cotton cloth (*mantas*). Tribute demands apparently were so high that they not only consumed much of the time of female householders but also disrupted cycles of feasting and textile exchange that ran on female-gendered labor (Espejo-Ponce and Restall 1997:232; Gosner 1997:223, 226). In reference to the female-led Tzeltal Revolt of 1712 in Chiapas, Gosner (1997:220) describes the rapacious Colonial laws and decrees as "an assault on the Maya moral economy."

Spaniards (particularly mendicant friars and *conquistadores*) sought to destroy all evidence of indigenous Maya writing, which was thought to be idolatrous. Diego de Landa, bishop of Maní, is famous for sponsoring an *auto de fe* in which untold numbers of precious books and wooden icons were burned. At the same time, Landa and other friars established a European alphabetic orthography for Mayan languages and effected a transition among Maya scribes from hieroglyphic and alphabetic writing. Landa also left behind copious notes on his impressions of daily practice (literally) within Yucatec Maya society. These "accounts" were written during the first generation after Spaniards gained political control of the Yucatán Peninsula (Tozzer 1941) and are an invaluable if highly biased and perhaps historically compromised record (see Restall and Chuchiak 2002 on problems regarding the authenticity of Landa's *Relación de las Cosas de Yucatán*). Despite the repression and impoverishment of the Colonial period, the tradition of indigenous literacy persevered from the Yucatán to the highlands of Guatemala. In the Yucatán, as late as 1837, histories were compiled by the "Spokesmen of the Jaguar" (a.k.a. *Books of Chilam Balam*), written in Yucatec Mayan from indigenous perspective but employing a European alphabet (Edmondson 1982:xii). During the sixteenth century, the great K'iché creation epic – the *Popol Vuh* – was written in K'iché using a Spanish alphabetic orthography (Christenson 2007:37; Tedlock 1985).

Archaeologists have barely touched the surface of Colonial archaeology in the Maya region beyond documentation of the monumental mission churches and cathedrals built with labor drafts and often of stone recycled from nearby precolonial monumental architecture. Graham (1998) provides an expanded discussion of Mission Archaeology and notable Colonial-period research includes Kepecs (2005) on Colonial salt production in the Yucatán; Alexander (2005) on *reducción* communities in Campeche; Pendergast and Graham on the excavation of the house of a Colonial-period *cacique* at Lamanai; Graham and Jones on the *visita* mission at Tipu (Graham et al. 1989; Pendergast 1993); Rice and Rice (2005) on Postclassic and Colonial settlement in the Petén Lakes district; and Palka (2005) on the Lacandon Maya of the Usumacinta drainage.

NEOCOLONIALISM IN THE MAYA REGION (1839–1950)

The start date for this temporal slice is pinned to the exploratory trips that led to the publication of *Incidents of Travel* written by John Lloyd Stephens and illustrated by his travel companion, Frederick Catherwood (Stephens 1993). Travel accounts were a popular

FIGURE 2.12 Nineteenth-century drawing by Frederick Catherwood of Copán Stela H showing Waxaklajuun Ubaah K'awiil wearing the net skirt of the maize deity.

literary genre in the mid-nineteenth century, and Stephens "wrote with humor and passion, with a lawyer's eye for detail, with candor, awe, indignation, exuberance, bravado, self-deprecation" (Ackerman 1993:1). Together, they traveled through most of the Maya region from northern Yucatán to Copán, visiting and describing countless sites. Catherwood, an architect by training, produced amazingly accurate and often haunting images of a civilization in ruins (Figure 2.12). Reversing popular opinion of the time that denied any genealogical link between the impoverished Maya living around the ruins and the architects and scribes of ancient times,

Stephens linked the living Maya population with the past and speculated accurately that the hieroglyphs were an ancient written form of modern Mayan languages. With this nineteenth-century spirit of exploration and recording, several others such as Teobert Maler and Alfred Maudsley traveled through the Maya region. They carried with them large-format cameras and took some of the best photographs of hieroglyphic texts chiseled into stone monuments that have ever been produced. Sylvanus Morley also sought to document texts written in stone before the ravages of time and chemical weathering completely erased them. Interest in the Maya region by foreign adventurers and early archaeologists was not divorced from Neocolonial espionage and intrigue, which is increasingly recognized as part of the political milieu within which Maya archaeology was born (Harris and Sadler 2003; Yaeger and Borgstede 2004:264–270).

During this time, attention turned also to the codices that languished in European repositories. Among the many notable breakthroughs of this period, Dresden librarian Ernst Förstemann cracked the numerical code of the bar-dot vigesimal counting system employed in complex calendrical and astronomical calculations, and Brasseur de Bourbourg rediscovered and published the remarkable quasi-ethnographic account compiled by Bishop Diego de Landa, the notorious sixteenth-century Franciscan friar stationed in Yucatán (Restall and Chuchiak 2002; Tozzer 1941).

Most important, this period represented a time during which living Maya populations began to rebound from the ravages of the Colonial period. A near demographic collapse had accompanied the sixteenth-century introduction of pathogens to which few had immunity, especially when coupled with the oppressive labor and tribute demands of the colonialists. As the process of nation-building took hold in the Maya region, some nations – such as México – embraced a hybrid national identity of *mestizaje*. Control of archaeological remains gravitated to these nacient nation-states (see Joyce 2003 for expanded discussion), but Maya people were poorly represented in the ranks of national bureaucrats. Between foreign researchers and local government representatives, the construction of written narratives and the daily management of iconic places of Maya deep history passed from the reach and influence of descendant Maya populations (see McAnany 2007a for expanded discussion of the Colonial aftermath).

POST–WORLD WAR II RESEARCH IN THE MAYA REGION (1950–1970)

The growth of anthropology departments in the United States during the post–World War II era translated into increased research – both ethnographic and archaeological – by foreign scholars in the Maya region. During this time, sociocultural anthropologists codified many core ideas regarding Maya *costumbre* and the close linkages between ritual and economic practice. Ethnographic research often is a solitary enterprise, but the Harvard University Chiapas Project, led by Evon Z. Vogt, involved a large group of undergraduate and graduate students – including Gary Gossen, Robert Laughlin, and Victoria Bricker – who continued ethnographic and linguistic research in the Maya region and trained students of their own. Evon Vogt, in particular, was fascinated by the parallels between archaeological and ethnographic materials. Even though this cross-fertilization often proved fruitful, there were missteps, such as the notion that Classic Maya cities were simply vacant ceremonial centers – inhabited only during periods of ritual practice. Also looming large during this time was the versatile British archaeologist, J. Eric Thompson, who conducted ethnographic and archaeological fieldwork in Yucatán and Belize; he did much to bring attention to the corpus of surviving codices (only three at the time – Dresden, Madrid, and Paris – named after the cities in which they are curated) as well as texts carved in stone and painted on pottery. Thompson staunchly maintained, however, that Maya script was purely logographic, rather than phonetic or syllabic (we now know that it was both syllabic and logographic). Thompson's pronouncement was damaging to decipherment efforts since elements of language are far more difficult to decipher with a purely logographic writing system. His pronouncement also was damaging to the career of a Russian epigrapher, Yuri Knorosov, who maintained that Classic Maya script had a phonetic component (see Coe 1992 for detailed historical analysis). Thompson had one other blind spot. Despite the 1946 discovery of the Bonampak murals – which featured a violent confrontation among Classic Maya warriors – Thompson promulgated the notion that Maya civilization was anomalously peaceful, an idea that would be reversed upon decipherment and greater attention to iconographic programs in royal contexts.

During this time, the five modern nation-states of the Maya region codified and elaborated procedures for investigating and preserving the ancestral remains of Maya societies. *Institutos* (government agencies such as the Instituto Nacional de Antropología e Historia [INAH] in México, which was created in 1939) were mandated with the management of research as well as tourism at Maya archaeological sites. Particularly within México, the restoration of monumental architecture – pyramids and palace complexes – relating to the increasingly glorified pre-Columbian past was perceived as both an integrative strategy of nation-building and a wise investment of tax dollars. Tourists from North America and Europe became increasingly fascinated by the mystique of stone "ruins" covered by tropical forest vegetation; the myth that the builders of this impressive civilization had disappeared mysteriously was born. While restoring the Temple of the Inscriptions at Palenque (Figure 2.2) in 1949, the great Mexican archaeologist Alberto Ruiz Lhuillier discovered a stairway leading from the floor of the temple-topped pyramid to the base of the structure where he encountered the royal tomb of a powerful ruler: K'inich Janahb Pakal ("great sun shield"; Martin and Grube 2008[2000]:162). This discovery displaced earlier notions that Maya pyramids differed from Egyptian pyramids in that they did not contain burial crypts. As Michael Coe (1956) was quick to point out, funerary pyramids (discussed in greater detail in Chapter 5) were an operative concept, at least among Late Classic royal Maya. The wealth of beautifully crafted jade objects interred with Pakal suggested that he had been a powerful and influential seventh-century ruler – a king rather than one of the calendar priests popularized by J. Eric Thompson. Unfortunately, this wealth – intended to adorn and sustain Pakal in his journey through the afterlife – also signaled to the unscrupulous that there was "treasure" to be gained by coring into the center of massive pyramidal constructions. The problem of looting persists to this day.

Foreign archaeologists with substantial institutional backing from U.S. institutions became active in the Maya region during this time. Gordon Willey, Bowditch Professor of Central American and Mexican Archaeology and Ethnology, worked through the Peabody Museum at Harvard University and initiated projects at Barton Ramie in Belize (where settlement pattern archaeology was first introduced to the Maya region), Altar de Sacrificios and Seibal in Guatemala, and Copán in Honduras (Figure 2.2). Edwin Shook and Linton Satterthwaite and then William Coe, of the University Museum at Penn, took on the large ancient Maya capital of Tikal in Guatemala – a site found to contain a hieroglyphic record of almost 600 years of dynastic rule. Dennis Puleston, then a graduate student, documented the sprawling settlement that sustained this capital and extended 4 to 8 kilometers from the monumental core with a structure density averaging about 112 structures per square kilometer (Puleston 1983:24). This project – along with several others – did much to overturn the notion of Maya cities as vacant centers. To the north, E. Wyllys Andrews IV, sponsored by the Middle American Research Institute at Tulane University, conducted broad-scale excavations at northern Late-Terminal Classic capitals such as Becan and Dzibilchaltún. The late florescence of the northern capitals forced Mayanists to grapple with the staggered quality of the so-called collapse. This period marked the end of Carnegie Institution projects in the Maya region. The last effort of Carnegie archaeologists at the Late Postclassic site of Mayapan revealed that a profound transformation had taken place between the Classic and Postclassic periods although the interpretation of that transformation – as a slide into decadence (Pollock 1962:17) – has been overturned by more recent Postclassic archaeology.

CURRENT MAYA WORLD (1970–PRESENT)

Across the Maya region, over two dozen different Mayan languages exist and, although many share cognates – such as the term *wits* for mountain – for the most part, they are distinct languages and not dialects of a single language. This fact, exacerbated by the struggle for survival that Maya people endured over the past five centuries, resulted in dampened levels of communication, political action, and cultural interchange across Mayan language boundaries. The Maya revitalization movement of the past three decades is reversing this trend (Fischer and Brown 1996; Montejo 2002; Warren 1998, 2002).

Victor Montejo, Jakaltek Maya and professor of Native American studies, expresses the hope of this movement most eloquently: "The current process of revitalization of Maya culture serves as the foundation point ... and gives us hope for the future, creating new forms of identity beyond the old models of survival and victimization. Our pride in our own heritage and our link with our ancestral past has reconnected the fabric of Maya culture, worn by centuries of neglect" (2005:xiii). Links to an ancestral past are now being forged anew – particularly within Highland Guatemala – although considerable tensions exist between descendant populations and those traditionally in control of Maya cultural heritage (Parks 2009; Parks and McAnany 2007).

Renewed interest and respect for indigenous Maya ways of knowing and seeing comes on the heels of the 1980s decade of brutal ethnic massacres endured by Guatemalan Maya people (Carmack 1988; Manz 2004; Montejo 1987; Sanford 2003; Smith 1990). As Montejo (2002:124) puts it, "Guatemalan history ... was written during the past two k'atuns (20 years each) with Mayan blood." This brutality was followed in 1994 by the Zapatista insurgency in Chiapas, México (Gossen 1994 among others) triggered by the passage of the North American Free Trade Agreement (NAFTA) – the final straw that broke the back of centuries of repressive economic inequality. Continued conflict over ownership and use rights to Maya ancestral lands extends across the entire Maya region from the Lacandon rain forest of southern México (Nations 2006:264), to the Mirador-Río Azul National Park in northern Guatemala, and the southeastern corner of Belize where an indigenous-run nongovernmental organization successfully sued the government of Belize to induce recognition of traditional land rights (http://www.law.arizona.edu/depts/iplp/advocacy/maya_belize; see also Wainwright 2008 for background). In the north, resurgence of expression of Yucatec Maya identity pivots around language and includes revitalization of writing traditions, artistic expression, and ritual practice (Guzmán Medina 2005). In the current Postcolonial era, the manner in which Maya people engage with their past, their present, and their future continues to be of intense interest to anthropologists, particularly in reference to polarized cultural frameworks such as *essentialism* and *constructivism* (Fischer 1999; Kroshus Medina 2003; Warren 1998).

The pan-Maya movement takes place in tandem with unprecedented levels of archaeological field research by nationals, foreigners, and collaborative efforts in all five countries of the Maya region (Figure 2.1). The efficacy of professional training for students of Maya archaeology within U.S. universities, in particular, has swelled the ranks of foreign archaeologists conducting field research in the Maya region. Heightened levels of tourism – and focused heritage tourism programs such as La Ruta Maya and Mundo Maya – have led to increased efforts by government archaeologists to enhance the appeal of ancient Maya places to tourists' sensibilities and limited abilities to "see" buildings unless they are restored. Unfortunately, Maya descendant communities participate in this multimillion-dollar heritage tourism industry primarily as vendors, staff at hotels and restaurants, site custodians, and sometimes as tour guides (see Breglia 2006; Casteñada 1996 for critical treatment of this situation as it exists at Chichén Itzá).

Publication has not kept pace with the mountain of primary data that has been generated as a result of both research and restoration projects, although published reports, syntheses, and topical books have expanded dramatically over the past two decades. The bulk of published material occurs within either English- or Spanish-language scholarly venues; there has been little effort to prepare curricular materials for Maya schoolchildren or deliver information via community outreach programs. As a result, there is only a very small pool of Maya descendants who have a sense of what archaeologists have learned about their ancestors. I sense that this situation is changing as Maya archaeologists develop a stronger social consciousness and Maya descendants begin to place demands on archaeologists for information sharing (see Parks 2009 and http://www.machiproject.org for more on outreach projects). Contemporary Maya archaeologists are more engaged with local communities, in general, and many try to ensure that the impact of archaeological field research on the surrounding populace is strongly positive in terms of identity, education, and economic opportunities (Bawaya 2006).

In terms of our substantive understanding of ancestral Maya society, the last 30 years have witnessed great strides among epigraphers and art historians in the decipherment of the grammar and syntax of America's most complex indigenous writing system – Maya hieroglyphic script (Houston and Lacadena Garcia-Gallo 2004). Unfortunately, looting of unprotected sites for the express purpose of extracting stone stelae carved with glyphs and pottery adorned with calligraphic and figural scenes also accelerated during this time. The application of scientific techniques – such as coring to retrieve pollen, sedimentary, and isotopic data, as well as attention to newly available satellite imagery – has begun to change dramatically our ideas about Maya landscape utilization (more on this in Chapter 3). Gone is the idea that the lowland landscape was sparsely populated during Preclassic and Classic times by *milpa* farmers who practiced a long-bush fallow. Rather, wet and dry lands alike were profoundly transformed and maintained as food-producing locales to nourish a population that may have exceeded five million by 700–800 C.E.. Unlike the pyramid-focused research of earlier eras, archaeologists now routinely survey and map residential structures of all sizes and surveys generally extend for a kilometer or more beyond the concentrated epicenter of monumental architecture.

ON LEARNING MORE ABOUT THE *LONGUE DURÉE* OF ANCESTRAL MAYA SOCIETIES

This introduction to Maya deep history and the milieu and methods of its study is intended to give the reader who is not familiar with Maya archaeology sufficient knowledge to forge ahead and tackle the remaining chapters that provide little in the way of culture history and intellectual setting but much in the way of an interpretive treatment of ancestral Maya social practices as they entangled with economic process. For the sake of brevity, many topics and periods have been treated far too lightly; a rudimentary web search will reveal the monumentality of published literature in Maya studies. For the reader who wants to pursue more detailed sources on Maya archaeology, the following are recommended: *The Classic Maya* (2009) by Stephen D. Houston and Takeshi Inomata (for the latest word on the Classic period, particularly courtly life), *The Ancient Maya* (2006) by Robert Sharer and Loa Traxler (an encyclopedic reference spanning all periods and topics of Maya archaeology), and *Ancient Maya: The Rise and Fall of a Rainforest Civilization* (2004) by Arthur Demarest (contains a heavy focus on western Usumacinta drainage sites examined within a cultural ecology and ideology perspective).

3

Feeding a Hungry Landscape

In archaeological monographs, it is common practice to preface survey or excavation descriptions with a section entitled "environmental setting" in order to set the stage for the cultural material to be presented. Historically, the "give-and-take" between environment and culture, in "settlement-pattern/processualist" terms, was perceived in terms of the environment doing the "giving" or setting the terms of interaction and the culture doing the "taking" or responding to the terms or limitations imposed by the environment (see Trigger 1989:303–311 for extended discussion). Under the rubric of "cultural ecology" (Steward 1955:30–42), this trend continued, but more recently "historical ecology" has promoted a more nuanced modeling of this interaction (Balée 1998; Balée and Erickson 2006; Bilsky 1980; Crumley 1994; Crumley et al. 2001). Within the earlier cultural ecology frame, economy was restricted to the methods by which an environment was managed and labor organized to extract and distribute resources. If one employs such a segmental perspective, nothing could be farther from ritual practice than economic behavior (see Isaac 1993:465 for more on this topic). According to Hawkes's (1954) fabled ladder of inference, archaeological economies were knowable whereas anything to do with ideology required

An earlier version of this chapter was presented at the Annual Public Lecture at Dumbarton Oaks, Washington, D.C., December 6, 2006, titled *Feeding a Hungry Landscape: Perception and Ritual Practice in Ancestral Maya Societies.*

a great inferential leap. Here, we diverge from this epistemology but not before tacking across these well-traveled waters.

The advent of landscape studies – although rooted in a decidedly Western perspective (Thomas 2001:168–170) – greatly expanded archaeological horizons. Distinctive environmental features – such as hills, caves, and locales of rock art – posed an uneasy fit with settlement archaeology, which emphasized camps, domiciles, and architecturally defined places of religious expression (see Anschuetz et al. 2001:171, 174 for expanded discussion). There was little conceptual space for a ritual landscape that had not been created by humans and may bear only ephemeral traces of human usage and artifact deposition. In calling for an experiential and phenomenological approach to landscape (Ashmore 2004a, 2004b; Ashmore and Knapp 1999; Thomas 2001; Tilley 1994), archaeologists have moved toward a deeper and more culturally contingent understanding of human interaction with the material world – whether that material world was heavily constructed or not. Ashmore (2004a:103), in particular, has discussed the newly blurred boundary between natural landscapes and constructed worlds. As Denis Cosgrove (1993:5), the influential geographer and doyen of landscape studies, put it: "landscape has come to denote a form of human signification. The visible scene and its various representations are regarded as constitutive elements in the complex individual and social processes whereby humans continuously transform the natural world into cultural realms of meaning and lived experience." Landscape is a social artifact "produced and reproduced through varying dimensions of spatial practice" (Smith 2003:25). This chapter continues along this track by examining Maya cosmologies of landscape and by focusing on the ways in which traditional Maya people today and probably in the past perceive of their lived space. As Dunning and Beach (2004:134) observe, perception [of landscape] is "one important component that has been missing from most considerations of the ancient Maya." Although there is demonstrated and pronounced variability in human–environmental interaction across the time–space continuum of ancestral Maya societies (Dunning and Beach 2004:132), here we consider prominent themes that underlie the social construction of landscape within the spaces of house, community, and field as well as the "natural" terrain of forest, wetland, hills, and caves. The goal is not to assert that Maya conceptions of landscape are timeless – in an essentialist fashion (Kroshus Medina 2003:355–357) – but rather to imagine ways in which landscape was integrated with social practice.

Landscape perception is an important part of figured worlds that "give meaning to people's interaction, [and] change historically in ways that are marked by the political struggles and social valuation of their users" (Holland et al. 1997:45). A discussion of prominent themes in Maya cognition of the cosmos and practices relating to that perspectival positionality provide the substance of this chapter. This cognition forms a basis for understanding that landscape is/was both an animate entity and the locale of a body of ritual practices that has been construed as "debt payment" in many discussions of Mesoamerican cosmology (Arnold 2001:81; Earle 1986:170; López Austin 1988, vol. 2:292; Monaghan 2000:36–39; Sahagún 1997:55–56, 74, 128). The cultural logic by which Maya people mapped on to their lowland landscape and devoted themselves to "the work" of servicing the debt owed to ancestors and deities provides a strong linkage between ritual and economy. Correlative to debt payment is the work of constructing an ordered landscape of house, community structures, fields, and orchards from a powerful and potentially dangerous wild landscape. Finally, we turn to the manner in which political agency – particularly during the Classic period – was enhanced through engaging metaphorically and materially with wild things and dangerous places as an expression of "naturalized" power.

PERFORMANCE-BASED THEOLOGY

In a theologically based study of ritual, Bell (1992:74) strives for an expansive definition of ritualization as "a way of acting that is designed and orchestrated to distinguish and privilege what is being done in comparison to other, usually more quotidian, activities." But even this liberal conception of ritual does not stretch far enough to encompass traditional Mesoamerican cosmologies in which the quotidian events of everyday life – such as planting a field or building a house – presented an occasion for ritual action and the performance, itself, far outweighed any body of religious orthodoxy in cultural importance. As Monaghan (2000:25, 26) has noted, Mesoamerican people did not radically separate faith and practice; nor did they conceive of a universe that was distinct from a divine being or host of supernaturals. The action-oriented nature of Mesoamerican belief systems translates into a kind of ritual practice in which, as both Barbara Tedlock (1982:6) and Alan Sandstrom (1991:300) have observed, ritual performance trumps abstract knowledge of theology, and religious pedagogy emphasizes practical epistemology over ideology. Thus, even though the term "religion" certainly can be applied to Maya belief systems, the word conjures images of a reified orthodoxy that refers restrictively to the solar aspects of royal Maya ritual and performance (more on this topic in Chapter 6). Here, we take a more holistic approach to landscape and social practice.

Just as ritual practice shaped the quotidian events of everyday life, so also "ceremony" can be perceived as another form of work. Monaghan (2000:32) notes that "instead of officiating at a rite, practicing a ritual, or performing a ceremony, officiants are [described as] 'feeding' or 'straightening' or 'sweeping.'" Among the Mixe of Oaxaca, rituals are simply called "work" and include the work of the dead and the work of the mountains (Lipp 1991:82, cited in Monaghan 2000:32). Among Yucatec Maya, Hanks (1990:364) records a linguistic expression, *meyah*, "work" that "applies equally well to what the shaman is doing in performing, what the farmer is doing in burning, and what a woman does in cleaning the household." Devereaux (1987:93–94) indicates that the Tzotzil Maya term for work, *'abtel*, refers to ritual work – such as preparing food for a fiesta – as well as subsistence practices. Sweeping and bathing, in particular, are perceived in a general sense as purifying acts, requisite to creating and maintaining socially constructed space (Burkhart 1997:33; Hanks 1990:364; Monaghan 2000:34). Clearly, "too often what is labeled as ritual by Mesoamericanists is based on a judgment about where an action lies on some scale of practicality or on which side of an empirical/spiritual, spontaneous/fixed dichotomy it falls" (Monaghan 2000:30).

Among traditional Mesoamericans, religion is work construed in active terms. As such, it cannot be surgically removed from the study of economy without damaging the contextuality of ritual practice. Moreover, because the object of ritual work is not to propitiate an abstract deity residing in the heavens, Mesoamerican religion possessed a pronounced locative aspect and a materiality that can be alien to utopian-based religions, such as Christianity (Arnold 2001:4, 5). In reference to the Highland Postclassic Nahua of the Basin of Mexico, Arnold (2001:18) argues persuasively that there was an emphasis on "performative and ritual labors involved in the process of occupying the land" (see Sahagún 1997:69–80 for list of performative practices). Indeed, the land itself was perceived as animate and, as such, required nourishment and sustenance as a consequence of human occupation; in effect, the landscape was perceived as capable of agency and of exhibiting a hunger that spurred ritual performance.

AN ANIMATED LANDSCAPE WITHIN A LAYERED COSMOS

" The earth is alive. We spend our entire lives defiling the earth, pissing on her and that is why she gets annoyed. That's why she wants to forsake us" (Sandstrom 1991:239). With these words, a Nahua shaman who Sandstrom refers to as "Aurelio" sought to teach the anthropologist about the earth as an animate and supernatural being. It seems that he also sought to share a kind of Latourian (1999:198) understanding of human interactions with nonhuman entities (or "actants" in the words of Latour). According to Monaghan (2000:27), part of the reason that the "natural/supernatural distinctions do not apply very well to Mesoamerica" is due to the fact that the supernatural was perceived as dwelling within the natural rather than having been the creator of the natural as in Judeo-Christian beliefs. As such, any feature of a landscape – particularly unusual features such as caves and lofty promontories – present an opportunity (or an obligation) to dialogue with supernaturals (Mauss 1967:14–17). As Bradley (2000:28) notes for prehistoric Europe, such distinctive locales are places where humans and supernaturals can come into contact. Eliade (1954:59, 95) referred to such places as "hierophanies" – locales where the sacred world shows itself. Within Mesoamerican cosmology, caves represent the archetypal hierophany – points of access to the powerful and dangerous vital forces that animate the universe (Brady and Prufer 2005:8). A specific cavern – perceived to be a place "where the greatest of saints and gods live and create rain clouds" – was named Paq'alib'al, which translates as "at the place of revelation of appearance" in K'iche' Mayan

(Christenson 2001:79, 84). Mountains and hills form an important complement to caves, as detailed later.

More than points of access to profound animate forces, however, the landscape itself was perceived as animate and given corporeal features. Monaghan (2000:27), taking his cue from indigenous Mesoamerican expressions, describes the analogy as follows: "the landscape is thus represented by corporeal images, so that mountains are like heads, valleys are creviced backs, caves are mouths or wombs, rivers are veins, water is blood or sweat, swamps are hearts, trees are hair, rocks are bones" (see also Sandstrom 1991:238). This equation between human anatomy and natural features defined the essential qualities of a deity for many Mesoamerican peoples: "what makes a god a god is the 'skin,' the 'bark,' the 'head,' the 'face,' or the 'mask'.... These surfaces might be wooden or stone images, but also places, such as caves (which, for the Q'eqchí, are the faces of the *tzuultaq'as* [earth lords]), altars, lakes, rocky outcroppings, and hilltops" (Monaghan 2000:29 in a survey of anatomical expressions of deity characterizations). In sum, humans and gods can be perceived to have entered into a "covenant of mutual obligation, phrased in an alimentary idiom" (Monaghan 2000:38).

The corporeal landscape represents the earth-bound realm, to be juxtaposed with a celestial realm that was equally subject to anthropomorphic constructions, and – pertinent to this study – deftly woven into a charter of political governance dating back to Preclassic Maya times (see Chapters 5 and 6). In reference to ethnographic K'iché conceptions of a layered cosmos, Earle (1986:168) states that

> below the surface of the earth is the Santo Mundo, or simply Mundo. There is a layer of fertile or accessible earth, with its special altars located frequently at the tops or edges of raised mounds, hills or mountains. Certain plains (*tak'aj*), canyons, and caves also have their Mundo shrines. In the Mundo reside the *tak xcamwinak'*, the deceased ancestors, as well as multiple manifestations of the Mundo spirit.

Within the "Mundo" layer of the cosmos, hierophanies – or places where the gods and ancestors reveal themselves – are the locales of shrines where offerings can be made to propitiate the forces that reside within. In this manner, "environmental setting" takes on a ritual significance and economic importance that is unimaginable if cognition and practice are not taken into consideration. The term "sacred ecology" (Berkes 1999) can be used to express the relationship among spiritual forces, landscape features, and humans.

Religious beliefs are robust constructs that often are resistant to change; however, ideologies also can be highly fluid instruments that are constantly reinterpreted and historically contingent. Certainly, Maya ethnographic conceptions – for instance, in reference to the layered cosmos cited earlier – bear the signs of 500 years of Spanish Catholicism, yet the manner in which earth-bound deities counterbalance solar deities likely draws from pre-Columbian beliefs. Duncan Earle recounts the interdependence between the deities of this layered dualism as understood by a K'iché Maya shaman.

> No more central dynamic dualism exists for Don Lucas than the Mundo, the spiritual embodiment of the fertile earth, and the sun, personified as Jesus, with his court of sky-bound companions.... [I]ndicting the religious reform groups for their lack of attention to the Mundo, [Don Lucas] explained that Jesus was all fine and good but of little use without the world for him to walk across. He asked me rhetorically, "Is it not the Mundo that sustains our lives, that provides the base for our corn, for our houses?"(Earle 1986:167, 169)

Sandstrom (1991:248) observed a similar wisdom among traditional Nahua cultivators of lowland Veracruz who, while acknowledging that the sun is the most powerful of all spirits, "make few offerings to the sun and seldom direct prayers to it." As Sandstrom (1991:286) explains: "The Nahuas are mother worshippers because fertility is life for horticulturists, and *tonantsij* [earth goddess in her Virgin of Guadalupe aspect], who springs from the pre-Hispanic past, is responsive to human needs."

In traditional Mesoamerican cosmology, the celestial and earthly layers – while quite distinct in terms of deities, association with the cosmos, and ritual practice – were not divisible; one cannot be ignored at the expense of the other. Rather, the two form parts of a whole; and both are united with respect to ritual performance. Both solar and earthly deities require "repayment" in the form of offerings, and solar deities were more likely to require the most precious of offerings – human life.

TROPE OF "ORIGINAL DEBT"

In an insightful juxtapositioning of Christian and traditional Maya cosmologies, Earle (1986:170) remarks that "Quiché are not born with original sin but rather 'original debt.'" In effect, ancestors and deities have already done the work necessary to bring humans into existence and give them a "piece of the material world" (Earle 1986:170). Throughout the lifetime of a human, this debt must be repaid to the extent that is possible. The K'iché Mayan term for "life" (*k'aslem*) is based on the root term "*k'as*," which means "debt" or "that which is borrowed" (Earle 1986:172). Some Mesoamerican creation narratives contain accounts of gods who performed heroic sacrifices in order to jump-start the solar cycle, such as the highland Nahua creation story of the immolation of Nanahuatzin (Sahagún 1950–1982, book 7:3–8; Taube 2000:302–303). Such stories provide a compelling morality tale as well as emphasize the immense debt that humans owe to the gods – one that can scarcely be repaid by an offering less precious than that of a human life. This precise sentiment was relayed to Earle (1986:163) by a K'iché Maya traditionalist who noted that "in [a human] death, a lifetime is paid back to the Mundo by the feeding of the body to it."

Frequent dialogue with the deities is maintained in an effort to ameliorate this debt, but an active rapport does not mean that humans enjoyed balanced reciprocity with the gods; rather, the interaction can be characterized as one of debt and merit couched in hierarchical terms (Monaghan 2000:36–39). Not only do the gods have the upper hand but, in many ethnographic accounts, the gods are described as extremely irritable and easy to displease. According to Monaghan (2000:33) "everyday activities – eating and drinking, excavating house sites, tilling fields – require one to act in a way that violates bodily balance and annoys, disrupts, and offends the gods … who are in turn described as touchy, sensitive to being slighted, and quick to punish." Whether among the Tzotzil of Zinacantán (Vogt 1976:50, 56–57), the highland Guatemalan K'iché (Nash 1970:97; Reina and Monaghan 1981:18, 26), the Lacandon of Chiapas (Boremanse 1993:333; Perera and Bruce 1982), the Q'eqchi' of Alta Verapaz (Carlson and Eachus 1977:39), or the Nahua of northern Veracruz (Sandstrom 1991:288, 313), traditional Mesoamerican people express great concern to avoid offense to easily angered gods and strive to secure the contentment of the gods through lavish offerings.

"Original debt" to the earthly gods was serviced in the course of daily practice and seasonal ritual at shrines located in the domicile, in community structures, in the fields, and at the boundary between field and forest (see Sahagún 1997:55–56, 74, 128 for specific Nahua examples). Placating the vital forces of powerful and dangerous parts of the animated landscape – rivers, wetlands, hills, and caves – often required special pilgrimage. Solar or celestial deities – more frequently under the purview of political hierarchies – were housed within monumental structures where sacrifices were offered. In many parts of the Maya world, Santos and Christ-focused rituals of the Catholic church have replaced older solar deities, such as the sun god, K'inich Ajaw. In deeper Lowland Maya history, solar deities such as the sun god were the object of elaborate stucco reliefs on the front facades of some of the earliest Maya pyramids and were instrumental in giving rulers a godly aspect (see Chapters 5 and 6). The constellation of saints and deities within the Catholic church, likewise, require lavish offerings and labor-intensive ritual practices; Annis (1987:85) reports that the success of Protestant evangelicalism among Kakchiquel Maya was due, in part, to "the practical advantages of a religion that venerates a god who is inexpensive to serve."

Among the Q'eqchi' of Chajaneb, the timing of ritual offerings and farming activities are closely interlinked. As Adams and Brady (2005:308–09) observe,

> most residents ... mark the beginning of work having to do with corn planting with ritual observances, whether these be house rituals, a special Catholic mass, a Protestant prayer service, or – in the traditionalists' case – *mayejac* [offerings] to the Tzuultaq'a. In Chajaneb during our observation, the participants began their preparations by collectively setting a date for making offerings to the Tzuultaq'a and for the work schedule.

Thus, the schedule of work and ritual go hand in hand and like many other aspects of the ritual economy are not divisible. At the end of the agricultural year, Earle (1986:163) records that, among the K'iché, "the earth spirits in charge of the brin[g]ing of the rain, the solar avatars (Jesus and the saints, the ancient K'iché heroes), and the Earth itself are 'paid,' 'fed' for their aid in sustaining another year of life."

Carrasco (1995:429) employs the expression "We eat the gods and the gods eat us" to characterize a relationship in which humans are sustained and nourished by the earth but also are obliged to provide nourishment to the godly forces that inhabit the landscape. These obligatory offerings mitigate the impact of humans on a landscape imbued with vital essence. Such symbiosis has been characterized as part of an intense mutual engagement, "almost as if gods and humans were members of a single moral community or participants in a universal structure of relationships. … [S]ociety does not exist apart from the gods" (Monaghan 2000:31; see also Sandstrom 1991:440–441 on the intimate relationship between earthly deities and humans). But, the covenant of debt and merit between humans and gods contains an unwavering sense of natural inequality. "Humans may eat the gods, but it is the gods who do most of the eating" with offerings often glossed as "payment" or "tribute" (Monaghan 2000:39). The asymmetry of this relationship harkens back to the forcible extractions of the Colonial period and farther back to tribute obligations as depicted on Late Classic Maya polychrome vessels (see Chapter 9). Given the longitudinal perspective of this study, one cannot help but wonder how much of the irritability of the deities is contingent upon historical circumstances of the pronounced social inequalities of past Maya societies. A kind of coevolution likely has occurred between social difference and religious cosmology. In other words, it is possible that Archaic and Early Preclassic gods displayed a more amiable temperament. This notion is difficult to assess but could be approached via a fresh look at Preclassic religious expression to see if the basic structuring principles of later times – debt and merit – can be discerned in figurine-based, Early Preclassic ritual practice.

Gender Implications

Linked to inequality in the terms of the covenant between humans and gods is the issue of gender construction. Specifically, are solar-linked deities primarily male except for those most closely associated with human reproduction, such as Ix Chel in Postclassic Maya theology and Mary, the mother of Jesus, in Christian cosmology? Can earth deities be said to be primarily female or do male qualities dominate in the lower realm also? Earle (1986) has expended some effort in linking, in a structuralist fashion, the solar aspects of K'iché ritual and daily practice with male actions and earthly aspects (Mundo) with female daily practice. Yet

> the Mundo as prior to creation and linked with the 260-day calendar round is a deity of the private household and the rhythms of the human birth and growth cycle. Its spatial locus is fixed, in or on the ground, within certain indestructible stones, dwelling in significant topographical features, all of these either without specific gender or with both sexes present. (Earle 1986:169)

Adams and Brady (2005) as well as Wilson (1995:53) also note that the earth deity is marked by both female and male attributes.

So, earth deities – including ancestral deities – are perceived to be either sexless or to combine the qualities of male and female. Earle (1986:170) explains the K'iché term for shaman ("mother-father") as follows: "Having passed through the cycles of solar time and having learned to become aware of the 260-day round of human time, he [Don Lucas] can truly be the 'mother-father' one, the man of both celestial and earthly days" (Earle 1986:170). Thus, the vital interlocking of both parts of the duality – celestial and earthly – seems to preclude a strictly female realm of deities.

Perhaps more to the point in terms of twenty-first-century inquiry is the question of the role of females in the "repayment" of debts to the deities. Q'eqchí ritual performance observed by Adams and Brady (2005) indicates that, ethnographically at least, cave rituals are "solely the domain of men, women are a critical element in the acquisition of ritual paraphernalia and offerings made outside of the cave. Participation of each person involved in petitioning the Tzuultaq'a is conditioned by gender" (Brady and Prufer 2005:10). Yet, such gender exclusivity may not have prevailed in the past. Artifacts that are strongly female-gendered – such as *manos*, *metates*, and weaving/embroidery implements – are commonly found in Late Classic cave assemblages, such as Actun Chanona (Figure 3.1; Peterson 2006), which is located at the head of the Sibun Valley, and in the deep crevasse of Aguateca in the Petexbatún (Ishihara 2007).

LANDSCAPE LOCALES OF DEBT PAYMENT

Above and beyond the monumental architecture that came to denote seats of power throughout the pre-Hispanic Maya region, there were

FIGURE 3.1 *Mano* and *metate* from the Great Platform of the cave of Actun Chanona in the upper Sibun Valley. Ceramic jar and bowl fragments likely collected recently by cave enthusiasts and placed near groundstone (photo courtesy of Xibun Archaeological Research Project).

many locales at which offerings were made to earthly and solar deities. Archaeological, ethnohistorical, and ethnographic accounts indicate that active locales of "debt payment" occur within domiciles, orchards, fields, caves and hills, cenotes, and wetlands (Earle 1986:157; Wisdom 1940:428, among others). Activities within culturally constructed domestic space are the topic of Chapter 4; however, preliminary attention is given here to ritual within these spaces. This is followed by a discussion of caves and pools as well as hilltop places in which English terms are paired with Classic Maya terms for such landscape features.

House, Orchard, and Field

In early ethnographic accounts of the domiciles of traditional Maya families in the highlands or the lowlands, domestic shrines form a ubiquitous component of house interiors (McBryde 1971:47; Wauchope 1938:142). In the Guatemalan highlands, McBryde (1971:47) reports that shrines were often decorated with pine boughs (as at field shrines) and a carpet of pine needles to kneel upon at the base of the shrine. The essential nature of house shrines leads one to wonder why more effort is not expended in identifying house shrines in archaeological contexts, a topic that is revisited in Chapter 4.

Beyond the interior house shrine, however, ethnographers record a second type of domestic shrine – one that is always located outdoors – and is well documented among K'iché traditionalists. Known as the "*warabal ja*," this locale for offerings has been described as the caretaker shrine for the house and is located at the border between the fields and the woods. As Earle (1986:166) observed, at the *warabal ja*, "Don Lucas asks for protection for those in the house, for abundance, and for the birth of new life. Here the Mundo is witness to the rites of marriage, to the initiation of new shamans, and to the asking for the 'birth' of the rainy season." Tedlock (1982:79, 83) shows that high pottery densities coupled with small-scale ritual architecture are prominent features of *warabal ja*. The location of these shrines – at the juncture between socially ordered spaces and wild places – is particularly significant as is the strong association of shrines with renewal and earthly forces. Given the relatively close packing of domestic structures in Classic Maya settlements, caretaker shrines – if they existed during earlier times – could have been placed at nonhabitable and nonfarmable locales such as caves. On the other hand, so little "distributional archaeology" (Ebert 1992; Rossignol and Wandsnider 1992) has been attempted in the Maya lowlands that dense and discrete concentrations of pottery sherds separate from residential compounds may exist but are seldom recorded. The discovery by Wells and Davis-Salazar (2008:200–210) of small field houses associated with high densities of censor sherds in the Naco Valley of Honduras strengthens the possibility of archaeologically visible field shrines. Certainly the high density of pottery sherds within many cave contexts indicates repeat visitation to locales that most certainly were associated with earth deities (Brady and Prufer 2005). On a larger political scale, the presence of stelae erected by the seventh-century ruler Smoke Imix God K around the edges of the Late Classic capital of Copán (Fash 1991:101) presents an interesting comparison with the *warabal ja*. This monumental version of "caretaker shrines," moreover, suggests that this concept was not alien to Classic-period populations.

In reference to the ethnographic distinction between shrines that are located within as opposed to outside of the domicile, Don Lucas explained to Earle (1986:167) that

> while the house altar has more say with his particular *santo* and for minor family issues, it is the *warabal ja* that has the greatest pull with the forces of the Mundo. Even though there is a Mundo part of the house altar, the "earth table" [*warabal ja*] is the place where the earth can be properly "fed." *Kol pom*, a pine-resin incense of local origin is only used in the outdoor altar, burned in a pile in front of the table.

While the presence of *santos* reminds us of the postcolonial character of the house altar, the concept of "feeding" the vital forces of the landscape by producing the redolence of smoky pine is strongly pre-Columbian (Morehart et al. 2005).

Because the lowlands is a mosaic landscape of hills and wetlands rather than one of strong topographical relief (the latter often demarcates arable from nonarable lands), it is possible that, in ancient times, outdoor shrines were placed in orchard areas that may or may not have been proximate to residences. Early Colonial accounts contain references to ritual offerings – including human sacrifice – that took place in orchards, particularly cacao and copal orchards (Jones 1989:151; Morley 1941:192; Scholes and Adams 1938:I:166). The residue of such activities would likely be reported archaeologically as isolated occurrences of broken pottery and possibly human remains.

Among the many cultural onslaughts of the Colonial period, the collapse of lowland Maya indigenous arboriculture – due to economic leveling, demographic crash, and blights affecting cacao trees (MacLeod 1973) – effectively eliminated outdoor shrines in the somewhat ordered landscape of orchards. Quadrangular fields, however, continued to be the site of ritual offerings that "fed" earth deities (see Vogt 1976 among others). For the Tzotzil of Zinacantan, Vogt (1976:55–59) describes a procession that toured a prepared field, in a counterclockwise fashion, stopping at each cross-shrine that had been built at the four corners and in the center of the field. Decorated with pine boughs, pine needles, and flowers, the cross-shrines accentuate the fact that the forest has been transformed into ordered, social space, and even though the role of pine in effecting this transition is not entirely clear, this species does play a critical part. The importance of pine in field rituals is all the more interesting given its ubiquity as archaeobotanical remains in excavation deposits (Crane 1996:269; Lentz 1991:Table 1, 1999:14; Miksicek 1991:Table 4.2; Morehart et al. 2005). As Vogt (1976:55) and others have noted, pine trees do not enjoy a continuous distribution in the lowlands but rather are restricted either to higher elevations or specific edaphic locales, such as the pine ridges of Belize. In either case, pine generally had to be transported to its locale of use, whether that use entailed incense burned as food for the gods, torches to be burned through the night or carried into caves, ritual adornment of shrines, or other more pedestrian uses.

Caves and Pools (*Ch'e'n*, *Ha'*, and *Nahb*)

The profound significance of caves (*ch'e'n*) – and related pools and sinkholes (*ha'* or *nahb*) – within Mesoamerican cosmology is inescapable and well documented. Less well understood, though, is the cosmological perception of wetlands – areas of shallow, still water that may or may not be seasonally desiccated. Here, caves and *cenotes* (Yucatec term for sinkholes) are discussed as sites of ritual offerings on the Lowland Maya landscape. Wetlands, because of their complex landscape evolution, are more difficult to characterize but are discussed in further detail later where evidence is provided indicating that all three landscape features appear to have been sites at which earth and water deities could be propitiated.

In a lowland tropical environment, there is no guarantee that water will be available when it is needed (see Lucero 2006). Lowland Mesoamerica – in particular – is characterized by a pronounced dry season from January to June. This meteorological pattern may explain why the earliest unambiguous sites of ritual practice are water shrines that date to the Early Preclassic period. Along the Gulf Coast, the pool located at the Olmec site of El Manatí contained a precious cargo of offerings that include jade artifacts, rubber balls, and carved wooden human busts, some as old as 1500 B.C.E. (Ortiz and Carmen Rodríguez 2000:75). Less than 20 kilometers from the Olmec center of San Lorenzo, this offertory site provides a sharp reminder of the fact that the practice of depositing offerings of highly valued materials into a pool of water – an act commonly associated with later times (i.e., the Cenote of Sacrifice at Chichén Itzá; see Coggins and Shane 1984) – was already established among Mesoamerican people by 1000 B.C.E. Likewise, on the Pacific side of Mesoamerica, the Early Preclassic cave site of Oxtotitlán contains a spectacular polychrome painting of a ritualist dressed as an avian deity and seated on top of an "earth monster" (Clark and Pye 2000:frontispiece). This occurrence, as well as the Middle Preclassic Chalcatzingo petroglyph of a seated figure inside a quatrefoil-like cave opening from which clouds emanate (Grove 2000:Figure 2), indicates that the association between caves and rainfall enjoys an equally deep antiquity in Mesoamerica. The representation of persons of distinction shown within caverns (for example, El Rey or "the king" on the Chalcatzingo carving), moreover, also highlights a long tradition of trained ritual specialists who were able to enter the liminal space of caverns in order to offer gifts to the vital earthly forces. As portals to the powers that provided (or withheld) seasonal rains critical to plant fertility and ultimately to human survival and reproduction, caves and pools (anthropomorphized ethnographically as mouths and wombs) constitute the earliest and most enduring locales of deity propitiation.

Throughout the lowland Maya region, the period of peak cave visitation coincided with the population maximum of the Late Classic period; however, the presence within caves of earlier deposits that predate local sequences of settlement (discernible from construction activity and midden deposits at surface sites) is increasingly recognized as a prevalent pattern (Brady 1997:608; Peterson 2006). This suggests that many caves served as pilgrimage locales before settlements were locally established. Pilgrimage to caves was likely a well-established Preclassic tradition since many parts of the lowlands, despite being underlain by limestone, contain few caves. Within the central band of the lowlands – from northern Belize west through the Petén all the way to the Usumacinta River – subterranean caverns are underrepresented relative to the extensive cave and *cenote* systems to the north, around the base of the Maya Mountains in the southeast, and in highland Chiapas, which is located in the southwestern part of the Maya region.

Even though pools – especially *cenotes* – may be incorporated into the social space of a settlement, particularly in the dry, northern

Yucatán (Brown 2006) and a settlement may be built on top of a natural or constructed cave location – as, for example, at Dos Pilas in the Petexbatún (Brady 1997) or Maax Na in northwestern Belize (King and Shaw 2003) – many caves are located in rugged landscapes that are not particularly habitable and require an arduous journey in order to arrive at the cave entrance. The caves of the Sibun-Manatee karst in central Belize represent this type of karstic landscape – one that was diametrically opposed to the socially ordered space of settlements (McAnany et al. 2002; Peterson 2006). The well-known cave of Naj Tunich, Guatemala (Brady 1989; Stone 1995), necessitated visitation via pilgrimage. Hieroglyphic texts within the cave chambers make it clear that this large, spectacular cavern was visited repeatedly; Stone (1995:112–116) has documented the hand of at least ten different artists who painted both glyphic texts and figural images on the walls of the cave. Emblem glyphs and long-count dates bracketing a time span of 692 to 771 C.E. (MacLeod and Stone 1995:156) represent standard written expressions of kingship and so impart a political purpose to cave visitation, although such visits could have been instigated by earthly concerns with crop and human fertility. The morally inverted and dangerous nighttime world of underground caverns, moreover, is aptly represented iconographically within Naj Tunich (see Stone 1995:146–148; more on engagement with dangerous powers later). Relevant to large caves such as Naj Tunich and Actun Chanona (the latter located in the Sibun Valley) is the notion expressed by Brady and Prufer (2005:12) that "political aspirations were expressed in legitimation ceremonies held in open and well-lighted cave spaces" while smaller caves with cramped interiors were the domain of local, ritual specialists.

Whether caves were large or small, shallow rockshelters or long caverns, these portals on the landscape were the domain of ritual specialists who by temperament and training could lead a pilgrimage and negotiate safe passage through the dark caverns lit only by flickering pine torches. Recently compiled ethnographic accounts of caves visitation (Adams and Brady 2005; Petroshyn 2005; Sandstrom 2005; Vogt and Stuart 2005) reiterate the critical role of specialists in cave ritual and the overwhelming association between caves and earth deities.

Hilltop Places (*Witsoob*)

In the mountainous topography of highland Chiapas and Guatemala, mountaintop shrines hold an important place in landscape cosmology and inevitably are conceptualized as riddled with caves and tunnels (Brown 2004; Vogt and Stuart 2005:166). In the more rolling topography of the lowlands, however, mountaintops are few and far between, restricted to the Maya Mountains of southern Belize and the eastern periphery of Guatemala. Prominent cone-karst features often contain artifacts; such is the case at "The Thumb," which is located within the Sibun-Manatee karst of central Belize (Figure 3.2a). The chambers that perforate the sides of this butte-like feature contain offerings of pottery, fauna, and marine shell; pictographs adorn chamber walls (Figure 3.2b and 3.2c). In the case of The Thumb – as well as many hills throughout the lowlands – there is no preserved summit shrine. Did the absence of mountains in the lowlands serve to fashion a landscape cosmology that did not ascribe great significance to natural mountaintops? The uncanny similarity between the sacred-mountain-and-shrine complexes of Tzotzil Maya and the temple-pyramids built by lowland Maya people was noted long ago by Vogt (1964:501). This parallel has been strengthened by epigraphic evidence that *wits* or "mountain" was a phrase used during Classic times in reference to ritual architecture, presumably pyramids (Stuart 1997:15). Finally, Preclassic antecedents for the notion of a mountain of abundance and sustenance have been revealed in the murals of San Bartolo where a corn maiden is shown carrying maize *tamales* from a flower-bedecked hilltop (Saturno et al. 2005:14–21). The ubiquity of iconographic representations of an animated and fertile *wits* in early Maya media reinforces the antiquity of the notion of an animated landscape. Just as many contemporary Maya people conceive of the "earth owner" as a fat, wealthy ladino (see Vogt 1976:16–17), so Classic Maya representations of an animated *wits* supernatural depict an opulently adorned deity that wears large jade earspools (Vogt and Stuart 2005: Figures 7.1 and 7.11). Such images acknowledge the richness of the earth but also the mercurial qualities of the earth deity who can share or withhold this wealth in a seemingly whimsical fashion. Metaphorically complex locales, mountains also are perceived as brimming with sustenance from the life-giving waters that flow from

FIGURE 3.2 Tall cone-karst locally known as (a) "The Thumb" is perforated by two pass-through caves that contain offerings of pottery, fauna, and marine shell. The walls of the major passage feature (b) red handprint pictographs and (c) charcoal latticework sketches, Sibun-Manatee karst, Belize (photos courtesy of Xibun Archaeological Research Project).

caves within mountains to the tree and flower species that grow upon mountain flanks (see Taube 2004). In the *Popol Vuh*, the Mountain of Sustenance is the place of the discovery of maize (Sachse and Christenson 2005). A metaphor used throughout Mesoamerica (e.g., the notion of Tonacatepetl in the Mexican highlands), the Mountain of Sustenance is a concept with deep roots in the Preclassic (Saturno et al. 2005).

Unlike the evidence for Early Preclassic water shrines along the Gulf Coast, there are no documented coeval mountain shrines from which we might infer that the onset of pyramid building in lowland regions represented an attempt to create a cultural landscape that contained some of the vital features absent from lowland environments. The Early Preclassic center of San Lorenzo was located on a terra-formed hilltop (Cyphers 1996:61–62, 66), however, and there is some evidence that hilltop locales were favored for elite residences from very early times and certainly through the Classic period in the Maya lowlands. Some hilltop locales likely witnessed a 2000-year cycle of changing use from initial shrine location to transformation into a residential compound and ultimately back to a ritual use when/if a large Classic-period pyramid complex was constructed. This sort of genealogy of place (de Certeau 1984:122) is suggested by the changing nature of the stratigraphic layers underlying Group A at Seibal; specifically, the presence of a Middle Preclassic quadripartite celt and bloodletter cache at the base of Operation 9(C)15 (Smith 1982:12, 243–245). Likewise, the North Acropolis and Mundo Perdido complexes of Tikal occupy prominent hilltop locations and contain deeply sedimented genealogies (Harrison 1999:48).

Specialized Extraction Locales

Systematic archaeological coverage of the Maya lowlands has revealed the presence of specialized extraction locales – such as *salinas* from which salt was harvested. The production of salt – either through solar evaporation or cooking down saline brine – was labor intensive but also highly productive. An ethnographic account of the extraction of salt from mineral springs near the highland Maya village of Sacapulas reinforces the animate qualities ascribed to this natural phenomenon as well as the logic of resource extraction, which was phrased in the trope of debt repayment. Reina and Monaghan (1981:18) describe a ritual conducted at the *salinas* to ask "pardon of the *nagual* of the *salinas* for any trespasses the *salineros* may have committed, and that he continue to supply them with salt." During a lull in the salt boiling procedure, furthermore, a *salinera* by the name of Rosa reiterates the prayer and again asks pardon for any trespasses that the harvesting of salt may have caused (Reina and Monaghan 1981:26).

RITUAL PRACTICE IN A LOWLAND LANDSCAPE

From the perspective of landscape transformation, the lowland Maya region has undergone profound changes over the past 3,000 years and is anything but a pristine tropical forest. Pollen and sediment cores extracted from wetlands and pools across the lowlands bear evidence of pronounced changes in vegetation, some anthropogenetically induced while others are linked to a rise in sea level, shifts in larger meteorological systems, or the natural succession of species (Beach et al. 2006; Binford et al. 1987; Brenner et al. 1990; Dunning and Beach 2000; Dunning et al. 1998, 2002; Hodell et al. 2000; Jones 1994; Leyden et al. 1996; Pohl et al. 1996; Rice 1993; Rosenmeier et al. 2002). The most dynamic landforms are shallow pools, many of which have been transformed over the past 2,000 years from open bodies of water to vegetated and seasonally desiccated *bajos* (e.g., Dunning et al. 2002, 2003, 2006). From the perspective of historical ecology, the so-called climax tropical forest of the Maya lowlands is more properly considered a forest undergoing an extended response to the massive impact of relatively dense habitation during the first millennium before and after the Common Era (Binford et al. 1987; Islebe et al. 1996). As in New England – currently a forested habitat – it is clear that the species composition of a second- or third-growth forest is dramatically different from that of a forest community that evolved without the determinative hand of human selection. For these reasons, more paleoecological studies will need to be completed in the lowlands before we can envision, in a detailed fashion, the kind of landscape that Archaic and Early Preclassic populations experienced.

Even though the details may be hazy, the general appearance of the second- to first-millennium B.C.E. landscape across which horticultural populations expanded can be envisioned. Rolling hills – some riddled with cave systems – alternated with lowlands containing perennial pools of water. The rivers that drain the eastern and western flanks of the Yucatán Peninsula were in place although their channels may have shifted over the centuries. Precious hardwood trees, such as mahogany, *sapadilla*, and *siricote* would have covered the hills, and riparian vegetation, including *amate* or the fig tree, would have graced the banks of river terraces. Small palms species that would come to have tremendous importance for house construction grew in seasonally wet areas, while clear pools of water supported water lilies and aquatic-loving palm species. Beneath this mane of "hair," was the crust of the earth itself, primarily white limestone – the color of bleached bone – that decomposed into a rich mollisol. Soils scientists consider limestone-derived mollisols to be some of the most nutrient-rich soils on the face of the earth. Meskell and Joyce (2003) have sought to bring attention to the physical embodiment of ancient Maya lived experience; however, the trope of corporeality can be extended much further than human experience. Landscape itself was perceived in bodily terms. This perspective provides an entry point for examining the lowlands with particular attention to how Maya people came to inhabit these lands.

"Veins" and "Blood" of the Landscape

Rivers have been equated ethnographically with veins and blood – channels through which vital fluids move (Monaghan 2000:27). Although Maya colonization of the lowlands is traditionally thought to have occurred via these channels (Puleston and Puleston 1971), in point of fact, the evidence of Early and Middle Preclassic occupation on river terraces is not overwhelming, be it the Usuamacinta or Pasión Rivers framing the western edge of the Maya region or the Rio Azul or the Sibun River that drain the eastern, Caribbean side. The upper Belize River valley where a cluster of 1000 B.C.E. settlements has been located around the site of Cahal Pech (Awe 1992) provides an exception as does the early canal system found by Pohl and colleagues (1996) along the Rio Hondo. The Usumacinta River contains scattered and small floodplain landforms that are suitable for agriculture and evidence of Middle Preclassic settlement has been found there (Houston, personal communication 2007). The Sibun River of central Belize, while supporting a well-developed floodplain, has a volatile flooding regime that coincides with the growing season; as such, it lacks the landscape stability attractive and essential to maize farmers. On the other hand, slow-moving river systems such as the New River, Belize River, and Río Hondo attracted a large number of early settlers (McAnany et al. 2002).

"Heart" of the Landscape

Middle Preclassic settlers gravitated to the high, drier ground proximate to stillwater pools or wetlands that provided a constant water source for humans and their crops as well as for other species – such as wild game – which could be hunted, fished, or collected. The

FIGURE 3.3 Classic Maya hieroglyph for cattail reeds, *puh*, a toponymic reference to the great city of Teotihuacan (redrawn by Josh Feola after Stuart 2000:503).

Mirador Basin – with its early, monumental constructions comes to mind (Hansen 1998). Northern Belize also supported a large network of Middle Preclassic villages situated on low ridgelines between landforms that are now primarily seasonal wetlands (McAnany 2004a). Within our Western postindustrialized society, environmentalists refer to wetlands as the "lungs of an ecosystem," but in fact thousands of acres of wetlands have been sacrificed in the name of development. In Mesoamerica, Mixtec reference to wetlands as the "heart" of the cosmos (Monaghan 1995:98) indicates the centrality of this landform in traditional Mesoamerican thought. This centrality is further highlighted by the fact that wetlands were synonymous with an indigenous concept of civilization during Classic and Postclassic periods. Place of the *tule* or cattails reeds (as in Tula or Tollan) signified a locale of great governance and well-developed artisanship in the Postclassic Mexican highlands. Closer to home, Classic Maya use of a hieroglyph for cattail reeds, *puh*, seems to have been a toponymic reference to the great Mexican highland city of Teotihuacan (Figure 3.3; Stuart 2000:502–506; Schele and Mathews 1998:39). Wetlands – or stillwater pools – provided an expandable metaphor with many levels of meaning and clearly this landform was of vital importance throughout Mesoamerica.

Scarborough (2003:111) has suggested that proximity to wetlands was the predominant pattern of Preclassic Maya settlement and one that can be contrasted with a later Classic-period attraction to hilltop settlement. While this contrast may be too starkly drawn (i.e., there are many Preclassic settlements on hilltops and plenty of Classic-period wetland-focused settlements), the concern of Scarborough is the contrasting manner in which water could be stored and managed through a perilously long dry season. According to Scarborough (2003:159), both types of settlement were dependent seasonally upon a "water system structured around reservoirs and swamp margins within a semitropical rain forest [that] resulted in a still-water adaptation." This concept captures, albeit using a Western technological riff, the same notion of Mesoamerican place making indigenously called the "place of reeds" or the place of still water. Both concepts can be stretched to include *cenotes* and *aguadas* as well as reservoirs that were constructed and terraformed from the quarry pits dug to provide construction material for nearby monumental construction projects as Scarborough (1998) has documented at Tikal.

Were ancient Maya communities situated close to the wetlands precisely to take advantage of the resources it offered? Kunen (2004:8) has proposed that such settlements, which she calls "*bajo* communities," existed in northwestern Belize. Tourtellot and colleagues (2003:39), on the other hand, have pointed out that settlements inevitably are situated on high, dry ground that is proximate to *bajos*. Since 40 to 60 percent of the land surface of the central lowlands is covered with *bajos* (Dunning et al. 2006:82), a spatial correlation is unavoidable. Whichever perspective one adapts, the pairing of the two appears to have provided the right combination for living well and prospering.

"Hair" of the Landscape

An upsurge in charcoal content and secondary species within dated pollen cores indicates that alteration of the forested uplands began as long ago as the second millennium B.C.E. (Dunning et al. 1998; Islebe et al. 1996; Jones 1994; Pohl et al. 1996). For farmers – or even hunters – the tall canopy of the semitropical rain forest provided neither prime habitat for game nor enough sunlight to grow desirable plants such as maize. On the other hand, valuable resources – for house construction, subsistence, and status-permeated performance – were distributed throughout the forest and could be collected by persons knowledgeable about the forest. Special knowledge and experience is needed to travel within a tropical forest as landmarks are few and far between; Classic-period representations of hunters wearing the broad-brimmed hat distinguish men with such a knowledge base (Taube 2003). In characterizing ethnographic Maya conceptions of the forest, Taube (2003:467) cites Guiteras-Homes (1961:287) who collected this impression of the forest from a Pedrano Tzotzil person: "The forest and the bush, the caves and sinkholes are feared by man, because in them he lacks the protective light and warmth of the sun." It appears that the darkness of the forest – in contrast to the bright sun within a maize field, for example – is capable of creating a sense of foreboding, a sense that one is too close to powerful earthly forces. This "mane" of the landscape represents a world in which principles of social order might be alien and the bright, protective light of solar deities did not penetrate.

Throughout the two millennia before and after the Common Era, many old-growth trees were felled across the lowlands. In their place, early successional species flourished along with economically desirable species – such as cacao, avocado, and nance. The forest became a managed habitat or a crafted mosaic (Dunning and Beach 2000:191; Fedick 1996) over which a modicum of social order could be implemented. Truly wild forested areas probably continued to exist only in areas that were inhospitable to arboriculture and agriculture due to steep grades or extremely broken topography, such as the high slopes of the Maya mountains or the Sierra Madre Oriental and the rugged terrain of the Chiquibul or the Sibun-Manatee karsts. These areas provided *refugia* for plant and animal species that radiated from these shelters to recolonize the lowlands during the less populous Postclassic period.

"Head" and "Bones" of the Landscape

The hills of the lowlands are subtle features when compared to the mountainous terrain of highland Chiapas and Guatemala that are inhabited by many contemporary indigenous Maya people. The graphic representation of what iconographers refer to as an "earth

FIGURE 3.4 Classic Maya "earth monster" shown with the grapelike clusters that denote a stony hill with cloud curls such as emerge from the mouth of a cave, Palenque, Temple of the Foliated Cross (redrawn by Josh Feola after Schele and Freidel 1990:240).

monster" (that includes the sign for *wits* or mountain) indicates that the concept of an earth deity personified in a hill feature was not alien to Classic Maya people (Figure 3.4). The fact that this toponym often references places within a built environment (Vogt and Stuart 2005:156) is not surprising given the paucity of impressive natural hillscapes in the lowlands.

Tourtellot and colleagues (2003:39) have noted that hilltops were favored locales for settlement and employ the term "hill subcommunities" to describe a residential pattern that is clustered around hills at the site of La Milpa. During the Classic period, in particular, high-elevation residences and temples appear to take on increased significance. On the eastern flank of the Maya Mountains – at the Classic Maya centers of Nim Li Punit, Lubaantun, Uxbenka, and surrounding satellite residences – high hilltops were the preferred residential location even though water, food, and supplies had to be carried up steep slopes. In modeling the flow of rainwater through large hilltop architectural complexes, Scarborough (2003:111) characterizes these constructions as having a "convex microwatershed" because water drained from stone architecture and paved plazas to fill reservoirs. Construction of and access to those reservoirs played a crucial role in the lived experience of community.

FIGURE 3.5 U-shaped outline of a *cenote* within which the rain deity Chahk is shown as a scribe holding a paint pot (likely fashioned from marine shell) and a quill, Codex Madrid, Folio 73b (reprinted courtesy of FAMSI).

"Mouth" and "Womb" of the Landscape

The attraction of water-filled *cenotes* as well as earth-filled but moist *rejolladas* (both are sinkholes) in the drier climate of northern Yucatán is obvious and such features are known to have been locales of offerings. Even though *cenotes* may represent portals to the realm of earth and rain deities (and representations in the Codex Madrid indicate that this was the case; Figure 3.5), they also are features around which many Maya settlements were established and prospered. Under the watery membrane of the *cenote*, all semblance of social order may fade but above the waterline, many *cenotes* were integrated into the social fabric of the settlement via peripheral temples, descending staircases, and other architectural features.

Caves, be they dry or wet, appear to be more universally conceived as powerful and dangerous places. Many were set off from settlements and accessible primarily to ritual specialists who often had to travel through a dark forest to arrive at the mouth of a cave that, today, requires technical equipment to access. In addition to being the residence of earth deities, the storm god, and ancestors, caves have been mentioned as the abode of the aged, deer-eared hunting god who required offerings to ensure a successful hunt and to compensate for the taking of an animal (Brown 2005; Taube 2003:473–474). As noted previously, many caves in the Maya lowlands were repositories of offerings long before a local population was established and so represent a palimpsest of use over many centuries. Brady (2006:119–122) has called attention to the fact that archaeological deposits within caves often contain very high densities not only of pottery but also of valuable items such as obsidian, greenstone *hachas*, and hematite. Caves of the Petexbatun region yielded a large number of items of personal adornment (Brady 2006:125; Ishihara 2007), possibly offerings to an earth deity who is always depicted – in both Classic Maya iconography and ethnographic accounts – attired in wealth items that cover a well-fed body. Given the richness of cave deposits, Brady (2006:126) rightly calls for more appreciation of the "tremendous economic importance of [cave] ritual in Maya society." Here, we situate such ritual within the larger context of Maya landscape inhabitation and the cultural economy that formed in relation to that landscape.

Specialized Features of the Landscape

Situating close to desirable resources – spiritual as well as material – was a strong motivational force in the founding of households across the lowlands. In many areas, the prevailing approach to inhabiting the landscape appears to have been that of balancing good soils with water availability. Included with the latter resource are animals, sources of wild protein that, like humans, tend to cluster around sources of water. This strategy appears to have underwritten the successful expansion of settlement into every corner of the Maya lowlands in which these two elements – good soil and water – coexisted. Landscapes with an altered equation – water that was difficult to access or thin soils – were not ignored but rather were inhabited with increased attention to what Scarborough (2003:114–115) has termed "labortasking." That is, special agricultural facilities might be constructed to create soil from mulched materials such as Kepecs and Boucher (1996) have documented in the northeastern Chikinchel region of Yucatán or to retain soils by terracing slopes as Healy and others (1983) and Chase and Chase (1998a) have recorded at Caracol, Robin (2002) and Neff (2002) in the environs of Xunantunich, Turner (1983) in the Rio Bec, Dunning and Beach (2000:197) in northwestern Belize and the Pasión Region of the Petén, and Liendo Stuardo (2002:64) in the Palenque region. If water availability was the issue, then rainwater cisterns might be constructed to store water through the dry season as in the Puuc regions (McAnany 1990) or quarry pits transformed into water reservoirs (Scarborough 2003). As population increased in the Maya region, more of the less than optimal niches were settled and the local resource equation modified by labortasking. As Scarborough (2003:6) has noted, "This kind of settlement expansion into potentially agriculturally productive settings, ones modifiable given increasing numbers of laborers and experiments in new landscaping technologies, was most pronounced during the Late Classic period."

The settling of the Sibun Valley provides a relevant case in point to this general trend. Although soils of the Sibun River terraces are annually enriched from floodwaters originating in the Maya Mountains, the flooding regime can be extremely volatile and coincides with the time of planting annual crops – such as maize and beans – at the beginning of the rainy season. Despite the attraction of this karstic landscape filled with cave chambers that contain Preclassic and Early Classic offerings, the valley lacks significant Preclassic and Early Classic settlement. This valley may have been shunned not because of a lack of water but because, for a maize farmer, there was too much of it at the wrong time of year. During the Late Classic when orchard crops such as cacao were in great demand, the valley was actively settled, likely by farmers who specialized in arboriculture, as do the current farmers living along the Sibun River. Thus, settlement of the Sibun Valley likely was spurred not by an innovation in landscape technology but rather by a specialization in tree crops.

Resource-specialized communities (Scarborough and Valdez 2003: 4–6) have been most commonly recognized for the Late Classic period but certainly were not restricted to this time. The stone-tool-producing settlement of Colha, for instance, dates back to the Middle Preclassic and likely even earlier (Iceland 1997, 2005). Its precocious origins may relate to the triad of valuable resources that are combined at this location: water, good although stony soil, and easily mined chert nodules of incomparable quality (Shafer and Hester 1991). This convergence resulted in what Potter and King (1995:19) refer to as a "specialized extractive/productive community specialization." Salt-production locales, situated on the edge of *ti k'ahk' nahb*, the fiery sea, as it was expressed hieroglyphically during the Classic period (Stephen Houston, personal communication 2006) increasingly are recognized as extremely important and highly prevalent resource-specialized communities (MacKinnon and Kepecs 1989; McAnany and Murata 2006a; McKillop 1995, 2002; Mock 2004). Ethnohistoric resources indicate that Postclassic polities actively vied for access to the large solar-evaporative *salinas* off the northern tip of the Yucatán Peninsula (Roys 1957:28–39), and the presence of Preclassic and Classic sites in the vicinity of the *salinas* suggests that there is considerable antiquity to their exploitation (Andrews 1983:119–125). At coastal Belizean salt-producing locales, a more labor-intensive technique of boiling salty water (*sal cocida*) was employed (MacKinnon and Kepecs 1989; McAnany and Murata 2006a; McKillop 1995; Mock 2004). Many of these locales date to the Late Classic period and seem to have employed this innovative technology in order to "capitalize" on a growing demand for a product – in this case, salt – that was not readily available to a burgeoning population in the interior.

Strategic location also can trump ready access to fresh water and good soil as is apparent at the Preclassic port facility of Cerros (Freidel 1979) and the Classic-to-Postclassic maritime trade depots situated on the coral reef islands along the Caribbean side of the lowlands (Graham and Pendergast 1989:11–12; McKillop 1996).

Resource-specialized communities likely were more common than was acknowledged under the old paradigm of Maya settlements as the ancient equivalent of Wolf's (1957:7–12) "closed corporate community" in which most subsistence and "hardware" needs were met by the household or community that sought to defend itself against the onslaught of taxation and rent demands from hegemonic forces. It now appears that we should be entertaining more dynamic models of ancient Maya production and trade that come closer to the ethnographic situation documented for Southwestern Guatemala during the first half of the twentieth century – a veritable hive of villages engaged in specialized production and woven together in "complementary and mutually dependent economic regions" (McBryde 1971:129–130; see also Reina and Monaghan 1981:13). As economic practice is situated within the duality of structure and agency, simply documenting the presence of specialized production is not sufficient. We need also to consider the constraints and opportunities afforded by the articulation of these activities with the "palace" economies in operation by 200 B.C.E. at seats of power throughout the Maya world. We turn to this challenging topic in the second half of this study (Chapters 6–9).

THE WORK OF ORDERING THE WILD AND CHAOTIC

The business of mapping on to the anatomy of a lowland landscape required engagement with and disruption of the vital forces of the earth. If traditional Mesoamerican theological concerns about the imbalance caused by such actions as well as the potential consequences (Monaghan 2000:33) provide a guide to understanding the past, then we need to envision a past replete with ritual practice – particularly offerings – designed to ameliorate the impact of humans on the earth and to compensate earthly deities for such invasive practices. The process by which a landscape is transformed from one of utilization via hunting, gathering, and collecting into a landscape of agricultural production has been referred to as kind of "domestication" (Hodder 1990); certainly, this term characterizes the transformation of the lowland landscape discussed above but a disruption or containment of earthly forces is also an establishment of social order and social space. Houses and fields, with their pronounced quadrilateral design, are paradigmatic of order (Monaghan 2000:35) to be contrasted with the chaotic structure and irregular form of wild places. According to Monaghan (2000:35), disordered places also are locales where social controls are lax and thus are "likely to be the settings of impropriety [particularly in] ... forests and wild areas, peripheries, and rocky outcroppings." Paradoxically, while the imposition of social order and the establishment of socially constituted

FIGURE 3.6 Copán Stela D, backside, showing a long-count date of 9.15.5.0.0 10 Ajaw 8 Ch'en or 736 C.E. with full figural substitution for bar-dot numbers. The figure on the upper right literally bears the burden of the *bak'tun* on a tumpline (drawing by and courtesy of Matthew Looper).

space (Hanks 1990:364) might disturb the deities due to its disruptive nature, the ritual offerings necessitated by such actions create and perpetuate the covenant between human and deities. The very work of transforming a landscape into one that houses and feeds humans exacerbated "original debt" and intensified ritual practice.

The Yucatec Mayan term *kuch* means "burden" or "cargo," the work of carrying a heavy load often suspended from a tumpline. Copán Stela D contains a fully figural long-count date that anthropomorphizes the numerical coefficients as bearing the burden of time – note the nine *bak'tun* (upper right) born as a tumpline burden (Figure 3.6).

Taube (2003:464) has called attention to the burden or *kuch* supported by upstretched arms in the Classic and Postclassic Pawahtun throne figures and suggests that they relate to a widespread Mesoamerican concept of public authority as a weighty burden, emblematic of the work and effort needed to maintain an ordered society. Arguably, such tropes build upon preexisting concepts and one inevitably finds that principles of social order are more stridently expressed in societies with a hierarchical structure in which the consequences of disorder translate into a loss of power and privilege for the ruling sector. The work of transforming a tropical forest environment into a pastiche of seats of power, villages, fields, and orchards must have been a considerable undertaking and appears to have been initiated during the early part of the Middle Preclassic period. The patterns and strategies of labortasking, as Scarborough (2003: 114–115) refers to it, in which a highly knowledgeable workforce implemented a wide range of labor-intensive tasks, provided the fuel that transformed the lowland landscape into a manicured domain that extended over a vast area.

In many areas, wetlands were absorbed into the web of socially constructed spaces, the intensive utilization of which required special offerings. Within the island fields excavated along the western margin of K'axob, for instance, we encountered offerings of marine shell adornment (Figure 3.7; Berry and McAnany 2007). Significantly, extensive excavation in the vacant terrain between the island fields and houses located on the higher terrain yielded no marine shell whatsoever. Apparently, the work of carving fields out of the wetlands and recursively cultivating the constructed surfaces was considered too invasive without the reciprocal offering of precious carved marine shell that might also ensure the continued fertility of the fields.

Elsewhere, there is evidence – particularly for the Classic period – of efforts to thwart the long-term deleterious consequences of farming hillslopes by constructing terracing and check dams (Beach et al. 2006; Chase and Chase 1998a; Dunning and Beach 2000:197; Healy et al. 1983; Turner 1983). Contrary to popular doomsday scenarios (e.g., Diamond 2005:157–177), the work of maintaining the fertility of the fields involved not only propitiating the earth deities but also careful landscape microengineering. During the Late Classic period, much labor appears to have been expended in order to accomplish

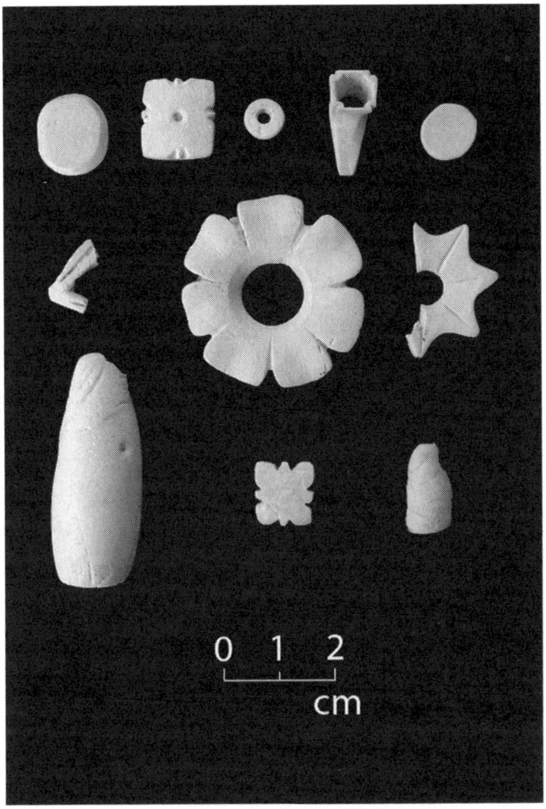

FIGURE 3.7 Marine shell adornments placed as offerings in wetland fields along the western margin of K'axob (photo prepared by Kimberly Berry, courtesy of K'axob Archaeological Project).

this goal and ameliorate the erosion processes initiated during the heady days of expansive Preclassic farming (Beach et al. 2006; Dunning and Beach 2000).

The frequent representation of Chahk, the rain deity, in the pages of the Codex Madrid (Figure 3.5) suggests that water – in the many capacities in which it was sought and utilized – was fraught with ritual concerns. Several scholars (i.e., Harrison 1993; Lucero 1999; Scarborough 1998; see also contributions in Lucero and Fash 2006) have suggested that water catchments and water management became a major concern of Classic-period populations. For Scarborough (1998:135), "The significance of modifying the urban landscape in the partial image of the ordinary water hole defines the extraordinary in Maya ritual." The centrality of water storage systems at Classic Maya hilltop capitals also suggests to Scarborough (1998:149) that the interpretation of the quatrefoil motif – commonly associated with cave or *cenote* openings – should be extended to include artificial reservoirs such as existed at Tikal. Lucero (1999:40–42), likewise, asserts that the presence of Classic-period royal iconography that dwells on aquatic themes – such the water lily that only thrives in clean water – demonstrates that elites were managing and controlling access to sources of potable drinking water. Certainly reservoirs and their less socially ordered counterpart *aguadas* are the result of engineered space. They also represent an attempt to regularize the supply of water in an environment in which there is not only a marked dry season but also a pronounced variation in the timing and intensity of the wet season. For these reasons, Postclassic representations of Chahk often portray a deity with a decidedly mercurial personality – both bringer and withholder of water. In effect, the wild and chaotic could refer to a particular untamed place on the landscape or to meteorological cycles that are beyond social control, regardless of the amount of labortasking. Ritual practice focused on Chahk – the bringer and withholder of rain – sought to assuage this deity, curry favor in the form of ample rainfall, and thus bring under social control a force that is not controllable, even with twenty-first-century technologies. Strong Preclassic antecedents for Chahk-focused ritual have been found in Campeche, México, at the site of Aguacatel in the form of a quatrefoil-shaped and stuccoed pool adorned with representations of fish, sharks, and Chahk (Houston et al. 2005).

How strong was the centripetal pull of the Preclassic- and Classic-period community, which is thought by some scholars to have been paradigmatic of social order and perhaps the repository of stored supplies of water and other essentials? Some have suggested that it was very strong indeed. For Lucero (1999:43–44), lords of central Petén held sway over their constituents by controlling the source of water through the dry season. For Taube (2003:479), the social order of the community conveyed a sense of security and separation from the moral and physical dangers of the wilds: "To be banished and forced into the bush was a situation of terrible consequence that placed one in moral as well as physical peril." On the other hand, engaging with the powers and dangers of the wilderness served to set one apart from the *macehualtin*, the common people.

TO WALK ON THE WILD SIDE

Sahlins (1985:73–79) notes Polynesian tropes of rulership that refer to the king as a stranger – not one of us – as "a shark that travels on land" (Handy and Pukui 1972:199). The decided inequality implied by rulership in addition to the rarefied pedigree of most hereditary rulers, in effect, ensured that rulers were not like common people. As such, they could engage with "the wild" with some measure of impunity, and, in fact, they were expected to do so. It comes as no surprise, therefore, that Maya rulers often took a royal title that included reference to *bahlum* (jaguar) or *k'inich* (sun-faced) and were carried through the forest on a jaguar-skin "vehicle" (Taube 2003:480; see especially, the depiction on Stela 2, Izapa). At large caves, such as Naj Tunich, Maya rulers might visit the solar deity in his "nighttime" home. To do so they traveled through forests, the abode of jaguars and the dangerous and unpredictable *way* spirits (Taube 2003:476). To move through the forest and visit caves with impunity served to mark these individuals as different, perhaps different enough to justify their power and influence over others.

In addition to rulers who could operate outside of socially constituted space, there were also hunters, warriors, nobles, and ritual specialists who routinely "walked on the wild side." Some of these persons are imaged or textually referenced on the cave walls of Naj Tunich, particularly the hunter who is represented by the hero twin, Hunahpu, and sports a broad-brimmed hat (Figure 3.8). At Naj Tunich, hieroglyphic reference is made to the arrival "*huli*" of royal individuals (MacLeod and Stone 1995:156), and even though a kingly form may be depicted on the walls of the cave, the lack of clothing (a primary indicator of status in Mesoamerican society) precludes identification of rulers. The quality of darkness within caves has a lot to do with their perceived supernatural power and danger. For the Ch'orti', dark spaces even within a domestic setting are propitious locales in which to contact supernaturals (Wisdom 1940:431).

FIGURE 3.8 Hunahpu, one of the hero twins, dressed in the broad-brimmed hat of a hunter and traveler. He wears the hip cloth of a ball player (painting on cave wall of Naj Tunich, Guatemala; reprinted courtesy of Chip and Jennifer Clark).

As Taube (2003:485) has noted, the Ch'orti' keep "idols" enclosed in dark spaces because "constant light is said to 'hurt' the santo" while darkness is considered protective and efficacious for ritual performance (Wisdom 1940:431).

ON FEEDING A HUNGRY LANDSCAPE

This chapter has introduced and developed conceptual material that lays the foundation for later chapters. Although broad in scope, the goal of this chapter is quite simple – to comprehend the "figured world" of ancestral Maya-lived experience in relation to the materiality of ecology. We began by noting the performance-based nature of traditional Mesoamerican theology – one that emphasizes action over internalized beliefs. Within this mindset, much theologically related performance is directed to the landscape where sacred forces are perceived to reside. Metonymic references to landscape as a human body further personalizes the landscape and anthropomorphizes the spirits residing within it. Although the interaction between humans and deities in Mesoamerica has been described as one of reciprocity, there is much evidence to indicate that the relationship was one of debt and merit with some scholars characterizing K'iché Maya, for instance, as born into "original debt." With sacrifice and offerings, humans could repay their debt to the gods; locales at which humans modified the landscape to create socially constituted space – houses, fields, and orchards – were prime areas for deity propitiation. Additionally, caves, pools, and hilltops can be understood as hierophanies – locales at which one could conjure supernatural forces. Although often located outside of the social space of settlements, and therefore potentially dangerous, such places were visited by ritual specialists and those marked as socially different.

The work of mapping on to the anatomy of the lowland landscape via settlement radiation indicates the central importance of pools and wetlands to Maya occupants. Access to a dependable water source and good soils was balanced against the attraction of specialized resources such as chert beds and salt-making opportunities. "Domesticating" the lowland environment required constant labor input and engineering efforts that thwarted the consequences of hill-slope erosion via terrace construction and mitigated the unpredictability of the water supply through construction of large reservoirs and small cisterns.

Areas outside of socially constituted space – particularly wild forests and distant caves – were perceived as locales of potent supernaturals and socially inverted practices. Rulers, hunters, and ritual specialists, among others, could traverse these spaces and did so with impunity. This ability marked them as different, powerful, and often dangerous – a topic to which we return. There was a pronounced materiality to landscape inhabitation that included dialogue between humans and supernatural forces perceived to reside in features of the landscape. This ecology suggests that a Latourian (2005) approach to reassembling the social by way of actor–network theory carries resonance with Maya ritual practice, a topic explored in later chapters. We turn now to the built environment of house, orchard, and field and the gendered social practice that sustained these spaces.

4

Gendered Labor and Socially Constructed Space

> Women are called in Quiché the *rajau ja*, literally "owners of the house," not because they legally own the physical place but because it is their action domain.
>
> Earle 1986:157

> You will be the heart of the house, you will go nowhere, you will become a person who goes nowhere. You become the banked fire, the hearthstone. Here our lord plants you, buries you.
>
> Nahua midwife addressing a baby girl in the *Florentine Codex*; Burkhart 1997:28

> Among the Lacandon, men pray whereas women prepare the ceremonial food.
>
> Boremanse 1993:340

> [T]he archaeology of the individual household is an essential building block in the reconstruction of past societies.
>
> Willey 1982:613 in the Foreword to an issue of *American Behavioral Scientist* dedicated to household archaeology, based on a Society for American Archaeology symposium organized by Richard R. Wilk and William L. Rathje in 1981

Within the last several decades, two research topics – germane to the study of ritually entangled economic practice – have witnessed significant growth within Maya archaeology. They are household and gender studies – the twin foci of this chapter. The former grew from recognition within ethnographic inquiry that households – while challenging to define – were a fundamental unit of farming societies (Orlove and Custred 1980:33; Wilk 1991; Wilk and Netting 1984; Wilk and Rathje 1982, among others). Within archaeology, the preservation of ancient dwellings suggested that archaeologists might also have a shot at understanding something of the activities performed by ancient householders (Wilk and Ashmore 1988). The cross-fertilization between ethnographic research – focused on what Wolf (1966:91, 97–99) termed "peasant households" – and archaeological research that increasingly focused on non-elite or nonurban residential contexts provided substantial methodological and theoretical underpinnings to this endeavor. Coeval and corollary to this increased focus on residential features outside of or on the fringes of monumental seats of power was an increased attention to agricultural features that constituted evidence that something beyond *milpa* agriculture had taken place in the Maya lowlands during the first millennia before and after the beginning of the Common Era (see Harrison and Turner 1978, among others).

While these salubrious developments signaled a maturation of field techniques and a paradigmatic broadening of research issues within Maya archaeology, they did not really transform our understanding of the social construction of labor in ancient Maya society. In contrast, gender studies in Maya archaeology – which followed on the heels of increased attention to gender and feminist issues within ethnographic research (see especially Reiter 1975) – focused on the social construction of gendered work regimes and status roles within ancient Maya society. Increased attention to households necessitated the new excavation of dwellings to produce primary data not hitherto available; however, gender studies could be based on the reinterpretion of old data in light of new perspectives (e.g., Miller 1988). Readily accessible representations of females existed in Classic Maya royal iconography and figurines; initial studies focused on the role of royal women, which was viewed as complementary to that of royal men (Joyce 1992, 1993). Deciphering the gender roles of nonroyal females might be inferred from patterning in the imagery of royal women but an assumption of uniformitarianism across such a wide social chasm is problematic, at best. Due to the paucity of readily accessible imagery, gender roles among ancient Maya commoners was and continues to be underdeveloped theoretically, although increasingly it is coming onto the archaeological radar screen as studies of artifact patterns are linked to considerations of gender (see Beaudry-Corbett and McCafferty 2002; Hendon 1996, 2002; Neff 2002; Robin 2002, 2003, 2006 for specific applications; and Ardren 2008 for a bibliographic overview). This chapter contributes to the study of gendered labor among nonroyal women and men.

Given the selected quotes that preface this chapter, it is clear that the socially constructed domains of household and gender are two highly convergent realms, the study of which is fraught with challenging issues regarding historicity, idealism, and essentialism. Most ethnographic and ethnohistoric sources throughout Mesoamerica indicate in an unambiguous fashion that the dwelling – especially the kitchen area – is female-gendered space (Burkhart 1997:28; Earle 1986:157; Hanks 1990:112; Shroeder 1997:16; Tozzer 1941:127–128; Vogt 1976:59; Wisdom 1940:120, among others). Rather than accept this notion at face value, archaeologists have considered whether this arrangement could be historically contingent and might have resulted from – among other factors – the heavy Colonial tribute demand for woven cloth (Espejo-Ponce and Restall 1997:232; Quezada 1985), which generally was produced within the dwelling compound. Greater reliance through time on maize tortillas in the diet – which increased the amount of time that women spent on food production (Blanton et al. 1981; Brumfiel 1991; Robin 2002:26) – tethered females more closely to grinding stones. Spanish-introduced concepts of gender hierarchy and gendered space also cannot be factored out of ethnohistorical and ethnographic accounts. Many factors could yield a highly varied pattern of gendered space and gendered work during ancient times (for critiques of gender essentialism, see Conkey and Gero 1991; Pyburn 1999). The statement of the Nahua midwife who referred to a newborn baby girl as "heart of the house" represents an expression of a perceived ideal and not an observed reality of the variable arrangements in which humans inevitably find themselves in response to unexpected and sometimes catastrophic events, such as an untimely death. Within the human life cycle, moreover, there is likely to be considerable variation in gender roles for both men and women, as Earle (1986:162) has observed among the K'iché and Neff (2002:50) has suggested for the Classic Maya.

Beyond historical contingency, cuisine trends, expressions of "ideal" gender roles, and life cycle transitions, however, there remains a strong linkage between female gender and the work regime in and around the domicile, on the one hand, and male gender and the work regime away from the domicile (e.g., farming, hunting, and fishing), on the other. Referring to the structuring capabilities of the house as culturally iconic, Bourdieu (1977:89) suggests that the house "is the principal locus for the objectification of the generative schemes; and, through the intermediary of the divisions and hierarchies it sets up between things, persons, and practices, this tangible classifying system continuously inculcates and reinforces the taxonomic principles underlying all the arbitrary provisions of this culture." In this manner, daily practice – especially gendered labor – and the physical container of the house can mutually reinforce each other. As Devereaux (1987:89–92) has discussed, among Zinacanteco Maya, gender is construed not in some essentialist – or even necessarily biological fashion – but rather by action and appearance, that is, by daily practice. The strength and durability of the linkage between gendered labor and the dwelling begs the question as to why the possibility that ancient houses were female-gendered space has not been actively engaged by Maya archaeologists who study residential compounds. The absence of this line of inquiry is all the more perplexing when one considers that many Classic Maya royal women are hieroglyphically linked with palatial, as well as pyramidal, structures at sites such as Yaxchilán, Chichén Itzá, Tikal, Caracol, Copán, and Dos Pilas to name a few examples (Tate 1992; Plank 2004; Josserand 2002; Krochock 2002; Martin and Grube 2008[2000]:46, 91; Chase and Chase 1987; Bell 2002; Houston et al. n.d.; Palka, Stuart, and Houston n.d., respectively). For the early Colonial period, Espejo-Ponce and Restall (1997:245) find ample evidence of wills written in Yucatec Mayan in which women inherited and bequeathed *solares* (a residential compound that includes a dwelling and surrounding yard). The strong association between Maya females and dwellings through time suggests that, despite important sources of variation, a linkage existed within Colonial society as well as in the royal sector of Classic Maya society and possibly within nonroyal residential contexts.

In this chapter, we examine the economic and ritual implications of viewing nonroyal houses as female-gendered space, an action domain as per Earle (1986:157) and a seat of power as per Burkhart (1997:26) of females. Trends in artifact patterns – especially bark beaters, spinning and weaving tools, *metates*, and swept debris – are examined with an eye to sharpening our understanding of the types of work regimes in which Maya females were engaged during Preclassic, Classic, and Postclassic periods. Mesoamerican females have been characterized as processors par excellence for they "processed unfinished materials into finished products: foodstuffs into meals, raw fibers into thread and cloth, sexual secretions into babies" (Burkhart 1997:35). Thus, it is critical to understand the centrality of action – *'abtel* or work among Zinacanteco Maya (Devereaux 1987:93) – in defining gender and the complementarity of male- and female-gendered labor. For archaeologists, this action-oriented approach poses methodological challenges as we must reason from archaeological patterns back to both the actions that produced them and the meaning ascribed to them (see Sweely 1999:162–162 for an example of the difficulties of such analytical "tacking"; and Hendon 2004:275 for programmatic recommendations).

The socially constituted space of the dwelling was complemented by extra-mural spaces that also were part of a crafted landscape: near-residential gardens, orchards, and fields. Ethnographically, increasing distance from the residence translates into increasingly male-gendered space and the places where extraction and production of unprocessed materials takes place (Earle 1986; Hanks 1990: 306–307). The possibility that this division of gendered space is an ancient pattern is considered, and archaeological data that are relevant to this question are reviewed.

As a prelude to Chapter 7 (on artisanship), the study of the house is then broadened to a consideration of the creation of value through household production activities, drawing on the approach of Munn (1986). Central to the creation of household-based value are not only artisan products but also participation and sponsorship of household and community feasts. This activity is considered through the lens of gendered labor.

We then step back to the creation of a house and examine how houses are "ensouled" or animated and, from a broader political perspective, how we can identify when the household becomes a unit of tribute collection. Throughout this chapter, the focus stays on the household as a primary unit of *production, performance, and identity.*

Royal palace compounds are not excluded from consideration in this chapter; however, because of their distinctive extractive relationship with lower-status households, they are more properly dealt with in Chapter 6. In the previous chapter, house and field were described ideally as paragons of social order that stood in contradistinction to the wildness of mountains and forested realms. Such social constructions of space were most dramatically illustrated in dwellings where the convergent trajectories of gendered labor and Maya households took form.

"HEART OF THE HOUSE"

If we consider the possibility that ancient Maya residences were female-gendered spaces – and that females were metaphorically considered the "heart of the house" – then a new universe of interpretive possibilities emerges. The dwelling, as a nexus of production, ritual, and identity, begins to assume interesting gendered properties. The goal of this examination is not to exclude male-gendered space and activities from consideration nor to reinforce gender essentialism; rather, the intended goal is to add the dimension of gendered labor to interpretive narratives for nonroyal domestic architecture and, in doing so, to fine-tune our understanding of the performance of domestic work.

In an examination of the religious significance of "housework" among Mexica women, Louise Burkhart (1997) identifies four recurrent work practices: sweeping, offering food and drink at the domestic shrine, preparing food, and weaving. Though separate in time and space from the Classic Maya lowlands, the Mexica region is an area for which there is detailed information on the topic of gender roles as recorded in early Colonial documents, such as the *Florentine Codex* compiled by Fray Bernardino de Sahagún (1950–1982). The description of Mexica women's work, moreover, bears a strong resemblance to an influential primary source consulted in the Maya lowlands, namely the *Relación de las cosas de Yucatan* compiled (only partially it seems; see Restall and Chuchiak 2002) by Bishop Diego de Landa (Tozzer 1941). Given our professed interest in the ritual entanglements of domestic work, Burkhart's analysis provides a compelling framework for considering female work regimes.

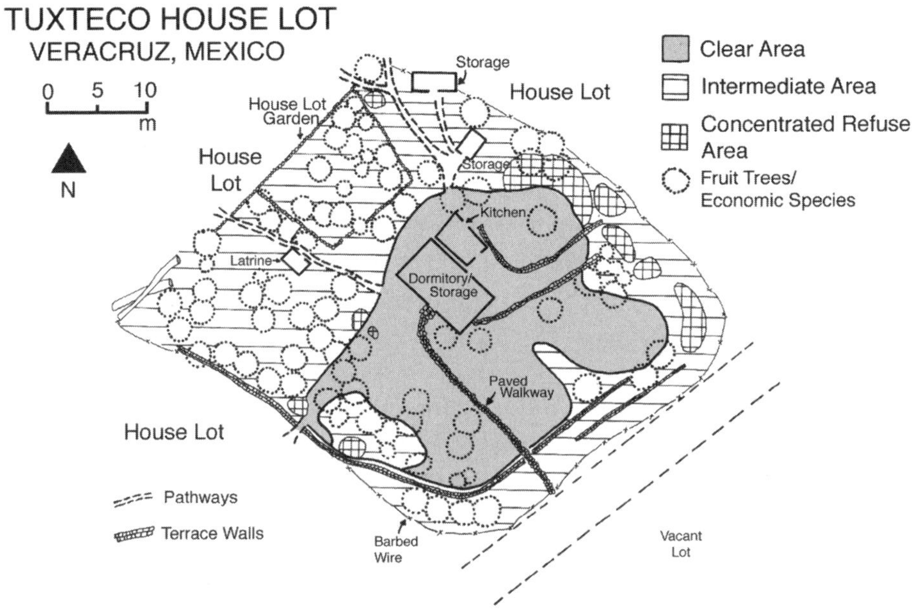

FIGURE 4.1 Tuxteco houselot, Veracruz, México; the Clear Area is maintained by the practice of female-gendered sweeping (after Killion 1990:204; courtesy of Thomas W. Killion).

Swept Away

In a section subtitled "The Power of the Brooms," Burkhart (1997: 33–37) describes sweeping as both an act of ritual purification (also recognized in the Maya region; see Hanks 1990:334–335) and as part of the daily work regime of Mexica women: "A housewife, rising before dawn to sweep away the night's debris, surely saw herself as an actor in the regeneration of order, dividing day from night and protecting her family from dangerous forces" (Burkhart 1997:33–34). "Sweeping the path" is a metaphor of ritual purification found repeatedly in the sixteenth- to nineteenth-century Yucatec Books of Chilam Balam (see especially, the Chilam Balam of Tizimin; Edmonson 1982:35–36, 101) as well as contemporary Tzotzil creation narratives (Gossen 1993:420). The action of sweeping within a domestic compound among contemporary Mesoamerican women serves to define the limits of the most highly maintained and culturally ordered domestic space (Killion 1990:204; Figure 4.1). Outside of the swept zone, garbage is allowed to accumulate and, often, garden spaces – crosscut by pathways – delineate the edge of broom-swept space. Indeed, the limits of the swept zone define a sphere of action that is created by female-gendered labor. Given the absence to date of archaeologically preserved sweeping implements (i.e., brooms), evidence of this gendered action in the past will be found not in the tools of the activity but rather in the fine details of the debris patterns created by sweeping, that is, by mapping the limits of the material that was swept away. As Killion (1990:Figure 8) has shown, piles of debris small enough to be propelled by a broom combined with tossed material accumulate at the limits of a swept area. Swept debris often exhibits edge rounding caused by the rolling and saltating motion to which swept objects are subjected. If the swept surface was a prepared floor – such as packed marl or plaster, which is and commonly was used to pave dwelling floors in the lowlands – then the limits of maintained space will contain small, rounded particles of flooring material. Such deposits are recognizable within extramural excavation units and often occur around the perimeter of a basal or building platform. At K'axob, swept debris is a common constituent of deposits located on the perimeter of floors. Small rounded pieces of white marl contrast sharply with the dark soil matrix in which they occur (Figure 4.2). Such deposits are not glamorous, but they are more than likely to be the material residue of female-gendered labor undertaken to maintain order and cleanliness in and around the dwelling. With closer attention to the micromorphology of deposits (Goldberg and MacPhail 2006), this realm of gendered labor can be documented.

Daily Offerings by the Three-Stone Hearth

As Burkhart (1997:38–40) indicates, Mexica women made offerings to deities and ancestors on a daily basis, and "the fire god was the focus of many domestic rites" (1997:40). Offerings of food and drink might take place at the three-stone hearth or at the household shrine. Likewise, Hanks (1990:112) considers the gendered labor of females to include the maintenance of fresh flowers and candles at the family shrine and tending the domestic cooking fire (which he describes as a "smoky, onerous job"). The domestic locales at which women conducted ritual practice tend to be found near the cooking

FIGURE 4.2 South Wall of Operation 11, K'axob, Belize, showing two packed marl/plaster floors that terminate in the center of the unit and are continued with a deposit of white flecks and small circular nodules that are the remains of swept debris (photo courtesy of K'axob Archaeological Project).

fire and before the family altar. As mentioned in Chapter 3, little effort has been expended in fine-grained site structural studies that might indicate patterning in the location of intraresidential shrines. There seems to be a tacit assumption that if a small structure – generally but not always found on the eastern side of the residential complex as per Becker (1971) – is not present, then the household had no shrine. But Becker noted that this plaza plan dubbed "PP2" at Tikal occurred only in elite residential groups and generally contained a distinctive mortuary assemblage, primarily of adult males (1971:178–179). During Epi-Colonial times, such expansive, wealthy residential compounds became few and far between, and altars often were placed within the primary dwelling. Ethnographers who worked in traditional Maya communities often stated that nearly every Maya house had a shrine, and some indicate that shrines were the first feature to be constructed in a house (Earle 1986:165). Unless we attribute this pattern to a sudden religious fervor induced by Spanish Catholicism, we must admit that a very large number of domestic shrines – key locations for female ritual performance – have gone undetected in commoner residences because they likely were built within the dwelling and not as stand-alone structures (but see contributions in Gonlin and Lohse 2007 and Plunket 2002 for studies of commoner ritual). The pattern of subfloor burials – particularly during the Classic period – may be signaling the presence and location of intradwelling shrines. Generally built of perishable materials, shrines are not likely to leave a signature that can be detected with the blunt edge of a shovel, the preferred tool of excavation in the Maya lowlands. Furthermore, there is likely to be regionally specific patterning in the placement of shrines within a dwelling that may or may not coincide with a particular suite of artifacts. Whether paved or packed earth, the floor under and around a shrine should bear a distinctive signature contrastive to high traffic areas; that is, it might be rich in ash, copal resin, or the macrobotanical remains of pine (shrine accoutrements noted especially by McBryde 1971:47). It is a special use area and, as such, should display a highly stylized and redundant material pattern.

The other site of female ritual practice, the hearth or kitchen (*k'oób'en* in Yucatec Mayan), "is a fundamentally female space, the place of fire, water storage, and food preparation and consumption" (Hanks 1990:329; Figure 4.3). Many activities co-occur around a hearth, which can be enclosed within a stand-alone kitchen structure or integrated within sleeping/visiting/storage quarters. In the lowlands of today and sometimes detected archaeologically, the kitchen often is located in a separate structure that is adjacent to a larger and more substantial dwelling where sleeping, formal visits, and storage take place. Both Burkhart (1997:29) and Hanks (1990:329–330) note the importance of the three-stone hearth as the quintessential cooking feature. Taube (1998:432), Reents-Budet (1998:78–81), and Freidel et al. (1993:65–67) have waxed eloquent on the cosmological significance of this metaphor of creation that pervades royal Maya iconography and texts. Ironically, only a limited number of ancient Maya kitchens with three-stone hearths have been excavated. Important examples include Proskouriakoff and Temple (1955) who report on the discovery of a Late Postclassic three-stone hearth in Structure R–86a at Mayapan and Fauvet-Berthelot (1986:195–197) who notes the presence of three types of fire features at the Late Postclassic

FIGURE 4.3 The kitchen (*k'oób'en*) in 1986 of Doña Eulalia Uc, whose husband Don Miguel was the INAH site guardian of Sayil, Yucatán (photo by author).

Highland sites of Mixco Viejo, Cauinal, El Talpetate, and Pueblo Viejo-Chichaj: a triangular hearth lined with three to seven stones, a U-shaped slab hearth, and a clay-lined hearth. As S. Coe (1994:166–167) suggests, a variety of pyro-features likely were employed for cooking, roasting, and steaming foods. Ball and Taschek (2007) propose that a portable, earthenware tripodal brazier be added to the suite of pre-Hispanic cooking facilities. Among the mid-twentieth-century Lacandon (Baer and Merrifield 1971:143–144), the three-stone hearth was employed only for *tortilla* roasting (using a griddle or *comal*) and the pot-based cooking of *masa* for *tortillas.* A separate "gruel hearth" – in which the pot was placed directly over a fire – was used for the preparation of liquid meals. If the three-stone hearth is thought of as the "tortilla hearth," then its presence likely increased through time as processed and roasted maize cuisine took on a larger role within Maya society. Interestingly, three-stone hearths or a symbolic reference to this archetypal feature have been found in ritual contexts from the Terminal Classic as far back as the Late Preclassic period. For instance, within the cave of Actun Chanona in the upper Sibun Valley, three-stone hearth arrangements dating to the Late-Terminal Classic period occur in three distinct locations

FIGURE 4.4 Symbolic three-stone hearth in the cave of Actun Chanona, upper Sibun Valley (photo courtesy of Xibun Archaeological Project).

(Peterson 2006; Figure 4.4). Despite their low visibility archaeologically, the mythical significance of three stones as a metaphor of creation and centering was present by the Late Preclassic period. Two published examples include (1) three unshaped stones found at the base of a lip-to-lip cache created during the ritual burial of Str. E-VII-sub at Uaxactun (Ricketson and Ricketson 1937:72–73; Taube 1998:441) and (2) another cache of three unshaped stones placed within a lip-to-lip cache during the dedication of a residential plaza space at K'axob (Harrison-Buck 2004:79). In the absence of a three-stone kitchen hearth, the best indicators of a female-gendered space, a *k'oób'en* in Yucatec Mayan or *c'oben* in Lacandon Mayan, remain an ashy floor, a distinct suite of chemical characteristics (see Manzanilla and Barba 1990:46), and artifacts of food preparation.

Sharpening the *Metate* and Making *Masa*

The female work of food preparation generally took place in the *k'oób'en* near the cooking fire and the grinding stone. We have already noted that three-stone hearths have not been commonly reported in pre-sixteenth-century lowland Maya residential contexts. In contrast, grinding stones or *metates*, while not overly abundant, are present throughout the sequence, although variable in frequency. In the Maya lowlands, the so-called turtleback *metate* was commonly used throughout the Classic period but was largely replaced by a three-legged *metate*, beginning in the Terminal Classic period. In the Nahua-speaking village of Amatlán, Sandstrom (1991:200) notes that each household buys a *mano* and *metate* with the expectation that they will "last a lifetime." The Yucatec Mayan landowner of K'axob, Concepción Campos, inherited three sets of grinding equipment (*manos* and *metates*) from his mother who had inherited them from her mother who had transported them from Yucatán to Belize (then British Honduras) when her family emigrated (Figure 4.5). This example indicates that grinding tools can be inherited and in use for more than one generation (which would depress their frequency in archaeological deposits). The three-generational duration of the Campos-family grinding tools, however, may be unusually long and due to the fact that Concepción Campos and his wife Elma do not use the tools but rather curate them as family heirlooms. In fact, Mr. Campos is quick to say that the only reason that he, rather than his sisters, has possession of the *metates* is because they showed no interest in inheriting the "old things." The fact that there are three *metates* suggests some functional specificity in the use of the grinding surfaces – an observation also made by McBryde (1971:47) when describing the daily work regime of Mayan women in southwestern Guatemala. A Late Classic burned and rapidly abandoned elite structure at the site of Aguateca (Str. M8–10) contained a total of 3 limestone *metates*, 3 igneous/sandstone *metates*, and 15 *manos* (Inomata and Stiver 1998:Figure 7).

FIGURE 4.5 *Metates* and *manos* inherited by Concepción Campos from his maternal grandmother (photo by author).

Given the potentially long use-life of *manos* and *metates*, a better indicator of grinding activity may be found in *metate*-pecking or sharpening stones. Often conflated with flint-knapping hammerstones (cf. Inomata and Stiver 1998:Table 1; Sweely 1999:161), *metate*-pecking stones generally are spherical and bear signs of battering over a large area (Figure 4.6). Hammerstones, on the other hand, tend to display percussion marks that are restricted to a rounded projection of the stone, since controlling the exact placement of the blow is critical for flaking a tool. When not in use, *metate*-pecking stones are cached in nearby spaces, such as the wattle weave of a kitchen partition or

FIGURE 4.6 Recycled bifacial tool with a pattern of spherical battering likely caused by sharpening *manos* and *metates*, from a Terminal Preclassic deposit at K'axob (photo courtesy of K'axob Archaeological Project).

between the stones of a masonry wall. When conducting ethnoarchaeological research during the 1980s among Tarahumara people in the Sierra Madre of Chihuahua, México, Robert Hard found that pecking stones used for sharpening *metates* were cached in the stacked-stone windbreaks built inside of winter-season rockshelters (R. Hard, personal communication 2005).

Metate-pecking stones are used daily by females so the stone quickly acquires evidence of use, generally in the form of a spherical battering or percussion pattern. Duncan Earle (1986:160) notes the constancy of women's daily work effort and McBryde (1971:47) observed that "[m]uch of a woman's day is spent grinding softened corn, coffee, cacao, and other things on it [*metate*]." The ever-present *rat-tat-tat* of *metate* sharpening muted by the early morning fog is reported by ethnographers and travelers alike who spent time in highland Maya villages before table-mounted hand grinders were widely available and affordable.

Archaeologists – taking their cue from Brumfiel's (1991) Basin of México study – might wonder just how much time ancient Maya women spent on the *metate* in the more distant past. The *comal* – a roasting slab used to toast tortillas – is absent from Preclassic deposits and not common through the Classic period. Was the preparation of *masa* – a moist corn flour necessary for forming tortillas and tamales (*wah*) – common during Classic times or only undertaken for special festive and offertory occasions? Taube (1989) has directed our attention to tamale or *wah* imagery found in palace scenes on Classic-period polychrome vessels that generally depict offerings to a royal person or a deity. Likewise, in the Postclassic Codex Madrid, there are many examples of *wah* offerings to the gods on the event of a calendrical ritual (e.g., Vail 2002:Almanac 103b–106b, Frame 6). On the other hand, corn-based gruels and stews can be prepared by softening dry maize kernels and do not require the laborious work of grinding. Given the ubiquity of large cooking pots in the lowland Maya region – particularly during the Late-Terminal Classic period when the size of cooking pots could reach 42 centimeters in height and 45 centimeters in girth (Figure 4.7) – it does seem that daily fare was more commonly liquid based. At K'axob where there is a nearly continuous sequence of occupation from Middle Preclassic through Terminal Classic times, the frequency of *metates* does increase through time (Ebersole 2001) in direct proportion to the size of cooking pots as though all aspects of maize processing (softening and cooking the kernels as well as grinding them) intensified through time. From other sites, there are osteological data that support the notion of increased maize processing and consumption during the Late-Terminal Classic period. A skeletal sample of 40 individuals from the site of Kichpanha revealed that the incidence of dental caries doubled and the severity of calculus increased between the Protoclassic and the Late Classic periods (Magennis 1999:141, 145). Magennis (1999:145) interprets this trend as indicative of a change in maize processing, possibly involving phytate removal. In short, there appears to have been changes through time in the amount of female-gendered labor involved in food preparation and that change was in the direction of an increased workload (see discussion in Isaac 1986:15–17). Additionally, the presence of *wah* imagery in Classic-period royal iconography hints that females were preparing tamales for more than just the occasional festive event but also as offerings to gods and ancestors. By the Late Classic period, labor-intensive tamale production likely also was a tribute obligation, the frequency and severity of which we can only approximate as will be discussed in Chapters 6 and 9.

FIGURE 4.7 Large, Late-Terminal Classic cooking pot found in an offertory context in a cave in the Sibun-Manatee karst. The vessel was inverted with a large kill-hole in the base of the jar. An inverted ring-based bowl was placed over the kill-hole (photo courtesy of Xibun Archaeological Research Project).

Making Cloth

The fourth cosmologically significant type of work for Mexica women was that of spinning thread and weaving cloth (Burkhart 1997:45–52). Likewise, in the Yucatec Maya region, imagery in the Codex Madrid indicates that such domestic activities typically were female-gendered (Vail and Stone 2002); the older goddess, Chak Chel, is commonly shown spinning or weaving (i.e., folios 102c, 102d). Several sources suggest that competency in weaving was an important learned skill not taken lightly. In Zinacantan, Vogt (1976:152) and Bricker (1973: 19–20) discuss the ritual humiliation and ribald joking to which incompetent spinners and weavers are subjected on Christmas Day. Burkhart (1997:51) suggests that a poor weaver who produces a "lumpy, lopsided weaving just may indicate a flaw in the cosmic fabric." Ethnographically and ethnohistorically, high expectations for female weaving prowess can be attributed to the fact that weaving was critical not only to clothe ones family but also to meet tribute payments and, in the case of many contemporary Maya women, to produce for a cash market. The political significance of cloth and the female-gendered labor that generally produced it has been discussed by many, but particularly by Weiner (1992) in reference to Oceania, by Silverblatt (1987) for the Andes, and by Little (2008) for highland Guatemala. Within Mesoamerica, the Colonial-period Spanish empire as well as the Postclassic Mexica empire are known to have made significant demands on female labor to produce surplus cloth for a tribute economy. The conspicuous display of large cotton *mantas* in Late Classic Maya royal iconography – in the Bonampak murals, for instance – insinuates that such tribute mechanisms – while operating at a smaller scale – were also present in the Maya region (Houston et al. 2006; Miller and Martin 2004). In Chapter 9, we return to this topic in detail.

For females, age, status, and placement in time appear to have played a large role in determining how much time was spent spinning a whorl or tied to a backstrap loom. Burkhart (1997:45) notes that the Codex Mendoza depicts girls of three to four years learning to spin and using a whorl with proficiency by five years of age. Prepubescent females (younger than 14 years) are not shown tied to a backstrap loom, which seems to have been a rite of passage, a signal that a female was of age to be married. Likewise, it is mature women who are shown weaving on the backstrap loom in Sahagún (1950–1982, Book 10:Figure 21). Burkhart (1997:48), following Sullivan (1982:14), notes that the act of weaving was perceived as carrying significant sexual innuendo (opening and closing of "the shed," thrusting of the shuttlecock, and so forth) and suggests that it may have been an activity considered more appropriate for a postpubescent female. Vail and Stone (2002:210) likewise note that there are two primary goddesses depicted in the Madrid Codex – a youthful Ixik Kab who is an earth and fertility goddess and the mature Chak Chel who is the patron of spinning and weaving, childbirthing, curing, and divining. The youthful goddess, they note, is seldom shown weaving (Vail and Stone 2002:219; see also McCafferty and McCafferty 1999:Figure 6.7 for an example of mature highland weavers). In fact, Vail and Stone (2002:204) propose that a "take-home" message of the Madrid Codex is that Maya women could be divided into two categories: "premenopausal women, whose sexuality was seen as a threat to men and in need of control, and grandmotherly figures associated with the security of the home." Presumably as a woman passed beyond her childbearing and childrearing years, more time could be spent pursuing the arts of weaving, divining, and assisting with childbirthing as Earle (1986:162) has documented among K'iche' women. The association of weaving tools and divining mirrors with the entombed mature female (in her sixties) who is thought to have founded the Copán dynasty (Bell 2002:97–99) suggests that the gender patterns found in the Postclassic Madrid Codex as well as ethnographically are relevant to understanding Classic Maya royal females.

Status seems also to have played a role in determining the amount of time women spent practicing the arts of spinning and weaving. Although ethnographically and ethnohistorically weaving is described as an important activity of women with no regard to status, an ever-increasing corpus of spinning and weaving tools found archaeologically indicates that elite and royal women left behind far more tools of textile production than did lower-status females (Chase et al. 2008; Halperin 2008, among others). Hendon (1997:44), for example demonstrated a positive relationship between household size/elaboration and the presence of textile production tools across three residential compounds at Copán. At Aguateca, a rapidly abandoned site, the presence and frequency of bone needles (n = 8) and spindle whorls (n = 13) within a single elite structure rivals the number of bone needles (n = 6) and spindle whorls (n = 5) found across several excavated earthen platforms at Barton Ramie (Inomata and Stiver 1998:Figure 6; Willey 1965:487, 500). For Barton Ramie, however, Willey (1965:402) does report the recovery of 42 drilled pottery disks that "presumably were used as spindle whorls," although they are larger than the formally shaped whorls (see Figure 4.8 for a comparable example from K'axob). Among the highland Mexica – where cotton

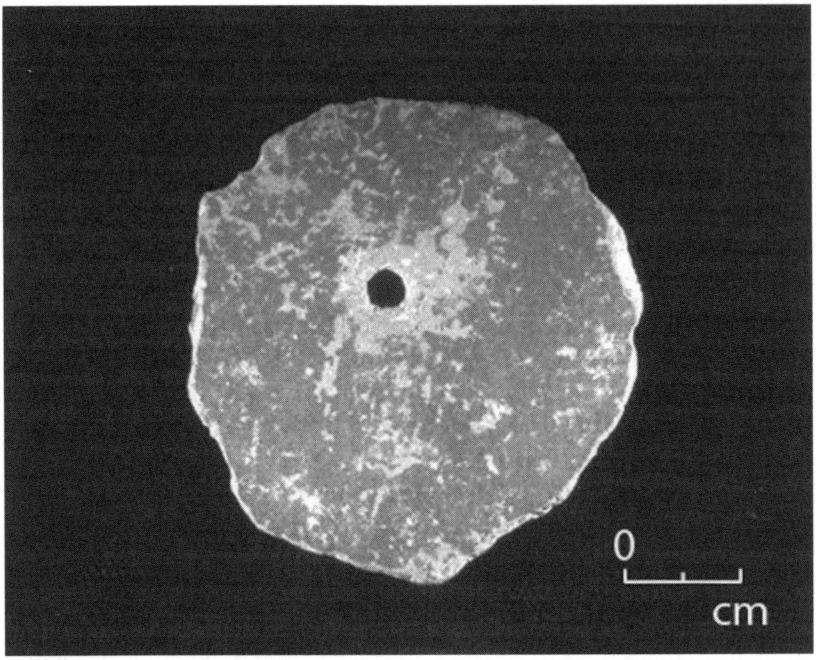

FIGURE 4.8 Circular pottery sherd with worn perforation, likely part of a spindle whorl used to spin a rough fiber such as maguey, from a Preclassic deposit at K'axob, Belize (photo courtesy of K'axob Archaeological Project).

had to be imported – Sahagún (1997:207–208) notes that commoner women spun maguey fibers to create clothing for their families; the spinning of cotton thread necessitated the use of delicate and radially symmetric whorls that were more likely to be part of a noblewomen's tool kit (see also Sullivan 1982:13). Both Parsons (1975) and Brumfiel (1991) provide archaeological corroboration for this statement, based on spot-find locations within the Basin of México, and it is likely that drilled pottery disks with an irregular circumference were used to spin maguey, much as Beaudy-Corbett and McCafferty (2002:60) have suggested for similar artifacts from Joya de Ceren. Parenthetically, Chase et al. (2008:128) have found evidence that circular drilled sherds also were used for backing mosaic earflares, which shows that pottery sherds could be recycled for multiple purposes.

Royal iconography showing elaborate *huipiles* worn by females – most famously those of Lady Xook of Yaxchilán – vividly indicates that the arts of weaving, embroidering, and brocading were fine-tuned among the upper segment of society. Dredging operations at the Sacred Cenote of Sacrifice yielded fragments of intricately brocaded cloth that are seldom preserved in surface sites (Coggins and Shane 1984:143; García L. 1981). The art of brocading, in particular, was practiced under the tutelage of a named goddess – Xochiquetzal among the Mexica and Ix Chebel Yax among the Postclassic Yucatec Maya – and likely was practiced more intensively and possibly exclusively in the homes of wealthy women who could secure the large blocks of time (during daylight hours) needed to adorn cotton cloth with the complex designs depicted in royal iconography. Hendon (1997:39) labels deer bone awls as "brocade picks" and finds that they are far more common in the large residential compound (9N–8) than in the smaller compounds at Copán. In the *Popol Vuh*, the art of adorning cloth is equated with that of adorning daily speech for public oration (Tate 1999:89; Tedlock 1985:72). Quite possibly, a commoner female spent the bulk of her time sweeping, preparing food, and assisting seasonally with agricultural tasks. Whatever time remained was used for spinning thread and weaving cloth possibly from maguey fibers. Royal and elite females, on the other hand, likely spent substantially less (if any) time on the mundane tasks of sweeping, processing/cooking food, and agricultural work, which would have yielded large blocks of time for spinning, weaving, and brocading. Mexica noblewomen, apparently, were exhorted to excel at weaving lest they be reduced to selling rock salt door-to-door (Sahagún 1950–1982:Book 6:96; Sullivan 1982:13–14).

Separate activity spheres for men and women have been noted by several Maya ethnographers: Earle (1986:158–160) for K'iche', Vogt (1976:58–59) for Tzotzil, Hanks for contemporary Yucatec (1990:111–112), and Landa for early Colonial-period Yucatec (Tozzer 1941:91). Likely, this pattern has earlier precedent. Although Hendon (1997:44) found scant spatial separation between male- and female-gendered artifacts in her sample of household artifacts from Copán, a distributional map of the spot-find locations of textile production tools at Aguateca Str. M8–10 shows little overlap between textile and scribal tools (shell ink pots, mortars, and pestles for pigment preparation), the latter considered generally but not exclusively to have been a male-gendered activity (Inomata and Stiver 1990:Figure 6).

Beaudry-Corbett and McCafferty (2002) have broadened the discussion of cloth making by considering the differences in tools and spatial requirements of making thread from a number of materials including maguey, feathers, hair, and cotton. At the southeastern Maya site of Joya de Ceren, maguey, cotton, and possibly feathers were spun but the spinning and weaving equipment for each material is differentially clustered. That is, textile production appears to have been somewhat specialized with some houses containing a sizable number of tools and others very few or different types of textile tools (Beaudry-Corbett and McCafferty (2002:Table 4.3). As Ceren is another rapidly abandoned site – although a village rather than a seat of political power as was Aguateca – the spatial signature of work activities is unusually crisp and allows us to glimpse the variable production practices among householders.

The spinning of feathers into an extremely fine thread is known from Contact-period sources such as Sahagún (1950–1982:Book 8:49, 1997:208). McCafferty and McCafferty (2000:47) suggest that certain small spindle whorls ("Type D" described as cupcake-shaped in cross section and often decorated with an avian motif) may be identified as whorls for spinning feathers. The distribution of these whorls in the Maya region is particularly intriguing as they occur at Terminal and Postclassic sites, many of which are thought to have participated in the so-called Cult of Quetzalcoatl, the feathered serpent (Ringle et al. 1998). For instance, Type D whorls are common at Cholula (McCafferty and McCafferty 2000:Table 6) and Chichén Itzá (Bolles 1977:239) and are also known from Dzibilchaltun (Taschek 1994:215–216, Figure 57) and Mayapan (Pollock et al. 1962:400, Figure 50). Significantly, a similar whorl with an avian motif has been recovered from a Terminal Classic deposit at the Hershey site in the Sibun Valley – a locale that witnessed probable contact with Chichén Itzá during the Terminal Classic period (Figure 4.9). A fabric woven of feather thread likely was used in special ritual costuming – possibly as part of a deity impersonation of the feathered serpent. Although the Terminal Classic period has been described as a time of lawless traders and raiders during which the status of women diminished (Joyce 2000a:109–115), the avian whorls suggest that female-gendered labor – possibly of feather-thread spinning – was integral to the success and expansion of

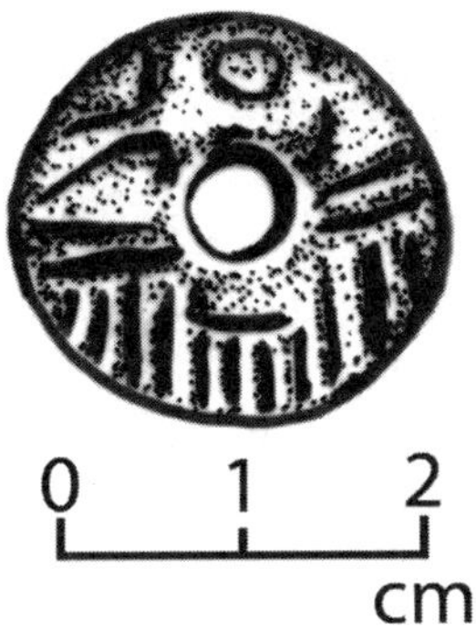

FIGURE 4.9 Terminal Classic spindle whorl with avian motif possibly used to spin bird feathers into thread, from the Hershey site in the Sibun Valley of Belize (drawing by Eleanor Harrison-Buck, courtesy of Xibun Archaeological Research Project).

Quetzalcoatl-related trading and ritual practices that swept across Mesoamerica around 800 C.E.

The avian whorls show how artifacts from female labor can track larger transformations within society and how female activities – while steady and repetitive on a diurnal basis – changed significantly over the *longue durée*. For instance, Preclassic lowland Maya sites, as a whole, tend to contain little in the way of formal spindle whorls (a pattern also noted for Formative and Classic-period Cholula; McCafferty and McCafferty 2000:42). Reporting on three limestone spindle whorls from a Terminal Late Preclassic burial of undetermined sex at Cahal Pech, Awe (1992:298–299) stated that the whorls represented the earliest known examples of stone whorls. If formally shaped whorls are indicative of cotton textile production, then their paucity during Preclassic times begs the question as to what Maya people were wearing. Recycled pottery sherds shaped into a circular form and centrally drilled are known from Preclassic contexts at Seibal, Cuello, and K'axob (Willey 1978:43; Hammond 1991a:176; Bartlett 2004c:271–272, respectively) and could have been used to spin maguey fiber. Preclassic people probably also wore bark cloth much as Tozzer (1907:29, Plate V, Figure 1) describes for the *fin de siècle* Lacandon Maya living in remote regions who made their garments from maguey fiber or from "the bark of a tree." Throughout Polynesia, bark cloth – called *tapa* or

FIGURE 4.10 Bark beater used to process bark into cloth/paper during the Middle Preclassic period at K'axob (photo by Michael Hamilton, courtesy of the K'axob Archaeological Project).

kapa cloth – was worn extensively and produced using a deeply striated paddle that is identical to the tool used in Mesoamerica (Figure 4.10). Archaeological support for Preclassic bark cloth comes from the presence of bark beaters in Middle Preclassic deposits at Seibal, K'axob, and Cuello (Willey 1978:80; McAnany and Ebersole 2004:318–319; Hammond 1991a:189–190, respectively). Clearly, bark-cloth technology existed in the earliest Maya villages on record. Although the paper cloth could have been used primarily for ritual purposes – as may have been the case during the Classic period – it also could have clothed the bodies of women, men, and children. The scant clothing worn by corn maidens in the Preclassic murals of San Bartolo (Saturno et al. 2005) lacks any quality of drapery, and the patterns on their skirts appear to have been stamped or painted rather than brocaded. The mural figures could well be wearing paper clothing. In traditional accounts of Mesoamerican paper production, making bark cloth or bark paper is described as female-gendered labor although men may collect the bark (Sandstrom and Sandstrom 1986:28–30; Lenz 1961:83).

On the other end of the temporal spectrum, Postclassic Maya sites tend to yield a preponderance of cotton spindle whorls – particularly from smaller settlements. At the Postclassic island community of Laguna de On (less than 500 meters in diameter), Marilyn Masson (2000:Table 5.21) recovered 34 spindle whorls, and Phillips (1979:64) reports that 61 spindle whorls were retrieved from excavations into Postclassic deposits on Cozumel Island. According to Masson and colleagues (2006; see also Masson and Peraza Lope forthcoming), the pattern of plenty is reversed at the Postclassic Maya capital of Mayapan where early excavations by the Carnegie Institution followed by more recent INAH excavations have yielded less than a dozen spindle whorls in total. Politically and economically, this paucity of thread production tools at the center of the Mayapan state suggests that cotton thread was an imported item – acquired either through trade or more likely tribute obligations. The upsurge in whorl frequency at Postclassic satellite settlements must have radically changed female labor and tilted daily practice toward increased spinning and weaving. This change could indicate the "democratization" of cotton apparel and a depression of maguey fiber clothing in the Maya lowlands (drilled sherd disks are not present at Laguna de On). Another major factor contributing to this pattern could have been the fact that tribute demands were stretched across a population depressed in size from Classic-period levels and, consequently, may have weighed heavier on each household. Masson (2000:165) indicates that cloth was exacted in tribute throughout the province of Chetumal, the political jurisdiction in which Laguna de On was located.

Far from an entity that was static through time and across space, the household itself exhibited considerable dynamism through time. Labor undertaken by the "heart of the house" changed significantly from Preclassic through Postclassic periods. As will be discussed in further detail in Chapter 6, status and wealth also greatly affected daily practice and the extent to which a female might be engaged in weaving fine cotton cloth or adorning cloth by brocading. Finally, age also had an effect on the activities that a female might undertake within the house, with certain activities, such as weaving, considered to be more suitable for a mature woman rather than an adolescent. One of the most ubiquitous classes of archaeological data collected from dwellings consists of pottery sherds. Given the emerging body of evidence that points to pottery production as a specialized craft of artisans, the topic of gendered pottery production and exchange is examined in Chapter 7 along with other artisanal crafts such as mat weaving.

INTO THE REALM OF PAK'ALBIL CHE'

As one moved away from the house into the realm of the orchard – *pak'albil che'* in Yucatec Mayan – and field (*kol*), one enters a "world of trails" as Sandstrom (1991:151) characterizes the village of Amatlán. Small paths (*yam b'eh* in Yucatec; Hanks 1990:311) emanating from house compounds are the central nervous system through which information, goods, and people travel continually throughout daylight hours. Sandstrom (1991:106) notes that trail networks emanating from the village of Amatlán encompass a 40-kilometer radius of named landmarks outside of the community. Although men, women, and children used the trail systems, the farther one traveled from the heart of a community, the stronger the tendency for the spaces along the trails to be perceived as the domain of male-gendered tasks associated with food production and resource procurement (Earle 1986; Hanks 1990:306–307; Wisdom 1940:44, 188). As Ashmore (2002:241) notes: "women and men may contribute to the others' activities in daily practice, they nonetheless hold distinctive ideal roles ... each as designated creators, of cloth and of cornfields." Males and cornfields do represent an iconic linkage, but, in reality, it is often the hunting and fishing that takes place on the way to or returning from the maize field that occupies a good part of the daily practice of males while away from home. Among the Nahua corn farmers of Amatlán, men teach their sons to fish before they train them in farming practices (Sandstrom 1991:128). Among the Lacandon, when a boy reaches the age of puberty, the event is celebrated ritually by offering a set of bow and arrows (rather than farming tools) to the gods. Tozzer (1907:169) translates the chant that accompanies this ritual as follows: "I am about to redden his set of bow and arrows, oh father. See his set of bow and arrows my son, oh father. When he is grown, he will make offerings to you. When he is grown, he will give you an offering of a fillet, oh father."

In effect, the culturally constituted space of the dwelling is complemented by extramural spaces that also are part of a crafted landscape: near-residential gardens, orchards, and fields – all connected via trail systems. With no shortage of land, expansive dendritic networks can develop in which fields and orchards that are several kilometers distant might be the site of predominantly male-gendered labor. As several archaeologists have noted, it is highly unlikely that such an expansive situation existed during the Late Preclassic and Classic periods when high population levels would have limited access to distant fields and promoted more intensive and continual use of near-residential fields and orchards (Johnston 2003; Killion 1990:210; McAnany 1995:78–79). We are only now beginning to grapple with the impact of this type of compression on gendered labor and tenurial arrangements among land holders (see Pyburn 1998 for a discussion of variation in the latter). If more of the work of farming – seeding, weeding, hoeing, and harvesting – took place close to the residence, then some of the ethnographically known proscriptions regarding women and corn fields may have been relaxed or nonexistent, particularly during periods of peak labor needs. Robin (2002) has suggested such a scenario for the Late Classic site of Chan No'ohol where hill-slope terraces, presumably intensively farmed, are located near residences.

Orchards represent a kind of socially ordered space that temporally is quite distinct from seasonally cultivated fields. Nations and Nigh (1980) documented an expansive kind of arboriculture among the Lacandon Maya – a type of silviculture, really – but it is likely that ancient Maya farmers were more spatially constrained in terms of orchard plantings. Unlike fields that are harvested and then must be replanted in order to bear another season of fruit, orchard species continue to produce fruit year after year, often beyond the life span of an individual. The period over which a fruit-bearing tree is harvested, moreover, is protracted in comparison with fields that normally have a narrow time window during which they must be reaped. Bert Faux, who managed the cacao grove surrounding the Sibun Valley site called Hershey (formerly owned by Hershey Foods, Inc.) explained that cacao trees bear fruit six to eight months of the year and can be harvested continually by a small labor force throughout this period. The measured pace at which fruit trees can be harvested may be one reason why Yucatec Maya women participate in the harvesting of fruit trees even though their "participation in other phases [of agriculture] is nearly nil" (Hanks 1990:111). Orchards frequently are located near the *solar* or houselot, which also facilitates female participation. The antiquity of near-residential orchards is suggested by the casts of fruit trees found in proximity to houses at Cerén (Lentz 1999:14). Lentz (1999:12) notes that fiber-producing perennial plants such as cotton and agave also were cultivated in the maintained space adjacent to the excavated dwellings of Cerén, which admits the possibility of some measure of female tending. Females also are variously associated with apiaries and the harvesting of honey. In Colonial Yucatec wills, Espejo-Ponce and Restall (1997:247) found that beehives generally were bequeathed to wives and daughters.

The qualities of durational reproduction and annual regeneration inherent in tree species – plus the permanence of their biomass – make fruit-bearing trees more like houses than fields. The permanence and presence of orchard species was deployed during Classic times as a metaphor of dynastic descent and continuity. The sarcophagus of K'inich Janaab' Pakal I provides the most vivid example of a "royal orchard" (see McAnany 1995:74–78; Schele and Miller 1986:284–285). In reference to Colonial-period Yucatán, Farriss (1984:469, 180) notes that the possession of an orchard constituted a statement of wealth and power and that elites "owned" (rather than having usufruct rights to) land with *cenotes* and *aguada,* which were of great value for fruit trees in the relatively dry climate of northern Yucatán. Given the quasi-permanence of orchards, it is difficult to imagine how an orchard could exist on communal-use land since, like a house structure, fruit trees – once planted – become part of socially constituted space for decades to come. De facto, orchards privatize land in the hands of the families who planted them. The social tension that can result from such privatization is clearly indicated in the Toledo district of Belize where contemporary Q'eqchi' and Mopan farmers sought to expand cacao production by establishing orchards on communal-use land (Wilk 1991:120). As more acreage was placed in orchards – which could be inherited or sold – some farmers began to resist this trend toward privatization as it engendered greater economic inequalities (Wilk 1991:120–121; Steinberg 2002:63).

Today as in the past, it appears that orchards signal wealth and access to resources that have been taken out of the communal pool. As a special kind of food production, orchards may have been under the tutelage of a deity. Martin (2006) notes that folio 15 of the Dresden Codex shows gods who are sprouting cacao pods and may be patrons of auspicious and inauspicious days for planting fruit trees.

MAIZE AND ITS DEITY

When a deity that is represented in the iconography of Maya polychrome pottery, royal sculpture, or codices can be identified with an activity such as brocading or planting fruit trees, it is likely that the activity or the fruits of that activity have undergone some measure of elite appropriation. Consider the fact that there is no recognized Maya deity of salt production despite the fact that an increasing number of specialized salt production sites have been identified in the Maya lowlands. We can presume that elites had an appetite for salt, but neither the method of its manufacture (evaporation or cooking) nor its essential quality as a residue apparently were conducive to the performance or portrayal of timeless dynastic power. In the Postclassic central Mexican highlands, the goddess of salt, Huixtocihuatl, is also the goddess of excrement and the shameless (Sullivan 1982:23) – hardly material for a royal charter.

In contrast, Classic and Postclassic representations of the maize deity (called Hun Nal during Classic times; Taube 1993:52) as well as royal persons dressed as the maize deity are relatively ubiquitous. Both young and paternal, the maize deity is the father of the hero twins (known as Hunahpu and Xbalanque in the Colonial epic, the *Popol Vuh*) but he is also shown as a young male in which guise he is thought to be analogous to an unripened ear of maize. His head is long and thin like an ear of maize and he sports an isolated lock of hair on top of his head that Taube (1985:172–173) calls a "tonsure" and likens to the silks of a corncob. The young maize deity wears the oft-discussed beaded loincloth onto which tubular jade beads were stitched to form diamond patterns. In both young and older representations, he is metaphorically decapitated (i.e., harvested), but after a period (of being stored as seed corn), he regenerates anew. This heroic saga resonates with royal identity, which leads Taube (1985:181) to suggest that "the tonsured young lord [maize deity] was considered as the founding mythical ancestor of the Maya elite. The *Popol Vuh* states that mankind originated from maize, a material personified as the Classic tonsured young lord." It comes as no surprise, therefore, that Chan-Bahlum, inheritor of the kingdom of B'aakal (commonly known as Palenque) is shown on the Tablet of the Foliated Cross as the personification of sprouting maize "as he stands upon corn growing out of a cleft Cauac head" and wears the garb of the maize god (Taube 1985:174).

Certainly, elites could not claim exclusive rights to the maize deity as maize was widely grown and consumed and the *Popol Vuh* does not state that only elites were made from maize, but there clearly is a royal riff that underscores the maize deity (see Chapter 6 for discussion of parallels between the embodiment of the maize god and of royalty). The iconicity of the maize deity – in both his youthful and mature guises – is matched by the cultural significance of the maize field. Echoing the words of Bourdieu (1977:89) in reference to the iconic nature of the house, Hanks (1990:313) indicates that among traditional Yucatec Maya, the *soólar* ("houselot") and maize field "stand alongside body space and deitic space as centrally important 'root' constructions. In their internal structure, temporality (development and duration), and symbolic significance, these places embody elementary principles, processes, and experiences." Even though the maize field lacks the permanence of the house or the orchard, it figures importantly in the spatial perception of a household because it "lies in an intermediate position between fully social and fully natural space" (Hanks 1990:307). As discussed by Vogt (1976:55–56), field rituals among Tzotzil farmers – designed to propitiate the earth and rain deities and thus ensure the success of a soon-to-be-planted crop – reinforce the social frame that has been imposed upon the forest by virtue of cutting and burning "wild" vegetation. A ritual circuit delineates the four constructed corners of the field and marks the center. Through male-gendered labor, a quadrilateral space is created from a natural form. As discussed in Chapter 3, such social practices can be perceived as offensive to deities at the same time that they are essential to human prosperity. Thus, Maya farmers counteract the imposition of socially constructed space with the observance of ritual practices that hopefully propitiated powerful, supernatural forces.

Returning to the issue of gendered labor, it is extremely difficult to know how much time, if any, females spent in the fields working with men in the deeper recesses of Maya history. Images of women and men working side by side in the rice paddies of Southeast Asia provide a model of mixed-gender work regimes in the context of intensive peasant agriculture, but this image may not be relevant to the Maya past. During the Colonial period, Espejo-Ponce and Restall (1997:248) report that tools such as machetes and hoes generally were legally bequeathed to sons, and Earle (1986:160) states emphatically that K'iché women never plant maize. Significantly, the Preclassic murals of San Bartolo depict females with offerings of processed maize – tamales – rather than raw kernels of maize and, by doing so, lend credence to the notion that gendered labor practices enjoy a deep antiquity in the Maya past.

VALUE TRANSFORMATION THROUGH HOUSEHOLDING

Many have stressed the importance of the household as a unit of production. Halperin (1994:143–145) traces the centrality of the household economy back to Karl Polanyi's concept of "householding," a form of economic integration equal in importance to reciprocity, redistribution, and market exchange. When householding coexists with more centralized forms of state finance, it also provides a theater of operations for resistance to the centralization of wealth. Notions of value – while somewhat slippery conceptually – provide an entry into the larger space–time frame in which householders, as constituents of a community, existed. For Munn (1986:273), the creation of value is essential to the viability of a community and its ability to act "as an agent of its own self-production" (see Touraine 1977:4). Among Gawan Islanders of Melanesia, the social practices of feasting, shell working, and trading serve to effect value transformations. Munn (1986:267) notes that value can be positively transformed and thus promote fame, wealth, and well-being, or negatively transformed and thus demote the above due to inefficacy or allegations of witchcraft that can bring about illness, death, and misfortune. The Kula exchange cycle – made famous by the early ethnographic work of Malinowski (1961[1922]) – is modeled by Munn (1983, 1986) as a kind of "exchange drama" (Bailey 1998:1) that transcends time and space so as to bestow fame on those who excel at it.

The study of ancestral Maya householding can be broadened to a consideration of the creation of value through feasting, production, and exchange activities. As Munn (1986) has shown, artisan products are central to the creation of value and those who physically craft objects – as well as those who create auspicious trade relations – can gain considerable renown. Regardless of whether products are made for internal consumption, gifting, trade, or to meet political obligations, this type of activity – in addition to food production – effects value transformations that are central to the health, well-being, and prosperity of members of a household. In effect, value transformation is what members of a household do; it is what gives meaning to daily practice (see also Wilk and Netting 1984:6–9). Householders transform raw ingredients (earth, seeds, ripened maize, clay, cotton, maguey, tree bark, and so forth) into socially valued items that may be consumed or used within the household, given away, traded, or politically extracted. In this manner, value – as culturally specific wealth and prestige – is created, maintained, and manipulated rather than existing inherently in an artifact simply because it is made of exotic materials or required great effort to produce (Bailey 1998:2; Graham 2002).

Because value is socially constituted, Munn (1986) stresses the intersubjective nature of value transformation. For example, success in the kula ring is dependent on much more than the quality of craftsmanship exhibited in a pair of shell armbands. Timing, navigational abilities, and oratorical skills are equally important. These social factors may be inferred archaeologically but, of course, cannot be directly observed. Nevertheless, it is worthwhile to think about the household not only in terms of its material output but also in terms of its social, intersubjective relations. We return to the topic of artisanship – so central to notions of value – in Chapter 7. Now we turn to a consideration of value transformation through household and community feasts – activities that are highly dependent on gendered labor (see Dietler 2001:90–93; Dietler and Hayden 2001:10–11) and that absorb a significant amount of the productive capacities of households.

Commensal Politics of Household-based Feasting

Among traditional Nuyoo households of Oaxaca, Monaghan (1996:511) notes that 420 households collectively sponsor 82 major fiestas per year; about 83 percent of households sponsor a fiesta in any three-year period. These are impressive figures when one considers that the Nuyoo peasant households would not be considered wealthy by most standards, yet a surplus is generated in order to participate in feasting events that are perceived as fundamental to the identity and reproduction of participating households and the community at large. In other words, sponsoring a feast effects a positive value transformation, and female-gendered labor can be viewed as a "structural fulcrum" in this value transformation (Gero 1992:16). Writing about early Colonial Chiapas, Gosner (1997:223) characterizes the fiesta cycle of the Tzeltal as "the central metaphor of the Maya moral economy. They [fiestas] symbolically linked the private world of hearth and home to the public domain of kinship and community." Such feasts were prepared with female-gendered labor among Tzeltal and Ch'orti' peoples (Wisdom 1940:44) and most traditional Mesoamericans. When these practices came under siege – as happened during the economic depression and rapacious Colonial practices of the eighteenth century – the sense of household and community well-being was shattered, and a full-scale revolt against Colonial powers ensued. Recognizing the central role of the sponsorship of feasts among Mesoamerican farmers, Wolf (1966:7) coined the term "ceremonial fund" in reference to the bank of labor and goods accumulated in order to cover the expenses of feasting. Rappaport (1968:153–157), a pioneer on the subject of ritual feasting, noted long ago that the central purpose of raising pigs among the highland New Guinea Tsembaga was to accumulate sufficient numbers for the yearlong *kaiko* festival. He later characterized this practice as "a ritual mode of production" (Rappaport 1984:410; see also Spielmann 2002, 2008). Closer to home, Vogt (1976:28–29) and Cancian (1965), have drawn attention to the fact that such sponsorship has an economic leveling effect in that households that can afford to sponsor feasts are significantly impoverished by doing so. Feasts are ubiquitous, expensive, and instrumental to the continued health, well-being, and prosperity of households and communities and, more important, of the persons constituting these social units.

What specific and proximate reasons for feasting existed in the Maya region? Many feasts are linked with an agricultural calendar and mark the beginning or end of the growing season. They are part of a larger ritual to supplicate or thank earth and rain deities and ancestors for their munificence and, as such, are part of the ritual logic of "debt payment" that cannot be slighted (see discussion of "debt payment" in Chapter 3). Since postcolonial times, some feasts are keyed to the Catholic-church calendar and the patron saints who guard over villages; the ritual practices of the Catholic religious hierarchy likely had some type of pre-Hispanic counterpart in royal ritual. Life-cycle transitions of household inhabitants (birth, marriage, and death in particular) provide an occasion for feasting as does the building or renewal of the house itself. For construction projects as well as agricultural work, feasting can constitute repayment to those who participated in cooperative work parties. While sickness within the house is not a cause for a feast, it does result in an outlay of the productive capabilities of the household as a healer is brought in to cure or restore balance to an ailing household member (more on this later).

Regardless of the immediate incentive for a feast, all such celebrations have a strong political dimension. As Dietler (2001:66) has argued, the opulence of feasts provides an excellent forum for the representation and manipulation of power. Although Munn (1986:18) argues that all "food giving" is basically a hierarchizing act, certain types of feasts seem to be more about power, whereas others are concerned with the promotion of solidarity within and among kin groups. Within the realm of commensal politics, Dietler (2001:75–88) distinguishes among three modes of feasting: empowering feasts, patron-role feasts, and diacritical feasts. The third mode – diacritical feasting – serves to separate a class or sector from the rest of society by virtue of a distinctive cuisine and the exclusive locale at which the feast is enjoyed. This form of feasting – which naturalizes societal differences and reifies asymmetrical relations of power (Dietler 2001:85–88) – is a topic of Chapter 6. Patron-role feasting – also called redistribution as per

Polanyi (1957) and Sahlins (1972) – is all-inclusive in that it involves the public display (and celebration) of the asymmetrical power that exists between unequal partners: namely, a patron and his/her clients. Although Dietler (2001:82–85) conceives of this mode as typical of the paramount chiefs of Africa and the *luau*-sponsoring *ali'i nui* of Hawai'i, it could pertain equally well to ancient Mesoamerica where kin leaders of large, expansive residential compounds commanded formidable resources that were periodically "redistributed" through the practice of commensal politics. Empowering feasts, the third mode, is intended to encompass all other types of feasting that, in a general sense, result in the empowerment or positive value transformation of those sponsoring the feast (Dietler 2001:76–82). This large umbrella includes many of the household-based feasts mentioned previously. As Dietler (2001:82) notes, the prevalence, ritual importance, and political significance of this type of feasting means that "a substantial portion of domestic agricultural production ... is regularly dedicated from the beginning to flowing outside the household and being consumed by people in other domestic units." In this fashion, households are "stitched together" into a ritual network of commensal politics. Such integration does considerable damage to the dubious premise of economically autonomous domestic units and highlights the false nature of a dichotomy between public ritual and domestic ritual. Households that feast together assuredly are linked economically, and feasting cannot be viewed as a kind of domestic production that has no political consequences or advantages to those who labor to organize and prepare the feasts. Feasting is a performance not only of household productive capabilities but also of alliance structures between households (Orlove and Custred 1980:32). Finally, as with many ritual practices, feasting reveals political schisms and struggles for hegemony (Dirks 1991).

As with other social practices, feasting is easy to hypothesize in reference to the past but more challenging to identify archaeologically. Nonetheless, archaeologists and art historians are beginning to take a more careful and contextual look at archaeological deposits. For instance, midden contexts might contain a higher-than-average frequency of high-value fauna elements and refittable sherds from drinking and serving vessels that suggests rapid deposit formation such as would occur following a feast (for feasting analyses based upon Maya archaeological deposits, see Brown 2001; Hendon 2003; Reents-Budet 2000; Wells 2007).

Appropriating Household-produced Value

The creation of value often equates with the production of surplus, and that surplus can be part of a "ceremonial fund," in the words of Eric Wolf, to be used at the discretion of the household (to propitiate deities, sponsor a feast, or both), and/or it can be extracted in the form of taxes or tribute. As discussed elsewhere (McAnany 2004b), such appropriative mechanisms are a prevalent characteristic of complex societies in which a politically dominant sector derives part or all of its wealth through appropriation from less powerful sectors. Commonly called the "political economy," such systems of appropriation can loom large and determinative in terms of household size and organization. As Orlove and Custred (1980) note, households do not exist in isolation but must contend with other more powerful households or estate-based units of production. Eric Wolf, who formulated a seminal definition of peasantry, seems to have become increasingly aware of the impact of appropriation. An early definition of "peasant" stresses the nonprofit, subsistence nature of peasant farming: "an agricultural producer in effective control of land who carries on agriculture as a means of livelihood, not as a business for profit" (Wolf 1957:1). Later, Wolf defined peasantry in relation to the appropriation of surplus: "rural cultivators whose surpluses are transferred to a dominant group of rulers that uses the surpluses both to underwrite its own standard of living and to distribute the remainder to groups in society that do not farm but must be fed for their specific goods and services in turn" (Wolf 1966:3–4).

For Wolf, the salient characteristic of peasants evolved from farmers who controlled their own land and produced for consumption rather than for profit to rural cultivators who lost control of some or all of their surplus due to appropriation by a ruling sector. Ironically, this definitional evolution likely mirrors actual changes in the relations of production as household production became enmeshed in vertical obligations. As householders are drawn into the tangled web of tribute or taxation, value produced by household members increasingly is transferred hierarchically. In relation to the transfer of household value (both goods and services) through appropriative mechanisms, four types of households can be proposed: (1) those that thrived in the absence of vertical appropriations; (2) those that relinquished household-produced value to politically dominant sectors; (3) those that appropriated such value and became the recipients of the labor of dominated sectors; and (4) those who both gave and received appropriated valuables.

A critical but unknown factor of ancestral Maya society is the presence and blend of these four types of arrangements and how they changed through time. The extensive horizontal exchange networks evident in Middle Preclassic lowland Maya households in addition to the underrepresentation of monumental architecture (see McAnany 2004b for extended discussion) lends credence to the notion that vertical appropriations, if present during this early time period, were not overly onerous and may have been restricted to labor obligations. By the Late Preclassic period, however, colossal construction projects, elaborate ritual practice, and the incidence of large residential compounds coalesced in a manner that suggests the vertical appropriation of goods and services increasingly was a fact of life, which persisted through the Colonial period. The severity of Classic period vertical obligations is not clear but has only recently been subject to scrutiny (more on this topic in Chapters 6 and 9). The Colonial period generally is thought to have been a time of the most rapacious tribute demands on households, particularly on female weavers from whom an ever-escalating quota of cotton *mantas* was requested. In reference to the 1712 Tzeltal Revolt in Chiapas, the father of Maria López – leader of the revolt – has been quoted as stating that "[i]n this time and occasion they were poor: myself and the others could scarcely put our hands on a single manta" (Gosner 1997:226). This situation represents an extreme example of appropriation of female-produced value – one that is more likely to exist within a sprawling imperial system such as the Spanish empire than within the closely packed and smaller-scale Maya polities. Nonetheless, Classic-period palace households, by definition, were recipients of appropriated goods and services. The construction and maintenance of lavish palace complexes exceeded locally available labor and members of palace courts surely were supported in the manner envisioned by Wolf – by the labor and perhaps "in-kind" contributions of surrounding families. The effect of such demands on household labor as well as household size can be significant. In Chapters 7 through 9, we turn to the complexities of artisanship and vertical appropriations. In reference to the four variations on the transfer of household value introduced earlier, we can envision the presence of elite and minor (or conquered) royal households that both rendered and received appropriations. Occupying a middle level in the power hierarchy, such households indicate just how entangled the flow of valued goods and services can become with multiple overlays of material transfers and labor obligations.

Labor Demands and Household Size

Although many factors contribute to the size and composition of a household, labor demands loom large in agricultural households, as many researchers have noted (Johnston and Gonlin 1998; Netting 1965, 1993; Wilk and Netting 1984; Wilk and Rathje 1982). The expansive residential compounds that are a prominent characteristic of Late Preclassic and Classic Maya communities – urban or rural – likely housed some variant of an extended family group. Johnston and Gonlin (1998:158) suggest that economic, rather than kinship, principles are the determinative factor in household composition when nuclear families coreside in response to labor requirements. This point is well-taken and can be expanded to a consideration of politico-economic factors as equally strong determinatives of household size. If labor needs increase because of the appropriation of household-produced value, then expansion of household size (and completed family size) provides a way of meeting extended obligations. Elsewhere, I (McAnany 1995:119) have suggested that this dynamic was at least partially responsible for the appearance of the large, Late Preclassic basal platforms upon which multiple structures were built.

Such expansion of residential space also signals the presence of a type of indexical communication (Blanton 1994:10) in which members of a household communicate their social identity (particularly rank and wealth) through house size, elevation, elaboration, and in the case of the lowland Maya, the nature of interred deposits within the house. Although hidden from view, the last kind of indexical communication indicates most eloquently the manner in which the creation of socially structured space was ritually entangled.

CREATION, CARE, AND FEEDING OF SOCIALLY CONSTRUCTED SPACE

As houses materialize social identity and the ability to create value, they become emblematic of the social standing of their occupants. The tendency for houses to outlast their residents also provides the domicile with an added intergenerational significance that many researchers have commented upon (see contributions in Joyce and Gillespie 2000). In traditional Maya cosmology, houses are animate entities and, just as mountains and pools provide hierophanic locales for offerings, so houses are conceived as entities that require sustenance, particularly at the time of their creation. As Monaghan (2000:31) states, "the act of feeding a house is not simply ceremonial or expressive, but a necessary step in its construction and maintenance. Just as no one would expect a horse or cow to thrive without being fed, so no one could expect a house to last without being properly maintained." Entangled with the construction of the house itself – which provides an index to the status of its occupants – is the offering of valuables – containerized food, precious stones, and so forth – to provide nourishment for the emergent entity. Even though Vogt (1976:52–55) refers to house dedication rituals in which the house is "fed" as "ensouling ceremonies," Carlson and Eachus (1977:50) observe that such house dedication rituals were not exactly voluntary; specifically, a Q'eqchi person related to them the belief that a house is like a jaguar or some other ferocious beast: "If it is not fed, the house will eat you. It wants its meat" (cited in Monaghan 2000:n15). The imposition of socially constructed domestic space, similar to the preparation of a maize field, appears to set in motion a series of ritual practices – not easily circumvented – involving the offering of valuables.

The prevalence of archaeological caches in domestic and nondomestic contexts (see Mock 1998 for an overview) indicates the pervasive quality of this practice that also appears to enjoy deep antiquity in the Maya region. Although Middle Preclassic caches are known – most famously the quadripartite-arranged cache of jade and pottery objects from Seibal (Willey 1978:97) – they became more prevalent during the Late Preclassic when, at communities such as Cuello and K'axob, they serve "to ensoul" plaza spaces surrounded by structures that have been built on top of large basal platforms (see Hammond and Gerhardt 1991:225–231; Harrison-Buck 2004). Such caches seem to indicate an increased concern with ensuring the prosperity of the expanded household through proper propitiation.

Marshall Becker (1992) has commented upon the similarity between caches and burials. Insofar as both can be interred under the surface of living structures, they may both be interpreted as ritual propitiations. Becker (1992:190, 193) suggests specifically that burials may be interpreted as offerings to the earth gods that provided the basis for rebirth and new life. Stephen Houston (personal communication 2007), however, notes that epigraphically caches and burials are signaled by completely different logographs. Elsewhere, I (McAnany 1995) have suggested that residential burial interments compiled a kind of genealogy of place and were instrumental in maintaining the social identity as well as the economic entitlements of house occupants through generational shifts. I would argue that the subset of family members who were placed in residential settings were more than just offerings to the earth deities and that Becker's (1992) notion is better suited to the many men, women, and children who were interred away from the residence in corn fields and orchards, and perhaps in caves. When a burial pattern is dominated by adult interments (in which males have the statistical edge, as is the Late Classic pattern), then I think that it is safe to say that the location of those interments speaks to indexical communication (as discussed earlier) rather than the propitiation of earth deities.

The death of an influential household member creates a break in the social fabric (McAnany 2010 among others). The opportunities and dangers that are incumbent upon the transmission of rights and resources that occurs upon death of a household leader probably contribute to the predominance of adult burials under many Classic-period dwellings (Welsh 1988:161–165). The interment of valuables along with the corpse signals the importance accorded to the mortuary ritual by the survivors and perhaps their hope that the journey to the afterlife will be a smooth road for the deceased. There are other, equally traumatic circumstances that also tear at the social fabric and endanger the health and vitality of the house and its constitutive members. These might include sickness, adultery, or accusations of witchcraft, anything that causes disease and disorder in the household. Ritual specialists might heal such a tear but household-produced valuables are expended in the process. Sandstrom (1991:235) describes the domestic healing role of shamans as "warriors in a life-and-death struggle against disease and disorder." In the Nahua community of Amatlán, four to six shamans serve a population of 500, a ratio of about 1:100 and the "majority of a shaman's professional activity is spent controlling *ejecatl* spirits, usually through cleansing rituals" (Sandstrom 1991: 233, 252). These "bad wind spirits" were primarily disgruntled ancestors who had not been properly attended to upon their death and afterward. The notion of cleansing or sweeping the house of malevolent spirits in order to restore balance and health to the occupants of a house is also recorded by Hanks (1990:335) for the Yucatec Maya: "In the *heéc lú?um* 'fix earth' ceremony, it [the solar] is an object of transformation which is swept clean of malevolent spirits." Lucero and Gibbs (2007) suggest that adult skeletons found on the floor of deep cave chambers may be persons who were accused of witchcraft and considered too dangerous and powerful to be buried near the afflicted community. Vogt (1976:196–197) discusses rituals of affliction and how shamans attempt to restore the balance and thus cure the afflicted household member. In short, the care and feeding of domestic space and its constitutive members is a realm of significant economic expenditure that takes place according to a social logic of ritual practice.

FINAL NOTE ON THE HOUSE

In this chapter, we have examined gendered labor in the socially constructed space of house as well as field and orchard. Although we have considered the house as an iconic entity – in the mode of Bourdieu (1977:89–91) – we have not reified the house at the expense of its occupants as have Lévi-Strauss (1982) and his followers. In a prescient characterization of Lévi-Strauss's aversion to kinship theory, Watanabe (2004:164) has the following to say: "The notion of the house as a corporate entity that seeks opportunistically to preempt spousal descent group ties serves his theoretical position well by corporatizing (however precariously) alliance itself at the expense of unilineal descent ideologies, corporate descent groups, and even prescriptive marriage rules, a development he then historicizes as the transition from kin-based to state-ordered, class-stratified societies." Whether one chooses to emphasize the manner in which householders build horizontal alliances or express descent ideologies, both practices were present in ancestral Maya society and played critical roles in the organization of production, the constitution of power, and the construction of identity. The last is particularly entangled with descent ideology as Watanabe (2004:161) indicates: "Clearly, Zinacantecos have a descent ideology that they use to differentiate themselves, their lands, and their community from each other and neighboring Maya and non-Maya communities." To borrow a term from Weiner (1992), the ancient Maya house – as both a nexus of alliances as well as the physical locale at which social memory and identity were reproduced through generations – became an inalienable possession, an heirloom to be passed to descendants who might modify and expand the house before passing it on to the next generation. These efforts are recorded in the sedimented stratigraphies – the materiality – of Maya domestic units. The work of ensouling, maintaining, and expanding the house might be accomplished by those who planned to occupy it – along with a little help from family, friends, and debtors. But the construction of monumental structures – residential or pyramidal – required the mobilization of a larger labor force and it is this type of ritual work to which we now turn our attention.

5

Ritual Works

Monumental Architecture and Generative Schemes of Power

There are few social processes in which the materiality of ritual practice is expressed more clearly than in the construction of monumental architecture. The mental image of a community of persons quarrying, transporting, and laying/packing stone or earthen fill in order to construct an edifice that is considered "monumental" even by twenty-first-century standards begets, to our secular mind, compelling questions. Who labored to build monuments so colossal and durable that even today they dominate the landscape of Mesoamerica? What were the identities of those who undertook the labor of construction – slaves, clients of wealthy royal families, or community members who volunteered their time and muscle to create a great temple to the gods? How were Maya pyramidal temples built and rebuilt? Some pyramidal temples contain tombs – afterlife "residences" of persons of renown – others don't. Some temples were built in a single-episode and massive construction event but most consist of "onion-skin" constructions, indicating that the ongoing practice of monumentalizing perhaps was as important as the finished edifice. Since most face onto large, open plazas, what purpose were these soaring structures meant to serve? Were

An earlier version of this chapter was presented at the Annual Meeting of the Society for American Archaeology, San Juan, Puerto Rico, April 29, 2006, titled *Ritual Works: Architecture and Generative Schemes of Power in the Lowland Maya Preoclassic Period.*

they theaters of power – icons of community identity, shrines to tutelary deities, solar observatories – or simply funerary shrines to dead dynasts? Once constructed, how did these imposing edifices alter daily practice much less social relations? Although the emergence and maintenance of hierarchy is not dependent upon monumental architecture and communities in which hierarchy is suppressed are quite capable of monumental constructions, there is no negating the fact that the construction of artificial mountains in the center of Preclassic Maya communities changed the dynamics of power and social relations. In this chapter, we explore how this happened and why monumental architecture – as an enduring landscape feature – is implicated in generative schemes of power. Because colossal architecture seems so entangled with institutionalized power – and institutionalized religion – it is often approached using a so-called structural paradigm as discussed by Giddens (1984; see also Fogelin 2007:62–66). Here, we fold into the traditional structure-oriented perspective, attention to practice in hope of more realistically sketching the outlines of human intentionality.

Work parties, in which several families come together to achieve a goal that a single family could not accomplish alone, are a time-honored method of mobilizing a large labor force (called "speaking *sa'a*" among Mixtec Nuyootecos; Monaghan 1996:508). Such voluntary and reciprocal arrangements result in a hoed field or a raised barn – significant group accomplishments but lacking the permanent landscape signature of monumental constructions. When communities began to construct (and reconstruct) monumental architecture, new spaces were created not only in a physical sense but also in a social sense, particularly in reference to fields of power, and – significantly – social memory (Rowlands 1993).

Within the Maya region, the onset of monumental architecture can and has been seen as a watershed event from which generative schemes of power – to borrow a concept from Bourdieu (1977) – emerged (see also Bradley 1998:18; Ricoeur 1984:87; Smith 2003:66–76). We find ourselves wondering how people who lived through this transition to "monumental time" (Ricoeur 1985:106) thought about it or whether it was a hinge point that, in retrospect, seems more auspicious than it did to those who lived through it. Within daily practice, perceptions of collective work, ritual performance, and, as I suggest in this chapter, inalienability reside at the core of this issue, and all come under scrutiny here.

Dietler and Herbich (2001:242–252) frame the concept of "collective work events" – the practice of bringing together a concentrated workforce to achieve what a single family cannot – along a continuum from reciprocal work exchanges to nonreciprocated work feasts in which lavish hospitality is exchanged directly for labor. Corvée labor, then, is modeled as a variant on work feasts in which a central authority possesses the moral muscle to call in labor obligations (Dietler and Herbich 2001:244). Such a framework suggests that a considerable amount of slippage and ambiguity exists between work feasts and corvée labor. With increased interest in practice and structuration theory, some Mesoamerican archaeologists have made an effort to situate interpretations of this process within the daily practice and figured worlds of the past and to move away from evolutionary and typological approaches to the construction of monumental architecture (Love 1999; Joyce 2004).

This chapter considers the onset of monumental architecture in the Maya region in light of both old and new anthropological formulations. In the course of this consideration, we revisit the well-tread insights of Emile Durkheim (1961[1915]) on the primacy of religion. Annette Weiner's (1992) challenge to the concept of reciprocity and her assertion that inalienable possessions are the oldest form of human "currency" provide space for considering monumental architecture as the ultimate inalienable and unmovable possession. We critically consider recent constructs that accord a role to male aggrandizers as prime movers in the promotion of hierarchy and its ideological materialization in monumental architecture (Clark and Blake 1994; Rathje 2002). As part of an engineered landscape, colossal constructions generally provide, above and beyond all else, performance space for ritual practice (Inomata and Cobean 2006; Schechner and Appel 1989, among others); the nature of this practice is explored later in this chapter. One of the most important functions of monumental architecture – "cosmological authentication" (as per Weiner 1992:99) – inevitably highlights societal differences, just as it also guards against the "forgetfulness of death and the dead" (Ricoeur 1984:87) and the defeat of hierarchy (Mitchell 1988), important issues in a consideration of the social consequences of building big. In order to set the stage for this discussion, we first consider the time frame of monumental architecture and whether or not the construction of colossal structures initially deviated from work parties in any significant fashion.

THE CONCEPT OF THE COLOSSAL AND ITS ANTECEDENTS

For a number of reasons, the Early Preclassic period (roughly 2000–1000 B.C.E.) is grossly underrepresented in the Maya lowlands proper where there is limited evidence of early villages before 1000 B.C.E. (see McAnany 2004a; McAnany and López Varela 1999 for reviews). After 1000 B.C.E., however, populations expanded throughout the Maya lowlands to construct well-built domiciles and, in certain places, low, circular platforms that were used for nonresidential purposes (Aimers et al. 2000; Hendon 1999). The construction of monumental architecture can be detected several hundred years later in El Petén, Guatemala (Mirador Basin, see Hansen 1998:63; Cival, see Estrada Belli and Rice 2006; Tikal, see Laporte 1989; to name a few examples) and elsewhere and was followed by a surge of highly elaborated monumental construction activity between 200 and 0 B.C.E. throughout the lowlands. Many elaborate pyramids – some with stucco-masked facades – were built during the Late Preclassic period – a time that generally is dated between 400/300 B.C.E.–250 C.E. Relative to other parts of Mesoamerica, monumental architecture (as well as sedentary farming communities) made a late appearance in the Maya lowlands, which can hardly be said to have been precocious in this regard. Throughout the trans-isthmian region (Gulf Coast and the Pacific Coast of Chiapas and Guatemala), in contrast, pyramidal construction was underway by 900 B.C.E., and the structures were formidable. At the Pacific Coast site of La Blanca, a 25-meter-tall pyramid was built at this time (Figure 5.1); Love (1999:139) notes that "the largest mound constructions in Pacific Guatemala are the earliest."

The sheer "bigness" of early pyramid construction is a strong characteristic of archaic states, and this trend is evident not only at La Blanca but also at places such as the Gulf Coast Olmec capital of La Venta (Complex C pyramid, 32 meters tall, built between 800 and

FIGURE 5.1 La Blanca Mound 1, a 25-plus-meter-tall pyramid constructed circa 900 B.C.E. on the Pacific Coast of Guatemala (courtesy of Edwin M. Shook Photo Archives, Ref. 3863, Universidad del Valle, Guatemala).

500 B.C.E.), Teotihuacan (Pyramid of the Sun, 65 meters tall, built by 100 C.E.) in the highlands, as well as pyramids built by lowland Maya populations, such as Structure N10–43 at Lamanai (33 meters tall, built around 300 B.C.E.; Figure 5.2), the gargantuan El Tigre pyramid at Mirador (55 meters tall, also built around 300 B.C.E.), and the newly identified Preclassic pyramid built along the base of the northern Puuc Hills at Xocnaceh (a 20-meter-tall structure situated on top of an 8-meter-tall building platform, dating between 700 and 300 B.C.E.; Gallareta 2005). The immense scale of these constructions bespeaks a desire to transform the landscape, to engineer a cultural topography that radically altered living space within the communities in which these colossal structures were built. This novel social practice, this lavish use of human labor for nonsubsistence purposes leads to many questions regarding the motivations behind the construction of monumental architecture and the consequences of these durable edifices.

FIGURE 5.2 Structure N10–43 at Lamanai, Belize, 33 meters tall and built around 300 B.C.E. (redrawn by Josh Feola after Pendergast 1981:41).

DEITY SHRINES AS COSMIC AUTHENTICATION

Given the fact that palace structures, sine qua non of a ruling class, are a later addition to Maya communities, one can reasonably ask who organized the large cooperative workforce necessary to build such colossal pyramids. Could these construction projects have been organized along the lines of kin-organized work parties – *faenas* – as they are known in Latin America (Long and Roberts 1978:4, 314; Sandstrom 1991:315) or *guelaguetza* in the Zapotec language (Beals 1970:234)? On these occasions, a copious supply of fermented beverages generally dulls labor fatigue and lends a measure of festivity. Such a model has been suggested for early monumental architecture in the Andean region (Burger 1992:75) and contrasts with the Olmec model proposed by John Clark (1997:223) in which muscular rulers coerced the labor of an underclass. Was there an implicit pledge of reciprocity on the part of the organizers or were pyramid builders performing ritual works – building a monument to the gods – in expectation of reciprocity from "on high" in the form of bountiful harvests and human fertility? In reference to Preclassic Lowland Maya E-Group architectural complexes – in which pyramid shrines occupy a pivotal position – Aimers and Rice (2006:92) note the deep history and centrality of ritual practice involving the "regeneration of the natural world through public ritual."

The paucity of tombs within early colossi suggests that early pyramids were shrines dedicated to supernatural forces. Pyramids as shrines to dead dynasts are not common during the Preclassic period. Given the proclivity of Maya archaeologists toward tomb discovery, many Preclassic pyramids have been probed for tombs with negative results. The list of Preclassic sites lacking internal tombs includes the Mirador Basin pyramids (Hansen 1998:89), the Mundo Perdido complex at Tikal (Laporte and Fialko 1990), Group H at Uaxactun (Valdés 1986), and Lamanai Structure N10–43 (Pendergast 1981:41–42). More diminutive but coeval, tomb-free pyramids have been documented at Cuello (Structure 35; Hammond 1991b), Cerros (Structure 5C–2nd; Freidel 1986a:3–6), and Komchén (Ringle 1999:187). As Ringle (1999:187) has noted: "Formative monumental construction [does not] appear to be accompanied by cults of individual rulers, which appear only later." Lucero (2007:423) has brought attention to the fact that not all Classic-period pyramidal temples "served solely as royal ceremonial stages" nor contain royal ancestors, especially those present at settlement centers in which there was no royal court, such as Yalbac, Belize. She argues for a more heterarchical and less hegemonic approach to pyramid construction and use, one that admits a role for nonroyals and grants agency to both elites and commoners in the selection of a specific temple to support (Lucero 2007:423).

Over 90 years ago, Emile Durkheim (1961[1915]:21, 80) argued that the "cult of ancestors" did not represent the earliest religion but was preceded by the formulation of animistic forces into coherent religious practices that he believed were rooted in the very primacy of human thought and action. For Durkheim (1961[1915]:347), temples and palaces were built because it was impossible for the sacred and the profane to coexist in the same place. As Fogelin (2007:59–61) notes, this structuralist opposition of the sacred and the profane meets with great skepticism in contemporary archaeological approaches. For instance, Bradley (2005) argues for the inseparability of ritual and utilitarian practices during the European Neolithic period. He envisions particular Iron-age structures – devoted entirely to public ritual – as standing for "rites of separation" between ritual and residence (Bradley 2005:165–190). Even within a more integrative approach, there is no denying the heightened value of things deemed sacred or cosmologically authenticated in the words of Annette Weiner (1992:99, 101). If early monumental architecture was dedicated to forces of the cosmos – and possibly conceived as debt payment – then the manner in which such colossal structures were entangled with political power and social identity becomes very complex. Brück (2001:655–656) critiques interpretations of monumental constructions – of the British Neolithic period – that rely on simple models of male aggrandizement and advocates more attention to the continuous creation and reinterpretation of monumental spaces. Following in the footsteps of Durkheim, Weiner (1992:41) situates political power at the center of the sacred. If we allow – for the purpose of this discussion – that early Maya monumental architecture was a type of sacred architecture and of a different character than Classic-period dynastic temples, then we can move toward a consideration of the fields of power negotiated and expressed through such ostentatious displays of human labor.

Monumental Architecture as a Durable, Inalienable Possession

In a work that challenges much of the received knowledge regarding cultural economies, Wiener (1992:17) suggests that the most ancient and powerful classification within human societies is not reciprocity but rather the distinction between alienable and inalienable possessions: those things that can and must be given away or traded versus those precious items that materialize the identity, the cosmological authentication, and the power of a family line or community. The latter can only be loaned and never fully alienated. Although seated within a Melanesian context, this far-reaching insight – triumphed by Godelier (1999, 2004) – has been applied to land inheritance on Yap (Egan 2004), to the materiality of inheritance in North American households (Arnould et al. 2004), and to ancestral U.S. Southwestern Pueblo societies (Mills 2004). In an ironic permutation of Levi-Strauss, Weiner (1992:102) maintains that totems are not only "good to think," they are good to keep! Weiner's (1992) argument is linked to the fabled Kula trading ring of Melanesian societies, which – as the astute reader is thinking right now – is not known to have been associated with the construction of monumental architecture. But

FIGURE 5.3 Late Postclassic Mexica warriors torching the pyramid of the conquered *altepetl* of Culhuacan in the Codex Tellerino-Remensis. Note the corpse bundle of an earlier ruler to the upper right of the burning pyramid.

what is monumental architecture if not a particularly large and durable type of inalienable possession? Its sessile nature gives it a great permanence but also a vulnerability since sacred structures must be protected from acts of aggression by those who would despoil them because of their powerful role in both cosmological authentication and community identity. A depiction of Mexica warriors torching the pyramid of the conquered *altepetl* of Culhuacan in the Codex Tellerino-Remensis (Figure 5.3) provides a powerful example not only of this vulnerability but also of the fact that a pyramid could "stand for" an entire polity – rulers and ancestors (note ruler and ancestor bundle shown in upper right of Figure 5.3) as well as commoners and the built environment itself. Even though a shrine can be violated or fall into disuse, its sheer size and durability mean that its impact on a landscape and the social relations of those who inhabit that landscape cannot easily be erased. In the words of Rathje (2002:36), social production has been successfully embedded. A sacred cloak or symbolic flute (Godelier 1999:133–135) might be stolen or destroyed, but a monumental construction contains a fixity that has been characterized as imparting disciplinary power or authority to a locale as well as engendering a transformation of the novel into the habitual (Foucault 1979; Giddens 1984:145–154; Love 1999:144).

Guarding against the Defeat of Hierarchy

As the ultimate inalienable possession iconic of a community, a monumental shrine provides a pathway to the deities, a sure road to cosmological authentication. But what's in it for the men, women, and children who spend countless hours working on shrine construction or for the influential families who organize the endeavor and cajole the community to provide labor week after week, month after month? Were laborers duped, were wealthy families led by self-aggrandizing males? Archaeologists have been grappling with these questions for decades. The sacred quality and cosmological significance of early shrines alludes to a consensus-based rather than a coercion-based mode of construction (see Feeley-Harnik 1985 on ritual work). Competition between groups rather than social divisions within groups likely provided the rationale for early shrine construction. In this regard, monumental shrines would have become a focal point for bounded groups and not the materialization of social difference within a group, as was the case for later dynastic shrines. Although social difference – manifest in mortuary practice – existed before the onset of monumental architecture, the very act of building such colossal structures appears to have accelerated and amplified social distinctions. Relevant to this process is Weiner's (1992:41) notion that political power can be constructed by keeping valued possessions safe and Godelier's (1999) observation regarding the power of sacred objects to engender consent, especially within hierarchical

FIGURE 5.4 Stucco masks of K'inich Ajaw on second terrace of Preclassic Structure E–VIIsub, Uaxactun, Guatemala (from Proskouriakoff 1963:5; reprinted courtesy of Oklahoma University Press).

social orders. Once a monumental temple was built and became emblematic of group identity and critical to continued prosperity, then extraordinary efforts might be taken to maintain and defend it and great power and position accrued through demonstrating the ability to do so. The prevalence of depictions of the sun god, K'inich Ajaw, and the principal bird deity – iconography linked to rulership during the later Classic period (K. Taube, personal communication 2005; see also Taube 1998:446–454) – on the stucco facades of earlier Preclassic pyramids suggests an entangled relationship between power and sacrality (Figure 5.4). Estrada-Belli and Rice (2006:73), likewise, sees precursors of kingship ideology in the Preclassic stucco façade of pyramidal Structure 1 at Cival, Guatemala. The pathway to strengthened fields of political power and economic difference, therefore, appears not to have been paved with acts of self-aggrandizement (that likely would have fallen outside of accepted social behavior in anything but a free-wheeling capitalist economy) but rather with an adroit manipulation of cosmological precepts. One can surmise that during the lead up to the emergence of archaic states, social difference had to be grounded in a cosmological charter in order to be naturalized and perpetuated. Archaeologists often pose the question: "How did human inequality emerge?" A more pertinent question might be "How was hierarchy, which seems to be a strong tendency within all primate cultures, defeated for so long in human culture?" The defeat of hierarchy at certain times and places (see Mills 2004; Mitchell 1988; Weiner 1992), in fact, may be a greater human accomplishment than "riding the wave" of amplifying societal difference generated by adroit demonstrations of power pinned to cosmological authenticity.

In today's world, attempts to defeat hierarchy are practiced through contestation and negotiation, using existing judicial and legislative mechanisms. Naturally, many scholars project our litigious times onto the past and suggest that the emergence of an ethos of monumentality and authority must have taken place within a highly contentious environment. There would have been many dissenting actors, the story goes, working to defeat hierarchy (cf. Love 1999:129). But as Durkheim (1961[1915]:244, 466) noted many years ago, the power of men/women with *mana* cannot easily be contested; sacred power provides a sure route to political power. Cosmic authentication provides a pathway to durable political power precisely because it is nearly incontestable.

Because of its permanence and inalienability, monumental architecture – as a materialization of sacred power – guards against the defeat of hierarchy. Over the long run, the durability of a large construction (and its association with monumental time) can naturalize its presence as well as the transformed and hierarchical relations of labor and production that serve to maintain such structures. In a very real sense, generative schemes of power are more efficacious when linked to that which is not easily contested and thus appear to be natural. In this manner, hierarchy could be reaffirmed continually by renovation and guardianship of sacred shrines. In discussing Preclassic Maya cityscapes, Ringle (1999:211) makes this point eloquently: "The sponsorship of religious cults was a third possible pathway to social complexity, involving neither the military costs of political administrations nor the reciprocal obligations of a tribute system. ... Cultic [sic] practice would have been especially valuable in providing a prior language of hierarchy and inequality that could easily have been transferred to the economic and political spheres."

In this way, monumental architecture could effectively block the defeat of hierarchy and be understood as a massive thing that unleveled the playing field of social and economic practice. Linked with sanctified charters, a structure that was built for the gods – on a scale larger than ever before imagined – provided a nearly uncontestable opportunity to display and maintain social difference for those who would claim guardianship of this most precious and inalienable community possession.

PERFORMING THE GODS

If the point of religion is "to make us act, to aid us to live" (Durkheim 1961[1915]:464), then ritual performance is the means by which such "aid" is delivered. The architectural pattern of Preclassic monumental architecture indicates that ritual performance occurred on a grand scale in large, open spaces – many but not all of which were successively closed in through the course of the Classic period. Ringle (1999:196–97) has commented upon this arrangement: "Another common Formative pattern ... was to place large platforms adjacent to local temples." Such large platforms sometimes were linked to ritual pathways or *sacbeob* at sites such as Cerros and Komchén and, later, to ballcourts as at Cerros, Pacbitun, and Colha (Ringle 1999:207, 209). At some Classic-period dynastic seats of power – such as Uaxactun – the open architecture of the Preclassic period is well documented (Proskouriakoff 1963:114–129). Within Structure complex A–V, a trinity of cardinally oriented shrines framed an open plaza and access does not appear to have been restricted. In contrast, later Classic-period construction at A–V resulted in architectonic space that was emphatically enclosed and to which access was restricted through narrow corridors.

What kinds of ritual performance took place at the large Preclassic platform and shrine complexes? Were they large-scale, historicoliturgical affairs the likes of which ethnographers record among highland Maya peoples (see Christenson 2001; Cook 2000; Vogt 1976, among others)? Or were they enactments of creation narratives, statements of cosmological charters that portrayed the fortuitous position of a community in relation to their deities – particularly supernaturals instrumental to the practice of maize agriculture and to biological fertility? The Preclassic murals from San Bartolo (Saturno et al. 2005), filled with corn "maidens" and the maize deity, would suggest the latter. The processional composition of much of the San Bartolo mural, moreover, affirms the idea that Preclassic *sacbe* features were constructed as ritual pathways.

Throughout the Mesoamerican Classic and Postclassic periods, "performing the gods" was a central element of rulership (Gruzinki 1989, among others). Classic Maya rulers often are shown attired in the raiment of a deity, such as the maize god apparel worn by both K'inich Janaab' Pakal I of Palenque on the lid of his sarcophagous and Waxaklajuun Ub'aah K'awiil on Stela H at Copán (Figure 2.12; see Houston and Stuart 1996 for a discussion of Classic Maya god impersonation). Importantly, on carved monuments, the name and title of the ruler generally accompanied the image so that there was no mistaking the action as that of a ruler impersonating a deity rather than an enactment of a creation narrative in which the actor was subordinated to the role. Bloch (1986:89) provides an illuminating discussion of the manner in which ritual performance can dampen challenges to social difference by folding it into a timeless natural order. As discussed elsewhere (McAnany 2001), Classic rulers – by virtue of their power – could impersonate deities but during the onset of monumental platform and shrine construction, it is more likely that deity impersonation provided a means to consolidate sacred (and political) power. Lucero (2007) also emphasizes the empowering effect of temple-related performances, regardless of time period or social position of the actors.

WHY BUILD MONUMENTAL ARCHITECTURE?

Among those who study the past, opinions vary significantly regarding the causal impetus behind this novel practice that occurred at many seemingly unconnected times and places. Mithen (1998:97, 104) has proposed that religious ideas require "external symbolic storage [i.e., materialization, as in pyramids] to help anchor them into a mind which has no natural home for ideas that cross-cut evolved domains of knowledge." Given this supposed universal need for external symbolic storage, Mithen would characterize pyramid construction as a kind of Upper Paleolithic art writ large. The pitfalls of overlaying such

Descartes-driven logic on the past have been discussed by Thomas (1998:155, 151), who questions the value of separating "a realm of mind and ideas from the world of material things" and suggests that the "defining characteristic of humanity is not the hardware within, but the relationships between persons." We might add that historically the relationship between humans and supernaturals has been an equally defining characteristic. Closer to home, Ringle (1999:198) sees causal grist in the external challenges of the Late Preclassic period in the form of increasing population levels and dwindling land availability, conditions that he contends "demanded some concentration of authority," which was materialized in Maya Preclassic building plans. Despite this invocation of authority figures, Ringle (1999:213) takes pains to stress that his "model emphasizes that monumental construction did not come from the expansion of the egos of local elites, but occurred within a framework of *regional* competition between neighboring regional cults." Lucero (2007:412) sees intracommunity competition over temple allegiance as well as the magnetism of ongoing temple-related performance as driving forces behind monumental construction. Douglas (1972:14) also stressed the role of ritual elaboration in the definition of group boundaries, and Moore (2004:83) has extended this notion to Andean mortuary practices. Building big structures – sacred or secular – has been interpreted by Joyce (2004) as a materialization of group identity rather than the strivings of male entrepreneurs for greater wealth and authority. In opposition to the thesis of Weiner (1992) and Godelier (2004:13–19), who contend that the ethic of "giving away" serves to mask strategies to keep ones most valuable possessions, several scholars have proposed that entrepreneurial "give-away" practices – especially feasting – provide a reasonable pathway to lasting political power (Clark and Blake 1994; Hayden 1995; Rathje 2002). Rathje (2002:36), specifically, models this trajectory as a two-step process in which competitive generosity leads to the embedding of resources in social production (such as pyramid building) that casts both the community and the "Nouveau Elite" in a favorable light.

Beyond the putative need for external storage, prevailing models either contrast or weave together two distinctive factors thought to have been vitally entwined with the onset of monumental architecture: group identity and the concentration of authority. The first factor deals with the boundedness of groups – horizontal divisions – while the second factor deals with vertical divisions within a group; it seems to have taken a synergism of both to generate the new "order" of rulership that emerged in the Maya lowlands.

CONSEQUENCES OF MONUMENTAL ARCHITECTURE

Although the intent of building mountainous temples to the gods may have been linked to intergroup competition, profound social and economic consequences resulted from engineering such topographic difference in the landscape. As Love (1999:144) has noted, monuments "warp social space" and modify daily routine. Social perceptions of difference were altered, and political fields within and between groups were significantly affected. Likely, work feasts that underwrote the construction of the early colossal structures were based upon an emergent grammar of social difference that included nonreciprocal labor obligations and the potential for exploitation (Dietler and Herbich 2001:242).

By virtue of their sheer size and durability, the materiality of monuments reinforces a notion of "monumental time" that generally becomes part of hierarchizing practices (Ricoeur 1985:110). By inscribing such features on the landscape, social memory (à la Connerton 1989) of hierarchy is stabilized and challenges to hierarchy likely diminished (see also Bradley 2000:104–109; Rowlands 1993: 141–142; Smith 2003:5). Such are the "unintended consequences" of building big; that which was novel becomes natural. Perhaps Love (1999:146) expresses this transformation the best: "monuments were more than purely religious; they functioned as symbols of power, wealth, and prestige. More than that, however, their effect was to redefine all sorts of activities, including economic practices." Whether one prefers to perceive monumental construction as symbolic or constitutive of authority (as per polarized discussion in Smith 2003:76), there is no denying that in the Maya region such colossal constructions were entangled with emergent practices of hierarchizing that codified economic inequality. The fallout of the establishment of a sacred, engineered landscape of monumental proportions included newly generated schemes of power that redefined social position and economic relations. As entitlement and disentitlement can be intimately tied to the built environment (Holland et al. 1998:44), so monumental architecture engendered change in identities and the figured world of ancestral Maya communities. The manner in which these changes resulted in a naturalization of authority is the topic of Chapter 6.

6

Naturalized Authority of the Royal Court

> So it was when the first people emerged. Jaguars accompanied some of them; coyotes accompanied some; weasels accompanied others. But those whom the jaguars accompany, these are the richest. Those whom the coyote accompany, these are not so rich. Those whom the weasel accompanies, these people are poorer. Those whom the fox accompany, these are the poorest, just as poor as those of the weasel. ... Those human counterparts of both the fox and the weasel, they do not live very long. ... Our Father long ago gave us dreams about our animal-soul companions. That is why it remains the same even today, that not all of us have jaguars as animal souls.
>
> Gossen 1993:428–429

This "true, ancient narrative" spoken by Méndez Tzotzek to anthropologist Gary Gossen in 1969 provides a matter-of-fact statement of the profound cosmological underpinnings of inequality in twentieth-century Maya society, complete with differential life-span expectations. To most Westerners who embrace the ethos, if not the reality, of equality, such a matter-of-fact statement that explains hierarchy as the result of a natural cause (i.e., animal soul companion) seems very foreign. Yet, the most powerful and enduring forces of

An earlier version of this chapter was published as "Shaping Social Difference: Political and Ritual Economy of Classic Maya Royal Courts," in *Dimensions of Ritual Economy*, edited by E. Christian Wells and Patricia A. McAnany, pp. 219–247. REA Vol. 27 (2008), JAI Press, Emerald Group Publishing Ltd., Bingley, UK.

hierarchizing are those that naturalize difference so that it is beyond dispute and something to be tacitly accepted. Such hierarchization has been described by Touraine (1977:461) as a type of historical action by which a cultural model is transformed into a principle of social order. Weiner (1992:16) views this transformation in highly familial terms: "siblings ... after they marry other spouses, reproduce by exchanging with each other and/or their respective children in order to authenticate intergenerational stability while exercising and enhancing the power of difference. The transformation of difference into rank and hierarchy is bound up with how women and men ... play out these multiple culturally reproductive roles." Thus, in the view of Weiner, social order is transformed by the active agency of siblings who manage to enhance the wealth and position of the family in a manner that is stable transgenerationally.

The ability of social difference to endure the *longue durée*, and to withstand challenges to hierarchy, is historically and certainly culturally contingent. In Western society where eliteness is defined as much by economic wealth as by "breeding," social mobility can be pronounced and contingent upon the vagaries of "the market." In nonindustrial and noncapitalistic economies, on the other hand, social distinctions – once established – tend to be more resilient to change. Social theorists have noted that, in the past, establishing difference and naturalizing inequality appears to have required more than economic muscle or raw power; difference had to be institutionalized into a kind of *social speciation* so that rulers became "stranger kings" (Sahlins 1985:73–79). A special link had to be forged with the dead and the gods (Helms 1998; Weiner 1992:119). Such direct links to the cosmological domain created a sacred charter, developed divine authentication, and provided a strong basis for authority.

But authority cannot exist in a vacuum, rather it must be materialized in inherited and labor-intensive items and performed through ritual practice. In this way, provisioning and consuming materialize a figured world that is central to managing meaning and shaping the interpretation of life experiences – complete with differences in social status and political authority. Ritual economy – as the materialization of values and beliefs through the acquisition and consumption of objects that facilitate symbolic communication – is central to the study of social difference and political authority. The inherited possessions of families – often linked with ancestors and gods – become what Weiner (1992:103) and others refer to as "inalienable possessions." Such possessions can be loaned but never given away for they embody the special status and position of those who possess them. Among Trobriand Islanders, "land, names, magic texts, and body and house decorations are among the [inalienable] possessions that belong to members of individual matrilineages" (Wiener 1992:26). From a slightly different perspective, Baines and Yoffee (2000:15) note that ruling elites manage to inscribe their legitimacy on the landscape through "specialization and unprecedented forms of inequality." As we shall see in the Maya region, authority was embodied in adornment, accoutrements of rulership and ritual performance, and regal names. Stone houses, sculpted architectural elements, ancestor-focused monuments, exquisite objects of artisanship, and likely land were considered inalienable possessions of royal lines. Stone houses – adorned with sacred texts and cosmologically rich iconography – provided the built environment within which social difference was shaped, performed, and reproduced.

Classic Maya society contained a plurality of social positions from royalty to captives, but the focus of this chapter is royal identity and the social fields of action that shaped and maintained that identity. The materialization of sacred authority provided robust underpinnings to hierarchy and established a charter of difference, a ritual logic that a privileged few simply were born accompanied by a jaguar. In the Maya area, as elsewhere, an ethos of difference was actively maintained by a well-developed aesthetic of authority that equated bodily beauty with power and persuasion (see Munn 1986:102; Turner 1980:130). In this way, a type of social speciation was actively embodied. Linked to solar metaphors and tropes of death and regeneration, royal lords and ladies not only embodied handsome deities, they actively channeled them and donned appropriate costuming and props. As Turner (1980:139) has noted in reference to the Kayapo of Amazonia, dominance and beauty complement each other and are conceived as a dynamic equilibrium. We explore the aesthetic of authority in relation to the royal body in further detail later.

The accoutrements of authority, from another perspective, are the luxuries of the wealthy, the "weapons of exclusion" (Douglas and Isherwood 1996:95). These items – by virtue of their concentrated presence, antiquity, the scarcity of the substances from which they were fabricated, or the many hours of labor that stand behind their fabrication – constitute powerful forces of exclusion that "make new divisions in society" and reinforce old fault lines (Douglas and Isherwood 1996:109). These "weapons" create what Wolf (1990:587) has termed "structural power." On the eve of the Spanish incursion, social divisions within highland Mexica society were powerfully and visually materialized through costuming; only elite persons had the right to wear cotton and feathers and to receive flowers (Anawalt 1981:28). Creating, maintaining, and regenerating the inalienable possessions that materialize the sacred authority of the nobility cannot help but become a predatory enterprise in which vertical transfers of goods greatly outnumber horizontal, reciprocal transfers. In the Bronze age Aegean, where early monumental architecture is primarily residential and contains ample storage facilities, there existed a writing system that explicitly "spelled out" the in-kind nature of vertical transfers; this arrangement has been dubbed a "palace economy" (Renfrew 1972:296). Although the visibility of subsistence storage in the Aegean case, the seemingly detailed administrative structure, and the overtly economic content of Linear B (Chadwick 1976:15–33) provide a striking contrast with the Maya region, nonetheless, the core of the concept – that those living outside of the royal court were entangled with palace provisioning and maintenance – resonates with the available information from the Maya region and will be explored in further detail later. The acquisitive practices of a palace economy provide the subject matter of Chapter 9.

The terms "royal court" and "palace" are subject to ongoing debate over their definition and strategic deployment within Maya archaeology (Christie 2003; Evans and Pillsbury 2004; Inomata and Houston 2001a, 2001b). Given the corpus of iconographic, hieroglyphic, and architectural information now at hand, it is clear that royal courts and palaces existed during the Classic and Postclassic periods, and possibly earlier. On the other hand, there will always be a certain amount of ambiguity surrounding the emergence of "seats of power" and indecision as to whether or not an elaborate Preclassic complex should be defined as a royal court, a palatial residence, or something else altogether. The distinction between an elevated, multiroomed palace roofed with a corbeled vault and a commoner residence built of perishable materials at ground level is starkly apparent, but there exists ambiguity in the midrange structures. As Chadwick (1976:69–70) has noted in reference to the Minoan/Mycenaean world, no one would question whether Evans was correct in using the label "palace" at Knossos or if Blegen used the term correctly in reference to Pylos, but "it is not so clear how small a palace can be." Since Mycenaean palaces are presumed to have been administrative centers, Chadwick (1976:70) uses the presence of written documents as the litmus test for defining a palace complex. To a certain extent, Mayanists have followed Chadwick's lead. Inomata and Houston (2001c:7) define the royal court in terms of the physical proximity of a ruler. Since one of the major signaling devices of a ruler was the commissioning of texts, any architectural complex that is asserted to be a royal court in the absence of hieroglyphic texts is suspect, at best. For palace structures, however, there is considerably more latitude as large structures at several Preclassic sites that predate the common presence of glyphic texts have been labeled palaces (e.g., San Bartolo [Saturno et al. 2005:4] and Chiapa de Corzo [Clark and Hansen 2001:27]). If the definition of palace is tethered to texts, then we are left with a very large residual category of substantial residences from the Preclassic through the Postclassic that must simply be called "elite residences."

This lower threshold terminological ambiguity can be circumvented by characterizing unusually large complexes relationally (meaning in their time and place) simply as "seats of power." This perspective mirrors what Marcus (1983) found to be an indigenous Mesoamerican notion of what we might call a "city" or an "urban" entity. In other words, a place is perceived primarily in terms of the power and charisma of its ruler or leader and perhaps secondarily in terms of its architectural mass or the quality of the ruling family's sacra. Although the expression "seated in office" is readily glossed in Classic period texts as referring to rites of royal accession, a corollary Yucatec Mayan term *kulá?an* refers to a person's core home, enduring place *-iknal*, or where he/she is seated, especially in reference to a man's stool (Hanks 1990:109). In this study, when there is ambiguity surrounding the appropriate label (i.e., whether to use the term "royal court" or "palace"), the more inclusive relational term "seat of power" is employed.

Notions of authority and power are difficult to separate from considerations of gender and hierarchy. As we dwell on the palace and the royal court – seats of power – we come face to face with images not only of royal men but also of royal women and children, particularly young males who often were called *ch'ok* or "young sprout" (Houston 2009). These are the images that gave rise to the gender construct of complementarity (Joyce 1992, 1993), a concept applied ethnographically to gender and work relations among Zinacantecos (Devereaux 1987:92). Devereaux (1987:89), however, forcefully argues that complementarity does not equal equality as "men's interests, autonomy and life prospects enjoy greater scope than do women's." This statement seems to accord well with evidence from the Classic Maya past in which noble females are imaged and hieroglyphically referenced in a subset of royal activities that include life-cycle rites of passage – such as birth, marriage, heir designation, and death – and less frequently mentioned in reference to martial activity, deity impersonation, and overt rulership (Josserand 2002:136, 149, among others). The dedication of royal architecture by women on behalf of maternal ancestors, however, appears to form the subject of hieroglyphic texts from both Structure 23 at Yaxchilán and Las Monjas complex at Chichén Itzá (Plank 2004; see also Josserand 2002; Krochock 2002; Tate 1992). Costuming as well as artifacts associated with palace structures and burial crypts reinforce the notion that crafting fine textiles was a critically important and female-gendered skill that promoted the palace economy (see also Hendon 2006). The manner in which royal female-gendered space and artisan activities materialized social difference is explored later.

Authority may be naturalized at the royal court and in elite households through cuisine and a type of feasting labeled "diacritical" by Dietler (2001:85–88). The ingestion of radically different foods or copious amounts of delicacies such as meat and chocolate emphasizes rather than masks social difference. Some types of differences in diet are detectable by isotopic analysis of skeletal remains; the somewhat equivocal data that have resulted from such analyses are discussed shortly. But social difference does not mean uncontested authority; in the final portion of this chapter, the ritualized means by which authority was contested at the end of the Classic period (ninth and tenth centuries) is examined. But first, we turn to the manner in which beauty and authority – especially ritual authority – was embodied and, in the process, substantiated an ethos of naturalized difference.

EMBODIED SOCIAL DIFFERENCE

In U.S. popular culture, there is a tongue-in-cheek expression that refers to "the beautiful people" and their opulent style of living, and social critiques often comment on the obsessive manner in which youth and beauty are worshiped. Although these predilections would seem to be culture-bound, in fact, they are more widespread across space and through time than one might imagine. Hierarchizing forces can generate a visual aesthetic of power that emphasizes youth, beauty, and vitality while disparaging decrepitude. In an essay entitled "The Social Skin," Turner (1980:130) argues convincingly that "wealth and beauty are closely connected notions among the Kayapo, and both refer to aspects of the person coded by items of prestigious ritual dress." In effect, beauty extends out from the social skin and is materialized in costuming and dance. According to Turner (1980:130): "ask a Kayapo ... why he dances, or indeed why the ceremony is being performed, and he will almost certainly answer, 'To be beautiful.'" According to Munn (1986:102), Gawan Islanders of Melanesia perceive beauty in slightly more political terms: "the beautiful person persuades by exhibiting his or her persuasive potency as a visible property of the self." Persuasive potency, as well as sexual potency, often is perceived as a manifestation of beauty and power (see Anderson 1972 for extended discussion). Relational and aesthetic aspects of the royal Maya body recently have become a topic of discussion (Joyce 2002, 2005). Houston et al. (2006:11–56) provide a comprehensive, anatomical treatment of the Classic Maya royal body that integrates images with linguistic and hieroglyphic texts, while Meskill and Joyce (2003) emphasize the disciplined manner in which concepts of royal beauty were imaged in Maya and Egyptian iconography. Here, we examine Classic Maya body aesthetics as a kind of diacritical marking of difference.

Maize, Mundane yet Magnificent

Based on royal iconography, the aesthetic of beauty in the Classic Maya world was embodied in the young maize deity, introduced in Chapter 4.

FIGURE 6.1 Sprouting ears on maize stalks drawn as the face of the maize deity on an Epi-Classic mural from Caxcaxtla, México.

Representing the fundamental processes of fruition, death, and regeneration, the appearance of the maize deity himself has been likened to that of a sprouting maize plant (Taube 1985:172–173; see also Houston et al. 2006:45–49) with a long, tapering forehead and a headdress that mimics corn silks. On close examination, the sprouting ears of corn on the maize stalks painted on the murals of Epi-Classic Caxcaxtla are the face of the maize deity himself (Figure 6.1). Although maize can be thought of as a basic "staff of life," there is nothing mundane or pedestrian about the maize deity who represents the epic struggle of humanity for survival and regeneration. As Miller and Martin (2004:25) have noted, "The Maya usually represented high nobility with the body and face of the Maize God, eternally young and beautiful ... with exaggerated nose, crossed eyes, and tapering forehead." The tapering forehead was achieved through cranial shaping that is found far more frequently in skeletal remains of elite individuals.

Herein lies the genius of the Maya aesthetic of royal authority crafted over the final centuries before the Common Era. In royal iconography, the maize deity is a royal entity, and royalty are shown in the manner of the maize deity. Although this deity represents fertility and regeneration, he is male (although some would ascribe him with androgynous David Bowie – type characteristics). Both male and female royalty are shown wearing the jade skirt of the maize deity (Houston and McAnany 2003:34; Joyce 2000a:78–82; Tate 1999:Table 5.1), which indicates that the persona of the maize deity – as iconic of death, fertility, and regeneration – could be assumed by both royal men and women. Although the royal associations of the maize deity are quite unambiguous, there is no getting around the fact that this deity is made of maize (as were the first progenitors), and corn is not exclusionary luxury cuisine but a plant that was and is widely grown and consumed in myriad ways all over Mesoamerica. In this respect, the maize deity is no more than the corn stalk in your backyard dressed in fine threads and adorned with jade beads. This ubiquity of maize probably explains the subtle conflation of cacao with maize in royal iconography – as cacao was more restricted in both cultivation and consumption.

Sun-faced Nobility

In addition to the royal appropriation of fertility and regeneration (or assumption of the burden of ensuring continued prosperity, depending on your perspective), there was the further issue of the diurnal cycle represented by the powerful sun god, K'inich Ajaw (Figure 6.2), and his nighttime counterpart, the enigmatic Jaguar God of the Underworld. As the ultimate natural power in the cosmos, the sun has been linked to authority in the earthly realm repeatedly through time and across space, including the sun kings of ancient Egypt, the U.S. Southeastern Mississippian kingdoms, and Louis the XIVth of prerevolutionary France. Of the 105 named rulers listed by Simon Martin and Nikolai Grube (2008[2000]) in *Chronicle of the*

FIGURE 6.2 The powerful sun god, K'inich Ajaw (adapted from Miller and Martin 2004:Plate 124).

Maya Kings and Queens, roughly a third ($n = 30$) bore regal names that included *k'inich*, "sun-faced or radiant," in their title. Colas (2003) discusses the manner in which the divinity of the king was reinforced through hieroglyphic appellation of the title *k'inich*, particularly in self-referential texts. Those who did not take the word "k'inich" in their title might closely identify with the sun deity and adorn themselves with images of K'inich Ajaw as did Itzamnaaj B'alam and Lady Xook of Yaxchilán who wear pendants of K'inich Ajaw on the extraordinary carving labeled Lintel 24 (Miller and Martin 2004:100). The sun god often is shown with T-shaped incisors, a dental feature that became increasingly popular among the upper sector of society during the Late Classic and often was accompanied by inlays of jade (the color green/blue symbolized "first" and "fertile") on canine teeth. The sun provided more than just a power trope for Maya rulers, some of whom also were described as possessing a radiance or vital force (*ip*) akin to the sun (Houston 2000:167; Houston and Stuart 2001:55), too hot to touch and too dangerous to be close to. The power and dangerous heat of a royal body – analogous to that of the sun – provides yet another diacritical that differentiated royalty from all others. This naturalization of power bears a strong similarity to concepts of African divine kingship discussed by Feeley-Harnik (1985) and to Anderson's (1972) dissection of political power in Javanese culture. The Classic-period term for a Maya ruler, *ajaw*, often was prefaced with the epithet, *k'uhul*, meaning "holy" or "divine," indicating that divine kingship was an operative concept during the Classic period. Looper (2003:203) has suggested that "even the likes of [hieroglyphic] parentage statements should be seen not as genealogical documents per se but as a trope which conveyed the sacred identity of a person through his or her divine bloodlines." Demarest and colleagues (2003:142–144) have extended the royal association with the power of the sun to include the strategic placement of a royal complex at Dos Pilas that straddles the east–west processional axis of the site (diurnal path of the sun) and was built on top of an entrance to a cave (the Underworld and nighttime abode of the Jaguar God of the Underworld). Along a similar vein, Bell (2002:103) has discussed the link expressed iconographically and artifactually between the Copán dynastic founders' tombs and solar/lunar deity complex.

The Fragrance of Power

In addition to possessing a body with extraordinary qualities of beauty and radiance unlike the ordinary commoner, Maya Classic royalty surrounded themselves with the fragrance of flowers (Houston et al. 2006:141). Maintaining a fragrant aura in a tropical climate where rapid biological decay rules the day is no easy feat, and palace scenes on polychrome vessels often show bouquets of flowers (Figure 6.3; see also Coe and Kerr 1998:Figures 27, 47; Reents-Budet 1994:52). But flowers have a more profound significance in Maya thought: Lacandon Maya declare that the gods were born from fragrant *Plumeria* flowers (Boremanse 1993:328). In the Mexican highlands, flowers

FIGURE 6.3 Scene on a polychrome cylindrical vessel showing a basket of flowers placed at the base of a throne, Tikal Burial 196 (from Culbert 1993:Figure 84; courtesy of University of Pennsylvania Museum).

are associated with sensual delights (McCafferty and McCafferty 1999:109). Such delights presumably were more highly refined among Nahua nobility who paid reverence to the flower-bedecked goddess Xochiquetzal ("flower-quetzal feather"), the patron of brocading and other "high" arts.

Dietary Distinctions

If the difference between nobility and others was as diacritically marked as the preceding discussion would suggest, did that distinction extend to the foods that nobility ate, how tall they grew, and what illness afflicted them? Skeletal, paleopathological, isotopic, and faunal information pertinent to these questions is accumulating but sample sizes are still relatively small and of unknown bias relative to the enormous time span and regional variation involved in any study of pan-lowland Maya patterns. In fact, initial evidence indicates that there are no dietary patterns that are consistent across the lowlands (Emery 2003:511–512), although the large, relatively crowded capitals do seem to yield more evidence of paleopathologies across all social strata as well as stronger indicators that the upper crust was enjoying a diet more enriched in maize and meat. There are three primary indicators of diet and health: (1) archaeofauna and archaeobotanical remains; (2) carbon isotopic ratios in human bone; and (3) paleopathologies that literally etched their mark on human bone. The data sort out in the following manner.

For the site of Caracol, the isotopic data for a large sample that includes individuals from both regal and commoner contexts clearly indicate the differential presence of what Chase and Chase (2001a:129) call a "palace diet" rich in protein and maize for "skeletal remains of individuals buried within. ... Classic period tombs located in Caracol's epicentral palace compounds." On the other hand, burials in dedicatory cache contexts within central Caracol do not display the signature of the palace diet and neither do the human remains from the satellite residences ringing epicentral Caracol. These residential groups "exhibit some of the worst dietary regimens known at the sites and are especially different from the diet found in the epicentral palaces" (Chase and Chase 2001a:130). So, for Caracol at least, it is clear that royalty, in addition to smelling different and looking different, also consumed a different diet. A similar study of the isotopic signatures of an essentially class-stratified sample of human remains from the sites of Lamanai and Pacbitun reached a similar conclusion with the added point that the signature of enriched maize consumption likely resulted from elite consumption of corn-fed animals, such as dogs and deer (Figure 6.4; Coyston et al. 1999:237, 239). Status-linked dietary differences – as detected in tooth decay – from Classic-period northern sites of Calakmul, Dzibanche, and Kohunlich are noted by Tiesler and Cucina (2003). Significantly, a lower rate of tooth decay among elite males relative to elite females at these sites suggests gender-based differences in diet, a distinction that was not present among non-elites in the sample.

The role of dogs in elite cuisine complicates isotopic signatures in intriguing ways. Tykot (2002:219) has found that "stable isotope analysis of dog remains from a number of Maya sites generally show similar

FIGURE 6.4 Spotted dog (left) and ensnared deer (right) from the Madrid Codex, folios 27d and 48b, respectively (reprinted courtesy of FAMSI).

values to their human masters, but some, especially in later periods, have even higher maize signatures indicating that they were specifically being fed large quantities of maize." Given the cumulative nature of isotopic ratios, higher maize signatures in dogs (or deer, for that matter) translate into higher maize signatures in those who consume the animals – a confounding factor in the interpretation of isotopic data. Since there were limited sources of protein from domesticated animals in the Maya lowlands, isotopic data – coupled with faunal data – shed new light on the dietary significance of the small, spotted dog of the Madrid Codex (Figure 6.4). Although Tykot (2002) alludes to a trend in which corn-fed dogs became more common during the Classic period, there is ample evidence of dog remains in midden deposits from Preclassic sites such as Colha and Cuello (Shaw 1999:94; Clutton-Brock and Hammond 1994). For the site of Cuello, the age profile of canines was particularly flat with most dogs surviving only one year of life, which is interpreted as clear evidence of animal husbandry (Clutton-Brock and Hammond 1994:824–825). While the sample of dog bones from Preclassic sites such as Colha, Cuello, and K'axob (Masson 2004) cannot be said to have been recovered from regal trash dumps, the recovered fauna did come from excavations in the heart of these Preclassic villages and likely represent the optimal diet that was locally available during the first millennium before the Common Era.

Regional diversity in diet – confounded by the biased recovery of high-status individuals – undoubtedly contributes to some of the unexpected patterns in isotopic data (Gerry 1997; Gerry and Krueger 1997. As Gerry (1997:62–64) has discussed, local population levels can impact the availability of wild game, and this factor could affect the amount of meat available even for the privileged few (cf. Emery 2004:94 and White et al. 2004:158 for dissenting views on the Late Classic "overpopulation environmental doomsday" scenario). Regardless of the presence or absence of a royal court, all indicators of diet and nutrition point to the fact that those living in a biologically rich environment – especially near coastal and wetland resources – enjoyed a more varied, protein-rich diet and, as a consequence, lived a healthier life. This pattern seems to have persisted from Preclassic through Postclassic times as indicated by Storey's (2004:134–138) discovery of the low incidence of paleopathologies at Preclassic K'axob, which is located astride a wetland and Seidemann and McKillop's (2007) description of the low incidence of dental pathologies within a burial sample from Postclassic Wild Cane Cay. On the other hand, Danforth (1997:136) compares the burial populations of the small Belize River community of Barton Ramie with the major capital of Tikal and the Pasión River capital of Seibal and finds that the incidence of childhood nutritional stress and anemia was considerably higher at Tikal and Seibal than at Barton Ramie.

Regardless of their privileged position, even the upper sector of society was hard-pressed to buffer themselves from periodic famine and pandemic disease. In a large sample of 128 burials representing both elites and commoners from the southeastern Maya capital of Copán, Storey (1999:177) found that the bones of elites bore evidence of similar frequencies of systemic infection and multiple hypoplasias (generally associated with nutritional deficiencies during childhood); the male elite sample contained evidence of having survived the highest incidence of infections, possibly from battle wounds. In effect, "no one was fully buffered and ... during periods of childhood and adulthood all individuals had impaired nutritional status" (Storey 1999:178). Analysis of skeletal material from Palenque by Márquez Morfín et al. (2004) reached a similar conclusion.

Regardless of the hazards of life without antibiotics – to which none was immune – male elites at Copán did manage to achieve, on the average, a significantly higher stature than commoners (163.4

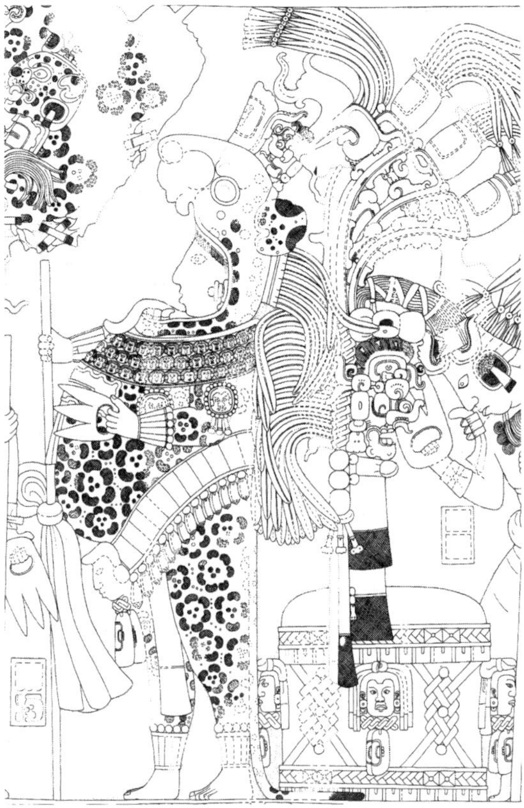

FIGURE 6.5 Generously proportioned Late Classic ruler of Tikal, nicknamed Dark Sun, as shown on the underside of Lintel 2, Temple 3 (after Harrison 1999:177; courtesy of University of Pennsylvania Museum).

centimeters as opposed to 160.1 centimeters [Storey 1999:176]; also see Danforth 1999 for review of earlier studies of height differences). The distribution of faunal material from Late Classic Petexbatún sites suggests a corrosion of status-based differential access to meat toward the end of the Late Classic period (Emery 2003:511), perhaps an indicator that authority structures were breaking down.

Although the noble ideal of beauty might have been the svelte maize god, images of corpulent lords and ladies in painted scenes and carvings have survived the ravages of time and looters. The super-sized ruler of Tikal, nicknamed Dark Sun, and shown on the underside of Lintel 2 of Temple 3 at Tikal (Figure 6.5), provides a case in point. Even when a royal person is shown in stone carvings as slender, their large size as revealed in mortuary remains can provide a reality check, as with the Lady of Cancuen who appears as a svelte mother of a young heir apparent in Panel 19 from Dos Pilas. Finger rings found in her burial crypt – encircling her finger – indicate the large diameter of the digits of this well-fed royal woman (Palka et al. n.d.). The enhanced nutritional status of royal lords and ladies likely gave them an edge in terms of longevity for there exists innumerable examples of lords whose venerable age is described hieroglyphically as reaching "four k'atunob" or in excess of 60 years. Famous examples include K'inich Janaab Pakal I of Palenque, Ruler 1 of Dos Pilas, and Itzamnaaj B'alam II of Yaxchilán (see Martin and Grube 2008[2000], and Tiesler and Cucina 2004 for additional cases of longevity). Thus, the long life expectancy of those with "jaguars as animal souls" as stated by Méndez Tzotek in the prologue is borne out archaeologically. Such longevity may be linked to the higher frequency of ritual feasting events among Classic Maya royalty during which varied and protein-rich foods that may not have been eaten daily – such as meat and chocolate – were consumed. In this way, political alliances forged and maintained through feasting were linked to longevity as a feature of social difference.

Authority Embodied in Performance

Among the Tzotzil Maya, the title *yahwal balamil* translates as "owner of the earth." As Vogt (1964:499) has related, this earth deity "currently [is] pictured as looking and behaving like a Ladino, especially a large, fat Ladino with piles of money." Rumored to live within a cave inside of one of the many sacred mountains within Tzotzil territory, the Ladino earth deity bears an uncanny resemblance to God L of ancient times (more on God L, the rich, aged, and lascivious trader and denizen of the Underworld in Chapters 8 and 9). Miller and Martin (2004:58–62) suggest that many scenes on Classic Maya polychromes in which God L appears can be read as an epic struggle for supremacy between God L and the hero twins or the maize deity (Hun Nal), the latter being the father of the hero twins. Ultimately, the good and beautiful triumph and subjugate God L, a lord of the Underworld. In Classic Maya iconography, Maya rulers stood or sat on top of the earth or *wits* (mountain) supernatural, further emphasizing their mastery over

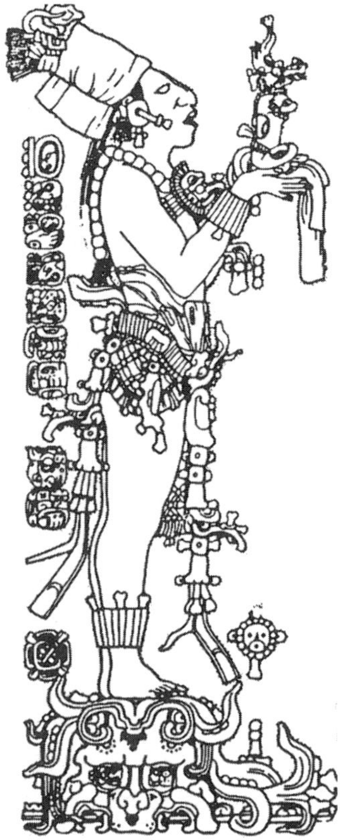

FIGURE 6.6 Maya ruler Chan Bahlum standing on top of an earth or *wits* (mountain) spirit, Temple of the Foliated Cross, Palenque (redrawn by Josh Feola after Schele and Freidel 1990:240).

earthly forces as well as those contained within the earth (Figure 6.6). The concrete implications of this mastery in terms of land ownership are discussed in the section "Lands of the Realm"; here it is sufficient to point out that this type of authority was explicitly claimed. As *wits-ch'een* or mountain-cave topography generally is located in the wilder, more inaccessible parts of the realm, Taube (2003:472) argues that the archetypal hero twins embody "two realms of authority: (1) Hunahpu, the king of the human community, and (2) Xbalanque, the king of the forest." Claiming mastery over both realms ensures that no stone is left unturned, perhaps no deer hunted, without royal knowledge and consent.

In reference to kingship at the Late Classic site of Quirigua, Looper (2003:200) suggests that there were two slightly different domains of power that are crucial to kingship: control of supernatural forces and monumental building enterprises. In Chapter 4, we considered the manner in which monumental works became entangled with political power; here, we turn to the control of supernatural forces through ritual propitiation of deities and deity impersonation. Houston and Stuart (1996) have shown that, like the Mexica of Highland México (Gruzinski 1989), lowland Maya kings dressed in the attire of deities such as the maize god or fire god and performed rituals on behalf of their kingdoms. Houston (2006:148) refers to this performance as a kind of "deity concurrence," which is referenced hieroglyphically in at least 50 separate texts. On such occasions, "divine essences came to visit, briefly, and were made animate by human flesh and motion" (Houston 2006:148). More than a propitiator of deities, however, the ruler was a caretaker and sustainer of the gods as materialized in the many images placed in temples and niches throughout royal courts (Looper 2003:200). The manner in which deities were cared for and communicated with generally involved ritual transformation on the part of the performer. Plank (2004:157) has discussed the "Starry Deer Caiman" hieroglyphic theme and its appearance in places that seem to have been used for ritual transformation, such as Yaxchilán, Str. 44, Palenque House E, and Copán Structures 22, 9N–82 (a.k.a. House of the Scribes), 9M–146, and 8N–66C. True mastery also included the ability to channel prestigious ancestors, a performance that was significantly enhanced by wearing and carrying sacra once possessed by ancestors (McAnany 1998). As Weiner (1992:6) so colorfully expounds: "When a Maori chief brandishes a sacred cloak she is showing that she is more than herself – that she *is* her ancestors [emphasis in original]."

SELF-CONSCIOUS DIFFERENCE OF THE REGAL COURT

Maya residential architecture does not fall neatly into discrete categories that can be labeled as housing for commoners, elites, minor royalty, and full-blown royalty. Given any one architectural characteristic, such as size, number of rooms, presence of benches, number of courtyards, and so forth, there is considerable overlap among

FIGURE 6.7 Palace of Labna constructed in the Puuc Region during the Late-Terminal Classic (photo courtesy of Tomás Gallareta Negrón).

categories. For this reason, Mayanists use words such as "continuum" when discussing residential architecture. Nevertheless, the manner in which regal architectural space was socially constructed is diacritically different from other kinds of houses (Figure 6.7). There is a self-conscious reflection and projection of authority that materializes social difference in a qualitative rather than purely quantitative manner.

One way in which this difference was asserted is through a break with the earlier architectural tradition of status through accumulation; that is, the forging of an earth-bound high-status genealogy through the superpositioning of structure renovations, expansions, and ancestor interments (see McAnany 1995:96–105). In contrast, many early cities and seats of power were deliberately created as a new and different kind of built environment (Cowgill 2004:534–537). As Plank (2004:235) has noted, during the Late Classic, regal architecture often was "newly built to display wealth and status." The scale, configuration, and elaboration of regal architecture so overwhelmed earlier traditions that perching on top of the residence of one's ancestors, while not unknown, apparently diminished in importance. In reference to Quirigua, Looper (2003:201) has suggested that the ambitious construction program undertaken during the reign of K'ak' Tiliw was necessary to establish a symbolic center for Quirigua that was "crucial to the cultivation of royal charisma." From a labor standpoint, these constructions required considerable input of human effort to quarry and transport raw materials, shape masonry blocks, build stone walls, mix and apply coats of plaster, and cut and shape wooden lintels (see Abrams 1994 for labor estimates). But the real statement of royalty lay in the fine finishing details; the carved lintels, panels, and benches; and the painted mural scenes. Because participation by a "public" was necessary to create a royal court, these structures have been called "public architecture." Undoubtedly, they were built by "the public," but there is nothing plebian about the use of or access to these buildings. The hieroglyphic corpus associated with court construction accentuates the exclusivity and sacrality of these spaces and their role as "weapons of exclusion," to use the words of Douglas and Isherwood (1996:95).

The antiquity of palace construction, per se, in the Maya lowlands is a matter of some discussion but an Early Classic example occurs in the lower levels of Structure B–2 at Uaxactun and dates to around 350 C.E., the first half of the Early Classic period (Laporte 1989; Valdés 2001:144), although the architectural elaboration of Group H suggests an earlier, Late Preclassic origin for palaces at Uaxactun. As Valdés and Fahsen (1995) have discussed, Uaxactun Groups A and B were focal constructions of the Early Classic royal court at Uaxactun with Structure A–5 taking on ritual significance as an acropolis while the structures of Group B assumed residential and administrative functions.

Indeed, a good part of a royal court must have been given over to administrative functions, although, unlike the distinctive C-shaped *audiencia* architecture of Andean Chimu sites, clues to administrative buildings within a royal court lay in subtle details, like the positioning of a built-in bench within a room, access patterns to a room complex, or the lack of associated trash debris (Harrison 1970). In a comparison between the Palace Group and other elite complexes at the Late Classic site of Aguateca, Inomata and Triadan (2003:173) note that "the Palace Group appears to have been more geared towards administrative and ceremonial functions than other residential units." Late Classic palace complexes, in particular, tend to contain a large number of structures that were not typical family dwellings or even dwellings at all; this pattern has been noted by Harrison (1970) for the Central Acropolis of Tikal, by Andrews and colleagues (2003) for the palace complex of Yax Pasaj at Copán, and by Inomata and Triadan (2003) for Aguateca. Shrines, boy's schools, dormitories, and reception chambers are popular assignations for these nondwellings. Oddly, storage chambers – used either for the items shown in tribute presentation scenes on polychrome vessels or for the voluminous and fragile headdresses, costuming, and backracks worn by royalty on ritual occasions – are seldom mentioned by those interpreting palace room function. In reference to storage, Smyth (1996:349) has suggested that rather than viewing the omission of storage chambers as a failure to identify a type of structure that – in Old World archaic states – is seen as critical to state development, we instead accept the fact that many Mesoamerican royal courts prior to the Mexica did not stockpile vast amount of goods but rather were provisioned through "appropriational storage." Specifically, goods and food were stored locally and then moved up the storage hierarchy as demanded. For royal courts located in a tropical environment where spoilage and insect/rodent infestation are chronic problems, this type of decentralized storage would have been especially efficacious.

Although royal courts may be unified by a display of self-conscious difference in the form of architectural size and adornment, architectural style and types of adornment are highly differentiated regionally. Royal courts in the southern Petén and Pasión/Usumacinta region are rich in carved hieroglyphic texts; however, the corbel-vaulted rooms are small and narrow. To the north, Puuc sites contain buildings fronted with stone mosaics and partitioned into large rooms roofed by expansive corbel vaults, but hieroglyphic texts are not as common (Figure 6.7). Even within Puuc architecture, there is tremendous diversity in the layout of royal courts among Uxmal, Labna, Kabah, Sayil, and Chichén Itzá (see Kowalski 2003 for extended discussion). The architectural expression of difference, therefore, seems to have existed not only between royal courts and other less distinctive dwellings but also among royal courts. How this difference translated into distinctive experiences and perceptions of royal courts – a type of study advocated by Moore (1996) – remains to be investigated in the Maya region.

One promising study by Liendo Stuardo (2003) indicates that differences may relate to a shift toward greater bureaucratization that originated with the Terminal Classic Puuc sites in northern Yucatán. Specifically, a comparative study of access patterns for six royal courts at the sites of Uaxactun, Palenque, Tikal, Uxmal, Labna, and Kabah revealed that the three northern (Terminal Classic) sites have shallower access patterns "which testifies to the existence of fewer subsystems for each building [and] indicates an apparent functional specialization among buildings." Since the Puuc buildings are those with fewer carved hieroglyphic texts, the suggestion that more of the northern "palace" complexes may have functioned as bureaucratic complexes is particularly intriguing. Carved palace texts, as we shall see, served many purposes but few, if any, could be considered bureaucratic.

Dedicated to Difference

The expression "writ in stone" conjures a notion of fixity, and, if a statement of dedication, an assertion that will not quickly fade or be erased (barring an act of violent defacement and such practices were not unknown in the Mesoamerican past). Literacy, in general, engenders social difference as it generates an "awareness of the process of abstraction and a concern with knowledge and value as explicit systems beyond the immediate contexts that generate them" (Comaroff 1985:143).

The permanence of carved stone and stone houses helps to create what Ricoeur (1985:106) termed "monumental time" or the time of authority figures, a chronological construct with great power to dominate. Such monumentality imparts a naturalized quality to stone-inscribed texts and their accompanying imagery. Carving a glyph block on a stair riser, a lintel, a doorjamb, a bench, a wall panel, an inset medallion, or a freestanding stelae served to define that architectonic space as imbued with a special quality of difference verging on the sacred. Although the events recorded might include a martial victory (or defeat), an end of a period, a birth, a rite of passage, a coronation, or a death (with a subsequent *och-k'ahk'* or fire-entering ritual), most texts explicitly served a dedicatory function (Stuart 1998). That is, they conform in syntactical structure to a sequence that includes an initial glyph, a verb, a possessed noun, a prepositional phrase, and the name of the possessor. This dedicatory genre was painted on the rim of polychrome ceramic vessels and also carved on stone slabs and wooden lintels that adorn royal courts. In a study of royal architectural contexts in which hieroglyphic compounds for dwelling – *otoot* – were employed, Plank (2004:236–237) found that not only did texts conform to the standard dedicatory sequence but that "dwellings" could be "owned" by humans, gods, and god impersonators, a further indicator of the wider range of relational arrangements within royal courts. The term *otoot,* it seems, was conceived as a "container" for animate substances. Vogt (1976) and others have documented the significance of dedicatory rituals that serve to ensoul and animate a new dwelling among Tzotzil Maya of Zinacantan. The ritual observed by Vogt (1976:52–55) included the burial of a black rooster beneath the floor of a newly constructed house, a ritual that Monaghan (2000:30–31) and others conceive as a type of nourishment for an animated structure. Dedicatory offerings – of food and precious items placed in pottery vessels – are part of a deep tradition in Maya society that reaches back to Preclassic times. *Otoot* dedications expressed in the sacred writing of hieroglyphic texts, therefore, represent an expression of difference couched within a time-established genre. At Yaxchilán, for instance, the dedicatory texts carved on the underside of lintels adorning Structure 23 record the ritual activation of the structure through (1) *och-k'ahk'* ceremonies (likely smoking with incense), (2) ritual binding of the southwestern doorway, and (3) the *t'ab'(?)* "ascending" of its "carvings" (an opaque phrase not fully deciphered; Plank 2004:51). Evidence of the ritual activation of this structure or its dedication as a building "owned" by the royal female Lady Xook was carved on the underside of stone lintels that brace the doorways. Only those permitted access to the dwelling of this powerful female were allowed a glimpse of the texts and figural scenes that assuredly are some of the most evocative images ever created by Late Classic Maya sculptors. Such a statement of difference cannot be called conspicuous consumption or propaganda for even its audience was highly circumscribed. Rather, it represents a very intimate statement of social self, the ability to command the labor of a sculptor who already must have had a legendary reputation among the royal courts of the Usumacinta Valley, and the permanence of social difference writ in stone. Perhaps this timeless quality also was the goal of the ambitious programs of stelae dedication undertaken sequentially by Waxaklajuun Ub'aah K'awiil of Copán and his eighth-century vanquisher K'ahk' Tiliw of Quirigua. Looper (2003:203) has suggested that that massive size of K'ahk' Tiliw's self-representations, "assert with increasing intensity the fixity and permanence of kingship at the site."

Upon death, noble members of the royalty court were distinguished by extraordinary mortuary ritual and distinctive mortuary crypts. As Fitzsimmons (1998, 2010), McAnany (1995, 1998), Weiss-Krejci (2004), and others have observed, ancient Maya mortuary ritual had a profound political dimension. The placement, construction, and dedication of a burial crypt as well as the interment of additional individuals within a crypt spoke to more than the passing of power between generations. These ritual constructions placed ancestors in the heart of the court and mitigated the danger to royal courts as influential members of a ruling family died and the liminal, interregnum time was negotiated both within the court and with powerful allies and adversaries. In a manner akin to the judicial court system of the United States, the authority of the royal court leaned heavily on precedent, and the debt owed to those who came before was actively acknowledged and celebrated. Anniversaries of the death of esteemed ancestors occasioned crypt rededication ceremonies, ritual feasting, and offerings, many of which were recorded hieroglyphically. Panel 3 of Piedras Negras, provides an archetypical example of the attention paid to royal ancestors by heirs. According to Houston and Stuart (2001:69), the three events recorded on Panel 3 include "(1) the *k'atun* anniversary of Ruler 4's accession of office and a ritual dance occurring two days later, (2) the death and burial of Ruler 4 after about eight years, and (3) over twenty years later, the culminating record, the rededication of Ruler 4's tomb as overseen by Ruler 7." While this type of ritual practice and the remembrance of ancestors was not restricted to nobility, the opulent manner and expenditure of labor and resources incurred through such celebrations was distinctive to nobility so that, even in death, social difference was preserved. Taube (2004:93) suggests that afterlife experiences, likewise, were perceived to have been different for nobility who could expect to journey to a solar, celestial paradise, sometimes referenced as "flower mountain."

Gendered Space in the Royal Court

The idea that a dwelling could be conceived as female-gendered space was introduced in Chapter 4 in reference to non-elite dwellings, and support for this notion was provided by way of reference to hieroglyphically documented examples of noble women who had dwellings and sacred spaces dedicated in their names. Based on mortuary and epigraphic evidence, Haviland (1981) proposed that certain dwellings at Tikal, particularly Group 7F–1, could be classified as dower houses. Mortuary and hieroglyphic evidence also combine at Dos Pilas to suggest that Structure L4–41 was the dwelling and burial place of the royal "Lady of Cancuen," probable wife of Dos Pilas Ruler 3 (Houston et al. n.d.). These examples are not anomalous and are joined by Yaxchilán Structures 23 and 11, which are identified in attached architectural texts as the *otoot* of Lady Xook and Ix Sak B'alam, respectively (Plank 2004:38, 50–51). Given the number of architectural texts dedicated by royal women at Chichén Itzá, these royal ladies of very Late Classic times, if not defining female-gendered space, were actively exerting their agency in dedicating ritual spaces to important patron deities in honor of female ancestors (Plank 2004:214).

In effect, glyphic texts make it abundantly clear that female-gendered space was an operative concept – and likely an ongoing expense – of Classic-period royal courts. Royal Maya princesses, like those of premodern Europe, were instrumental in forging durable alliances between seats of power through marriage. For instance, a blue-blooded princess from Dos Pilas – namely Lady Six Sky, a.k.a. Lady Wac Chanil Ajaw – was sent to revitalize the royal court of Naranjo at the close of the seventh century. She is one of few royal females to be represented (as in Stela 24) in a martial pose, that is, standing on a captive. When women of a foreign dynastic line married into a royal house – as did the Lady of Cancuen who married into the royal house of Dos Pilas – separate dwellings appear to have been constructed for these "stranger queens" and the entourage with which they no doubt arrived (see also Plank 2004:53). Mortuary data suggest that, once married and after producing an heir, a royal woman tended to stay in her new home, even if her spouse died before her. Hieroglyphic texts and burials alike suggest that the construction of gendered space within royal courts involved significant resource and labor investment. An embodiment of alliance structures, these spaces often were ritually dedicated with sacred texts that served to emphasize the distinctiveness of the social persona who resided within. But what of the activities that transpired in royal courts, in both gendered and ungendered spaces? With this question in mind, we turn to an examination of the palace economy.

MATERIALIZING DIFFERENCE THROUGH PALACE ARTISANSHIP

Although Maya royal courts were organized quite differently from those of the Minoan/Mycenaean world, both can be considered to have operated as variants of a palace economy. The economic arrangements within a palace economy include local production and consumption, centrifugal transfer of artisan production from the palace (in the form of gift giving, alliance building, tribute, and trade), and vertical and centripetal transfers to the palace from satellite domestic units as well as from other fiefdoms that were subjugated politically and/or conquered militarily. The lords and ladies of a realm invariably exercised a certain amount of control over the lands of the realm, a factor that contributed significantly to feeding palace residents and staff. But, first we examine artisanship and royal identity, specifically, the social and ritual practices that embodied royal identity and served to bolster the palace economy. Then, manifestations of the principle of divine rulership on the countryside around a seat of power are approached with an eye to understanding how the palace was provisioned locally with food and goods. In Chapter 7, the artisan discussion is extended to nonregal dwellings that appear also to have embraced a similar ethos of artisanship and identity. Overt aspects of vertical transfers to the palace – that is, taxation and tribute – form the subject of Chapter 9.

The Weaving Bone of ...

The formal dress of royal Maya women was beautiful and sumptuous, finely embroidered with intricate designs. If current weaving patterns are any guide to the past (Holsbeke and Montoya 2003), textiles encoded a world of cosmological meaning (see contributions in Miller 1988 for seminal thoughts on this topic). In Chapter 4, we reviewed the evidence (or lack thereof) for weaving in lower-status Classic dwellings and arrived at the conclusion that – although cotton could be widely grown in the Maya lowlands – material indicators of cotton spinning and weaving are more commonly found in high-status residences. This pattern, coupled with the great deal of time and drudgery involved in processing raw cotton into spinnable thread, suggests that processing time – rather than availability of raw material or difficulty of spinning – was one of the primary factors restricting cotton spinning and weaving during Classic times. Persons of lower social position likely were engaged in cleaning cotton bolls for royal ladies. Hieroglyphic evidence only serves to strengthen the association between weaving and royal identity. Miller and Martin (2004:94) note that "connection between weaving and high status is reiterated on the fine bones from more than one kingdom inscribed with *upuutz' b'aak*, 'the weaving bone of,' followed by the name of a royal wife" (see also Houston and Stuart 2001:64).

These personally monogrammed tools of the trade often are found in mortuary contexts, although many have been looted and thereby severed definitely from their context of social meaning (e.g., see contextless study by Dacus 2005). Such an extremely personalized tool kit is an indicator of the extent to which a female's identity was entangled with her prowess as a weaver and hints at the fact that this particular female identity as artisan had implications far beyond weaving textiles to clothe the royal family (Hendon 2006). The importance of finely woven *mantas* or *tilmatli* in Mexica tribute, trade, and alliance building is well known (see Anawalt 1981:27–32 on Aztec clothing). In early Colonial Yucatán, Spaniards commented favorably on the linenlike quality of cotton *mantas* woven presumably by elite females (Morley 1941:155) who, according to the sixteenth-century Franciscan friar Bishop Diego de Landa (Tozzer 1941:127) worked in groups, strapped to backstrap looms, likely in shaded courtyard spaces. This transformation of raw cotton – as well as feathers, agave, and just about any other spinnable material – played an extremely important role in the political economy of the palace. Although palace prestation scenes painted on polychrome vases invariably depict men offering textiles to a seated male ruler, women produced the textiles and were ultimately responsible for their quality.

Several depictions of royal women wearing elaborately embroidered *huipiles* – Lady Xook of Yaxchilán being the most famous image – indicate that the technical skill and artistry of weaving among royal women existed on a level of connoisseurship and also reinforces the notion that weaving and royal female identity were tightly intertwined. The reconstructions offered by Thomas Tolles (Looper and Tolles 2000:39–104) of 54 intricate and distinct Late Classic woven *huipil* designs based upon known monuments and pictorial polychromes provides evidence of the skill level under consideration here. Females seem to have taken their identities as weavers into the afterlife in contrast to royal males who might boast of the number of captives taken during martial campaigns in their hieroglyphic title string – thus indicating that captive taking was part of male elite identity – but they seldom were buried with battle regalia (see McAnany 2001:136–138). Some extremely important gender constructs – of masculinity and femininity – appear to have been materialized in death accoutrements, but this area of study has received scant attention (see Ardren and Hixson 2006; Houston 2009 for important contributions).

A salient example of a royal female buried with weaving bones and brocade picks comes from Tomb 3 of Yaxchilán. The mortuary crypt was placed beneath the floor of the central room of Structure 23, and appears to be that of well-known Lady Xook. The following burial items were placed with this 40- to 45-year-old female: 3 cacao beans, 81 bone needles, 2 bivalves, 431 greenstone beads, 1 greenstone disk, 34 obsidian blades, 4 greenstone earspools, 3 pearls, and 1 bone awl incised with glyphs (García Moll 2004:269). Even though the greenstone and pearls likely were part of her raiment, the bone needles, bone awl, and obsidian blades were tools that she probably used during her lifetime. Although obsidian blades are rarely discussed in terms of female tool use, these sharp-edged flakes would have been an indispensable cutting tool for weaving and brocading in the same way that a seamstress or tailor needs a sharp pair of scissors.

Another example of a royal female buried with weaving gear comes from a tomb deep in the bowels of the Copán acropolis where a mature woman (likely in her sixties) was laid to rest amid three concentrations of bone needles – two placed on the eastern side of the tomb along with a bone spatula and one in a central deposit that also contained "tabbed jade and shell rings that may have served as loom weights" (Bell 2002:97). Tools for dyeing textiles also were placed in the tomb: two small pigment grinding stones on the western side of the tomb and two miniature jars for pigment storage near the entrance to the chamber (Bell 2002:99). The woman in this so-called Margarita tomb is thought to have been the wife of K'inich Yax K'uk' Mo' (fifth-century founder of the Copán dynasty) and the mother of K'inich Popol Hol (Bell 2002:99). Just as the goddess, Chak Chel, is depicted in the sixteenth-century Madrid Codex as a mature female weaver and seer, so 11 centuries earlier this female progenitor of a dynastic line may also have practiced divination – two slate and pyrite mirrors were placed in her burial crypt (Bell 2002:99; Nielsen 2006). While the mirrors, no doubt, indexed aesthetics of courtly beauty, they also are acknowledged to be tools of divination and so suggest an identity for this woman as one who engaged in both weaving and divination. The continued importance of this Early Classic royal woman to her descendants long after her death is indicated by the fact that access to her tomb was maintained through at least two subsequent and expansive building programs during which the present Copán acropolis began to take shape (Bell 2002:96); some of the weaving and sewing tools may have been offerings left during tomb revisitations.

These two examples of royal females buried with the tools of textile production are complemented by the recovery of similar tools (often broken) from excavation of high-status residential compounds (e.g., Chase et al. 2008; Halperin 2008; Hendon 1997). Krochock (2002:160) has noted that 31 spindle whorls were recovered from excavations by Bolles (1977:237) at Las Monjas complex of Chichén Itzá. Although Krochock (2002:160) suggests that this complex was the palace structure of a royal female whom she calls Lady Ton Ajaw, this interpretation is confounded by the martial subject of the painted wall murals, the physical features of the second-story rooms (many of which contain wall niches for deity images) and the fact that in situ hieroglyphic texts cite the dedication of deity shrines by women on behalf of their female ancestors (Plank 2004:179–225). Regrettably, Bolles (1977:237) provides no contextual information whatsoever regarding the provenience of the whorls, many of which contain carved avian designs, which may indicate that they were used to spin thread made of bird feathers (as per McCafferty and McCafferty 2000:47). Plank (2004:214) suggests that the whorls may have been used to spin thread for cloth used to dress the "numerous god images that were undoubtedly housed in the niches of the Second Story [of Las Monjas]." A distinct possibility, this example represents a kind of production

FIGURE 6.8 Stone mosaic of a textile diamond pattern on the West Building of the Nunnery Quadrangle at Uxmal (photo by author).

for ritual consumption that is analogous to the *ritual mode of production* discussed by Spielmann (2002, 2008). To the south in the Andean region, female weavers sequestered in the royal *aqllawasi* of Cuzco wove cloth specifically for imperial ritual practice. The trope of weaving is invoked in Maya hieroglyphic and ethnohistorical texts in reference to the wrapping of bannerstones (stelae) and tying of sacred bundles; the under–over weave pattern itself (*pop*) is a symbol of authority. Carved in stone mosaics, this pattern decorates the front of several Puuc structures such as the West Building of the Nunnery Quadrangle at Uxmal (Figure 6.8; Trevelyan and Forbes 2002). Plank (2004:180) suggests that entire building facades may have been "dressed" for ritual events as was the case in the Inka imperial capital.

Because of the poor preservation of textiles in a humid tropical environment, cloth production must be inferred from iconographic depictions and production tools. Regardless of the lack of textile preservation, however, we cannot lose sight of the fact that much of this female-gendered practice went into the production of what likely were considered inalienable possessions in the same sense that Weiner (1992) used the term. Many of the elaborately embroidered *huipiles* and cloaks worn by royal women and the capes and tunics worn by royal men were inherited possessions as were their jade jewels, headdresses, warrior regalia, and deity impersonation costumes. The tropical environment did impose a "shelf life" on perishable items but it is likely that even in a tattered state, folded and placed in a wooden box, the *huipiles* of Lady Xook – textile masterpieces in any culture – would have been considered precious and inalienable.

Not all textiles were produced to be held as the inalienable possessions of a royal house; many left the palace compounds as gifts, symbols of alliance, tribute offerings to dominant royal courts, or possibly in outright trade arrangements. We can presume that certain elite or royal women were particularly well known for the fine quality of their textiles, which would have been highly desired. In the Postclassic Mexican highlands, textiles were exchanged among elites on the occasion of betrothals, births, funerals, and religious holidays (McCafferty and McCafferty 1999:113). Textiles lubricated the political economy of the palace, and elite female identity and social difference were materialized in these aesthetically pleasing woven constructions.

Crafting Authority

While the authority of elite females, no doubt, was enhanced by their prowess in weaving and brocading, the crafting of authority within a palatial – or even a residential – context was not restricted to textiles or to women. According to Sahagún (1950–1982, Book 8:45), Mocteuczoma II told his children who were not in line to inherit the throne to "learn well" the skills of artisans (cited in McCafferty and McCafferty 1999:111). That Mesoamerican palaces were places of artisans is only now beginning to be appreciated despite the long-standing accounts of the cultural importance given to the skills of artisanship by the Postclassic Mexica (who referred to the earlier Toltecs as the great artificers) as well as the Postclassic Mixtec who prized craftsmanship (Pohl 2003). Folan, Gunn, and Domínguez Carrasco (2001:234–244) have suggested that the royal court of Calakmul – specifically Structures II and III – were veritable hives of craft production. A well-crafted item materialized elite identity and authority as nothing else could do. Traditionally, archaeological literature on craft production differentiates primarily between independent and attached specialists, the former working independently to produce for exchange while the latter is attached through vertical obligations to a higher authority for whom items are crafted (Brumfiel and Earle 1987:6). In reality, craft production encompasses several variations, two of which include elite and commoner artisans for whom quality – not quantity or efficiency – is the critical factor. Output might be very low and crafted items may not leave their place of crafting (i.e., they could become inalienable possessions of a household), or they may be given away as gifts as often as they are exchanged; nevertheless, the identity and authority of the artisan is profoundly entangled in the materiality of that which is crafted (see expanded discussion of this point in Chapter 7). The weaving bones of prominent females provide a telling and personalized example of the manner in which a woman could enhance her agency, and her legacy after death, through prowess in textile production.

We have dwelt at some length on textile production because (due to the lack of archaeological preservation of textiles) the authority of ancestral Maya female weavers has been somewhat underappreciated (see Joyce 2000a for review). But artisanship was ubiquitous in the palace sector among both males and females. After conducting a wear-pattern analysis of stone tools from the epicentral structures of Aguateca, Aoyama (2007:24) found evidence that "artistic and craft production appears to have been a common pursuit among Classic Maya elites at Aguateca, including courtiers of the highest rank and even members of the royal family." To this evidence culled from excavations, we can add sculptors, painters, calligraphers, and especially potters who produced the most ubiquitous and durable material remains. These artisans may have been the same courtiers who are shown on polychrome palace scenes as formally receiving tribute, keeping account books of tribute, and fulfilling other kinds of bureaucratic roles (discussed in more detail in Chapter 9) that kept the palace operating. Hieroglyphic and ethnohistorical evidence has been marshaled in support of the notion that many of these artisan roles were male-gendered (Clark and Houston 1998). Given the strong ethnographic evidence of female-gendered pottery production in the Guatemala Highlands (see Reina and Hill 1978, among others), however, it is difficult to imagine a Maya past without female potters. In reference to royal calligraphy carved into stone, there is evidence that up to eight calligraphers might work on a piece (Stuart 1989) and leave the signature of a group effort in their carved names; signed pieces also are known from figural polychrome pottery. These signatures have been translated as those of males (although the pronominal referent may be nondeterminative rather than assertive). Regardless of this semantic ambiguity, signed pottery and stone carvings are analogous to monogrammed weaving bones in that they indicate just how profoundly the identity of the artisan was entangled with the crafted piece.

There are indications that by the Postclassic period, artisan production had became more commercialized – a quality of statehood that is akin to the Holy Grail for some anthropologists (see Smith 2004:77). During lowland Maya Classic times, however, Miller and Martin (2004:65) propose that "the conflict between agricultural and commercial wealth" was played out metaphorically in the oppositional values, personalities, and appearances of the maize god and God L. The former was associated with the agricultural wealth sustained by a bounteous harvest, whereas the latter was symbolic of wealth accrued by the shrewd trading of luxury goods such as cacao, cotton, and jade. This conflict is discussed at greater length in Chapter 8, particularly in reference to a distinction between Classic and Postclassic Maya economies as proposed several decades ago by Sabloff and Rathje (1975). This topic deserves to be revisited in depth. Here, I can only allude to the profound economic changes that characterized this transition.

Lands of the Realm

Any treatment of a palace economy would be incomplete if it did not consider the link between the authority of the royal court and the lands and people of the realm. Here, a classic ethnographic study of Lozi royal kingship conducted by Gluckman and cited in Isaac (1993:443–444) may be relevant. "Commoners think of themselves as permanently indebted to the king for the land on which they live and its wild and domesticated products which sustain them. The Lozi say this is why they gave tribute and service to the king" (Gluckman 1959:61–62). The perceived indebtedness to the king is reminiscent of the "original debt" (discussed in Chapter 3) in which humans can find themselves in relation to deities. The structural parallel between deities and rulers can expand, it seems, to include the lands of the realm and is most acute when a ruler is perceived as sacred or *k'uhul*, as in the Classic Maya case. The fact that Maya rulers were depicted standing on top of *wits* deities (Figure 6.6) can be interpreted to mean that they asserted eminent domain over their realm. In effect, they were *yahwal balamil* or "owner of the earth" much as Tzotzil Maya today perceive the earth deity to be a wealthy, touchy Ladino who controls vast material wealth. Any requested tax and tribute then becomes part of a debt owed in return for using the lands of the king. There is no hard evidence to support this suggestion, and there were plenty of areas within the Maya lowlands that likely were beyond the reach of divine rulers; nevertheless, the ethos of sacred rulership – which certainly existed during the Classic period – carries certain implications. In the Mediterranean region, the Mycenaean case – for which there are plenty of economic texts – is instructive. There, the king is never cited as owning the lands of the realm, although Chadwick (1976:116) opines that "in a monarchical society all property is ultimately held by others at the king's pleasure."

It may seem simplistic to reduce the constant negotiations, petitions, and compromises that must have been part of the daily routine at royal courts to a simple, hierarchical version of a patron–client relationship but there is some hieroglyphic support for this construct. Houston and Stuart (2001:56) note that hieroglyphic compound *u-chab-j-iiy'* (which occurs in statements in which a subordinate ruler is linked with a superordinate) is based on a Tzotzil root *chab,* meaning "his spreading of manure/cultivating." In other words, an agricultural trope was used for supervision. Thus, a hierarchical relationship seems key to understanding a political interaction that is phrased in agricultural terms. Controlling and governing subordinates was perceived as akin to cultivating land – and both were the source of great wealth. Although higher-order control of land might be asserted by a sacred ruler with rare contestation, control of the people inhabiting and using that land could never be taken for granted but must be constantly cultivated lest families decamp for "greener pastures," as seems to have occurred repeatedly throughout the Preclassic, Classic, and Postclassic periods based on the cyclic patterns of polity waxing and waning. As Wilk has noted in reference to wealth differentials among Q'eqchi' Maya of southern Belize, control of labor is the critical factor in accumulating wealth; the material trappings are the products of that control. "Wealth in pigs and a large house are the attributes of a particular social position – being the head of a household cluster. This social position and the material wealth are the products of the head's control of the labor of junior members of the cluster" (Wilk 1983:111).

Based on the large size of plazas located near royal courts – some of which probably accommodated up to 20,000 people (such as the West Plaza of Tikal), ritual performance that was regal in scale and theatrical in effect took place close to royal courts and likely served to woo a constituency in order to maintain a well-populated realm. Large-scale feasting events constitute another type of enfranchisement or solidarity-building ritual; however, available evidence indicates that feasting at the royal court tended to be an exclusive rather than inclusive practice.

PARTY IN THE PALACE

Elsewhere (McAnany and Plank 2001:94–97), I have discussed the daily needs of the palace in terms of food preparation. and, in an earlier study of ethnohistorical evidence from early Colonial Yucatán (McAnany 1995:137–139), I discussed how female commoners were obliged to provide domestic labor in the homes of nobility on a rotating basis (also see Gero 1992 for a discussion of gender ideology and feasting at Queyash Alto, Peru). When a large feast was under preparation, labor needs would have skyrocketed, and we can imagine that the ability of royal females to amass enough labor to grind the needed maize and cacao, shape the tamales, ferment the balché or corn beer, roast the meats, and so forth, provided a test of their charisma, the loyalty of their followers, and/or the muscle behind their calls for assistance. A scene from the Calakmul murals is relevant here: a royal female clothed in a diaphanous, cartouche-adorned *huipil* is shown reaching toward a large *olla* of *atole* borne on the head of a crouching female who is clad in very simple clothing (Boucher and Quiñones 2007:Figure 3). Might this show preparation of cuisine for a banquet? The feasting that transpired in royal courts appears to have been primarily among peers, and even though the prepared foods probably were not foreign to Maya commoners, the cuisine was labor-intensive to prepare (featuring items such as tamales or pipián sauce, the latter made from ground squash seeds), or difficult/expensive to acquire (such as hunted game or cacao) and thus was consumed much less frequently or not at all by commoners. Did this constitute a "hierarchical cuisine" in the sense that Goody (1982:133) has discussed in reference to Western Europe and Imperial China? Without putting too fine of a point on it, we can probably assume that much of the food described by Sophie Coe (1994) in *America's First Cuisines*, in fact, was elite cuisine because it was described by Spaniards who were being feted by indigenous royalty among the Mexica and throughout the Yucatán. Even so, the amount of meat served during these special feasts apparently was much less than Spaniards – with a palate attuned to domesticated cattle, sheep, and goats – were accustomed to eating, and they complained of the perpetual Lenten diet of the Americas (Coe 1994:153). As discussed earlier in this chapter, in the section "Dietary Distinctions," isotopic data from Classic-period faunal remains indicates that a shortage of meat at royal courts was alleviated, to some extent, by "kept" dogs and deer that could be corn-fed in preparation for a feast or a ritual offering (White et al. 2004:158).

In addition to a sixteenth-century description of feasting practices by Bishop Diego de Landa (Tozzer 1941:92) in which he emphasizes the frequency and opulence of this form of commensal politics, there are frequent references to anniversary celebrations in the hieroglyphic corpus, and we can assume that a large feast in the royal court was a part of such celebrations. A nighttime feast at the royal court of Piedras Negras – in which a chocolate drink was served – is specifically mentioned on Panel 3, and the text is accompanied by a carving of a throne room filled with honored guests from nearby Usumacinta kingdoms (Houston and Stuart 2001:69–73). In the Colonial K'iche' document called the *Popol Vuh*, there are innumerable references to feasting, and Tedlock (2002:167) suggests that the compilers of the *Popol Vuh* may themselves have born the title *nim chokoj*, which means "great convener of banquets" or "master of ceremonies," and could also have held the additional office of *k'amalb'e* or "road guide," a term for a marriage spokesperson (Tedlock 2002:167). From the *Popol Vuh*, this passage highlights the role of feasting in royal marriage arrangements: "They began feasting and drinking over the blossoming of their daughters. This was the way the ones they named the 'Three Great Houses' stayed together. They drank their drinks there and ate their corn there, the payment for their sisters, payment for their daughters. ... They ate, they feasted inside their palaces" (Tedlock 1985:183).

Such feasting among peers – with persons of equal status with whom a marriage alliance might be negotiated – fits within what Dietler (2001:85–88) terms diacritical feasting: a type of commensal politics that serves to separate a class or sector from the rest of society by virtue of a distinctive cuisine or exclusive locale at which the feast is enjoyed, in this case, within a palace context. But such feasting is about more than delayed reciprocity or bride price; it also served to reinforce existing power relations and establish new alliances. A variant on what Firth (1983:101) calls "indebtedness engineering," feasting creates a network of obligations that could be called in at a later time, if needed. Feasting as practiced in the Mexica imperial capital of Tenochtitlán is thought to have served to impress territorial nobles and enfranchise them into the imperial system.

A growing number of Maya scholars (e.g., Houston et al. 1992; Reents-Budet 2000) have suggested that the massive dumps associated with palace complexes – often containing a high number of conjoinable vessel sherds as well as a high density of faunal material – may not be the result of long-term accretional discard but rather of concentrated episodic events, in effect party refuse. Palace complexes at Tikal, Palenque, Altun Ha, and Buena Vista del Cayo, for example, feature nearby associated dumps that may have formed from a series of massive discard events following palace feasts. LeCount (2001:947) has interpreted the variation in form among ceramic assemblages from Xunanatunich as indicative of the relative importance of private feasting events – specifically those involving chocolate drinking. The cylindrical vase form was found in inflated proportions relative to other vessel shapes near the Castillo pyramid complex. Hendon (2003:226–227) argues, based on locational patterns in ceramic forms, that feasting – and preparation for feasting – was a central activity of elite residential compounds at Copán and provided a "vehicle for competition."

In summary, it seems that increased attention to midden deposits associated with palace architecture is yielding insights regarding the ubiquity – and perhaps in the future the periodicity – of feasting events. Diacritical feasting materialized social difference in a spectacular manner. Feasting practices certainly promoted solidarity among those who ruled and likely smoothed over many grievances and sutured political fractures. Despite such practices, the authority of those who ruled could be and was contested, particularly during the eighth and ninth centuries.

CONTESTING THE NATURAL AUTHORITY OF THE COURT

Dirks (1991) has suggested that, contra Durheim's notion of ritual as reinforcing social order, ritual practice in southern India can provide a venue for contesting and subverting power. Rather than accepting ritual as constitutive of social order, Dirks (1991:219–220) situates ritual in a world of hegemony and struggle and views the formulaic qualities of ritual practice as a potent arena for the construction of power and a site of struggle between authority and counterclaims. Although one is hard-put to detect ritual practice that is clearly antistructure in the carnivalistic sense discussed by Kelly and Kaplan (1990:121), evidence is mounting that there was an assault on the natural authority of the royal court particularly during the Late-Terminal Classic period when social instability rocked the world of Classic Maya nobility.

Looper (2003:200) characterizes the elaboration of the sacred center of Quirigua undertaken by K'ahk' Tiliw as an effort to promote "an image of economic prosperity for the polity, fostered by the king's leadership." Indeed, the construction of new monumental shrines and the carving of new stelae provided material evidence that all was well and prospering in the realm. In contrast, the ritual burning of monumental shrines and defiling of ancestral tombs could create a mood of despair and economic depression, a failure of the ruler both to safeguard the inalienable possessions of the royal line and to provide a prosperous livelihood for those of the realm. The potent images of Mexica warriors torching the pyramid of a conquered *altepetl* (Figure 5.3) bespeak the reality of this ritual assault on the natural authority of a royal court in ancient Mesoamerica. Among lowland Classic Maya, such assaults on authority are recorded in statements of royal captive-taking as in 738 C.E. when K'ahk' Tiliw of Quirigua succeeded in contesting the power of his overlord at Copán by taking Waxaklajuun Ub'aah K'awiil, ruler of Copán, captive and sacrificing him. Royal iconography and texts indicate that captives generally were marched back to the royal courts of the victors, stripped of their finery, and subjected to humiliation and sometimes torture. The ballcourt appears to have been the place at which captives were displayed and possibly made to play a mock game. Taube (2003:481) suggests that the chaos of warfare – often conducted in the forested areas between capitals – was offset by bringing a captive into the royal court to play the ballgame and ultimately be sacrificed, specifically that this practice represents a "vivid portrayal of channeling dangerous alien powers – in this case the foreign captives – for the spiritual well-being of the community."

In reference to the K'iche' Maya play – Rab'inal Achi – Tedlock (2002:174–177, 2003) examined the manner in which the cup of cacao drink offered to a captive before he is sacrificed is a tropic inversion of the rituals of betrothal, structurally identical but with tragically different results (see epigraph at beginning of Chapter 9). A marriage alliance between two houses can bring the peace, but the sacrifice of a noble captured during martial conflict can only bring more conflict.

To the eyes of an archaeologist who excavates an ancestral seat of power more than a thousand years later, efforts to terminate the authority of a court may appear only as subtle signs in excavated deposits. Joyce and Weller (2007) suggest that the so-called squatter deposits found in palace precincts during the Terminal Classic at both highland and lowland Mesoamerica sites are interpretable as active repudiation of authority or, at least, resistance against existing political authority. Other indicators interpretable as challenge to extant hierarchy include an unusual density of charcoal along the front face of a pyramid, a burned stucco facade, a disturbed tomb, or scattered human remains that bear evidence of high status in the form of inlaid teeth and a cranium shaped to resemble that of the maize deity. Such archaeological finds are the result of ritual activities to eliminate, rather than to maintain, a social order and have been suggested to have been the cause of a disturbed tomb at Yaxuna (Ambrosino 2003) and the scattered human remains at a site called Hershey in the Sibun Valley of Belize (Harrison-Buck et al. 2007).

The natural authority of the Late Classic Maya court also was under assault from the growth and expansion of a new ideology materialized in circular shrine structures that appear to have been related to the expansion into the Maya region of highland Mexican religious and mercantile practices centered on a deity called Quetzalcoatl (Harrison-Buck 2007; McAnany 2007b; Ringle et al. 1998). Thought by some to have heralded a trend toward greater commercialization of the Maya economy, circular shrines were constructed during the Terminal Classic period at strategic locales in which a prized commodity – such as cacao – could be harvested or extracted. Whether this new ethos of mercantilism completely undermined the authority of Classic Maya nobility or simply weakened an already precarious power structure is not completely clear, but the manner in which ritual and commerce appear to have been wedded in this new ideology effectively contested the authority of Classic Maya royal courts.

7

Social Identity and the Daily Practice of Artisan Production

> Truly now,
> Double thanks, triple thanks,
> That we've been formed, we've been given
> Our mouths, our faces,
> We speak, we listen,
> We wonder, we move,
> Our knowledge is good, we've understood
> What is far and near,
> And we've seen what is great and small
> Under the sky, on the earth.
> Thanks to you we've been formed,
> We've come to be made and modeled,
> Our grandmother, our grandfather.
>
> On the making of the first humans by the Maker, the Modeler, from *The Popol Vuh*; D. Tedlock 1985:147 trans.; see also Christenson 2007:199 trans.

And so it started – according to the K'iche' Maya book of genesis – when the Maker, the Modeler, first formed humans and gave the species the ability to speak, to know, to see, and to give reverence to their Maker. This generative action of making and modeling would be recapitulated by Maya descendants of the first Grandmother and first Grandfather every time a potter crafted a water jar, a weaver finished a *huipil*, and a stone worker polished a jadeite earflare. Crafting objects – a quintessential human activity – is an intimate and creative process regardless of whether the object is crafted according to ancestral or cutting-edge techniques. Notions of personal identity, gender roles, and position within society are profoundly entangled with crafted objects that provide a mirror, a materialization, of complex situational and relational forces that underwrite the very process of fabrication. The first humans described in the epigraph for this chapter were able to know, to see, and to wonder; in other words, they were able to learn. In like fashion, the knowledge and skills necessary to craft items – to be culturally competent in this manner – were learned from elders through direct instruction and by observation. With the hindsight perspective of archaeology, the fact that a craft such as pottery jar fabrication could by fashioned with very few changes over a time span as long as 200 years indicates that such skills and knowledge passed through generations of potters with remarkable replication. The very ethos of artisanship itself is a social construct historically referenced in the Maya region as "*costumbre*" – cultural convention – that can include an *oficio* or economic specialization that makes one "an active guardian of the unique community heritage" (Reina and Hill 1978:19). But *costumbre* drills deeply into the entangled metaphysics of crafting as Reina and Hill (1978:233) observe: "For Indian [*sic*] potters, religion and economics are not separate categories. Rather, they have become one: there is religion in pottery making, in selling, and in all aspects of existence." As we shall see, Maya ritual performance often is a vital part of crafting in the same way that Bradley (2005:33, 210) has argued in reference to prehistoric Europe. As a result of this entanglement, the expression "ritual mode of production" has particular salience when applied to practices of Maya artisans (Spielmann 2002 after Rappaport 1984[1968]).

Perhaps more than any other topic within archaeology, the study of crafts and of artisans speaks to the agency of those who produced crafted items as part of their social practice. After all, the fabrication of tools was once considered the watershed event that separated the sapient line from primate cousins less inclined toward the manipulation of their material environment. We are a species of makers, of modelers. As archaeologists, we tend to focus on the finished product and the debris piles left by the creative process of crafting. Increasingly, however, archaeologists are calling for more attention to the agency of the makers themselves and the social and political relations within which their productive efforts were situated (Clark 1995:286; Costin 1998:4; Dobres 2000; Hruby and Flad 2007; Ingold 2000; Shimada 2007; Tringham 1996:235–236, among others). The cultural competency involved in making things for others to use or wear, in crafting objects in an expert fashion, has been called "craft specialization." With a direct channel to the cultural logic of V. Gordon Childe, this topic has suffered the misfortune of having been too close to Adam Smith (but see Smith and Schreiber 2005:189 for a contrastive viewpoint). Perhaps because we sense that making things is an innately human proclivity, it does not seem a stretch to conceptualize past artisans as having operated according to the same logic that shapes production within a capitalist ethos. In this manner, artisans of the past have been converted into faceless producers akin to assembly line workers who toiled alongside the *Vanity Fair* of Victorian England's conspicuously consuming elites. Such culture-bound models have come under fire (see Clark 1995; Costin 1998; Inomata 2001), but they are part of the history of this study, still wield tremendous influence, and thus cannot be ignored. Consequently, a selective history of how archaeologists have wrestled with this King Kong of a topic is provided here, to be followed by an in-depth examination of artisanship in ancient Maya society – both at home and at court.

PROXIMITY OF ARTISANSHIP TO CAPITALIST PRODUCTION

In our study of past economies, there is a perilous tendency to "naturalize" capitalism and to impute to past fabricators the same goals and principles that have underwritten the global expansion of capitalism. Two of these principles – well illustrated by Adam Smith's (1991[1776]:5) description of a factory for producing pins – are standardization and efficiency, which were conceived by Smith as a further development of a primordial division of labor. Within capitalism, these goals of production apply primarily to items deemed utilitarian or those that could be produced within an assembly line mode of production as opposed to the fabrication – or as we tend to say "creation" – of items construed as artworks. The latter are produced in a manner that is opposed to standardization and efficiency and with an emphasis on singularity and labor intensivity.

Thorstein Veblen is most often cited as the first to comment upon these two contrastive modes of production, particularly in relation to the importance of luxury goods among the leisure class; those items that promote "invidious comparison" (Clark and Parry 1990:319 on Veblen). Veblen's *Theory of the Leisure Class* (1934[1899]) is squarely seated within the social climate of late nineteenth-century capitalism with no pretension of validity for noncapitalist systems of production. Yet, the archaeological study of crafting, for the most part, can be characterized as having operated within a paradigm only slightly modified from Smith and Veblen, both of whom offered astute but culture-bound analyses of capitalist modes of production. Under the "Smith–Veblen" paradigm, there is an emphasis on standardization and efficiency (S & E) of production for utilitarian goods. This emphasis comes through clearly whenever an archaeological study of production technology is undertaken.

Second and following Veblen, archaeologists are prone to dichotomize material items into two classes: utilitarian and prestige (also called status or luxury). Utilitarian goods generally are thought to be amenable to analysis according to principles of S & E, while those deemed prestige or luxury are analyzed according to principles of skill intensivity and connoisseurship in which the value of an object increases in direct proportion to the amount of time expended in crafting and sometimes the distant and exotic nature of the raw material (see Malinowski 1961[1922]:173 on hypertrophy and Helms 1993:13–18, among others). So, the split (as methodologically applied) between utilitarian and prestige goods seems to be rooted, at least partially, in the analysis of capitalist forms of production. Of course, labor-intensive production of highly valued goods that often are linked to status is not exclusive to capitalism but can be found in just about all kinds of economies across the cultural spectrum (see Malinowski 1961[1922]:173 in reference to the Trobriand Islands and Clark and Parry 1990 for a comprehensive survey based on the Human Relations Area Files). Likewise, ancient crafters sometimes *were* guided by principles of efficiency and standardization (see Wright 1998 for a Mesopotamian example). Masson and Rosenswig (2005:381) note, furthermore, that standardization per se – as in Maya Postclassic pottery production – could be the result of a small group of crafters with a large distribution net or spatially dispersed artisans fabricating objects for which canons of technology and decoration are widely shared. Significantly, the split between utilitarian and prestige goods may have little validity for past contexts in which artisans construed the practice of crafting in terms that were more akin to pursuing a vocation and did not encompass the capitalist contrast between assembly line and artistic production. Much conceptual work remains to be done in order to disentangle the archaeological study of crafting from the cultural logic of capitalism.

No doubt the most influential twentieth-century archaeologist to weigh in on the topic of crafting was V. Gordon Childe (1950:11) who envisioned full-time specialists to have been a hallmark of the urban revolution in the "Old World." Childe clearly was in a quandary regarding the urbanization process in the Maya lowlands as the following quote shows, "the minimum definition of a city, the greatest factor common to the Old World and the New will be substantially reduced and impoverished by the inclusion of the Maya" (Childe 1950:9). Regardless of his underappreciation of civilizations of the Americas, Childe proposed global benchmarks for urbanization. The presence of full-time specialists formed benchmark number two. Childe imagined that the rich surpluses generated by the "urban revolution" liberated craft specialists from patronage relations, a trajectory that, as Tringham (1996:234) has pointed out, proved to be false again and again. Moreover, the stark distinction that Childe imagined between Neolithic self-sufficient villages and urban interdependence of production activities has now come to be viewed as the "economic fiction of self-sufficient social groups" (Clark 1995:270). In reality, there was greater interdependence among Neolithic villages than Childe imagined and urban entities can exist and thrive independent of the presence of full-time specialists. Unfortunately, the shadow of V. Gordon Childe looms large and much ink was spilled during the last half of the twentieth century by archaeologists trying to persuade colleagues that a particular archaeological context constituted full-time specialization and thus prima facie evidence of civilization in the Childean sense. Case studies that provided a method for such evaluations – such as Evans (1978) – became touchstones upon which archaeological inferences were constructed.

During the 1980s, Earle (1981) and then Brumfiel and Earle (1987) codified two types of specialized production – independent and attached – based on demand structure and relations of production. Conceptually, this codification shifted emphasis from the number of hours per day involved in production (that is, full-time or part-time) to the origins of the social demand for crafted objects. As an independent crafter, one produced for an "unspecified demand crowd," while an attached specialist produced for a patron to whom she/he was "contractually bound" and likely resided in close proximity (Brumfiel and Earle 1987:5). Conceptually refreshing for its time, this framework was expanded considerably by Costin (1991:8–9); however, it suffers two major limitations: (1) it does not encompass the full range of social relations under which specialized crafting occurred/occurs, and (2) in placing emphasis on demand structure, it flirts dangerously with the cultural logic of supply-and-demand capitalism, which cannot be assumed to have greased the wheels of "industry" in the past (see Clark 1995:279–287 for extended discussion of this topic and Lewis 1996:359 for a defense of the universal applicability of "social origin of demand"). Not long thereafter, the lack of fit between this framework and archaeological case studies became an object of discussion among archaeologists. Sinopoli (1988, 1998, 2003), for instance, noted that in the case of Vijayanagra (a medieval empire in southern India), specialization might be more accurately characterized as administered and could be centralized or noncentralized; moreover, administered production – which most closely approximated attached specialization – might be arranged on a purely voluntary basis. To further complexify artisan activity, there likely were types of specialization that were neither independent nor attached but rather embedded within kinship structures (as with pottery and panpipe production near the Andean city of Tiwanaku; Janusek 1999) or conducted by elites themselves (rather than their minions) who crafted highly valued items for the purposes of keeping, gifting, trading, or as tribute obligations as was the case on the Northwest Coast of North America (Ames 1995), at the lowland Maya site of Aguateca (Inomata 2001), and among the Mixtec of Postclassic México (Pohl 2003). In a similar spirit of amplifying our knowledge of production relations and contexts, Feinman and Nichols (1995) note that in ancient Oaxaca very intensive production took place within a domestic context. This observation conflicts with earlier Childean assertions that intensive production should take place in a factorylike environment as is the case with capitalist production. Based on ethnoarchaeological data on Luo pottery production in Kenya, Dietler and Herbich (1989:129) also note that "household industry is capable of an astonishing volume of production."

As the archaeological study of past fabricators approached the end of the twentieth century and the influence of V. Gordon Childe mellowed to intellectual legacy, archaeologists were really no closer to understanding ancestral makers and modelers. Formal models had limited reach and an abstract quality that belied the reality of the topic under study. A dramatically expanded archaeological and ethnographic record indicated a wide array of social and political relations within which items might be crafted and also situations in which attached and independent specialization coexisted side by side as relational postures adopted by a single crafter. Although standardization and efficiency might be serious concerns for maintaining factory production, these principles bore little salience for artisans who crafted using inherited recipes and techniques that had been handed down for generations and often stressed conservatism over innovation (Reina and Hill 1978:231).

On the other hand, archaeologists found plenty of evidence of skill-intensive items that had been produced using methods that pushed the edge of the envelope in terms of existing technologies. When linked to prestige, the significance of a crafted piece often resided in its uniqueness. To repeatedly produce unique pieces, one must innovate, an example being Late Classic Maya pictorial polychromes – a few even signed by the artist who created them (Stuart 1989:156–157; and more recently Reents-Budet 1998:74–75). Can ancestral technologies that were both traditional and innovative be married under a unified theory of craft production? Moreover, if the antiquity of craft specialists and thus societal interdependence was much greater than Childe had imagined – as it has been shown to be – then how do we explain the emergence of household, village, and urban interdependence that accompanies (or preempts) artisan production? Issues of interdependence and cooperation are key here as several authors have noted. According to Costin (2004:209), "Specialization is as much a social relation as it is an economic one, as it diminishes autonomy and creates new kinds of interdependences that underwrite complex forms of social integration." When conceived in this manner, should we view specialization as part of a general cultural evolution toward an economy of scale as Stanish (2004) suggests, or should we look to models that emphasize the materiality of ritual practice as Spielmann (2002) has suggested? These are very large questions that demand not only greater problematization but also extremely fine-grained archaeological studies of artisan-related contexts. Taking stock at the fin de siecle, Costin (1998:13) urged increased attention to artisan identity. The time was ripe for practice theory.

CRAFTING À LA MARX, BOURDIEU, GIDDENS, AND LATOUR

Social theory owes a great debt to Karl Marx, whose pioneering foray into the social relations of production continues to inform our constructs about past economies. Although explicitly interested in how relations changed upon the advent of capitalism and naïve in reference to ethnographic and archaeological materials relevant to noncapitalist economies (see discussion in Halperin 1994:15), Marx – nevertheless – struck a resonant chord in his analysis of capitalism as a mode of production in which producers were alienated from their products. For Clark and Parry (1990:297), the single most important characteristic of craft specialization is the alienation of producers from their goods whether voluntarily (as in independent specialization) or as a consequence of patronage-based production. With this Marxian perspective, the right of alienation over goods (Clark 1995:286, 298) or, as Giddens (1984:258) would phrase it, control of "allocative resources," becomes the central feature of the study of craft production. This framework for studying specialization goes a long way until we come up against the crafting of what Weiner (1992) refers to as inalienable goods and Godelier (1999) as the enigma of the gift. These are items such as elaborate and labor-intensive feather cloaks produced by the finest Polynesian craftpersons for an elite cadre. Such items materialize the power and "beauty" of a ruling cohort and were intended to remain inalienable possessions. The same kind of production likely underlies the elaborately brocaded *huipil* worn by Lady Xook on Lintel 24 of Yaxchilán (see further discussion in Chapter 8). The skill involved in its production surely indicates that it was made by a specialist artisan – perhaps Lady Xook herself – but alienation of that garment (voluntary or involuntary) probably was not part of the production plan. Once again, we are confronted with an exception to the rule, which leads us to agree with Sinopoli (1998:170) that "relations between institutions and craft producers were localized and situational."

Dobres (2000:127) characterizes social agency and practice as the "the heart and soul of technology." The active nature of crafting links readily with the concept of human agency; the repetitive practice and learned sequences that result in a highly skilled craftsperson provide a good working definition of Bourdieu's *habitus*. As Dietler and Herbich (1989:161) show by reference to contemporary Luo potters, craft production often is highly conservative, and the technology of production itself encodes a tremendous amount of social information akin to what we would call style but tend to restrict to the decorative field. Focusing on the process of crafting, Ingold (2000:68) argues that "the forms of objects are not imposed from above but grow from the mutual involvement of people and materials in an environment." On a fundamental level, the social practice of crafting is a generative process that entangles people possessing particular knowledge and skills with earthly materials. Because of this special skill and knowledge base, the goods that result (alienable or not) can be perceived as cultural or symbolic capital, a notion popularized by Bourdieu (1977:89, 171–173) and applied to elite Late Classic crafters of Aguateca (Inomata 2001:324).

So, there is power in crafting even within the framework of traditionalism in which much craft production occurs. But the "regulated improvisation" to which Bourdieu refers coexists with traditionalism and yet can result in innovation. In this regard, Lewis (1996:364–365) notes that innovation is inherently risky and increases the likelihood of production failure. Nonetheless, many items destined to circulate within a prestige or political-economy sphere are characterized by intricate and delicate designs that push the limits of technological possibilities and require an inordinate amount of skilled labor. For Lewis (1996:364–365), this assumption of risk by a patron sponsoring the crafting process is a key factor that distinguishes attached from independent production. From another perspective, we might observe that when crafting becomes entangled with prestige and competition, there is a premium on creating unique – if highly risky – goods. Generally, within such contexts, sufficient wealth (or surplus) exists to underwrite replacement "costs" should an innovative experiment fail. This type of production is radically different from that practiced by traditional Luo potters of Kenya who most often describe their craft as *tich matek* ("hard work"; Dietler and Herbich 1989:148) or traditional Maya potters of highland Guatemala whose attitude toward their craft was characterized by Reina and Hill (1978:251) as follows: "all the parties involved in pottery realize that to work through *costumbre* is a way to sustain life, although it does not create wealth." In these contexts, innovation can and does occur, but crafting techniques also can remain stable over hundreds of years.

Certainly, one can argue that traditional pottery production in postcolonial Guatemala is linked in a very clear and historically contingent manner to cultural survival. As such, this situation indicates the social and political entanglements that both constrain and enable artisanship and play a role in the valuation of traditionalism and innovation. Reina and Hill (1978:258) provide an insightful commentary on the social difficulties of an innovative Chinautla potter who in 1953 began to make figurines (called "urban ware") rather than traditional vessel forms: "For years Margarita and her adoptive family could not bring her marriage arrangement to a successful conclusion. One day – after her grandmother had died and after a great deal of pressure from her aunt – Margarita decided to change her public image and began to work on *tinajas* [traditional water jars] only. Within six months she was properly married." In other words, to become an innovative "maker and modeler" in Chinautla at this time was to step outside of socially acceptable behavior and to risk ones chances of successfully negotiating the rite of passage to adulthood and motherhood – marriage. Despite the observation by Reina and Hill (1978:262) of great "intellectual excitement among potters producing [innovative] urban wares," there were social ramifications to the rejection of reflexive daily practice (*costumbre*) in favor of artistic figurine crafting for an urban market. This example suggests that, in the deeper past, the contexts in which innovative crafting came to be valued also may have represented a break with the more traditional *habitus* of artisans. I dwell at some length on these differing ethos of artisanship because both were present in ancestral Maya society in which certain crafted goods – such as water jars – could retain the same form and technique of production for a thousand years while other goods – such as pictorial polychrome cylindrical vessels – were produced for less than 200 years. Innovation in form and surface decoration of the latter is consonant with their classification as Late Classic Maya prestige items that, as discussed in Chapter 9, were closely linked not only with social status but also with political competition.

The foregoing discussion is not intended to draw an absolute contrast between traditional and prestige goods nor to assert that traditional crafts are stodgy and unimaginative while items crafted with prestige or political competition in mind are innovative and artistic. One could cite plenty of examples to the contrary; the main point here is that the social and political context of production plays a very large role in crafting an ethos of artisanship and in setting parameters regarding traditionalism and innovation.

Crafting skill is only part of the story when it comes to goods made to circulate within prestige spheres. When items are fabricated to be moved within the context of political interaction and competition – as in the famed Kula ring of Melanesia – crafting is vitally important but so is the social history of an object (Kopytoff 1986:66–68). The story of who formerly possessed an item such as a shell arm band becomes as important as the quality of the crafted item. After Trobriand Islanders had a chance to read Malinowski's (1961[1922]) analysis of their storied trading network, several islanders commented that Malinowski had overemphasized the role of "magic" in Kula transactions and underemphasized the power of oratory – telling well the story of the social life of a shell item – in effecting a trade (Firth 1983:101). To be sure, the social context of conveyance is well developed within prestige spheres and, as in the Kula ring, can form a sphere that is partially or even totally distinct from other realms of trading and exchange. It is the political uses to which laboriously crafted objects are put that tends to result in this diacritical marking. Douglas and Isherwood (1996:95) describe prestige goods as "weapons of exclusion," while Clark and Parry (1990:296) refer to "conspicuous production" and Veblen (1934[1899]:68–101) to "privileged consumption" by a leisure class. All of these constructs represent attempts by social researchers to deal with what Appadurai (1986) termed the "social life of things" and how these materialities create and maintain social difference as veritable instruments of power relations. Latour (1999, 2005) has pushed this line of reasoning even further by ascribing agency to crafted things, noting how the construction of something as pedestrian as a speed bump changes human action. Characterizing human lives as existing within a web or network of human–nonhuman interaction, Latour comes close to (re)capturing the power and animism ascribed to nonhuman entities in traditional Mesoamerican cosmologies. Moreover, the bidirectionality of influence between humans and nonhumans – here referring specifically to crafted items – highlights an important message of this chapter. Namely, humans may be the crafters of objects but, once crafted, an item takes on a life of its own and the power to influence human interaction.

Suffice it to say that human crafting – especially that subset labeled "craft specialization" –is a topic as complex and varied as the social and political relations within which it is embedded. There is a need for more grassroots study of crafting – perhaps ethnoarchaeological – so that general frameworks may rest on firmer empirical foundations. In reference to his study of contemporary flint knappers in Irian Jaya, Stout (2002:696) comments that such studies do not provide answers about the past but allow us to frame productive questions. With these considerations in mind, we turn to ancestral Maya artisans.

ARTISAN PRODUCTION IN A "VALUE-ADDED" ECONOMY

As in all human societies, ancestral Maya crafters had a healthy appreciation for the social and political life of goods and the potent manner by which identity was expressed through crafted items. As Maya society flourished through the two millennia on either side of the Common Era, the number of craft specialties no doubt also grew so that "the body of users [was] significantly larger than the body of producers" as Dietler and Herbich (1989:148) have noted for specialized pottery producers in Luo villages. In the spirit of a reappraisal of older Childean notions, we can justify discarding the notion that Maya communities – or even households – were self-sufficient. Like the Neolithic villages envisioned by Childe, ancestral Maya communities also have been subjected to the fiction of self-sufficiency. Our archaeological methods are still developing in reference to discerning fine details of crafting, such as whether it was practiced on a household or community-wide basis (or both); however, future research, no doubt, will indicate that there was greater interdependence among Maya communities and more circulation of goods than generally thought. Some of our clearest examples of the preponderance of crafting activities at ancestral Maya sites – of stone tools at Colha, of court paraphernalia at Aguateca, of multiple village crafts at Ceren – have come to light because of the durability of lithic debris in the first example and rapid site abandonment due to extraordinary circumstances in the latter two cases. These examples represent the tip of an iceberg that will be fully revealed only with state-of-the-art sampling, retrieval, and analytical techniques.

In Chapter 4, the idea that households produce value in the sense of transforming raw materials into socially valued goods that can be worn, lived under, eaten, and so forth was introduced. Analogously, crafting is a very direct way of creating value that either stays with the house or circulates through trading, gifting, or tribute. Specialized skill and knowledge of material transformation is the human quality that creates this "added value." In this chapter, crafting in ancestral Maya society is examined in relation to the value of skilled work, as a dialogue with the deities, and as a potent constituent of social identity.

The Value and Prevalence of Skilled Work

The pervasive, Colonial notion of *costumbre* as it relates to the totality of existence as well as craft production among traditional highland Chiapas and Guatemalan Maya people was introduced earlier and will be elaborated later as it relates not only to an ethos of production but also to the manner in which ritual practice and identity are entangled with craft production and serve to establish parameters around the construction of value. The point here is not to ignore 500 years of repressive Colonial overrule but to propose that the Colonial Spanish term *oficio* (one's trade, function or religious office) provides a more insightful point of origin for engaging with the identity of ancient artisans than many other constructs.

In a survey of Colonial Yucatec Maya linguistic evidence for artisans, Clark and Houston (1998:44) found three relevant terms: *ah men*, "he who occupies himself, he who engenders"; *ah bolon hobon*, "he of the nine or many colors" (employed for female and male crafters); and *ah chuuen,* "he, the artificer." These terms clearly reflect the concept of artisans as creators, artificers of things of value, especially in reference to weaving and painting goods of many colors. When Clark and Houston (1998:41) tried to determine the exclusivity of these occupations, however, they were forced to conclude that "everyone was probably a specialist, or potentially so. Every competent adult in Yucatec society could probably practice a variety of crafts should he or she so choose, or circumstances dictate." While keeping in mind that the Colonial sources consulted by Clark and Houston were compiled by Spaniards interested in extracting large quantities of goods deemed valuable – such as cotton *mantas* – nevertheless, the notion that crafting was part of the identity of every culturally competent adult differs significantly from prevalent constructs that construe crafting to be either the last resort of land-disenfranchised farmers (who become independent specialists) or a pastime of minions who produce under the thumb of powerful and charismatic rulers (attached specialists). In reference to the Colonial period, Roys (1943:46) likewise has commented that a "man might make many things for his own use but manufacture for sale only the one thing for the production of which he was specially trained or naturally adept." Here, we can assume that Roys used a male pronoun as a gloss for both male and female crafters since female weavers produced one of the most desirable categories of goods – namely textiles – during the Colonial period.

The prevalence of skilled artisans who crafted highly valued goods appears to have been more widespread – at least during the early Colonial period – than is often supposed, which leads one to suspect that the transmission of crafting skills and knowledge between generations was an integral social practice that served to maintain a high level of cultural competency. The notion of apprenticeship and the concept of scaffolding in the learning and performance of artisan skills are highly relevant to archaeological artifact studies (see Crown 2007 for an example from the U.S. Southwest) and also have been applied to ethnoarchaeological cases (i.e., Stout 2002 on knappers in Irian Jaya). Tedlock and Tedlock (1985:121) propose that there exists a dialectical relationship between language and technology with K'iche' Maya artisans. Avoiding the term *costumbre,* the Tedlocks, nevertheless, suggest that there are metaphors or tropes that cut across media to express "intertextualities within and among such arts as instrumental music, storytelling, prayermaking, dream interpretation, divination, weaving, housebuilding, and horticulture" (Tedlock and Tedlock 1985:123). Such metaphors encode social practices of living, making, and modeling and can only be acquired through learning. Although one *oficio* may differ from another – that is, one may be a potter while another is a weaver – there are themes and a logic, one could call it *habitus*, that crosscut and unify the practice of crafting into a materialized whole. Moreover, among traditional Maya craftspersons, the process is conceived as an intimate interaction with natural forces that are animate in the same sense as was discussed in Chapter 3. Part of the value of crafting comes from this struggle with natural forces. Guatemalan Maya potters express it best when they relate that "'clay does not let itself' (*el barro no se deja*) be manipulated; the 'clay is alive.' Therefore, 'the clay is hard to dominate. It is a *lucha*, a struggle, but once it is fired the struggle ends and *se logró*, success follows. We potters must be able to dominate the clay as it resists its transformation'" (Reina and Hill 1978:236).

Artisanship as Dialogue with the Deities

There is another aspect of crafting that has only been alluded to thus far – the entangling of production with ritual practice. As the epigraph to this chapter indicates, the original creators are referred to as makers, modelers, and weavers; these generative acts are recapitulated when humans craft goods. Because of the manner in which crafting transforms raw materials, such creative acts must be done carefully and with proper respect for earthly supernatural forces, that is, there needs to be a dialogue with the deities while crafting is underway. Moreover, one of the best ways to initiate and maintain a dialogue is to offer (or sacrifice) to deities a precious thing, such as human blood or a beautifully crafted item – painted paper or woven cotton. In a nutshell, crafting can be viewed as godlike behavior, a transformative act and, therefore, a necessary occasion for making offerings.

Spielmann (2002) following Rappaport (1984[1968]) has characterized the entangled nature of crafting as a "ritual mode of production" and notes its prevalence among small-scale societies (those with complex social and political structures but lacking the trappings of a state) in which a large portion of societies' productive efforts may be channeled into the crafting of ritual paraphernalia and amassing of food and gifts for ritual feasting. Interestingly, some of the most aesthetically pleasing and technologically innovative types of crafting are undertaken in the context of a ritual mode of production, and these items – if not ritually deposited in a cache context – may circulate as heirloom pieces for many generations (see Spielmann 2002:200–201 for discussion of "enchanting objects" and Weiner 1992:83 on the production of ritually charged bark cloth). Some kinds of crafted items – such as deity icons or bark-cloth skirts – are more ritually charged than others and therefore are produced within more diacritically marked conditions. The well-known description by Bishop Diego de Landa of the ritual seclusion and auto-sacrifice surrounding the crafting of wooden icons in sixteenth-century Yucatán provides a case in point (Tozzer 1941:159–161).

Costin (1998:5) looks to the inherent risk of failure involved in the crafting process and to the desired efficacy of the crafted good to explain the entanglement between ritual and crafting, asserting that such links serve "to ensure the technical success of the manufacturing process or to imbue finished objects with the appropriate qualities and powers." In light of the discussion of Mesoamerican cosmology in Chapter 3, it may not be technological failure so much as supernatural testiness that supplicants hope to avoid by careful attention to ritual practice during the crafting process. In this regard, Reina and Hill (1978:232) provide a particularly evocative description of a potter's ritual in Highland Guatemala:

> Early in the morning, before the firing, the potter will walk into the countryside to visit a specific sacred site in the mountains, and there she will conduct a ritual of personal *costumbre*. She may proceed alone or may seek the help of a *chimán* (shaman). She attempts to maintain a balance with the elements of the universe. Potters believe that, if these personal rituals are observed, Nature will provide the raw materials for pottery production. Thus, devotion, reverence, and offerings enter into this experience and, through the ritual, the potter relates to the universe in submission and feels herself a part of all life.

The potter may not be hedging her bets before tackling a particularly recalcitrant bit of clay or attempting an innovative vessel form; rather, she performs ritual practice in order to situate herself (in her *oficio*) in the grand scheme of things, to maintain a dialogue – supplemented with offering and chants – with the deities. Tedlock and Tedlock (1985:129) make a similar observation about ritual practice among Highland Maya weavers: "Weavers pray before they begin work, invoking both celestial and earthly deities and explicitly situating their work within the *caj xucut caj, caj xucut ulew*, 'four corners of sky, four corner of earth.'" Weavers, like potters, are concerned with the link between their craft and the larger forces of life and structures of the universe, which, if not propitiated, can lead to dire consequences. Potters reported to Reina and Hill (1978:236–237) that the "process of pottery making is fragile (*algo delicado*)" – precisely the same term that indigenous Maya peoples use to refer to Ladinos and to deities, both of whom represent powerful and dangerous forces that cannot be controlled but only managed through careful attention and handling.

These examples indicate a linkage between Maya ritual practice and crafting (see Bradley 2005 for examples from prehistoric Europe). But while traditional artisans may be concerned to avoid offending the gods through trespass that occurs due to material transformation, some ancient Maya artisans are thought to have capitalized on the trope of crafters as creators with a capitol "C." In reference to the fabrication of Late Classic pictorial polychrome vessels, Reents-Budet (1998:71) suggests that the "elevated social identities of some of these artisans, in part created by a perceived connection between them and the gods of Creation, lent prestige to their crafted items." The creation scenes painted on some polychrome vessels are further interpreted as reinforcing this connection (Reents-Budet 1998:77–85). Inomata (2001:331), likewise, sees a link between crafting and supernatural power among elites of Late Classic Aguateca who left behind evidence of skilled crafting activities in nearly every elite structure excavated. Can these two radically different ethos of crafting observed from different points along the time continuum of Maya society be reconciled? That is, can an ethos of *costumbre* in reverence of animistic forces coexist with an ethos of human divinity, of making and modeling in impersonation of the great creation deities? Given the dedication to difference among Classic-period elites (see Chapter 6), this latter ethos likely did coexist with one akin to what Spaniards termed *costumbre*.

Beyond crafting as *costumbre* or as deity impersonation, however, there is a further and direct link between crafting and the ritual cycle. Reina and Hill (1978:248) note that crafters prepare goods for rituals and fiestas that can occupy up to one-third of the calendar year. In a manner that is directly analogous to Spielmann's (2002) discussion of the ritual mode of production, tremendous productive efforts – beyond food and drink – are poured into the crafting of new and distinctive items for ritual practice and the gifting that generally accompanies such rituals. In San José Petén, for instance, "a special effort is made each year to produce new vessels for cooking ritual food" (Reina and Hill 1978:249). Likewise, Arnold (2005) notes that specific pottery is produced for the annual *gremio* celebration of potters in the Yucatec town of Ticul. In short, the entanglements between crafting and ritual practice exist on several different scales from personal *costumbre* to community feasting.

Artisanship as Identity

According to Munn (1983:302), the old adage – you are what you eat – should be expanded to include what you craft and what you trade: "I argue that this ranking [of shells] encodes the long-term hierarchizing process, or continual resynthesis of spacetime through which men define their own value in the system." Referring to the crafting and circulation of shell adornment in the Kula trading sphere, Munn sees the ranked identities of the Kula traders as constitutive of a participant's success in negotiating the trade of shells that – on the basis of raw material, fabrication, and social history – are items of ranked value. In this manner, crafting and circulation of goods creates and defines value, encodes hierarchy, and frames identity. Ironically, in current anthologies (Insoll 2007), the manner in which hierarchy and identity are manifest through crafting is remarkably undertheorized; the waters are poorly charted beyond the Marxian construct of labor alienation. Archaeologists have just begun to grapple with the manner in which artisan identity can be part of what Munn (1983:302) refers to as "the long-term hierarchizing process." Costin (1998:11) has acknowledged its presence in middle range and chiefdom societies: "it is likely that much of the production that took place within elite households was accomplished by elite household members themselves." Inomata

(2001:321), faced with ubiquitous evidence of elite artisan production in domestic contexts, has also weighed in on the topic: "skilled crafting, along with the privileged knowledge encoded in the products, formed an important part of the high culture that served to distinguish the elite from the rest of society." Ironically, crafting as part of elite identity is a concept with deep indigenous roots within Mesoamerica. Postclassic Mexica crafters reverently referred back to the legendary Toltecs as artificers par excellence and Mixtec elites were known for their ability to craft gold and other precious materials. Somehow, the deep antiquity and ramifications of artisan-as-part-of-elite-identity for Preclassic and Classic Maya society have not been addressed until recently. Clearly standing outside of the framework of independent and attached specialists, elite artisans craft for a diverse demand crowd that includes their immediate family as well as political allies and enemies and, in some cases, trading partners. Their labor-intensive goods serve to differentiate, to create, and to maintain hierarchy in the manner explored in detail in Chapters 6 and 9. In what follows, we return to a consideration of artisans and elite identity but now turn to artisan identities that are not so explicitly framed within the hierarchizing process.

The perfect complement to the Aguateca case cited earlier would be ancestral analogues to the community specialization documented ethnographically. Given the difficult work of piecing together the story in the absence of contexts of extraordinary preservation or complementary texts, the analogues have been slow to materialize (but see Ball 1993; Bartlett et al. 2000; López Varela et al. 2001; contributions in Masson and Freidel 2002; Rice 1987a; Shafer and Hester 1991; Sheets 2002, among others). Existing examples tell us several things: (1) production beyond that needed for immediate household use existed; (2) clay procurement zones for pottery production could be extremely circumscribed; and (3) distribution spheres were highly variable in areal extent. How can these archaeological observations enhance an understanding of artisan identity? A circumscribed clay procurement zone around K'axob as documented by Bartlett and colleagues (2000) could be interpreted in several ways, but the pattern bears an uncanny similarity to an observation by Reina and Hill (1978:238) that clay was not found in markets or sold as a commodity because it was conceived as part of the identity of a place and an artisan. Likewise, village potters did not imitate vessel forms made in other villages because, as merchants maintained, "It is not right to take an object away from its place of birth" (Reina and Hill 1978:238). Copying a form known to have been made exclusively by a particular village was thought to destroy the identity of the vessel and of the artisans who had traditionally made the form. Based on ethnoarchaeological observations among contemporary potters in Latin America, Arnold (2000:333, 370) proposes a 3- to 4-kilometer threshold for clay acquisition; this model could be used archaeologically to identify "community signature units." Dietler and Herbich (1989:150) note that clay and temper generally are collected within 2 kilometers of the house where production is to take place. Furthermore, Luo artisans are recognized by their "characteristic combinations of technological, formal, and decorative features" that Dietler and Herbich (1989:150) term "micro-style." Thus, place and material are critical factors of vessel and artisan identity. Since there is initial congruence between ethnographic expressions of artisan identity (via specific clay sources and vessel forms) and archaeological patterns of clay utilization, it is worth investigating the possibility that artisan identity was entangled with specific resource locales and technologies, in much the same manner as Stout (2002:702) documents *hereditary quarrying rights* among Irian Jaya flint knappers.

Crafting of stone tools throughout the community of Colha as evidenced by the presence of more than 100 concentrated debitage piles (Shafer and Hester 1991:81) likewise suggests that the ethnographic model of communitywide specialization has relevance for the past. Again, Reina and Hill (1978:19) provide commentary from an ethnographic perspective:

> the technological specialty may be weaving, basket making, rope making, and so forth. The crucial fact is that, no matter which specialty is established, all able members are expected to practice the same community-defined specialization. Making the traditional pottery of the community not only defines a person as a potter but also serves as the mark of membership in the corporate body.

In the Maya lowlands, evidence of specialized stone-tool crafting can be linked in a straightforward fashion with sources of prime chert, and production debris is readily detectable even if one is fixated on royal tombs, which often were encased in lithic debris (see Moholy-Nagy 1997 for more on this topic). Maya crafting of pottery, the most ubiquitous artifact class known and the best-studied ethnographically (see Arnold 1971, 1985; Reina and Hill 1978; Thompson 1958, among others), has been more difficult to characterize as a community specialization. The operating assumption has been that all communities of the past produced a basic repertoire of pottery with a limited number of serving wares being produced in a specialized manner. In point of fact, there are few data to support this assumption, and there is extremely limited insight into the identity of pottery artisans other than the elite artisans who signed their unique pictorial polychrome creations.

PRODUCING GOODS AT HOME, AT COURT, AND ELSEWHERE

Artisan production within the Maya lowlands often was seated within the home (be it commoner or palatial), although specialized extraction and processing sites certainly existed for quarrying chert and processing nondurable goods, such as salt. Due to the domestic context of production, specialization that is embedded within and forms part of the identity of kin groups (as per Ames 1995 and Janusek 1999) more aptly characterizes Maya crafting than the starkly bipolar construct of independent versus attached specialization. There were likely very few artisans who crafted for an unspecified demand crowd and conversely few compliant minions toiling under a demanding royal patron who coerced production from their skilled hands. Social and political relations were more richly complex and generative of agency. As discussed previously in this chapter and in Chapters 6 and 9, artisan production was part of elite identity, and often the goal of production was possession in perpetuity rather than alienation, especially for items such as well-crafted and symbolically charged personal adornment. Miller and Martin (2004:121) describe Maya royal courts as places of "artists and scribes" and note that courtly objects and monuments were crafted not only "in the service of a courtly culture, but within and by it."

To the query often posed by archaeologists regarding the degree to which elites controlled the production of everything from obsidian blades to brocaded *mantas*, Clark (2003a:35) opines that "[c]ontrol [over production and exchange] is easy to conceptualize but difficult to demonstrate." In reference to items known to have been highly desired tributary goods (i.e., cacao, cotton *mantas*, jadeite, quetzal feathers, and *Spondylus* shells), we can postulate some degree of elite control of production and consumption based upon hieroglyphic, iconographic, archaeological, and ethnohistorical information (see Chapter 9). But for items that were not clearly linked to the political economy of Classic-period Maya interaction, control over production and exchange is much more difficult to demonstrate. To posit control, one often is forced to take some profound leaps of faith (e.g., see Clark's [2003a:50–54] detailed critique of the model of Ixtepeque obsidian control by Classic Copán elites proposed by Aoyama [1999]). On the other hand, some contexts are strongly suggestive of either independent or attached production. For instance, evidence of initial-stage jadeite working in modest compounds at Late Classic Cancuen (Kovacevich 2007), as discussed later in this chapter and in Chapter 9, is highly evocative of attached production because three lines of evidence converge: (1) a symbolically charged raw material coupled with (2) evidence primarily of preform fabrication from jadeite boulders, (3) within the context of what is likely a commoner residential compound. In short, there is a broad horizon across which social and political arrangements of artisan production could occur. One way to proceed with this expansion is to examine what is known regarding different kinds of artisans who practiced their *oficio* in the Maya past.

Artisan Production across Social Identities: Age, Gender, and Status

Even though the practice of crafting durable goods in ancestral Maya society was widespread, age, gender, and status exerted considerable influence over who produced what. For instance, pottery might be produced within both elite and commoner residences but pottery decorated with painted hieroglyphs and throne scenes could only have been produced by someone with scribal training and a specific knowledge base that was not widely disseminated throughout Classic Maya society. Other bodies of knowledge and skills were gender linked by virtue of their prevailing mode of transmission from elder to younger females or males. For instance, from all available accounts, food processing on a *metate* plus spinning and weaving appear to be female-gendered activities. Males certainly were capable of learning either skill but the context in which learning took place (within gender-segregated pedagogical spheres) rendered it less likely that a male would learn such skills, just as females might be less likely to learn hunting strategies. Age also played a role in the practice of crafting as a person cycled through culturally recognized life stages. An individual might gain proficiency in a craft as she/he approached adulthood, maintain a plateau of highly developed skill reinforced by routinized practice through adulthood, and then lose competency as mature adulthood advanced and eyesight, strength, and manual dexterity began to fail. Thus, for persons skilled in crafting, there was a life cycle to the crafting process itself that was not unlike the notion of a *chaîne opératoire* (steps and choices that effect the transformation of a material from a natural to a fabricated state) so popularized by Lemonnier (1986:149). The resulting *habitus* of crafting created a "cultural technology" informed by knowledge and practice (Lemonnier 1986:154). In ancestral Maya society, these skills and frameworks of knowledge could be transmitted with remarkably accurate replication through countless generations. As archaeologists, we focus on the end result (e.g., pottery sherds that we can recognize as "Maya" and assign to a time period); less often do we stop to contemplate the age, gender, or status of the maker through whom the cultural technology was transmitted.

In an effort to link craft skills with gendered labor, Clark and Houston (1998:34) examine the pronominal gender linked with crafting in Colonial Yucatec Maya dictionaries. As in prefeminist English, Yucatec Maya speakers of early Colonial times seem to have employed male pronouns as a default unless an activity was diacritically female (see also Jackson and Stuart 2001:222 on glyphic use of *aj-* as a gender-neutral agentive prefix). Clark and Houston (1998:40) summarize crafting activities in Colonial Yucatán as follows: "women spun thread, wove cloth, made nets, and probably also plaited mats and baskets. For their part, men made pottery, worked wood, wax, stone, and leather, and practiced many minor arts such as making flutes, shields, bows and arrows, and probably gourd vessels." There are few surprises here except for two categories, those of making pottery and gourd vessels, which, based on ethnographic examples, might be expected to have been female crafts. Even Clark and Houston (1998:37) express surprise that there are 22 unambiguous references in the Colonial Vienna and Motul dictionaries to male potters and wonder whether the heavy tribute load placed on women weavers during the Colonial period by Spanish overlords shifted the practice of pottery (and gourd?) vessel production exclusively into a male-gendered activity realm. Since pottery production appears to be a category of gender-conflicted and perhaps historically contingent roles, let us begin with a consideration of this craft, which has produced by far the most ubiquitous class of archaeological evidence in the way of pottery sherds. An examination of what we now know and might in the future discover about the identity of potters in reference to status, gender, and age is followed by a consideration of other selected crafts, namely: stone-tool makers; lapidaries; weavers and paper makers; plaiters of baskets, mats, sacks, and nets; gourd carvers; shell, bone, and hide workers; wood carvers and carpenters; architects and masons; and scribes, painters, and carvers. The intent is not to survey in a comprehensive fashion the archaeological literature pertinent to each type of artisan – which would exceed the page limits of this book – but to explore existing sources for information pertinent to the daily practice and identity of ancestral Maya artisans. The following discussion is partitioned by types of crafted items, but there is full acknowledgment that crafting activities often co-occur and produce a material pattern of multicrafting, which is amply demonstrated archaeologically in the contributions to Shimada (2007).

Potters at Home and at Court. An additive technology, crafting pottery through the working, modeling, and firing of clay is a transformative process that most clearly typifies the notion of *chaîne opératoire* (Lemonnier 1986:149). Unlike stone-tool making, the many steps and choices intervening between a ball of unshaped clay and a fired artifact allow for an almost infinite range of human creativity and variety. From this perspective, the long-term stability of many traditional pottery forms is quite remarkable. For example, Reina and Hill (1978:163 [Figure 26]) note the production of a duck effigy vessel form – called a *pichinga* – at San Luis Jilotepeque and comment that it was on the verge of extinction in the 1940s but had made a strong comeback by the 1970s. A similar vessel form was found in Preclassic deposits over

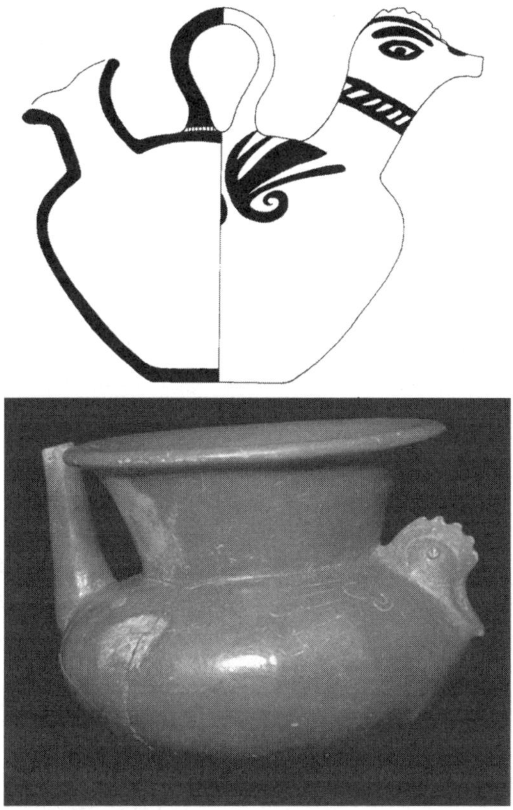

FIGURE 7.1 Duck effigy pottery vessels from San Luis Jilotepeque, Guatemala, circa 1970 (top) and K'axob, Belize, circa 300 B.C.E. (bottom). (Top image after Reina and Hill 1978:Figure 6; bottom photo courtesy of K'axob Archaeological Project.)

2,000 years earlier at the lowland Maya site of K'axob (Figure 7.1; see López Varela 1996:211 for additional discussion). At Preclassic K'axob, there are many vessel forms that remained stable – in terms of paste, form, and surface decoration – for hundreds of years. Thus, it is hard to overemphasize the power of tradition in the Maya region and the manner in which identity is/was materialized and maintained through the process of crafting (Bartlett and McAnany 2000). For Reina and Hill (1978:231), these material patterns signify *costumbre*, a type of *habitus* that emphasizes "emulation and conformity." This ethos of crafting appears to predate and coexist with another that was overtly linked to the hierarchizing process in Classic Maya society.

Dedication to status difference among Late Classic Maya elites resulted in a distinct "school" of pottery production. Ball (1993:259) refers to two discrete production contexts as "palace schools" and "village traditions." Coggins (1975:32) first proposed the notion of a site-specific local tradition of polychrome painting for the great Maya capital of Tikal. The idea continues to resonate within Maya studies and has been elaborated by other art historians such as Reents-Budet (1994). A skill- and knowledge-intensive craft with considerable intertextuality with carved monuments, the pottery of recognized palace schools emphasized fine serving wares, such as cylindrical vessels and bowls (Figure 7.2). It is these potters that Rice (1987b:21) characterizes as possessing "exceptional technical skill." Reents-Budet (1998:71) suggests that the bifurcation of pottery production into two schools may have been formalized as recently as 600 C.E. or the beginning of the Late Classic period when skills of literacy and figural painting supplanted more basic and often script-free cosmological themes that dominated the more widely dispersed Early Classic polychromes. Though this may be the case, Loughmiller-Newman (2008) shows that the widely acclaimed artistry and innovations of Late Classic pictorial polychromes were tempered by adherence to specific canons regarding figural and textual layout, size, and composition.

Is the other, more ancient and enduring, context of production actually a village tradition as Ball (1993:259) has suggested? Certainly, the antiquity of pottery production can be traced back to the earliest Preclassic villages known in the Maya lowlands, but as time went on, the size of Maya political capitals grew to urban proportions and, in many areas, villages were engulfed within larger political networks. "Community" production may be a more accurate descriptor of the counterpart to "palace schools" and can be grounded ethnographically in the characteristics of community potters observed by Arnold (1971:26, 39) in twentieth-century Ticul. Both "schools" likely shared the cognitive categories of form identified from hieroglyphs painted on Late Classic polychrome vessels: specifically, *u lak* or *u hawante'* ("his dish" and "his wide dish"), and *y-uch'ib* ("his drinking vessel"; Houston et al. 1989:722; Reents-Budet 1994:72–87). There exist intriguing similarities and differences between the two "schools" in terms of the production of serving wares. Ceramic types (defined by form and surface decoration) such as Chinos Black-on-Cream or

FIGURE 7.2 Late Classic polychrome vessel from Buenavista del Cayo, Belize, featuring the maize deity and a hieroglyphic band beneath the rim that identifies the vessel as that of the ruler of Naranjo (photograph © Justin Kerr, K4464).

Cabrito Cream Polychrome were produced by both community and palace artisans, although, as Reents-Budet et al. (2000:101, 107) have noted, vessels from the hand of the former group of artisans lack hieroglyphic texts (but sometimes contain "pseudo-glyphs") and exhibit a more limited color spectrum. Thus, available materials and access to restricted realms of knowledge resulted in a distinctive skill set for palace artisans, and their crafted goods materialized this hierarchizing process. Nonetheless, these two "schools" are best envisioned as two ends of a continuum rather than discrete and non-overlapping social contexts of production. Vectors of pedagogy, politics, and wealth might co-occur in distinctive ways along an *n*-dimensional continua of variation. For instance, Ulua marble vessels provide an example of a distinctive co-occurrence of the following: a highly restricted and highly valued raw material; long-term and localized skill in working the hard stone into bowls; a canon of shared iconographic elements; and places of production that Luke and Tykot (2007:315) characterize as social rather than political centers.

Even though ceramic serving wares are uniquely amenable to analysis according to "school" and distribution generally mimics production (i.e., vessels made by palace artisans are found in palace contexts and those by community artisans in nonpalatial contexts), the pairing of artisan with vessel and depositional context is far less clear-cut for the essential but not status-linked category of jars used for cooking, water transport, and storage. The answer to the question, "Who made the palace water jars?" cannot be determined at this time. If and when this question can be answered, we will understand much more about the economic linkages between royal courts and their surrounding populations.

Aside from the presumably male "signatures" such as that of Ajmaxam who is thought to have been a member of the Naranjo palace school (Reents-Budet 1998:74–75 [although it should be noted that most of the vessels bearing his name have been looted, so definitive evidence of provenience is lacking]), there are few indicators of the gender of ancestral Maya potters. In the future, if DNA can be retrieved from fingerprints impressed into clay we may be able to answer the important question of the gender of pottery artisans. Likewise, the age of artisans is extremely difficult to know from archaeological evidence alone. An apprentice model seems most appropriate for this craft and would bring together older and younger craftspersons who may have worked together on the same vessel, undertaking different stages in the *chaîne opératoire*. A practiced artisan would have executed steps – such as painting – that require a high level of skill while other steps requiring less skill but lots of time might be given to an apprentice. In this regard, it is informative that "among the techniques of decoration the most time-consuming and physically tiring process is burnishing, a fact readily pointed out by the potters themselves" (Dietler and Herbich 1989:155). Thus, it comes as no surprise that the photograph of a Maya potter burnishing a large jar (Figure 7.3) features a young girl and bears the following caption: "San Miguel

FIGURE 7.3 Young girl from San Miguel Acatán burnishing a *tinaja* with a river-worn quartz pebble (from Reina and Hill 1978; photo courtesy of Ruben Reina and Robert Hill).

Acatán girl burnishing a *tinaja* with a river-worn quartz pebble" (Reina and Hill 1978).

Judging from ethnographic accounts, there likely was a seasonality to pottery production, which often is characterized as a dry-season craft since it is much easier to dry and fire pottery during this time of year (Arnold 1985:Table 3.2; Reina and Hill 1978:64, 76). Production levels are extremely difficult to gauge. Guatemalan community potters have been clocked at "an average weekly firing of twenty to twenty-five vessels of various forms and sizes during the dry season" and, in the specific case of jar production at Santa Maria Chiquimula, between "one and three dozen regular undecorated *tinajas* per person or family each week, usually approaching the lower figure in the rainy season, the higher in the dry season" (Reina and Hill 1978:64, 76). During the populous Classic period, one could expect comparable production levels. Foias (2002:235–236) and others suggest that control of community-based artisans was seated at a very local level. Distribution spheres likely were smaller than that for the palace school vessels, which were transported long distances as part of diplomatic relations. Dietler and Herbich (1998:255) note that among traditional community-based Luo potters, approximately 94 percent of pots are "consumed" within 15 kilometers of the regional market at Ng'iya. Judging from the density of pottery sherds excavated from Preclassic and Classic period Maya sites, community-based artisans maintained a brisk trade in pottery.

Did some ancestral Maya communities specialize in crafting pottery, effecting a "site specialization" as per Rice (1991:262)? Archaeological studies of clay sourcing through Instrumental Neutron Activation Analysis (INAA), petrography, and other methods indicate a pattern of localized source signatures (Bartlett et al. 2000; Reents-Budet et al. 2000). Rice (1987c:84), furthermore, has noted the pronounced regionalization of Late Classic pottery, which suggests that the population rise of the Late Classic period resulted in an expansion of the number of communities producing pottery. Along this vein, Ball (1993:255) has suggested that unique combinations of ceramic types – called complexes – can be used to identify discrete Late Classic production and distribution communities in the upper Belize Valley. Perhaps the present cannot be used as a guide to the past, but it is noteworthy that Maya pottery production in mid-twentieth-century Guatemala took place in 24 pottery-production centers within an area of about 60,000 square kilometers (Reina and Hill 1978:Map 2). Within these centers, potters produced both everyday water and cooking jars as well as finer serving wares (both "site" and "functional" specializations as per Rice 1991:262–263). Extrapolating from this information to the Maya lowlands, which extend over about 225,000 square kilometers, there could have been as many as 90 or more specialized pottery-production locales (including both palace schools and community-based artisans). Admittedly, open firing areas, as opposed to a production feature such as a kiln (see López Varela et al. 2001), can be difficult to identify archaeologically. Regional programs of materials sourcing (Bartlett 2004, among

FIGURE 7.4 Chipped stone eccentric of deity K'awiil made by a master craftperson and redeposited in a Postclassic context at Laguna de On, Belize (photo courtesy of Marilyn Masson).

others) provide another avenue toward the identification of pottery-production areas as well as recognition of regional marketplaces at which exchange occurred (Dahlin et al. 2007). If we can achieve greater resolution of production and trading locales, we cannot help but come to a deeper understanding of the identity of the potters who crafted the hundreds of thousands of vessels that archaeologists recover in the much-reduced state of pottery sherds.

Knappers of Siliceous Stone and Volcanic Glass. As a subtractive technology, flint knapping results in serviceable tools, weapons, and eccentrics (the last term refers to difficult-to-produce and unusual forms that include profiles of the serpent-footed god, K'awiil, Figure 7.4).

The large and durable debris piles generated by repeated crafting in a prescribed location is an added bonus of flint knapping. Unlike pottery artisans for which there is evidence for two schools of production – palace and community – such a split is not so starkly indicated for stone-tool makers. Rather, proximity to high-quality chert and trade linkages for acquiring distant obsidian seem to have been genuine factors determining skill level. There is a greater democracy to attaining skill at flint knapping since it is not dependent upon training in the scribal arts (calligraphy and figural painting) or any other realm of knowledge that was culturally restricted based on status. One needed access to flint-knappable material (while obsidian had to be imported, chert was ubiquitous – although variable in quality – across the limestone substrate that underlies the Maya lowlands), a good teacher, some natural skill, and lots of time to practice.

Since flint knapping is a reductive technology, error rates are readily detectable. Errors can indicate the neophyte status of a knapper, but they also occur when highly skilled knappers attempt to produce a form that stretches the technological limits of flint knapping, such as a trident-shaped eccentric with an interior hole or a North American Folsom point (Clark 2003b:230). In reference to a survey of modern male flint knappers, Clark (2003b:230) observes that "the relationship between skill and production is remarkable." In effect, higher levels of skill are achieved as a function of intensity and length of time over which production skills are practiced, a pattern also observed by Stout (2002:705–711) in reference to flint knappers of Irian Jaya and by Eerkens (2000) within an experimental context. Only a highly skilled flint knapper could attempt to craft an object that stretched the limits of the technology. Such objects for which there was a heightened risk of error or complete failure – as with eccentrics in the Maya lowlands – tend to be found in elite and monumental contexts at which the crafted objects were interred ritually as burial accoutrements or cache offerings (but see Masson 2000:92–93 for an unusual example of an heirloom Late Classic god K'awiil eccentric reinterred at the Postclassic island site of Laguna de On, Belize; Figure 7.4). The many eccentrics interred with Late Classic elite male burials at Altun Ha such as burials E–1/1, E–1/3, and E–54/9 (Figure 7.5; Pendergast 1990:vol. 3) provide a compelling example of the prestige that was associated with this most difficult to

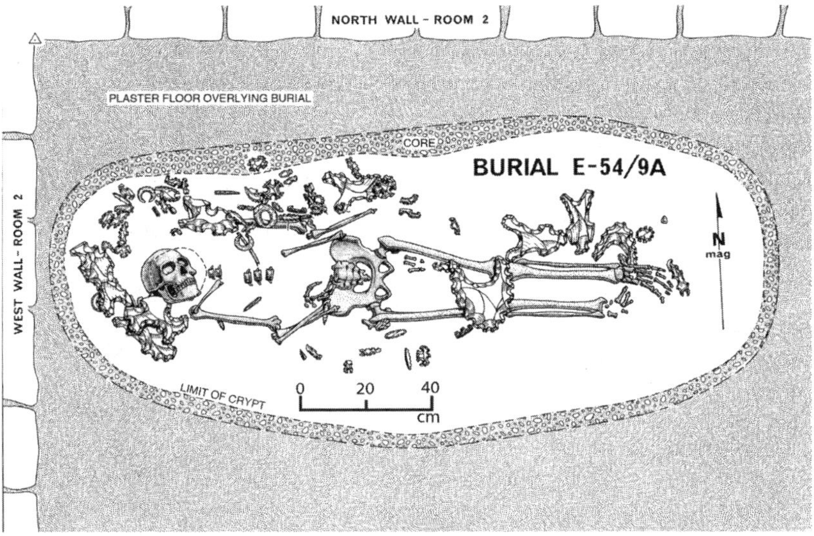

FIGURE 7.5 Late Classic elite Burial E–54/9A at Altun Ha with stone eccentrics placed as burial accoutrements (redrawn by Josh Feola after Pendergast 1990, Volume 3, Figure 66).

produce chipped stone artifact. Altun Ha is located within a zone of extremely high-quality chert; flint knappers – who could have resided at Altun Ha or the famed tool-producing center of Colha located only 25 kilometers to the north – used superior but locally available material. The true value of the eccentrics came not from a foreign origin for the raw material but from the "value added" by flint-knapping virtuosos who pushed the limit of forms that can be chipped from stone. For Tikal, Moholy-Nagy (1997:296), likewise, notes that there is "no simple correspondence between the distance over which the raw materials were transported to Tikal and the function of the finished artifact. Imported fine-textured chert and gray and green obsidian were used primarily for utilitarian artifacts, while a large class of elite ceremonial artifacts, the so-called eccentric flints, were made almost exclusively of locally available chert."

The association between eccentrics (made of chert or obsidian) and elite monumental and burial contexts suggests that some measure of elite patronage may have been involved in the production of these valuable and skill-saturated specimens. The higher levels of risk and error could have been underwritten by elite patrons in the manner suggested by Lewis (1996:359). Specific locations of eccentric production – whether at court or in simple residential contexts – currently are not known; thus, it is not possible to address the issue of whether elites produced eccentrics for their own ritual purposes or "commissioned" pieces from lower-status artisans. Potentially, specific locales of eccentric production are knowable; Titmus and Woods (2003:141, Figure 9.10, 145) have identified "eccentric notching flakes" which are "removed by indirect percussion from within the different types of notches required to create the eccentric design." Greater attention to the attributes of debitage will permit the identification of locales of virtuoso eccentric production.

One Maya site for which exhaustive lithic analyses have been conducted, Colha, reveals dynamic trends in artisan production and status. Extensive research at this flint-knapping center indicates that large debitage deposits (a.k.a. workshops) are widespread across the site and associated with a range of residential types and ritual deposits. King and Potter (1994:81–84) make a case for the high status of Late Preclassic flint knappers whose production debris can be found around the edges of modern *aguadas* (ancient quarries) very close to the monumental core of the site and whose participation in ritual macroblade reduction, bloodletting, and caching is strongly suggested from an excavation unit (Operation 2012) atop a small Preclassic pyramid. Moreover, during this time period one of the most popular tool forms to emerge from the Colha workshops – the stemmed macroblade (Figure 7.6) – can be found at sites as distant as Chiapa de Corzo, 500 kilometers to the west (Hester and Shafter 1994:59). By the Late Classic period (the Early Classic is poorly represented in the deposits of Colha), however, the status of stone-tool makers appears diminished. Production was dispersed throughout the community, flint-knapping debris piles accumulated off the sides of residential platforms in the manner of talus slopes, and deposits indicate that households specialized in items such as smaller stemmed blades and oval bifaces. Residential compounds involved in crafting tools often lack finished stone retaining walls and no cache deposits equivalent to the Late Preclassic cache bearing a blood-stained macroblade have been found (King and Potter 1994:81–84). Hester and Shafter (1994:60) suggest that the diminished status of these extremely skilled crafters may be attributable to their Late Classic political subjugation

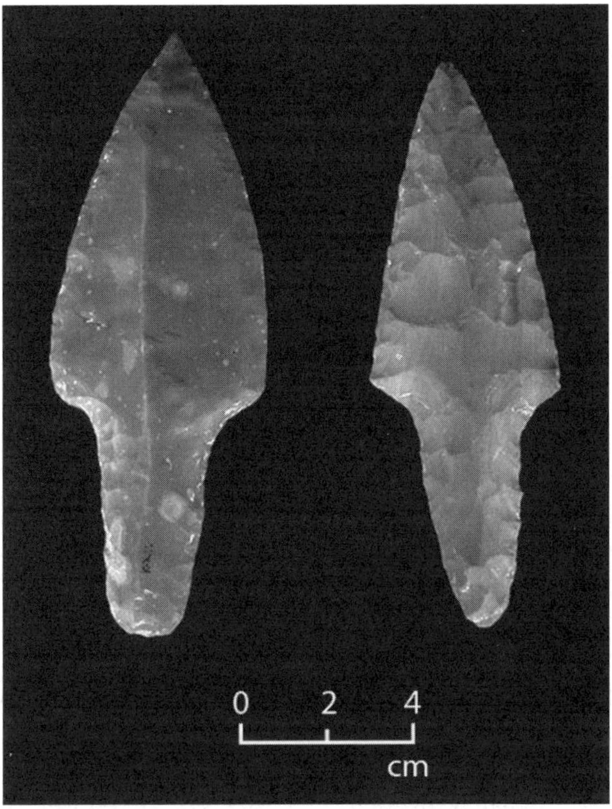

FIGURE 7.6 Stemmed macroblades crafted in the workshops of Colha and deposited in an Early Classic dedicatory cache at K'axob (photo courtesy of K'axob Archaeological Project).

to the larger capital of Altun Ha where, as we have already seen, elites had a healthy appreciation for the fine points of flint knapping.

More modest debitage piles that are nonetheless indicative of intensive crafting of stone tools beyond levels required for family use have been documented and continue to surface from many parts of the Maya lowlands (e.g., see Lewis 2003), and analysts have concerned themselves with documenting the intensity and duration of production and also with interpreting the social relations of production (generally within the independent-attached paradigm). Moholy-Nagy (1997:307) has focused attention on the formation processes that generate and result in the transport of debris piles by noting that the "composition of the chamber burial debitage deposits [at Tikal] is almost identical to that of special-purpose lithic dumps. It differs markedly from household middens by a virtual absence of finished artifacts and a scarcity of sherds." Although this statement has generated controversy because it calls into question the integrity of debitage piles, it also has the effect of reminding us that so-called ritual deposits of debitage that envelope tomb burials, in particular, should be understand as workshop debris piles that were transported and recycled as tomb linings.

Because volcanic deposits do not occur in the limestone bedrock of the Maya lowlands, obsidian was imported predominantly from three sources in the Guatemalan highlands (see Clark 2003a for a review of twentieth-century Mesoamerican obsidian studies). As an unusually homogeneous, translucent, and sharp raw material from a distant source, obsidian later was characterized as star or meteor excrement (*citlalcuitlatl*) by Nahuas (Karttunen 1983:35 cited in Taube 2000:290). In the Maya lowlands, obsidian may have been traded as preformed polyhedral cores since the preponderance of obsidian artifacts in the Maya lowlands consists of debris from blade reduction as well as fragments of prismatic blades. Across Mesoamerica, the core-blade tradition can be traced as far back as the Middle Preclassic period (about 1000 B.C.E.; Clark 1987; Johnson 1991; McAnany 2004c), and it continued unabated through the Postclassic period (see Dreiss and Brown 1989, among many others). Changes did occur, however, in the dominance of source areas provisioning the Maya lowlands, and trends can be detected in the greater abundance of broken blades in modest residential contexts of the Late-Terminal Classic period (Rice 1987c:84). The ancient political capitals that dotted the lowland landscape appear to have used their alliance networks to acquire obsidian – probably as polyhedral cores – which was then distributed via gifting and trading to households and more distant communities. Artisans residing at large political centers likely reduced polyhedral cores to blades, which were then further distributed. Over 30 years ago, Sidrys (1977:97) noted that large centers generally exhibit obsidian densities that are six times greater than those of smaller sites. This differential availability coupled with a highly structured reduction technique suggests that the crafting of obsidian was more entangled with power relations and its distribution was more likely to have been marketplace-centralized in a manner that was evocative of early Colonial descriptions of obsidian-blade crafters who practiced their trade in the Mexica marketplace of Tlatelelolco (Clark 1989:310).

Finally, issues of age and gender of stone-tool makers require discussion. Considerations of skill, strength, and manual dexterity as discussed for the life cycle of potters applies equally, if not more so, to flint knappers. A period of apprenticeship, generally structured by family connectivity, likely typified the learning of this craft. Cross-cultural ethnographic as well as experimental studies have focused on chipping stone as a male-gendered activity. Given the upper-body strength that females developed as a consequence of *metate* use, there is no reason why females also could not have practiced the craft of flint knapping in the past (see Gero 1991 for critique of the androcentric bias in our narratives of past flint-knapping activities). Certain stone tools – such as *metate*-pecking stones and likely bark beaters – were used extensively (and perhaps exclusively) by females. A central issue to consider in resolving this question is the probability of gender-segregated learning spheres (the engine that drives gender complementarity as originally noted by Devereaux 1987). A corollary issue is the daily practice and workload of ancestral Maya females, which appears to have increased steadily through the Classic period (see Chapter 4) and may not have contained scheduling space for a type of crafting that produced large debris piles of sharp-edged waste material that could be hazardous to small children.

Lapidaries and Makers of Groundstone Tools. Clearly related to the skills of working stone through chipping, the shaping of personal ornamentation as well as tools such as bark beaters, *manos*, and *metates* required extensive use of time-consuming techniques, such as string-sawing, grinding, and polishing. Because of the protracted time needed to fashion an item of personal adornment – such as earflares made from a semiprecious stone like jadeite – these items often took on hypertrophic qualities (as per Malinowski 1934) and became entangled with power relations within prestige spheres (see Chapter 9 for more on the political economy of jadeite). In the Maya lowlands, the addition of inscribed glyphs confirms the exclusive nature of certain items of jadeite ornamentation that could only be finished in this fashion within the context of a royal court where a scribe/sculptor

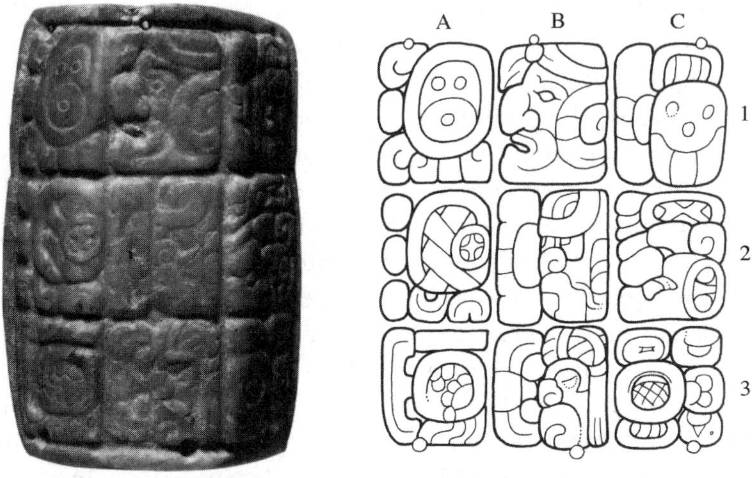

FIGURE 7.7 Jadeite cube (8.2 centimeters tall) from Palenque carved with a text that refers to the *yax* ("green/new") cube as the *yikatz* or "burden" (C1) of a ruler of Pomona (C2–C3; adapted from Miller and Martin 2004:234).

was in residence (Figure 7.7). The jadeite cube shown in Figure 7.7 is particularly instructive as it was part of a tribute burden offered to Palenque by a ruler of nearby Pomona (Miller and Martin 2004:234). In reference to jadeite, a two-tiered production sequence is suggested to have existed at Cancuen. The laborious initial process of sawing and grinding was conducted at modest residences; in contrast, jadeite ornaments were finished, worn, and discarded (or deposited as funerary accoutrements) in upper-status residences (Kovacevich 2007). Although jadeite was not exclusively an elite item, it is found in far greater quantities and was shaped into more intricate designs – and inscribed with literacy-based design elements – within royal contexts.

As a result of this disparity, we can imagine that there existed the equivalent of a palace school of lapidaries who embraced an ethos of artisanship that emphasized social difference in a manner similar to the palace school of pottery production. Status played a role in shaping the identity of these artisans and their crafts. As the evidence from Cancuen shows, stone workers of both high and low status worked in relatively close proximity to produce symbolically charged bodily ornamentation and accoutrements of rulership. Such proximity suggests that a model of attached production – as discussed earlier – is not inappropriate for fine stone working. Additionally, there likely existed community-based stone crafters who produced grinding stones and bark beaters that were fabricated from both local and more distant materials – limestone, granite, and vesicular basalt, in particular. Of the age and gender of those who specialized in sawing, grinding, and polishing stone – and whether they formed a subset within flint knappers or maintained a separate artisan identity – we have few clues and can at best, envision identities that mirror those of flint knappers.

Weavers and Paper Makers. Weaving, perhaps more than any other craft, indicates the difficulties inherent in the term "specialization" – which suggests that a small subset of society produces for a larger subset of consumers. Of female weavers in Inka society, Costin (1998:129) explains that all "women in the Inka empire were cloth-producing 'specialists,' since it was their obligation to produce thread and cloth beyond their own needs, for the use of their households and the state." This inversion of craft specialization – in which all produce for a few – indicates the profound manner in which textile production can be viewed as part of a gendered performance of culture. Judging from ethnohistorical accounts of the Spanish Colonial period in the Maya region, it seems clear that an imperial process (not unlike the Inka example) entailing expansion of a weaving industry for the purposes of tribute extraction was effected. From Colonial tribute records compiled for the Maya Highlands during the period of 1549–1750, Feldman (1985:59, Table 12) documents 21 cotton-growing towns and 34 cotton-weaving towns. Only five towns were listed as growing as well as weaving cotton, which indicates that most of the towns that paid tribute in woven *mantas* had to effect trading transactions in order to acquire the raw material (cotton) to spin thread and weave textiles. In a manner that was reminiscent of the Mexica empire, Spanish imperial administrators used to their advantage the fact that knowledge of textile skills was widespread among Maya females at the time of Spanish incursions.

As discussed in Chapter 4, spinning thread and weaving cloth may not have been skills that were ubiquitous among females during Preclassic and Classic times. Based on the disproportionate association of spindle whorls with elite architecture, cotton cloth appears to have been made and worn primarily by elites until the Postclassic period at which point whorls became more widely distributed. The weaving and spinning of maguey fibers, likely by female family members, probably provided some of the clothing and bags needed within communities outside of elite compounds. Age-appropriate weaving activities – as discussed in Chapter 4 – characterize Postclassic and Colonial sources, reinforcing the notion that weaving activities constituted part of a carefully calibrated cultural performance. Despite the rapaciousness of Colonial tribute demands, weaving remained an artisan activity of considerable status, and women could accrue renown through the creation of a highly desired, technologically superior, and symbolically laden *huipil* or *manta*. The manner in which gendered power and textile crafting intersected at the Classic Maya court is discussed in Chapters 6 and 9. Tedlock and Tedlock (1985:124–125) point out the continuity, during the Colonial period, of brocading and describe the designs on the lordly cloaks of the *Popol Vuh* as "a mixture of iconic, indexical, and symbolic aspects." The symbolic import of brocaded designs apparently did not escape Spanish overlords who in the sixteenth century issued a royal warrant prohibiting Maya apparel that bore brocaded designs (Tedlock and Tedlock 1985:125). This historical detail highlights not only the complementarity between weavers and scribes but also the manner in which cloth production, in the words of Weiner (1992:50) gave females "a domain of authority and power in their own right."

Because social practices most likely were reproduced through gender-segregated pedagogical realms, spinning and weaving became female-gendered. But what of paper making? Unlike spindle whorls, bark beaters are commonly found in Preclassic deposits at both villages and emerging political capitals (Garber 2001; Hammond 2006; McAnany and Ebersole 2004:319). As such, paper making represents a very old Mesoamerican craft and may have provided the earliest clothing. As late as the nineteenth century, bark-cloth tunics were worn by Lacandon Maya living in remote areas (Tozzer 1907:29). Mesoamerican paper production differs little from Polynesian methods and tools, which entail removing the inner bark of certain trees (often a species of *Ficus* or mulberry), soaking the bark in water, and then laboriously beating it to the thinness of paper. In the Maya region, paper appears to have been used extensively at royal courts for recording everything from incoming tribute to the astronomical cycles of Venus. As depicted on Lintels 24 and 25 of Yaxchilán, paper could also be used for ritual sacrifices – folded, placed to catch blood droplets, and subsequently burned as an offering to the gods. Lowland Maya paper making appears to have disappeared – along with hieroglyphic writing – soon after Spanish missionaries established a foothold in the Yucatán Peninsula. There is no term for a paper maker in Yucatec Colonial dictionaries (see Clark and Houston 1998:34), indicating the disappearance of this craft by the seventeenth century. To the west, in the Mexican state of Puebla, the craft endured and paper making survived into the twentieth century when Lenz (1961) observed the process of paper making within several villages of Otomí speakers. According to Lenz (1961:83), "Both sexes procure the raw material for the 'paper' making, but its actual manufacture is only done by the women." Lenz (1961:83) goes on to describe the fact that the "harvest" was brought in at the very end of the dry season – during the months of April, May, and June – indicating that this craft, like pottery making, had a pronounced seasonality.

If Lenz's observation of paper making as female-gendered can be extended to the lowland Maya area – and there is no guarantee that it can – then it was a female-gendered craft that was "as old as the hills" and yet, over time, became linked with quintessential court activities such as calligraphy and painting. Just because paper was used at court, however, does not mean that royal females took on the arduous task of beating tree bark into paper. Since the locale of paper production is directly indicated by the presence of bark beaters, the simple question of where paper was made should be answerable, even if we cannot detect the fingerprints of a royal princess on a shattered bark beater. We might also entertain the possibility that, over time, paper making became a specialty item produced for courts in the river valleys flanking the lowlands. The *Ficus* spp. thrives in riparian habitats, and one Late-Terminal Classic site in the Sibun River of central Belize, in particular, contains an unusually high number of bark beaters from modest residential contexts (Figure 7.8).

Plaiters of Baskets, Mats, Sacks, and Nets. In refutation of typological classifications of artifacts, Ingold (2000:56–57) waxes eloquent on how the form of a basket emerges: "One could say that the form unfolds

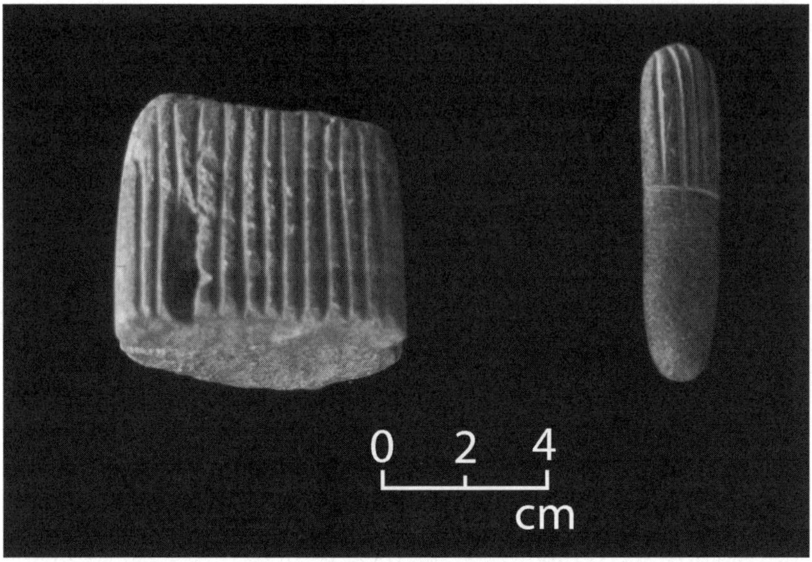

FIGURE 7.8 Bark beaters from a site called "Churchyard" in the Sibun Valley of Belize (photo courtesy of Xibun Archaeological Research Project).

within a kind of force field, in which the weaver is caught up in a reciprocal and quite muscular dialogue with the material ... the form of the basket emerges through a pattern of *skilled movement*, and it is the rhythmic repetition of that movement that gives rise to the regularity of form." Certainly one of the oldest crafts practiced by humans – the plaiting of palm fronds, cattails, maguey, and other types of leaves and fibers – yields containers, floor coverings, seating, bedding, and nets for catching fish and small game. Although an old craft, plaiting leaves scant archaeological evidence (but see later discussion) and so is largely inferred from Classic-period imagery and ethnographic accounts. Yucatec Maya Colonial dictionaries lack a term for basket makers and mat makers (Clark and Houston 1998:34), which leaves one to wonder whether the craft was considered an *oficio* or an activity in which one might engage at certain stages of a life cycle.

Petate or mat making was practiced well into the twentieth century within Kakchiquel communities of highland Guatemala where Annis (1987:47–48) notes that *petate* making was done by those too old to farm or weave or too young to have land. According to Annis (1987:47–48), the craft is not as strongly gender-linked as is weaving

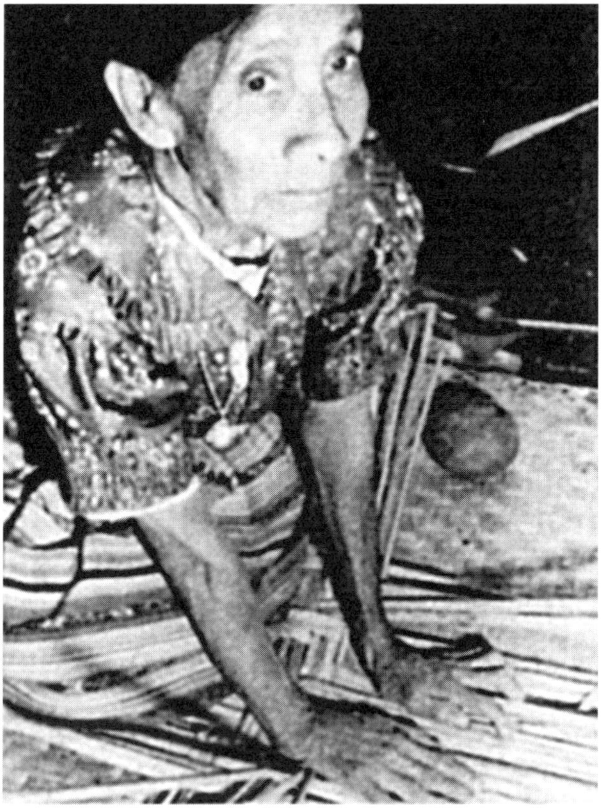

FIGURE 7.9 Kaqchiquel Maya woman sitting on a *petate* mat of her making with a pounding stone used to flatten *tul* reeds (from *God and Production in a Guatemalan Town* by Sheldon Annis, copyright © 1987, courtesy of Sheldon Annis and University of Texas Press, photo by Mitchell Denberg).

and farming although the accompanying photo (Figure 7.9) of a woman seated on a reed mat of her making strikes a poignant and familiar message of an elderly woman whose hands have become too arthritic and eyesight too clouded to weave and brocade. In order to contribute to the household, she takes on the task of plaiting mats, the larger and coarser scale of which do not require fine manual dexterity and keen eyesight. In the photo – next to her frail figure – is the pounding stone, which is used in a "muscular dialogue" with the *tul* reeds that must be beaten flat to create a woven mat. Approximately the same size and shape as the *metate*-pecking stones described in

FIGURE 7.10 Two variants of the Yucatec Maya month, Pop, that feature the woven mat motif, a symbol of royal authority (redrawn by Josh Feola after Coe and Van Stone 2001:43).

Chapter 4, the pounding stone bears the same formal appearance as many stones that are excavated archaeologically; few survive the sorting process at the screen in order to be examined for traces of grass phytoliths although these tools represent one of the few direct indicators of mat making.

In the ancestral Maya past, mat making must have been widely practiced. Colonial tribute records (1550–1821) of 106 townships in eastern Guatemala indicate that 22 specialized in making *petates* (Feldman 1985:55, Table 11). The plaited mat symbol of Classic through Colonial period iconography and associated rhetoric represent authority, most often expressed as "he of the mat" or *ah pop* (Figure 7.10). So, the mat symbol was implicated minimally in royal charters. Like paper making, the raw material for mats is large and bulky and not likely to have been transported farther than was necessary. Unlike paper making for which suitable raw material could be distant from a royal court, reeds and palm fronds are plentiful throughout the lowlands. Thus, mats could have been crafted proximate to most Maya sites, likely by those of either gender and perhaps of several *k'atunob*.

Gourd Painters and Carvers. Like mat making, there is no Colonial Yucatec term for "makers of gourd drinking cups" (Clark and Houston 1998:34), yet the craft flourished through the Colonial period in the Guatemalan highlands where the town of Rabinal gained notoriety for its carved gourds (see epigraph to Chapter 8). Gourds – both the calabash tree and the *Lagenaria* spp. vine – thrive in the lowlands, so the lack of a Colonial gourd-carving tradition cannot be explained on ecological grounds. Obviously a postharvest activity, gourd working bears many structural similarities to pottery production – particularly to Terminal Classic and Postclassic pottery on which elaborate scenes and designs were carved prior to firing. Skill in carving or painting on a three-dimensional surface is a learned and practiced skill in which proportionality figures prominently, so skilled decorators likely were practiced adults. As to gender and status, few clues exist. Since an early Mesoamerican pottery form called a *tecomate* mimics the spherical shape of tree gourds, pottery is thought to have been patterned after gourds. Poorly preserved fragments of painted gourds – some mistakenly identified as bits of painted paper – have been reported from tombs and caches throughout the Maya region. The 13 fragmentary painted gourds found at the sixth-century site of Cerén (Beaubien and Beaudry-Corbett 2002:162) provide a remarkable instance of gourd recovery.

Shell, Bone, and Hide Workers. Almost every site in the Maya lowlands contains at least one item of shell adornment – such as a bead or a tinkler – and a bone tool or artifact of bone adornment. Hide working, on the other hand, is generally diagnosed by virtue of wear patterns on the tools used to work hides. Where were these items made, by whom, and how specialized were these crafting activities? Bone- and shell-working debris, commonly found in Preclassic sites (see Isaza 2004 and Bartlett 2004b for examples), appears to have been become more restricted during the Classic period when access to marine products and large, terrestrial fauna was more sharply circumscribed. For instance, Teeter (2004:191) finds evidence for bone working in only four contexts at Classic-period Caracol structures (B88, B108, B118, and the "Barrio"). Based on wear patterns on tools and modified shell and bone excavated from the rapidly abandoned Aguateca, Emery and Aoyama (2005, 2007) opine that most (elite) inhabitants of Aguateca engaged in bone and shell artifact crafting. With an artisan in every elite home, this pattern contrasts with that of Caracol although the differing conditions under which the sites were abandoned must be kept in mind in addition to the emphasis on the excavation of royal residential contexts at Aguateca. With more such examples and fine-grained analyses, it will become obvious whether or not shell and bone working took place in both elite and commoner contexts during the Classic period; likely the incidence will always be greater among high-status members of society. The product of hide workers – jaguar skins, in particular – are much in evidence in Classic period carvings and paintings but can be detected archaeologically primarily by high-powered microscopic wear-pattern analysis of tool edges. Active practice of hide working has been suggested for the "Toltec-ish" royal crafters of Aguateca (Aoyama 2007) who either were also hunters or had forged a trading relationship or tributary link with hunters. The gender of these crafts – if they represented gendered labor – is more difficult to fathom. There is scant evidence with which to even hazard a guess, although Clark and Houston (1998:40) suggest that leather working was a male-gendered activity.

Wood Carvers and Carpenters. Like gourds, paper, and textiles, the organic nature of wood compromises its preservation in the biologically active tropical environs of the Maya lowlands. Nonetheless, some extraordinary wooden items have been discovered such as wooden boxes, bowls, and benches from caves (Pendergast 1974; Peterson 2006; Prufer 2002) as well as in situ architectural elements, such as the carved door lintels of Temples 1 and 3 at Tikal (see Figure 6.5). During the Early Colonial period, the carving of wooden deity icons in Yucatán was so significant (and observable) as to elicit a hand wringing and detailed description by Bishop Diego de Landa (Tozzer 1941:159–161). At that time and place, carvers of wood were called *ah pol* "he who carves" or *ah hot'* "he who sculpts," the latter apparently referring to a "hard point making lines in a surface" (Clark and Houston 1998:43). It is hard to imagine a Maya past in which wooden objects – intricately carved of beautiful tropical hardwoods – greatly outnumbered the more durable pottery, stone tools, and ornaments of semiprecious stone and shell that are recovered archaeologically, but it is possible that they did. There were the literate carvers who worked in the palace tradition – the *ah hot'* – and left behind magisterial royal carvings such as Lintel 2 of Temple 3 at Tikal (Figure 6.5) and the carpenters – the *ah pol* – who made things such as bowls, boxes, and perhaps deity icons for their community. Were they generally male artisans? Possibly, but such a statement is based upon analogy with ethnographic/ethnohistoric accounts rather than relevant archaeological evidence.

Architects, Stone Masons and Carvers, Stucco Modelers, Scribes, and Painters. The legacy of Maya architectural skill is permanently inscribed on lowland landscapes as a palimpsest of monumental and more modest stone and earthen constructions that began shortly after 1000 B.C.E. and continued through Colonial-period church constructions. Without a doubt, there were palace schools of architecture as each Preclassic, Classic, and Postclassic seat of power was built in a distinctive fashion although drawing from a shared canon of architectural principles, such as room proportionality, design, balance, and use of the corbel arch, to name just a few salient architectural concepts. The means by which the great cities were constructed – by organizing the labor of hundreds, if not thousands, of people to do everything from quarry stone to mix plaster – surely is one of the less told stories of Maya civilization (but see Abrams 1994 for a discussion of labor and energetics). The full range of knowledge and artisan skill was employed in these monumental works although the final finishing-work of the stone mason, carver, stucco modeler, or painter generally receives the most acclaim by contemporary students of Maya architecture. Their artisanship was complexly entangled with the political aspirations and legacy-building dreams of whomever wielded authority at the seat of power in which they lived and/or labored. The architects and finishing crafters likely were members of the *literati* who worked in groups composed of apprentices and master crafters. According to Miller and Martin (2004:121), "Carvers often worked together on monuments – up to seven signatures could appear on the same stone ... artisans' names and elevated titles often place them within the elite class and doubtless quite a number were of noble birth." Stone masonry and stucco/plaster surfaces are not restricted to elite contexts, however, and enjoyed a wider distribution, particularly during the Preclassic period. Once again, it seems most realistic to imagine a broad base of cultural competency in stone building and stucco/plaster working at the community level with a smaller subset of persons – educated at royal courts – who pushed the limits of the medium and effected innovations in scale, patterns of vaulting, types of tenoning, and application and content of decorative facades. These materialities of spirituality and power resulted in the larger-than-life stucco masks of Preclassic pyramids, the tall, narrow temples of Tikal, the mansard roofs of Palenque, and the wide, spacious corbel-vaulted rooms of the Puuc sites, to name just a few of the distinctive and innovative architectural characteristics of these ancestral Maya seats of power.

Much has been written of Maya scribes, painters, and sculptors who pushed hieroglyphic script and a naturalistic rendering of form farther than any other indigenous American peoples (e.g., Herring 2005). Our understanding of Maya grammar, syntax, and semantics is under constant expansion and refinement (see Houston 2000 for a turn-of-the-century review of Maya epigraphy). The exulted and most important sacred status of writing and painting, the most diacritically marked of artisan skills, was deeply encoded in Maya hierarchizing via a creation narrative. In the *Popol Vuh*, most crafts are mentioned as practiced before the era of true human beings except for "writings or figures (*tz'ib*) rendered on blankets or cloaks (*c'ul*) or on paper (*wuj*)," which do not occur until the story moves into the human era (Tedlock and Tedlock 1985:124). Classic-period scribes (generally imaged as well fed) were painted on polychromes and shown wearing a balloon headdress stuffed with pen quills; they can be identified as male and all known scribal signatures contain the pronoun "*ah*." Given the significant complementarity between writing and brocading, however, the elaborate symbol system woven by females into Maya brocade designs deserves greater study. In the Andean region, Urton (1997, 2003) has shown that knotted *khipu* and woven tunics encoded complex sets of mathematical and status-linked information.

Specialized Production of Consumable Items

Beyond the production of crafts, there also existed specialists with skills such as salt processing, cacao and tobacco cultivation, hunting and trapping, healing, calendar keeping, name giving, and midwifery–skilled persons who produced valuable consumables or provided valuable (socially consumable) services. Even harder to detect archaeologically, such specialists nonetheless were indispensable to the cultural and biological reproduction of a community. Over the past few decades, sites at which salt processors worked and the equipment that they used has come into focus, initially for researchers focusing on the northern coast of the Yucatán Peninsula (Andrews 1983) and more recently for those investigating coastal Caribbean sites in Belize (Andrews and Mock 2002; MacKinnon and Kepecs 1989; McAnany and Murata 2006a; McKillop 2002). Unlike pottery production, salt production is more visible at its place of production than its place of consumption, particularly when the *sal cocida* or cooking method is used. The diagnostic artifact inventory of sockets, spacers, and solid cylinders has helped to pinpoint production locales. Some archaeological salt-processing locales also contain residential features; however, others, such as Wits Cah Ak'al in central coastal Belize, contain scarce evidence of a residential component and probably were visited seasonally over centuries (Murata 2010).

A detailed ethnographic study of traditional Highland Maya salt processing by Reina and Monaghan (1981) provides an account of salt production that may be relevant to the past. In Sacapulas, according to Reina and Monaghan (1981:32), the craft of salt making "is closely tied with one's place in the society, community identity, and economic well-being. It is not only a job, but *costumbre*. It is a mission that has been entrusted to them by the *nagual* of their leader, the Ahau Canil [culture hero in migration epic], and links them with their past." According to Reina, the same *habitus* that pervades artisan activities also informs salt processing. During the period of ethnographic study, males and females worked as a complementary team to extract and boil the salt water from saline springs but informants remembered a time when females were not allowed near saltworks (Reina and Monaghan 1981:17). The salt of Sacapulas – especially the highly desired dark variety – was traded widely and it is not inconceivable that in the past coastal Belizean salt was traded 150 kilometers or so inland to the central Petén. Wright (2005:563) has suggested that elevated $^{87}Sr/^{86}Sr$ levels found in the Tikal burial sample may be the result of ingestion of sea salt. Additional support for large salt distribution networks comes from early Colonial-period Guatemala where the coastal salt-making community of Iztapa traded their salt – transported via tumpline – 200 kilometers into the highlands (Feldman 1985:76–78, Figure 14).

Data have been slow to accumulate, but it is becoming quite likely that there also existed communities that specialized in crops – such as cacao and tobacco – that were highly desired at royal courts. The political economy of cacao is discussed in Chapter 9. The dispersed settlement pattern of the Caribbean coastal zone coupled with its rich alluvial soils renders this area a prime suspect as a specialized cacao-growing region, to be counted along with the better known cacao-producing regions of Tabasco, Ulua, and Soconusco (McAnany and Murata 2006b, 2007). Likely grown amidst high-canopy trees, cacao can be harvested over a very long period of time; thus, a family could manage, harvest, and possibly transport the valuable cacao seeds. Ethnohistorical data from Belize and elsewhere (Jones 1998; MacLeod 1973) corroborate the importance of cacao in the early Colonial economy and, of course, epigraphic evidence is replete with examples of its high value in Classic Maya society (see Chapter 9 for more details).

The role of tobacco in the ancestral Maya past is less well understood. God L – associated with trading and the Underworld – is often shown smoking a fat cigar as on the Temple of the Sun at Palenque (Figure 7.11). Houston and colleagues (2006:114) have identified glyphic compounds for tobacco (*k'utz*) and tobacco powder (*may*) in Classic-period inscriptions, the latter on small flasks colloquially called "poison" bottles. There is a growing sense that tobacco use was very common in Maya society but, as yet, no tobacco seeds have been identified in archaeobotanical remains (Lentz 1999:13). Both tobacco and cacao – and probably other crops as well – may commonly have been grown as specialized crops, with production exceeding that needed for family use. Intimately linked with landscape and growing conditions, agricultural products grown for the purpose of trade or in response to tribute obligations represent a kind of focused land use by those already in the "business" of making a livelihood through farming.

Hunters and trappers interact with their environment in a manner that is different from farming. There are few images of farmers in Classic and Postclassic royal iconography, but hunters or a personification of the god of hunting appear in quite a few scenes – most notably in the black-and-white drawings painted on the caves walls of Naj Tunich (Stone 1995:198); the guardian of game is thought to have resided in caves (Taube 2003:474). At Naj Tunich, one of the hero twins – Hunaphu – is dressed in the broad-brimmed hat worn by hunters plus the hip cloth of a ballplayer (Figure 3.8), indicating the complex interplay among the practices of hunting and ball playing

FIGURE 7.11 Tobacco-smoking God L carved in stone on the Temple of the Cross, Palenque (redrawn by John Feola after Schele and Freidel 1990:241).

and places of the Underworld such as caves. Taube (2003:473) emphasizes the association between the hunting god and the gods of night and darkness, which he attributes to the dark and menacing nature of the forests that are frequented by hunters in search of deer, peccary, and jaguar. Of course, the association between hunters and nighttime could also be attributed to the efficacy of nighttime hunting. The hero twins are famous for their exploits with a blowgun, and their youth and beauty – along with their desire to avenge the death of their father – were considered archetypal ideals of Maya royalty. By extension, their hunting activities may also have been considered proper royal pursuits. Elites – as diacritically marked persons – traversed the forest with impunity (see Chapter 3). For the Alta

Verapaz, Feldman (1985:90) provides a fascinating description of the trapping – but not killing – of quetzal birds at water holes for the purpose of feather extraction. The status of the trappers is not indicated.

Finally, there are specialized identities that can be subsumed under the heading of social or ritual specialists. This list is a long one indeed and includes such *oficios* as astronomers, calendar keepers, healers, name givers, and midwives. Encompassing both genders and a profoundly wide range of skills, these specialists were present both at court and in communities and were an indispensable part of ritual cycles, rites of passage, and family crises. Court astronomers and calendar keepers produced a written record – in hieroglyphic texts – on carved monuments and painted codices. The former have been much diminished by the decontextualization and commodification of modern looting, whereas the latter were greatly reduced by the destructive nature of time and the Colonial conquest. Until relatively recently, the footprint of ritual specialists was barely detectable, but an upsurge of archaeological research in caves has brought this type of ritual activity into focus. The density of materials deposited as ritual offerings in the deep recesses of caves is significant. Brady (2006:119–125) provides a detailed comparison between artifact densities in the caves below Dos Pilas and surface deposits from excavated architecture and midden contexts. Artifact density is much enhanced in cave contexts, which suggests that cave visitation occurred frequently. We can imagine the significance ascribed to ritual practice that took place within these Underworld chambers – whether that practice was aimed at maintaining balance or effecting a change in an existing, undesirable situation.

How Much Evidence Constitutes Proof of a Specialized Skill?

The material left in caves provides an unusually crisp signature of specialized ritual activity but what of the everyday surface contexts – residential floors and midden deposits that archaeologists frequently encounter? How much evidence needs to be found in order to argue that artisans were at work? Judging from our few contexts of extraordinary preservation due to rapid site abandonment – Aguateca and Cerén – artisan activities routinely go undetected because the long-term process of site abandonment tends to strip away much of the relevant material. Inomata and Triadan (2000:60–64) note that the best evidence of artisan activity was found within floor and plaza surface deposits rather than midden and burial contexts. Unfortunately, floor deposits are more typically devoid of significant material at sites that were abandoned over a long period of time. A further sobering thought comes from Lewis (1996:377) who suggests that because of "the technical intricacies often required in the production of status-legitimizing items, production output may be quite low and by-products few." Certainly the seminal studies of artisan production at Tikal were based upon modest counts of artifact debris (Becker 1973; Haviland 1974).

As we strive to bring into better focus the identity and places of artisans, we must also contend with transformational and maintenance processes that result in the movement of debris piles – a particularly serious issue for sites with long occupational spans; some Maya sites were occupied continuously for close to 2,000 years. As Clark (2003a:27) observes, "[a]s an inferential matter, occupational specialization is tied up with issues of waste and waste management." Moholy-Nagy (1990, 1997) has drawn particular attention to this aspect of site formation, arguing that most workshop identifications are actually transported dump deposits, including most of the lithic debris lining royal tombs at Tikal as well as some of the caches. This point is well taken and makes it clear that unmasking the identity and place of ancestral Maya artisans involves much more than restructuring our problem focus to include "agency"; it entails more sophisticated analysis of maintenance and depositional processes, more attention to microdebris and floor chemistry, and, of course, wider sampling nets when one is selecting units for excavation. Serious attention to methods will alleviate the impasse that Clark (2003a:30) referred to with the following witticism: "We cannot continue to live with the modified adage that 'one man's workshop is another woman's garbage.'"

CONCLUDING THOUGHTS

Ironically, the methods and logic by which ancestral Maya society was materially reproduced over several millennia remain a frontier within Maya archaeology – poorly charted terrain for which hieroglyphic sources provide only tantalizing hints. The dissonance between the cultural logic of artisan production documented ethnographically/ethnohistorically as opposed to that embraced by archaeologists – informed by the relations of production within capitalism – is great but the chasm can be spanned. Here the notion of self-conscious "tacking" (Geertz 1979; Wylie 1993:24–25) between the known and the unknown may provide a productive approach for thinking and modeling a past in which interactions between people and crafted goods were profoundly entangled and contextualized in a more complex fashion than exists in economies in which goods are commoditized. As Sabloff (2005:90) has noted, "for all Precolumbian Mesoamerican peoples, technology was not a separate sphere of knowledge and activity but a deeply embedded part of all aspects of their culture."

8

Places, Practices, and People of Commerce

> **K'IWIK** 1: tianguis, feria o mercado o plaza, donde venden y compran...; **k'iwik likil kon ba'ba'l**: feria o mercardo donde se venden muchas cosas ... **2. K'IWIK SOTS' U KONOL NA** 11: bazar, mercado ...
>
> Barrera Vásquez 1995:405

And so goes the entry for *k'iwik* – a word for places at which things are bought and sold – in the dictionary of contemporary Yucatec Mayan compiled by Alfredo Barrera Vásquez. What is the antiquity of this term and of marketplace practices in the Maya region? And what can we say about the antiquity of the role of trader in ancestral Maya society and of their connections to royal courts and palatial precincts of power? These questions – so integral to the puzzle of ancestral economies – defy easy answers. The interrogation begins with an allegory or morality tale about traders pieced together by an epigrapher and an art historian and then moves on to consider media of convertibility, evidence of marketplaces, and approaches to reading the economic biography of things.

ALLEGORICAL SHAMING AND REHABILITATION OF GOD L

One of the extraordinary facts of artisan activity across Mesoamerica resides in the methods by which crafts were transported from their place of fabrication. Many products were loaded on to a back-rack (*cacaste*) or into a large net bag and shouldered by means of a

FIGURE 8.1 Epi-Classic version of the merchant deity God L from the murals of Cacaxtla, México (drawn by and courtesy of Simon Martin).

tumpline across the forehead. Alternatively, goods could be transported via canoe if feasible. No other means of transport existed save the palanquins upon which royalty were carried by porters. The antiquity of the *cacaste* backframe is made clear by the Terminal Classic murals of Cacaxtla, found far west of the Maya lowlands, that depict the intrepid God L – patron of traders – with a *cacaste* loaded with precious items such as quetzal feathers (Figure 8.1). He surveys a cacao tree laden with pods and a nearby maize plant that is fecund with corn cob-shaped images of the maize god. Far from being a relict of the distant past, however, *cacastes* were still used to transport goods – especially pottery – to markets in highland Guatemala well into the twentieth century (Reina and Hill 1978:208; Figure 8.2). This mode of transport places an upper limit on the weight (probably not more than 85 pounds) that could be traded at any one point in time (Reina and Hill 1978:208). As Sanders and Santley (1983; see also Drennan 1984) note, this restriction did not apply to canoe transport,

FIGURE 8.2 Highland Guatemalan traders transporting pottery to market via *cacaste* backracks (from Reina and Hill 1978:208; courtesy of Ruben Reina).

particularly the large cargo canoes known to have been used during the Postclassic period.

In a seminal publication, Sabloff and Rathje (1975) maintained that the economy of the Postclassic Maya world was more highly commercialized than that of the Classic period – with more bulk trading over longer distances and more involvement on the part of elites. Subsequent research has born out the thesis of an increasingly commercialized society throughout Postclassic Mesoamerica (see contributions in Smith and Berdan 2003b), and, of course, the Postclassic Maya deity of traders and travelers – Ek Chuah – was described in the sixteenth century by Bishop Diego de Landa

(Tozzer 1941:107). It is difficult to gauge the extent to which Classic-period Maya economies were commercialized, particularly if one uses the definition of "commercial" adopted by Plattner (1989:175) to refer to the use of "money to effect economic exchanges" (more on media of convertibility later). But changes do seem to have occurred near the hinge point between the Classic and Postclassic periods. Seats of power and population shifted to coastal or more strategic and canoe-accessible locales, the pattern and quantity of traded goods such as obsidian changed significantly, and artifacts indicative of textile production – namely spindle whorls – increased dramatically in frequency. Moreover, identity as a trader – once seemingly scorned by royalty – seems to have been embraced. We learn from Colonial accounts that one of the royal Cocom princes was spared certain death when Postclassic Mayapan was sacked and burned because he was absent, presumably on a trading mission in Honduras (Tozzer 1941:37). A second example from early Colonial times is provided by Matthew Restall (1997:185) who translates a Yucatec legal document of 1580 in which Diego Pox makes a claim on his father's estate with the following statement: "I have also sustained my father, for four times I went to trade in Bacalar, that I might bring cacao, half of which I gave to my father, as the principal men of my cah [town and community] well known [*sic*]." These accounts suggest that trading activities were subsumed within a Postclassic-Early Colonial elite identity.

Trading as a royal occupation arguably is traceable to the latter part of the Classic period. The collapse of the authority of sacred rulers in the southern Petén and a greater openness to a pan-Mesoamerican amalgam of trading and ritual practices in the northern Yucatán contributed to this transformation of social roles. Representations of God L are particularly sensitive to these changes. In the Cacaxtla murals, God L appears as a stately caped and capped figure (Figure 8.1) but earlier Classic-period depictions are not so flattering. Piecing together an ancient narrative from a series of pictorial polychromes, Miller and Martin (2004:58–61, 76) tell a Classic-period tale of the manner in which the hero twins brought down the arrogant and wealthy God L, stripped him (literally) of his finery, and forced him to pay tribute to the sun god (presumably, a thinly guised reference to a sacred ruler). This morality tale can be interpreted to suggest that wealth – in the absence of sacred power – is somehow immoral and must be controlled. This story also conveys the sense that Classic period rulers were wary, perhaps jealous, of the power and wealth that came from trading activities, which they may not have directly controlled but upon which they were greatly dependent, particularly as a materialization of social difference. Long-distance traders would have brought raw materials and finely crafted things to royal courts and palatial precincts and also to local and regional marketplaces. The wealthy god of trading – God L – was not an exulted or handsome member of the Classic Maya constellation of deities but rather is depicted as elderly, wrinkled, and lascivious, with Underworld connections. Moreover, Maya royalty are seldom shown smoking tobacco, but Classic God L often puffs on a fat cigar with smoke scrolls prominently displayed (Figure 7.11). As a traveler of wooded trails between settlements, the itinerant God L's cigar smoke probably kept the mosquitoes at bay, a trick that archaeologists working at sites in the middle of the forest know well.

So, what does the story of God L tell us about the ethos of trading in Classic Maya society? His stately representation in the Cacaxtla murals suggests that the intersection of wealth, religion, and political power was shifting at the end of the Classic period in the direction of greater engagement with the movement of materials and an embrace of what Bailey (1998:1) calls the "exchange drama." The morality tale also conveys a deeply seated suspicion and wariness about trading as an activity and an *oficio* among Classic-period elites. Trading activities must have been a fact of life at Classic royal courts where über-elites sought to acquire highly valued things such as quetzal feathers and *Spondylus* shells from afar, but see Chapter 9 for alternative methods of acquisition. The punitive overtones of stripping God L of his fine clothing suggests that interaction with traders was somewhat taxing for Classic Maya rulers who, after all, would have commissioned the figural paintings that depicted the denigration of this wealthy resident of the Underworld. While everything that came into and went out of royal courts probably was carefully counted and controlled, there likely was much that circulated beyond the radar of royal oversight. Only God L – and traders as his human counterparts – knew the details of this vibrant and wealthy sector of the economy. In principle, all that exists within the fiefdom of a sacred ruler belongs to that ruler who is a supernatural delegate on earth; this principle renders bureaucratic control a moot point. In reality, there are deals to be made and wealth to be accumulated by both bureaucrats and astute traders. Regardless of whether or not there existed elaborate bureaucratic oversight, every ruler would have been well aware of the untapped wealth that flowed through her/his kingdom. In this regard, the flamboyant display of rich attire by God L constituted a kind of "in-your-face" reminder of the wealth that existed outside the control of rulers. Highland Mexica of Postclassic times did not allow such an affront and carefully regulated the type of clothing that traders could wear, in essence, forbidding them from conspicuously displaying their wealth as if they were members of the noble class. This type of parable is not unique to the Classic Maya world and illustrates a widespread and persistent tension between traders – who affect the conveyance of crafted/harvested goods (and acquire wealth in the process) – and rulers who accumulate wealth and transform it into material accoutrements of authority.

SPHERES OF CONVEYANCE AND NOTIONS OF EQUIVALENCIES

The movement of goods throughout Maya society was a complex and layered affair and involved what Rowlands (1993:149) terms the "transformation of value through movement in space/time." Given the appetite for prestige goods from afar among elites and nobles, *spheres of conveyance* (Bohannon 1955) likely existed, meaning that water jars probably did not circulate in the same trading sphere as quetzal feathers and jadeite. Of course, everyone needed water jars so trading spheres were not coterminus with social difference. Feldman (1985:23) suggests that spheres of conveyance existed in highland Guatemala on the eve of Spanish incursions, and their presence is known among highland Mexica where they were backed by sumptuary laws that added muscle to the differentiation of the noble class from the rest of society based on permitted costuming and accoutrements. Among highland Mexica, we also know that there were several different types of traders who worked local and distant markets, and we can only assume that similar roles existed in the Maya region from very early times. Dahlin and colleagues

(2007:367) provide one of several reviews of Yucatec Mayan terms for traders. Those dealing with prestige goods from distant lands might also trade in goods that were more locally available and not so restricted in their distribution.

Despite the convertibility and high value of cacao, there was no "gold standard" in ancient Maya society, meaning that "money" *sensu stricto* did not exist. Agreed upon equivalencies and exchange rates, no doubt, fluctuated in response to supply and demand (which generally are linked to harvest cycles, availability of raw materials, and political relations). Halperin (1994:88) provides an extensive review of Polanyi's concept of equivalency, which he employed to circumvent use of the term "price" in reference to noncapitalist forms of exchange that are not driven by the "forces of supply and demand in a price-making market system." Here, I note that Halperin used the term "market system" in its formal economic sense to refer to price-setting forces that are specific to capitalist production; she is not referring to exchange transactions within localized marketplaces. Equivalencies clearly existed among the Mexica; for instance, a single cotton *manta* could be exchanged for 100 or more cacao beans (Boone 1994:87). Red shells, copper bells, and axes, as well as cacao are noted as money-like media of convertibility in Yucatec documentary sources of the Colonial period (discussed in Piña Chan 1978:43–44). We can assume that similar equivalencies existed during the preceding Classic period, but have no way of calibrating ratios of exchange or equivalencies in the absence of explicit documentary sources. The notion of equivalency is central to effecting an exchange – be it a gift exchange or a ceremonial exchange of arm shells as in the Kula ring – and is deeply contextualized and situationally contingent. Notions of fairness, prosperity, and wealth all flow from the notion of equivalency. Indeed, Firth (1983:89) considered the notion so central that he critiqued Mauss (1967) for failing to develop an inquiry into equivalencies because of his focus on spiritual bonds between things.

To establish an equivalency is to forge a ratio-based relation between two unlike things. With this convention, things that theoretically are widespread across a landscape – pottery for instance – can circulate and be exchanged for items crafted from a raw material that is more restricted in distribution, such as marine shell, obsidian, or salt. Lemonnier (1986:176), Firth (1983:101), and others have pointed to the significance of this interdependence that perpetuates sociality among communities. Concepts of both convertibility and interdependence contain overtones of social covenants – arrangements that exist as a result of mutual consent and no doubt effect mutual (although perhaps not equal) benefit to participants. But what and where were the material contexts – the places – in which such transactions played out? Where could one participate in the theatricality of exchange drama, so aptly described by Hutson (2000) for Mexica marketplaces? Pictorial images of God L seated within palace precincts provide an image of the material context of "high-end" long-distance trading transactions, and there is increasing evidence that large-scale marketplace trading also occurred within the ubiquitous plaza spaces of many Maya centers.

COMMERCE AT MARKETPLACES AND FAIRS

Although images of God L provide insight on the role of traders in Classic Maya society, there is no parallel Classic Maya iconography showing bustling marketplaces, although the vivid murals discovered at Calakmul certainly emphasize dyadic exchange (more on this later). Contemporary marketplaces in highland Guatemala – at communities such as Santiago Atitlán (Figure 8.3) – provide a wealth of potential analogy to the past, although the validity of that analogy to certain parts of the Yucatan has been questioned. Restall (1997:185), for instance, asserts on the basis of documentary sources that open markets did not exist in Colonial-period Yucatán, although specific references to marketplaces are cited in documentary sources footnoted in Tozzer's edition of *Landa's Relación* (1941:96). Piña Chan (1978:43) considered the presence of Yucatec markets to be indisputable (see also Fernandez Tejero 1997). Significantly, several sources cited in footnote 424 of *Landa's Relación* refer retrospectively to the great marketplace of Chichén Itzá and thus suggest the possibility that the political balkanization of the Postclassic period actually dampened marketplace exchange (see following discussion of isomorphism between political spheres and supply zones).

Archaeological sites generally contain sizable plazas where market exchange, among other activities, certainly could have taken place. The spatial triangulation of churches, marketplaces, and soccer fields

FIGURE 8.3 Periodic marketplace at Santiago Atitlán, July 7, 2007 (photo courtesy of Walter E. Little).

in contemporary Maya communities is mirrored in the past by the proximity of pyramidal shrines to large open plaza spaces and formally delimited ballcourts (Fash and Fash 2007), which suggests a long-standing intersection of ritual, athletic, and economic activities. For Santley (2007:179), the presence of large, open plazas at archaeological sites in the Tuxtla Mountains of southern Veracruz provide *prima facie* evidence of marketplace activity. In the Maya region also, many archaeologists suspect that such spaces accommodated the performance of many different types of activities, including commercial. Jones (1996:91) interprets the East Plaza of Tikal as "the principal marketplace of Tikal" based on its open architecture and U-shaped structures, an observation collaborated by Coe (1988:73). Wurtzburg (1991) argues for the feasibility of interpreting the low, rectangular stone alignments of the Mirador Plaza at Sayil as remnants of market stalls. A similar pattern has been detected and interpreted in an identical fashion at Chunchucmil (Dahlin et al. 2007:372), Pueblito (Laporte and Chacón 2007), and other Maya sites as well. Dahlin and colleagues collected soil samples from the putative marketplace at Chunchucmil. Subsequent geochemical analysis indicates spatial clusters within which levels of phosphorus as well as zinc and iron are elevated beyond the level of background control samples (Dahlin et al. 2007:373–376). Using soil chemistry at the Honduran site of El Coyote, Wells (2004) was able to identify activity loci relating to production and possibly exchange. If formation processes and historical factors of land use can be adequately controlled, a geochemical approach to identifying places where food items were bulked and processed or crafting took place holds great promise.

At Calakmul, Campeche, intriguing pictorial and glyphic evidence of what is interpreted variously as banquet preparations or trading activities (including the exchange of salt) has been discovered on wall murals from the North Acopolis (Chiik Nahb) complex (Boucher and Quiñones 2007; Martin 2007a, 2007b). The vibrancy of the murals is striking, particularly the image of a women shown in stride wearing a diaphanous blue *huipil* adorned with large pictorial cartouches (Carrasco and Colón Gonzalez 2005:40). Mural scenes emphasize interactivity between persons – as if to indicate the face-to-face transactional nature of Maya exchange activities (or the value of personal charisma and persuasion in pulling off a successful palace feast). Martin (2007a:15–24) reads the associated short hieroglyphic strings as linking a person with a thing (possibly a traded thing) – that is, a person of salt, of corn, of tobacco, and of delicate and thin-walled pottery vessels. In a scene that includes the hieroglyph for salt, a seated woman wearing a strapless blue *huipil* holds a green sphere (possibly a squash) over a woven basket (Martin 2007b). Seated opposite is a male who wears a broad-brimmed hat and holds a ladle. The currently known 18 murals feature (pictorially and glyphically) prosaic items such as tamales, atole, cylindrical vessels, and textiles (Boucher and Quiñones 2007; Martin 2007b). Interestingly, although the North Acropolis is near colossal pyramidal Structure II – the ritual heart of Calakmul – the things that are changing hands are not quetzal feathers or jadeite, nor are they things that are constitutive of royal identity, crafted with labor intensivity, or transported from far away. Rather, the exchange of more pedestrian items is the subject of the murals; this fact has stoked the fires of contrasting perspectives that favor interpreting the subject of the murals either as banquet preparations (Boucher and Quiñones 2007) or as marketplace activities near the epicenter of Calakmul (Martin 2007b).

Maya hieroglyphic texts differ famously from the corpus of Mesopotamian cuneiform in providing scarce detail of exchange activities – documentation that is a staple of cuneiform texts. But, as hinted by the Calakmul mural glyphs, such opacity may be lifting. Although the reading is not secure for a number of reasons, Maya epigrapher David Stuart has tentatively identified a glyph compound within a title string painted on an unprovenienced Late Classic cylindrical vessel that might be read as *aj k'iwik* or "he/she of the market/gathering place" (D. Stuart, personal communication November 2008). Non-elites – or even nonroyalty – are seldom referenced in Classic Maya hieroglyphic texts so, if such a title did exist, the referenced person would have been elite and probably affiliated with a royal family. For instance, scribes – who generally exhibited elite identity – were referenced as *aj ts'ib* ("he of the painted text"; Coe and Van Stone 2001:13). So, a title such as *aj k'iwik* would have referenced an elite person who managed/supervised a marketplace or was an active trader and spent considerable amounts of time in a marketplace.

Even if Classic period nobles did not exercise hegemonic control over the exchange of goods within their realms, markets or fairs likely were held – even if only periodically – at these large and impressive seats of power, as Freidel (1981:378–379) has suggested. Indeed, it is difficult to imagine how a concentrated population of 30,000 to 60,000 people could be supplied with basic goods in the absence of a marketplace (a pertinent discussion of scale and economic complexity of Maya cities can be found in Chase and Chase 1996). An observation on highland Guatemalan marketplaces is pertinent here: "the market is not an institution 'owned' by the *pueblo* or the *municipalidad*; rather, the political system acts as a custodian. An officer known as the *fiel* supervises activities, collects a daily fee from each vendor for the rights to sell goods or to rent market stalls, and sees that everyone observes appropriate behavior" (Reina and Hill 1978:207). In this instance, the marketplace is monitored but not possessed by political authorities, but the collected fees certainly enrich the entity hosting the market. The catchment area for a local marketplace can be quite large. For southwestern Guatemala, McBryde (1971:Map 15) shows trade links that extended over 25 miles (40.2 kilometers) from a production locale to a marketplace for large *tinajas* and cooking *ollas* – all transported on *cacaste* backracks. Even though there is no need to throw Thiessen polygons of 40-kilometer radii over the Maya region, it is clear that – given the populous conditions of Late Classic times – supplying households in the *absence* of marketplace activity would have been extremely challenging.

PATHWAYS OF CONVEYANCE TO AND FROM A MARKETPLACE

The distance and travel conditions over which things are transported to and from a place of exchange frame the relationship between artisans/growers and marketplaces. Conceivably, the number of different Mayan terms that exist for pathways might be linked to the periodicity of their use. In Yucatec Mayan, for instance, Hanks (1990:311) notes the terms *noh b'eh* (open or great road), *yam b'eh* (small path), and *ek' b'eh* (rough trail or black dark road). Although there is no definitive evidence that roads were used for commercial purposes, the most parsimonious explanation suggests multipurpose functions that encompassed commercial, ritual, and martial uses (see Chase and Chase 2001b, among others). For the highland site of Xochicalco, Hirth (2000:187) argues for the presence of markets at two plazas (South and Coatzin plazas) based on their proximity to the dendritic road network of Xochicalco and to the Plaza Ceremonial. Thus, both roads and plazas can be envisioned as richly textured and polyvalent spaces, sites of contestation as well as covenantal cooperation.

Because the burden of transport fell on the backs of traders, assistant porters, and likely slaves, location (and distance between locations) played an important role in the complex and multitiered trading network of ancestral Maya times. Locales situated strategically in reference to a resource or a crafted good assumed great importance – such as Cancuen, located at the base of the Alta Verapaz, where jadeite was reduced from boulders to items of adornment (Demarest et al. 2004). Chunchucmil, an Early Classic site in the northern Yucatec plains, is argued to have been a gateway and major market center (Dahlin 2003; Dahlin and Ardren 2002:267; Dahlin et al. 2007) in part due to the diminished focus on regal–ritual architecture. Doubtlessly, there are many other examples of strategically positioned gateway as well as resource-specific sites that existed in zones of salterns as well as amid cotton, cacao, and tobacco-producing areas. Likewise, locales of superior clay and chert – Colha, Belize, for instance – likely sponsored trading as well as production activities. Although sacred authority emanated from large seats of power, such places should not be construed as having formed the exclusive prototype for all Maya central places (see Dahlin and Ardren 2002:275). As the soft focus of archaeological method improves, we will be in a better position to comprehend the manner in which landscape, crafting, and marketplace came together to create an ancestral Maya economy.

READING THE ECONOMIC BIOGRAPHY OF THINGS

Certainly, archaeologists would love to be able to pick up a potsherd or piece of obsidian and "read" when, where, and by whom the artifact was crafted, the circumstances under which the artifact may have changed hands during its use-life, and how that changing-of-hands affected its final disposition in a context amenable to preservation and retrieval by an archaeologist. Kenneth Hirth suggests that study of the economic biography of things may be more fruitful than efforts to pinpoint the location of marketplaces. "Archaeologists have had difficulty in identifying the appearance of market institutions through central Mexico. The primary reason for this has been their concern with identifying *marketplaces* rather than trying to measure the effect of *market exchange* on the movement and distribution of resources" (Hirth 2000:184, emphasis in original). Hirth (2000:188) reasons that the presence of marketplace exchange reduces assemblage variability within and among residential locales because things are freely available for exchange in the marketplace, regardless of the socioeconomic status of the consumer. For Xochicalco, he examined the distribution of "foreign" ceramics (clay, form, and style discernibly not local) as well as obsidian from several different sources and found a pattern of ubiquitous distribution throughout residences of varied size and architectural elaboration. From this pattern, Hirth (2000:189–194) reasoned that marketplace exchange existed at Xochicalco.

The "market effect" on the distribution of crafted goods (also called supply zone and distributional studies) has been applied in the lowland Maya region following the pioneering study of Robert Fry (1979, 1980) at Tikal. More recent distributional studies – focused as well on the question of marketplace exchange – have included Chichén Itzá where Braswell and Glascock (2002) conclude that obsidian was exchanged within a bounded and administered marketplace during the Terminal Classic period. They note the dynamism of distribution patterns, with a different regional pattern emerging during the Postclassic period. Temporal dynamism and spatial complexity also form the conclusion of a comprehensive study of lowland Maya supply zone patterns (based on ceramic characteristics) undertaken by West (2002). So, the economic biography of things is a complex matter, and no single distribution model provides a perfect fit for the manner in which things were crafted and changed hands across the Maya region throughout 2,000 years of crafting and trading. If this complexity of evidentiary material tells us anything, however, it is that places, practices, and people of commerce varied widely across time and space, as noted by Braswell and Glascock (2002:46). Blanket, global statements regarding the commercialization (or not) of Maya ancestral economies (e.g., Smith 2004:Table 1) should be approached with great caution.

The study by Braswell and Glascock (2002) also indicates that power relations can intersect with trading spheres in a fairly direct fashion. This finding is echoed in the Mexican highlands where researchers have found close congruence between Aztec political spheres and distribution zones for pottery sourced through instrumental neutron activation analysis and stylistic types (see Minc 2006; Nichols et al. 2002, among others). The notion that trading occurs more frequently among persons who share identity – whether ethnic, political, or both – is echoed in the analysis of pottery distribution patterns of the Late Postclassic period in the Petén lakes region of Guatemala. There, Cecil (2004) found that areas defined on the basis of archaeological and ethnohistorical sources as ethnically Itzá or Kowoj yielded different and non-overlapping source signatures (based upon inductively coupled plasma emission spectroscopy or ICPES). These examples, and many more could be cited, indicate the key role of materials analysis in assessing the congruence (or not) of the complex spatial signatures of social/group identity, political allegiance/hegemony, and the economics of crafting and trading. Going to ground or, in this case, into the chemistry of sherds and other source-sensitive things spatializes trading and consumption patterns in a manner that deepens and contextualizes interpretation that, otherwise, tends toward general statements regarding the linkage between political power and economic practices (also see Masson et al. 2006; Smith and Schreiber 2005 for useful reviews).

CONCLUDING THOUGHTS

The lesson of God L suggests that there were substantially commercialized sectors within ancestral Maya society and that these sectors exhibit evidence of conflictive relations with political authority during the Classic-period. The conflict between the mythic power of the ruler (expressed by the dual tropes of the handsome young hero twins and the sun god) and the commercial wealth of traders (embodied in the flamboyant dress and aging body of God L) provides intriguing insight to Classic Maya society and may explain why hieroglyphic texts directly relevant to economic concerns are underrepresented. This glimpse into the arcs of political power and economic wealth suggests that much of the received wisdom regarding the limited degree of commercial activity in ancestral Maya society rests on shaky grounds.

New evidence of marketplace activity – iconographic, architectural, and chemical – is coming to the fore and may solidify what many researchers have already suggested, that ancestral Maya economies contained places of exchange. Economic interdependence, rather than autonomy, appears to have been the prevailing riff. Studies of the biography of things – through a variety of techniques, including chemical sourcing, stylistic analysis, and archaeological patterns of deposition – are yielding finer resolution of age-old and somewhat intractable archaeological questions regarding who traded with whom and how crafting as well as trading were constrained and enabled by political entanglements.

The subject of political entanglements is dealt with head-on in the following chapter, which addresses the political economy of Classic royal courts. Under examination is the manner in which royal families and their entourages were provisioned, particularly with items indicative of skill intensivity and exclusionary knowledge – objects that can be understood as instantiating authority. In Chapter 9, we see how artisanship colluded with political ambition to both engender and support hierarchy.

9

Flowery Speech of Maya Tributary Arrangements

Is this what you eat from, sir
what you drink from, sir?
Could this be
  the skull of my grandfather?
Could this be
  the skull of my father?
Is this what I am looking at
  what I see before me?
Then won't this also become
  a work of some kind
    an artifact
this bone of my crown
  bone of my head
carved in back
  and carved in front?
Then it'll be sent down there
  to my mountain
    my valley
ending up as an even trade for
  five score seeds of pataxte
    five score seeds of cacao
paid by my children
  my sons
at my mountain
  my valley.

Recited by José Coloch
of Rabinal [Tedlock
2003:176–177]

Why begin a chapter on Maya tributary arrangements with an excerpt from the K'iche' Mayan dramatic play called *Rab'inal Achi* or "The Man of Rabinal"? In the passage cited here, Cawek – who has been captured in battle by a warrior from Rabinal – is offered a last drink of chocolate that is served to him in a carved calabash cup. Knowing that he is to be sacrificed, he contemplates the fact that his skull may be carved and used as a drinking cup before being returned to his home community in return for a sizable tribute ransom of cacao and *pataxte* (a semiwild form of cacao) seeds. In this passage, the entwined nature of warfare, captive taking, and tribute is intimated by flowery prose. This evocative soliloquy spoken by a captive about to be sacrificed alludes to mirror strategies of alliance and warfare that were deployed to finance ancestral Maya kingdoms. The evidence for and cultural logic of tribute – particularly tribute ransom – as a form of state finance is the substance of this chapter. We begin by examining extant literature on state financing.

CONSIDERING STATE FINANCE

The means by which early civilizations were financed has been a topic of some interest since social theorists began to look back to the Roman Empire. Arguably, one of the first scholars to codify terminology for understanding noncapitalistic economic systems was the economic historian Karl Polanyi (1957:248) who seems to have come close to addressing taxation and tribute with a concept called "appropriative movement" from "dispositions." Defined as "a one-sided act of the hand, to which by force of custom or of law definite appropriative effects are attached" (Polanyi 1957:248), this concept draws on the vertical and centripetal characteristics of state financing. The mechanism that Polanyi (1957:253–254) provides for state financing is that of "redistribution" under which "the allocation of goods is collected in one hand and takes place [is redistributed, that is] by virtue of custom, law or *ad hoc* central decision." The mechanism of redistribution, familiar to all, later became a cornerstone of evolutionary typologies of social forms thought to be characteristic of chiefdoms in particular (see Earle 1977 for critique). In contrast, states or civilizations were thought to be characterized by systems of market exchange rather than by redistribution although Polanyi

(1960:330–331) noted that all three "patterns of integration" – that is, reciprocity, redistribution, and market exchange might – coexist. But a royal court cannot be financed through market exchange; a more effective means of building a fund of power (as per Malinowski and Sahlins) was required as was some wrestling with the notion of a political economy. In reference to Hawaiian chiefdoms, Earle (1977) noted that the term "redistribution" – which conjures an image of goods flowing into a central repository and back out again as needed – did not come close to accurately characterizing the methods by which Polynesian chiefdoms were financed (see also Yoffee 2005:22–31). Goods did flow into the chiefly coffers but then were consumed within the household of the chief, given to subordinates as awards for loyalty or military prowess, or dispersed through lavish feasting, all solely at the prerogative of the chief. In effect, political power and patronage intervened to thwart the return flow of goods intimated by the prefix of repeated action in "re-distribution." In retrospect, it is clear that Polanyi struggled to characterize early states that did not utilize a money-based standard for transactions and accounting. In an apocryphal statement worth repeating, Polanyi characterized the Minoan/Mycenaean economy as possibly "the only case on record in which a literate community eschewed the employment of money for accountancy" (Polanyi 1960:341; also cited in Renfrew 1972:297). As has become apparent with extended research of literate communities of the ancient Americas, states can deploy several means of financing and can keep track of transactions without reference to a money standard (some system of equivalencies always exists).

In an effort to clarify the discussion of state finance within the Inka political economy, D'Altroy and Earle (1985:188) further developed Polanyi's (1960:343, 346–349) notions of staple finance and the prestige sphere within staple finance in order to create a distinction between staple finance and wealth finance. The former entails "obligatory payments in kind to the state of subsistence goods such as grains, livestock, and clothing" while the latter "involves the manufacture and procurement of special products (valuables, primitive money, and currency ...) that are used as a means of payment" (D'Altroy and Earle 1985:188). This emphasis on the stuff of state finance rather than its mode of acquisition moved the discussion of state finance in a more concrete direction and probably created a false dichotomy, but it raised the consciousness of archaeologists by stipulating that all states require some type of financing. The real questions then involved how and with what states were financed. Blanton et al. (1996) continued to refine the tradition of dichotomous processes by analyzing the emergence of states within Mesoamerica as the result of two contrastive types of political action: exclusionary (as in the Maya lowlands) and corporate oriented (Mexican highlands). Once again, luxury or wealth items were contra posed against staple items with the acquisition of the former being a strong characteristic of exclusionary political action, while staple items supposedly formed the backbone of states that operated within a corporate ethos.

Although the strong neo-Marxist trend within mid-twentieth-century economic anthropology (see Wilk 1996:92–98) was not as prevalent within archaeology, Marxian constructs filtered into archaeology through use of ethnographic analogy and theoretical models. The following definition of peasantry, offered by Wolf (1966:3–4), was widely accepted by archaeologists: "rural cultivators whose surpluses are transferred to a dominant group of rulers that uses the surpluses both to underwrite its own standard of living and to distribute the remainder to groups in society that do not farm but must be fed for their specific goods and services in turn." This "bottom-up" predatory view of hierarchy in which those at the top benefit from appropriating the labor and services of subordinates led to a generation of scholars who asked large questions regarding the ontogeny of inequalities in wealth and power (see Stanish 2004). This line of research is primed by underlying questions regarding how (and why) social mechanisms working against the establishment of hierarchy failed. Thus, Trigger (2003:375) states that "a defining feature of all early civilizations was the institutionalized appropriation by a small ruling group of most of the wealth produced by the lower classes." After a survey of those mechanisms within early states, Trigger (2003:385) concludes that "almost nothing is known about how the Maya upper classes extracted surplus wealth from commoners. The vastness of state projects and the opulent life of Maya rulers suggest, however, that the Maya upper class, and kings in particular, did it very effectively." In the pages to follow, epigraphy and pictorial representations are brought to bear on just how Maya rulers did it.

STATE FINANCE FROM THE PERSPECTIVE OF MAYA TEXTS AND ICONOGRAPHY

As hieroglyphic decipherment progressed through the 1970s and 1980s, the general consensus among epigraphers and art historians was that the texts did not contain economic information. There was little chance, it seemed, of discovering an analogue to Mesopotamian cuneiform tablets, which have been characterized as the "cash register receipts of the ancient Sumerian world" (Paul Zimansky, personal communication 2005). Rather, Maya texts revealed new information about Maya royalty – their names and title strings, royal marriages, royal warfare, and their profound investment in the materiality of privilege.

Coincident with this decipherment came the recognition that Maya civilization, like many states of the past and present, was heavily vested in warfare. And so a discussion ensued as to the purpose of that warfare; that is, whether it represented ritualistic combat – undertaken for the purpose of securing captives for sacrifice along the lines of Mexica warfare – or whether Maya martial practices had a more pragmatic goal, such as territorial expansion or labor sequestering (see Webster 2000 for a comprehensive review of this topic). The obvious emphasis on live captive taking favored ritualistic combat and moved Maya statecraft away from a linkage between warfare and state finance. It soon became clear, moreover, that even divine rulers, such as the son of the great K'inich Janahb' Pakal I of Palenque, could be taken captive. One ruler, Waxaklajuun Ub'aah K'awiil of Copán, not only was taken captive but was sacrificed by the victorious captor, K'ahk' Tiliw Chan Yoaat, ruler of a kingdom that had been subordinate to Copán. Captive taking, in fact, seemed central to the identity of Classic Maya nobility as their titles often contain phrases such as "Aj Baak (*aj b'aak*), 'Captive-taker' or Baah Pakal (*b'aah pakal*), 'Head Shield'" and can include a count of captives secured over the course of a reign (Miller and Martin 2004:26–27). Were these epithets a boast of martial prowess or an indication of the deep religiosity of warriors bent on offering precious human life to the gods? Perhaps there exists yet a third alternative.

Concomitant with expanded knowledge of the martial and masculinist ethos of Classic Maya nobility came the comprehensive

FIGURE 9.1 Painted throne scene on a cylindrical polychrome vessel showing caped tribute messengers, from the tomb of Late Classic Tikal ruler, Jasaw Chan K'awiil I (Bur. 116; after Culbert 1993:Figure 68A; courtesy of University of Pennsylvania Museum).

documentation of the corpus of Classic Maya pictorial polychrome vessels by Justin Kerr. The Late Classic Maya polychrome painting tradition was highly sophisticated and temporally restricted (see Reents-Budet 1998:72–76, among others). Unfortunately, the cylindrical pottery vessels (commonly called vases) on which pictorial scenes and hieroglyphic texts were painted are in great demand on the illegal antiquities market by those with sizable disposable incomes. The great allure of these vessels stems from the fact that they (1) are portable (and so easier to smuggle across international boundaries than are megalithic stelae); (2) contain hieroglyphic texts (and thus provide a privileged view into the world of Maya *literati*); and (3) often depict court scenes complete with an enthroned ruler and courtiers that were painted in a naturalistic style and with an emphasis on social hierarchy and difference (Figure 9.1). Kerr (1989–2000) perfected a system of roll-out photography and set about photographing polychrome cylinders, whether looted or provenienced. Based on this sample of 176 Late Classic vessels, Reents-Budet (2001:213) found that the most frequently depicted courtier on these painted narratives is the *k'uhul ajaw* (divine ruler) himself who occupies a central and elevated throne position surrounded by attendants and supplicants. Although these compositions provide us with vivid, unparalleled images of the ancient Maya royal court, one is left wondering why so many palace presentation scenes – showing the "king at work" – were commissioned and, furthermore, why they were later interred with the deceased. Although with looted items, we will never know the full backstory, a preponderance of those recorded as part of an archaeological excavation were discovered within tombs. Figure 9.1, for example, was found in the royal tomb of Jasaw Chan K'awiil, the great warrior king of Late Classic Tikal who reigned from 682 until around 734 C.E. The well-fed ruler at the top of the composition – shown receiving offerings – could be Jasaw Chan K'awiil himself. Do such palace scenes represent interactions between palace nobles and territorial nobles who have come to pay homage to the divine ruler or is there a more coercive undertone to the palace presentation narratives?

Work on partially deciphered hieroglyphic texts indicates that the latter is a distinct possibility (see also Foias 2004:149). Despite earlier notions regarding the lack of economic content in Maya hieroglyphic writing, more recent decipherment reveals references to the machinations of a political economy organized around the royal court and, most important, sequentially linked to warfare (see review in Houston 2000:173–174). Stuart (1998:410–416) notes that the co-occurrence of the so-called step glyph with axe events (warfare) often also includes references to *patan* (tribute or labor service) and to *ikats* (cargo or burden born in Tzeltal Mayan), most notably on Naranjo Stela 12. Although the step glyph has not been deciphered securely, it probably reads *t'abayi* (Houston, personal communication 2007), and refers to an ascension of some sort and possibly the offering of gifts and tribute. Likewise, Stela 32 from Naranjo not only depicts a staircase leading to a throne but also contains a text that refers to the delivery (*ya-k'a-wa*) of tribute (*i-ka-tso-[o]*; Houston and Escobedo 1996:468; Le Fort and Wald 1995:112). The step symbol further emphasizes the hierarchy so clearly indicated on the pictorial imagery of polychrome vessels as in that of the vessel from Tikal (Figure 9.1), in which two figures ascend hieroglyphic steps to offer precious green quetzal feathers and a platter heaped with valuables to a seated ruler. Such hierarchical compositions with associated texts is particularly notable when the *ikats* is identified as that of another *k'uhal ajaw* as on Stela 12 from Naranjo in which the phrase *yi-ka-tsi* (his cargo) is followed by the title of the conquered lord of Yaxha (Stuart 1998:414). Of further interest is the fact that the "foot-ascending-steps verb," or semantic variants of it, occurs repeatedly on glyph bands painted on ceramics and other objects (Stuart 1998: 412). This suggests that many of these objects were crafted and inscribed either as part of a vertical transfer from a subordinate to a superordinate or to create a material memory of such a transfer. Architectural staircases present the perfect spatial geometry in which hierarchy, and thus social order, is showcased and performed. As Stuart (1998:414) notes, "warfare and captives are dominant themes of inscriptions on steps [of royal courts]." Houston (1998:360–361) suggests that the staircases themselves – often overbuilt in proportion to surrounding architecture – are profoundly dramaturgical and were locales for spectacles such as "the heaping of tribute ... or the display of captive[s]."

Additional clues to the workings of Classic Maya political economy come from the identification of the standing and kneeling persons in the Tikal court scene (Figure 9.1) who are attired in oversized white capes (unusual attire in a court scene) trimmed with brocaded sky bands and feather edging and who wear necklaces of jadeite and large *Spondylus* spp. shells, as well as headdresses of quetzal feathers. Elsewhere, persons wearing this attire are identified as *yebeet*, "his [bird] messenger" (unfortunately on a looted and therefore unprovenienced vessel); the messenger and the cacao that he offers is identified as coming to the royal court of Tikal from a lord of Calakmul (Houston et al. 2006:243, Figure 7.22). These two Maya capitals – Tikal and Calakmul – were mortal enemies; in fact, the major achievement of Jasaw Chan K'awiil of Tikal is generally considered to have been a decisive victory over Calakmul. Whether the presentation of cacao tribute resulted from that victory or another, we cannot determine because there is no context, no provenience, for this critically important vessel.

Reference to "bird messengers" has been found at royal courts with a strong tradition of martial activity, such as Caracol and Naranjo, where the phrase *y-ebet papamil*, "the messenger of papamil," has been recorded although the identity of "papamil" is currently unknown (Houston et al. 2006:244). These examples pale in comparison to the scale, pomp, and grandeur of the *yebeet* of the Bonampak murals, however. The walls of Room 1, traditionally thought to depict an heir-designation scene (Miller 2001:210), actually seem to showcase tribute-related figures clad, once again, in large white capes with finely adorned edging, *Spondylus* shells, jadeite ornaments, and quetzal feathers. Bags of cacao, totaling at least 40,000 beans, are conspicuously displayed in front of the throne on the end-wall mural (Houston 1997). As Houston et al. (2006:248) note, despite the finery in which these figures are clad, the few who are named with an adjacent hieroglyphic band are not called by a personal name but rather by their messenger role; specifically, one band reads *ybeet chak-ha ajaw* or "messenger of the Red or Great Water Lord." The lasting impression is that these messengers will be relieved literally of their sumptuary items by the attending "lord-on-high" and will then return to their home court, having fulfilled the role of emissary for their liege who could not or would not present the tribute personally.

Walking tribute bundles (Houston et al. 2006:247), the messengers clearly advertised the fine quality of the woven textiles and the lapidary works of art with which they were adorned. We have no way of knowing whether each human tributary bundle stood for a set number of folded *mantas,* bundles of quetzal feathers, or boxes containing jadeite ornaments and *Spondylus* shells and so currently have no way of gauging the quantities of tribute transfers. Drawing upon early Colonial records from Highland Guatemala, Feldman (1985:57) notes that, in addition to the standard *manta* of tribute, there were two special types: an extra large *manta* called *szuunum pati* in Xinca and a white *manta* called *tzotom zu pom chigul* in Kaqchiquel. Although highly speculative, it is tempting to see the tribute messengers of the earlier Classic period as wearing a variant of these ethnohistorically documented tribute *mantas.*

Another uncertainty of the known corpus of tribute narratives involves the movement of more pedestrian goods such as tumpline *cargas* filled with maize. Houston and Stuart (2001:69) observe that scenes of tributary interactions between lords and inferiors painted on polychrome vessels often include platters brimming with *tamales* (*wah*) and bowls of *pulque* (*chih*), an alcoholic beverage brewed from the agave plant. Taube (1989) originally identified *tamale* presentation imagery in court scenes, and it could be that the prepared *masa* of *tamales* was symbolic of a large volume of maize that was transferred between courts during a tribute-paying event. In the terminology of Polanyi (1960) and D'Altroy and Earle (1985), the tribute transfers could have consisted of both staple and wealth items.

In summary, the wall murals of Room 1, Bonampak, can be interpreted as a display of the great pageantry of tribute presentation although the location of the home of the Red or Great Water Lord – who is presenting the tribute in absentia – is unknown as is the underlying motivation for such a lavish presentation (but see discussion that follows). So too, many Late Classic polychrome pottery vessels provide a narrative of tribute presentations, offerings to overlords by subordinates who, by virtue of military conquest or diplomatic arrangements, send their messengers to "ascend the steps" with "gifts" for a publicly acknowledged superior. Ultimately ending their "social life" as funerary accoutrements, these vessels symbolize not only the wealth accumulated by victorious rulers with shrewd instincts of statecraft but also the impoverishment and anguish of those who were forced to relinquish their wealth and position in Late Classic Maya society. Tragically, many of these visual narratives of political domination have been ripped from their archaeological context by looters, smuggled illegally to dealers operating in wealthy, politically dominant twenty-first-century states, and ultimately purchased by private collectors and "public" museums eager for a piece of the past. Perhaps more than any other artifact class, Maya-painted polychrome vessels have been commodified and come to stand for the dark side of capitalism wedded to Colonial-style economic predation and an acquisitive romanticism about the past. Just as they appear to have represented the triumph of hierarchy and dominance in the distant Maya past, so today these vessels symbolize the political dominance of antiquity-consuming countries over less affluent antiquity-producing nations within which early states once reigned.

STATE FINANCING, CAPTIVE TAKING, AND TRIBUTE RANSOM

What was the motivating force behind these tributary offerings? How was a ruler cajoled or coerced to relinquish the wealth of a kingdom and perhaps some of the inalienable possessions of a royal family? From accounts of Mexica imperial statecraft, we know that simply the threat of a military campaign was enough to reach a tributary agreement with a less powerful *altepetl* (variant of a city-state). It is doubtful, however, that an imperial army consonant with the size and threat of the Mexica existed in the Maya lowlands where a situation of multiple polities (of varying power and influence), rather than a primate polity, prevailed. Nevertheless, Maya tribute presentations do seem to have been linked to "axe" or military events, and there is clear evidence that high-ranking nobility were captured during those events. We have already reviewed the death of the early eighth-century ruler of Copán as a result of capture but that "sacrifice" may have been the exception rather than the rule. As Freidel (1986b) noted, captives – especially royal captives – were more frequently captured than killed. Miller and Martin (2004:170) note that, in several instances, captives of noble rank appear to have survived a period of captivity and returned to their throne obviously in a much-diminished status and burdened with new tribute obligations. For instance, Yich'aak Bahlam ("Jaguar Claw") of Seibal was captured by Dos Pilas in 735 C.E., yet there is a reference to his rule at Seibal with a long-count date of 747 C.E. (Martin and Grube 2008[2000]:61, 63). Likewise, Palenque ruler K'an Hoy Chitam II was captured by Tonina in 711 C.E. but apparently was restored to the throne of Palenque and ruled until 720 C.E. (Miller and Martin 2004:183). A miniature wall panel from Temple 21 at Palenque features an unusual carved scene dated to 731 C.E. in which the successor to K'an Hoy Chitam II – Akul Ah-Nab III – manages a huge tribute bundle (González Cruz and Fernández Martínez 1994; Stuart 1998:413). This scene suggests the possibility that even a decade after the death of the once-captive ruler, Palenque still serviced a tribute obligation to Tonina. Likewise, the jadeite cube (Figure 7.7) that is inscribed as the burden or *yikatz* of a ruler nicknamed Sunraiser Jaguar of Pomona and was excavated from a tomb at Palenque includes a calendar round date (A1–A2) that postdates the death of the Pomona ruler.

The notion that a royal enemy is more valuable alive than dead is reinforced by the fact that "*chuhkaj*, 'he is seized/roped,' is the most common of all verbs referring to warfare" (Miller and Martin 2004:166). A captured member of a royal family or a high-ranking warrior and/or scribe represented the wealth of a vanquished kingdom and could be used to extract that wealth in the form of goods, labor, land, advantageous marital alliances, and so forth (Miller and Martin 2004:166). European history of more recent medieval and even Renaissance times is full of such accounts. As the wages of war took their toll on one kingdom after another, rulers such as Richard the Lion-heart, Jean of France, and Francis I of France were held for a "king's ransom" (Gillingham 1978; Knecht 1994; Tuchman 1978). According to Tuchman (1978:84), the taking of high-ranking captives for ransom in fourteenth-century England and France "became a commercial enterprise." A young princess could find herself betrothed to the sworn enemy of her father as happened to 11-year-old Isabelle who was "sold" for 600,000 florins to the Visconti family of Milan in order to cover the three million *écus* that her father, King Jean of France, owed to King Edward as a result of being taken captive in 1356 at the Battle of Poitiers (Tuchman 1978:201). Held for ransom for four years, King Jean's release was secured by substituting high-ranking French hostages in order to ensure that payments on the ransom would continue. Since the king died before payment was complete, the substitute captives were never officially released and at least one married into King Edward's royal family (Tuchman 1978:214). The reversal of fortunes engendered by royal captivity was eloquently expressed by King Francis I who was taken captive by the troops of Emperor Charles V at the Battle of Pavia in 1525. In a letter to Charles V, Francis wrote: "You may be sure, should it please you mercifully to offer the ransom which the imprisonment of a king of France warrants, that, instead of acquiring a useless prisoner, you will turn a king into your slave for ever" (Knecht 1994:226). Once taken captive, a sovereign might have to mortgage his kingdom, sacrifice the future of his children, and offer his most loyal subordinates as hostage substitutes in order to secure his release. Once released, a ruler either accepted the new vassal status of his kingdom or engaged in endless battles (as did Richard the Lion-heart) to regain some measure of supremacy and autonomy.

Small wonder then that Maya rulers did not personally present tribute at the court of their victors but rather sent their "messengers" dressed in tribute raiment. Sometimes, they physically couldn't attend because they were the captives for whom the tribute ransom was offered. If the ransom was offered toward the release of a valued captive warrior or scribe (Johnston 2001), there was little sense in endangering the security of the ruler via a personal appearance when the tribute goods, themselves, were the desired object of the transaction. Depending upon the political climate, the mobility and personal freedom of high-ranking Maya persons might have been restricted. In certain cases, travel outside of the security of one's kingdoms could pose great peril. The text of the hieroglyphic staircase of Copán obliquely refers to the capture of Waxaklajuun Ubaah K'awiil by the ruler of Quirigua as having taken place in a setting away from any semblance of social order. The distance between royal courts could be less than 50 kilometers, and so it is obvious that martial campaigns often took place against one's neighbors, which may explain why dressing as "stranger" warriors from Teotihuacan proved so popular during the Classic period (Miller and Martin 2004:166; Stone 1989).

This form of tribute – tribute ransom, in which there was an interchangeability between people and goods and tribute obligations could extend over decades – may have been more common among Late Classic Maya kingdoms than is indicated by the limited hieroglyphic corpus (see also Graham 2006:118–119, in press). In a tropical climate where long-term storage of perishable items is rendered difficult, the recursive nature of tribute ransom could ensure a cyclic infusion of fresh supplies into royal courts. As European examples indicate, conditions for the release of hostages could include continued tribute payments until the military strength of the vanquished state was rebuilt to the point of challenging such a predatory arrangement. This variant of "appropriational storage" à la Smyth (1996:349) or "supply on demand" as outlined by LaLone (1982) for the Andean world solved many of the challenges to state finance that are faced in a humid, tropical environment. From this perspective, a royal hieroglyphic title string that indicates the number of captives taken by a warrior-ruler is not so much a boast of martial prowess as it is a proclamation of the ability of that ruler to bring "home the bacon." Just as U.S. congresswomen and -men jockey for lucrative highway pork-barrel funding to fuel economic growth and security for their home constituencies, so ancient Maya warriors fought to bring highly prestigious captives back to their constituents and to display them in the triumphal setting of ballcourts and plazas. Such captures translated into great prosperity as tribute ransom "flowed in a golden stream to nourish the economy" as Tuchman (1978:307) has characterized fourteenth-century England. Throne scenes on polychromes that show a ruler graciously accepting such "gifts" likely represent the culmination of this process of state finance, the largesse of successful captive taking. Low-status captives, while not the stuff of lucrative ransom, might still have served to swell the ranks of available labor within the victorious polity. Likely occupying slave status, captives could be offered in sacrificial ritual practice to deities and ancestors, as isotopic studies by Cucina and Tiesler (2003) would seem to indicate.

Houston and colleagues (2006:243) suggest that captives could be taken by subsidiary lords and given as tribute to an overlord; in effect, offering a "gift that keeps on giving" and one that circumvents the obligation of the subsidiary lords to provide tribute goods. Stela 12 of Piedras Negras (Figure 9.2) shows Ruler 7 sitting atop a sea of captives accompanied by a text that celebrates two triumphs over the site of Pomona "in collaboration with his vassals from neighbouring La Mar" (Martin and Grube 2008[2000]:153). This monument provides support for up-the-line transfer of captives as does the battle scene in Room 2 at Bonampak, if the captives were ultimately destined for the royal court of Yaxchilán where the overlord of Bonampak resided (Houston et al. 2006:247–249).

The practice of tribute ransom is mirrored in mythic Maya narrative. Just as nobility possessed the radiance of the sun god and the handsomeness of the maize god, so God L exhibited the human characteristics of affluence, vanity, and self-magnification. As a patron of trade and tribute, God L resided in the powerful Underworld. As mentioned in Chapter 8, Classic period imagery (again on polychrome vessels) refers to a confrontation between God L and the hero twins during which God L is taken captive, stripped of his finery, and forced to pay tribute to the sun god (Miller and Martin 2004:58–61, 76). For Martin (2006:171), "[t]his obligation evidently served as a key paradigm for tribute payment in the mortal world." Significantly, the parable of God L condones the taking of captives and extraction of tribute and, furthermore, characterizes God L as one who needed to be taken down a few notches. He is a character out of balance, with too much hubris and too much investment in luxury. Miller and Martin (2004:58–59) conjecture that "his [God L's]

FIGURE 9.2 Stela 12 of Piedras Negras showing Ruler 7 sitting atop a sea of captives (after Maler 1970–1976, reproduced courtesy of the President and Fellows of Harvard University).

affluence and lavish palace furnishings were the objects of desire for worldly kings, who needed to extend lavish hospitality while keeping the palace economy afloat. Despite disdain for God L's luxury, Maya kings aspired to live as he did." Like the bird messenger emissaries of the rulers from whom tribute was demanded, God L also possessed a messenger bird "13 Sky Owl" (*uxlahuun chan kuy*), who perched on the brim of his hat (Miller and Martin 2004:58–59). So, the tributary arrangements of state financing by which Classic Maya rulers both thrived and perished possessed a mythic reality and mirrored the epic struggle between the hero twins – children of the maize god – and the vainglorious God L.

FIGURE 9.3 Fenton Vase from Nebaj, Alta Verapaz, Guatemala, showing a scribe seated to the ruler's left who appears to be keeping a tally (© Trustees of the British Museum).

COLLECTING AND COUNTING TRIBUTE

Alongside the mythic trope of Classic Maya tribute, the reality of incoming goods and captives accumulating on the steps of the ball-court meant that someone had to keep a count of things. Just as Polanyi was perplexed by Mycenaean civilization in which the written word was not extended to a standardized monetary system, so scholars have wondered why at least one of the surviving four codices does not contain some type of accounting. The elaboration of counting systems – including the invention of zero – is an impressive part of Maya intellectual tradition. Likewise, where are the accountants in the many palace presentation scenes painted on polychrome vessels? In point of fact, accountants do not seem to have been differentiated from palace scribes who appear in many of the painted throne scenes, generally seated to the ruler's left. The so-called Fenton Vase, excavated from the Alta Verapaz site of Nebaj (Figure 9.3), shows a scribe/accountant, who is seated on a throne to the ruler's left and may be recording tribute tallies on a flat, rectangular surface. The scene is evocative of Renfrew's (1972:296) description of Mycenaean Linear B tablets: "The in-payments include carefully calculated tribute assessments, together with a record of any deficit in the actual payment." On the Fenton Vase, the pen quills stuck into the bulbous headgear of the accountant – and the other four persons as well, including the ruler – identify this scene as a group of scribes. To the ruler's right, a kneeling supplicant offers what might be a *Spondylus* shell. Between the supplicant and the ruler, there is a pile of stacked feather-edged capes topped by a large bowl possibly filled with *wah* or *tamales*, although the contents lack the characteristic identifiers, either "corn-curls" or dripping sauce (Taube 1989:41). For this tribute presentation, there are no white-cloaked "messengers"; instead, high-ranking scribes/ accountants, possibly from another kingdom, offer tribute. The presence of five glyph bands and five persons suggests that the emissaries might be named with their personal titles; however, Stephen Houston (personal communication October 2005) notes that only the glyph band to the ruler's right is composed of "legible" glyphs, while the other bands contain primarily pseudo-glyphs and are not readable. Even though the tribute emissaries remain nameless, the collegial tone of this scene suggests that there were significant variations on the performance of tribute presentation. Factors that could shape this encounter might include the conclusiveness of the martial victory, whether the atmosphere at court was highly conflictive, whether tribute demands were perceived as unduly burdensome, and most important the probability of being taken captive while in hostile terrain.

Other images of likely accountants appear on looted examples of painted pottery. For example, Coe (1978:Figure 16) shows what appears to be an accountant with a long tally scroll. Whether the "counter" of tribute and the "collector" of tribute were conflated into one role or generally separated into two roles is unclear. Ethnohistorically, among the K'iche', the person in the "collector" role held the title of *ajpop k'amja*, "Keeper of the Reception House Mat" (Tedlock 1985:315). Braswell (2001:312), following Casas (1909:615–616), identifies the Keeper of the Reception House Mat as "king-elect," an indication that the role of tribute collector was one of extremely high status and not that of a lowly palace functionary or bureaucrat. The profound significance of tribute collection to the survival of the K'iche' state resides in the fact that the last K'iche' to hold this noble title, Don Juan Cortés, traveled to Spain in 1557 in an effort to persuade the Spanish Crown to restore the right of K'iche' lords to collect tribute (Carrasco 1967; Tedlock 1985:315). Reents-Budet (2001:214) suggests that a Classic Maya version of the *ajpop k'amja* is represented by the presence in palace scenes of a high-ranking individual shown close to the enthroned *k'uhul ajaw*. Jackson and Stuart (2001:225) further suggest that the hieroglyphically attested title of *aj k'uhun* may refer to one who guards, keeps, or oversees tribute production and presentation for a named ruler.

TRIBUTE OFFERINGS

Provisioning the royal courts of the Classic Maya must have been a daunting task that was achieved through a combination of production at court and on lands controlled by nobles, trading arrangements, and extraction of tribute. Chapters 6 through 8 deal with the first two categories of provisioning, while this chapter handles the third. There are five tribute items that are written or imaged repeatedly in Classic Maya sources. The paradigmatic five are cacao, cloth, jadeite, *Spondylus* shell, and quetzal feathers. Doubtlessly, there were countless other items requested in tribute payments that are not included in pictorial imagery or, if included, are shown in a manner that is so subtle as to elude a reading. Rare Ulua marble bowls come to mind (Luke 2008; Luke and Tykot 2007). Among the main five, there exist dramatic contrasts in terms of availability, crafting intensivity, and knowledge base necessary for crafting.

Cacao (a derivation of the Classic Maya hieroglyphic expression *ka-ka-w[a]* as per Stuart 1988) is the seed of a tropical forest understory species, *Theobroma cacao* L., and can be grown wherever there is no danger of frost and adequate moisture, even in moist *rejolladas* in the relatively dry northern Yucatán (Gomez-Pompa et al. 1990; Kepecs and Boucher 1996; Perez Romero 1988). Concentrated production of high-quality cacao was restricted to the alluvial soils of river valleys in the lower Usumacinta delta, along the southern Caribbean Coast, and the piedmont flanks of the Pacific Coast. Cacao can be understood to have been a naturally circumscribed resource.

Cotton cloth, on the other hand, is fabricated from gendered labor. Like cacao, cotton probably could be grown in many parts of the lowlands, but unlike hydrophilic cacao, cotton (*Gossypium hirsutum*) prefers a hot and somewhat dry climate and, significantly, is tolerant of salty soils. The fact that it grows as a wild perennial bush along the littoral of the Yucatán Peninsula has prompted some plant biologists to suggest that the Yucatán was the location of its initial domestication in Mesoamerica (Piperno and Pearsall 1998:151). The saline-tolerant character of cotton may explain why cotton pollen has been retrieved from the upper strata of wetland island fields, such as those adjacent to K'axob (Jones 1999), where gypsum infiltration is widely considered to have posed a challenge to Late Classic farmers. The transformation of cotton into cloth involved the tedious separation of cotton fibers from their constituent plant parts and cleaning of the cotton bolls. The time and tedium of this processing step explains why the cotton gin was heralded as one of the most significant innovations of the late eighteenth century. Clean cotton fibers likely were delivered to palace precincts where skilled female labor (as discussed in Chapters 4 and 6) set about spinning and weaving the fibers into cloth. Of all the items of tribute, cloth may be the most labor intensive or closely matched with the labor involved in the crafting of jadeite ornaments.

Jadeite appears to have been offered at court in finished form, a topic that is revisited later in this chapter. As a semiprecious gemstone, the only jadeite sources currently known for Mesoamerica occur in the metamorphic rock found in the southeastern corner of the Maya region, near the Motagua Valley of Guatemala (Foshag 1984:Figure 13; Hammond et al. 1977). As a demanded item of tribute, most royal courts would have had to engage in trade just to secure the raw material from which to fabricate jadeite beads, pendants, earspools, and so forth. Excavations at Cancuen indicate that this ancient capital was in the "business" of supplying worked jadeite preforms that were removed from boulders via string-saw technology (Kovacevich 2007). Items of jadeite actually inscribed with some variant of the *ikats* or "tribute" glyph are known from Piedras Negras (Burial 5) as well as Palenque. From the latter, *ikats* jadeite was found in a tomb within Temple 12 (Miller and Martin 2004:234; Figure 7.7) and, in another temple, the sarcophagus of K'inich Janahb Pakal of Palenque (Houston and Escobedo 1996:467, Figures 2 and 3).

A similarly complex blend of trade and tribute probably existed for *Spondylus* spp. shells, a deep-water bivalve available off both the Caribbean and Pacific Coasts (*Spondylus americanus* Hermann and *Spondylus princeps* Broderip, respectively; Andrews IV 1969:25–26; Vokes and Vokes 1983:62). Unlike shallow-water conch (Caribbean *Strombus* spp.) – which also was utilized extensively for personal adornment as well as for trumpets – *Spondylus* inhabit deeper waters and so harvesting is more specialized (see Pillsbury 1996:317–319 for review of *Spondylus* habitat). The relative inaccessibility of this bivalve undoubtedly enhanced its value as did the spiny protuberances on the exterior of the shell and the translucent orange, red, or purple of the shell interior. It arrived at royal courts essentially unmodified and often was worn as a pendant or as part of a belt ensemble. Unmodified *Spondylus* shells also are found in elite burials and caches and are thought to represent fertility and renewal. The paired "clam shells" of *Spondylus princeps* often were used to hold small, precious objects (i.e., the "jewel boxes" of E. Wyllys Andrews IV [1969:25]) as in a cache placed within Caracol Structure A6–2nd around 70 C.E., where both halves of a *Spondylus* shell formed a container within which a solid jadeite mask covered with red hematite was placed (Chase and Chase 1998b:315).

Today, quetzal birds with their long, elegant green tail feathers are an endangered species that live in the Alta Verapaz – a cloud forest region of limestone karst where the lowlands meet the igneous mountains of the Guatemalan highlands. Additional patches of suitable habitat apparently once extended to the west all the way to southern Oaxaca and south to Panama (Gasco and Voorhies 1989:67). Thompson (1964:32) notes that, for the Alta Verapaz, there seems to have been some control over trapping rights at locales where the birds came to drink and Feldman (1985:90) asserts, based on ethnohistorical documents, that "killing quetzal birds was a more heinous crime than murdering quetzal feather collectors." Apparently, birds were trapped at waterholes during the dry season using an ingenious trap that allowed the bird to escape but not with its tail feathers (Feldman 1985:90). Only lowland sites situated close to the Alta Verapaz, such as Cancuen, would have been positioned so as to be reasonably close to this extremely valuable resource. Others would have acquired the feathers through trade or gifting in order to satisfy a tribute demand. Alternatively, royal headdresses of the vanquished court could have been stripped of quetzal feathers with the intention of replacing the feathers with glistening fresh ones when the fortunes of the court were reversed and key ritual performances could resume. The same could also be said of jadeite and *Spondylus*, that is, royal treasuries may have been emptied of their inalienable possessions in order to ransom a captive ruler or high-status warrior.

Behind-the-Scenes Tribute Offerings

Beyond the paradigmatic five, royal courts surely sought to enhance their provisions and position by preying opportunistically on vanquished kingdoms. Variations in tribute demands likely were adjusted to accommodate historical and local contingencies that produce product-specific artisans, variations in resource structure, soil differences, natural plant distributions, and population clines (see McAnany 1993 for further discussion of these factors).

The ethos of artisan production that existed throughout the Maya region, as discussed in Chapter 7, meant that certain communities produced extremely fine-quality goods by virtue of the repetition and reproduction of social practice that engendered a concentrated and multigenerational pool of skill persons. The carved gourds of the highland town of Rabinal (Figure 9.4) provide an ethnographic case in point and to that example we can add pottery made in distinctive forms and with specific finishes, woven mats, wooden bowls and boxes, and so forth. When one of these socially constituted production locales fell victim to tribute extraction, then artisans likely produced for the royal court of the victor in addition to satisfying local demands and participating in trading systems. Up-the-line transfers through voluntary or coercive giving can move items that show extraordinary crafting – such as the chert eccentrics crafted at Colha – to distant royal courts, perhaps even to Tikal.

Based on accounts of Mexica tribute, Berdan (1996:125–126) shows how royal courts also were consumers of geological and mineralogical raw materials. Given artisan production at court plus the need for food-processing equipment and condiments, Maya royal courts needed a wide diversity of supplies including pigments for paints and for dyeing thread, clays with suitable firing properties, temper – such as volcanic ash – for pottery production, granite for *metates*, slate for carving, amber for ornaments, pyrite and magnetite for mirrors, obsidian for cutting, abrasive materials for sanding, and salt for flavoring foods. Every one of these items is naturally restricted in its distribution and so would have to be secured through trade or the establishment of tributary obligations. Few would have been locally available within the area controlled by any one lowland kingdom.

FIGURE 9.4 Carved gourd from the highland town of Rabinal, Guatemala, held in the hand of Cawek of the Forest People in a performance of the Maya drama, *Rabinal Achi* (reprinted courtesy of Dennis Tedlock).

Soils, physiography, and intensity of land use would have created differences in the availability of economic plant species as well as animals. The natural habitat of the *amate* fig tree, from which bark paper was made, is a riverine gallery forest. Rubber (*Castilla elastica* or *'uulej* in Itzaj) is intercropped with ground species in *milpas* of the Petén Itzaj, indicating that this tree requires ample moisture (Atran and Ucan Ek 1999:Table 2.2). Precious hardwoods from old-growth forests – *sapote*, *ceiba*, and mahogany, for instance – would have been few and far between in the populous landscape of Late Classic-period Petén but were needed for carving lintels, fabricating portable boxes, and possibly god images. Tropical pine, likewise, enjoys a restricted distribution but is essential for nighttime lighting (pine torches) and also appears to have played a crucial role in ritual activities. Animals of the high bush – tapir, jaguar, macaw, and parrots – were highly desirable for their meat, skins, or feathers and detailed faunal and isotopic data now indicate that consumption of marine fish occurred at interior locales (Stanchly 2003; White et al. 2001). Many of these items would not have been locally available to royal courts but could be demanded as tribute. As mentioned previously, staple goods, such as maize, squash, and beans also could have been transported via tumpline over the relatively short distances between royal courts. Although there do not seem to be any textual references to this type of transfer, it would have been of vital importance if a harvest failed due to insect blight or lack of rain or because the size of the royal court had outstripped the capacity of the sustaining population to support it. Raiding the food stores of one's neighbor is an activity as old as food production itself.

Finally, labor services – including captive laborers – were fundamental to the operation of the court. Laborers were needed in the kitchen for food preparation and also for construction and maintenance projects. The specialized needs of the royal court for litter bearers, torchbearers, water carriers, and so forth translated into a huge labor sink so that an almost infinite number of laborers could be absorbed into the vortex of the royal court.

POLITICAL ECONOMY OF TRIBUTE GOODS

Although we can be assured that the scope of items transferred through tributary mechanisms was much broader than the paradigmatic five – cacao, cloth, jadeite, *Spondylus* spp. shell, and quetzal feathers – the fact that these five items are imaged and referenced repeatedly in Classic-period sources suggests that they formed an archetypal set of items that royal courts were expected to possess in abundance. They are emblematic of successful feasting, luxurious clothing, and symbolically charged personal adornment. The performance of nobility, power, and supernatural intercession simply was not possible without them. As Geertz (1980:129–130) notes in reference to kingship in nineteenth-century Bali, the extravagance of state ritual was a measure of the king's divinity and the well-being of the realm; in effect, the king was a human ideogram. In this light, the social practices standing behind the political economy of these five tribute items deserve a bit more discussion.

Harvesting the Food of the Gods (*Theobroma cacao* L.)

In 1956, J. Eric Thompson stated that the "food of the gods" – so named by Carolus Linnaeus himself – was all but invisible archaeologically (1956:101). The most perishable of the archetypal five tribute goods, cacao became more visible at royal courts once its glyphic compound was deciphered (Stuart 1988, 1989) and its chemical residue identified (Hall et al. 1990; Hurst et al. 2002). The phonetic syllables of *ka-ka-w[a]*, with the final "a" silenced, are now widely recognized as one of the most ubiquitous glyph compounds of the Late Classic period. They occur most frequently on the cylindrical polychromes, many of which portray tribute scenes, although the glyph compound itself generally forms part of the dedicatory name tagging of a vessel and does not directly address the issue of tribute. Nevertheless, such scenes provide a vivid display of the tribute drama on a vessel that could be marked as one in which an item of tribute was consumed.

Notably, the *ka-ka-w[a]* glyph occurs in the murals of Bonampak, Room 1, where tribute "messengers" process along the walls and sacks of cacao labeled hieroglyphically as to content and amount are stacked against the throne on the end wall (Miller 1997). Mention of cacao is less frequent on carved stone monuments but does occur on the well-known Panel 3 from Piedras Negras in which a nighttime banquet where cacao was served is recorded (Martin and Grube 2008[2000]:149). In the soliloquy from the play *Rab'inal Achi*, quoted at the beginning of this chapter, the captive Cawek states that his skull, after having been carved into a cup resembling a Rabinal carved gourd, might end up as an "even trade" (meaning tributary ransom?) for fivescore seeds of *pataxte* (*Theobroma bicolor*, a "wild" cacao cultivated on the Pacific Coast by Pipil-Nicarao groups; Young 1994:24–26) and fivescore seeds of cacao paid by his children, his sons of his home valley. Here, we get the sense that tributary ransom could be extracted posthumously. That is, if the Great House that Cawek called his home valley desired the return of his skull, they would have to ransom it with 200 cacao seeds. Perhaps cacao was such an important part of tributary relations because it was foundational to so many transactions, particularly those between noble houses. Ethnohistorically and ethnographically, in the Maya highlands as well as Yucatàn, cacao drinking was/is integral to betrothals, marriages, and anniversaries (Tedlock 2002; Thompson 1930:80, 1956:104). In Colonial Yucatán, affairs of state could not be settled properly without drinking chocolate as in the negotiation of territorial boundaries among the Xiu, Cocom, and Cupul families in 1557. Not only was cacao drunk to seal the agreement, but sacks of cacao were given as gifts (Morley 1941:159; Roys 1943:178–86) – all this, in an area that was too dry to grow cacao except in collapsed sinkholes. In essence, no state banquet could take place without drinking cacao. Within pre-Columbian royal courts, the preparation and serving of cacao assumed a formal protocol akin to Japanese tea ceremonies (see McAnany and Murata 2007). Sophie and Michael Coe (1996:50) popularized the Late Classic polychrome vessel court scene in which a well-dressed, jade-adorned female froths cacao prior to serving. Like textile production, the preparation and serving of cacao drink were female-gendered practices, and females might prepare large amounts of the beverage – using a number of different recipes – for banquets. The female-gendered labor implicated in cacao drink became so rigid during Colonial times that daily preparation of a morning chocolate drink by a male was brought forth as evidence in judicial court that the husband had been bewitched into "unnatural behavior" by his wife (Few 2002:32–33). Although the production of cacao was not female-gendered in the manner of textile production, the preparation and serving of the chocolate drink appears to have been solidly in the female orbit and to have been ritualized in a manner that accrued status to females, particularly within Classic Maya royal courts.

Outside of regal settings, it is likely that females also prepared the chocolate drink; the frequency of imbibing chocolate among nonelites probably was linked to the ability to grow cacao locally and/or acquire it through trade. Where conditions for cacao trees were desirable – the lower Usumacinta Valley and the southern Caribbean valleys of the lowlands proper – cacao quaffing may have been a common occurrence. On the other hand, commoners living in areas where cacao cultivation was more difficult – northern Yucatán and central Petén – probably restricted their consumption of cacao to celebrations during rites of passage and other significant events. Living amongst cacao trees may have incurred occupational hazards; evidence is emerging that jockeying for control of cacao-producing valleys was a subtext of Classic Maya geopolitics.

The textual record of royal courts that occupied the "gateway" to the lower Usumacinta and Belize zone orchards – Palenque and Naranjo in particular – reveals an unusually high ratio of martial events in proportion to diplomatic and marriage events (see Martin and Grube 2008[2000]:21 for graphic display of this pattern and McAnany and Murata 2006b and 2007 for further discussion). Up until now, it has not been clear to what extent such martial events affected the daily lives of Classic Maya people actually living amongst the orchards since, ironically, the production areas tend to contain limited textual records. Just as Sidney Mintz (1985) has characterized the Caribbean islands historically as a sugar factory for Europe, the cacao-production zones beyond the royal courts could have been controlled as "chocolate factories" to underwrite the palace economies. It is clear that the early Colonial ruler of Tah Itza – the central Petén island kingdom and the last to fall to Spaniards in 1697 – exerted a large measure of control over cacao production in the upper Belize Valley and along the southeastern side of the Maya Mountains (see Jones 1989:102, 1998:35 for further discussion of early Colonial cacao production; also McAnany and Murata 2006b). So, the link between sweetness and political power, so adroitly framed by Mintz, could easily be extended to the pungency of cacao. Although not sweet like sugar, cacao was a highly desired luxury good and a mildly addictive stimulant.

Research in the Sibun Valley of central Belize suggests that during the Late-Terminal Classic period, this cacao production locale, in the words of Mintz (1985:xvi), became "caught up in the skeins of imperial control" spun in distant capitals. That is, sites in the upper valley closest to the Petén capitals emulated Petén architectural styles and layout, down to the construction of a small ballcourt in the shadow of the largest pyramid, while those in the lower part of the valley – near the navigable inner channel of the Caribbean – expressed architectural and possibly political affinities with northern Yucatán by way of circular shrines (Harrison-Buck 2007; Harrison-Buck and McAnany 2006; McAnany 2007b; McAnany et al. 2002, 2005;

Thomas 2005). In a fashion parallel to the sugar production and export industry of the Caribbean region, the appetite for this food of the gods appears to have engendered spheres of political influence and domination with clear architectural expression. Theoretically, the manner in which cacao production locales were dominated probably differed significantly from the martial conflict between the royal militias. Likely, the process resembled a type of colonization and met with both collusion and resistance by local rulers whose status would have been enhanced by a connection to a royal court, while, at the same time, the additional labor required to cultivate, harvest, and transport cacao destined for a royal feast would have placed a new burden on the colonized. These labor demands would have fallen on the shoulders of ruling families and followers, and likely did not increase their popularity among local constituents.

In regard to the labor profile of cacao harvesting and transport, it is notable that the period during which cacao can be harvested is unusually protracted and can last for up to eight months. Unlike the labor-scheduling crunch involved in bringing in a maize harvest, a small amount of cacao can be picked every day for months on end. Concomitantly, small batches can be fermented and sun-dried before being packed into tumplines for transport to their locale of consumption. The cacao presentation scene in the Bonampak murals is informative in this regard. The sacks of cacao are labeled hieroglyphically as "5 *pih kakaw*," the unit "*pih*" probably representing a count of 8,000 (Houston 1997). The Nahuatl term for the same count is *xiquipil*. Since the mural shows five bundles placed at the foot of a large throne on which a royal family is seated, the total count of presented cacao beans would have been 40,000. The standard cacao *carga* or load carried by a porter is reported to have been three *xiquipil* (or three *pih*), which means that the cacao beans presented in this scene could have been transported with relative ease by two to three porters. "Five *pih kakaw*" could represent a standard tribute amount offered to a Classic Maya royal court during a single presentation event or simply an amount chosen by a mural artist to fill a composition. Nevertheless, this mural, in conjunction with the protracted harvesting cycle of cacao, admits the possibility that royal courts were supplied continuously with a few large sacks of cacao. At any one point in time, this demand would not have been onerous, but, over the long run, the constancy of the demand could have taxed production levels and transport capabilities. Cacao, thus, provides an excellent example of a political economy based on "appropriational storage" (Smyth 1996:349) in which a highly desired luxury good could be stored on trees, harvested and processed over a prolonged period of time, and transported up the line in response to tributary demands, an occasion of gifting, or as part of a trading arrangement.

Burden of Cloth Tribute on Female-Gendered Labor

Cloth, *yubte'* in Yucatec Mayan (Barrera Vásquez 1995:981), is probably the most ubiquitous item shown in tribute presentation scenes, whether folded and stacked, wrapped around a bolt, or worn by tribute messengers. In tribute scenes, cloth is generally displayed with detailed edging as on the vessel from Tikal (Figure 9.1), where tribute emissaries wear sumptuous white capes that drag on the floor and are edged with a sky-band design (likely brocaded) finished with feather trim. The size of the *manta* is impressive as is the fine quality of handwork displayed on the edging. Based on the quality of textiles and the paucity of spinning and weaving equipment in Late Classic commoner residences, tribute *mantas* were produced by elite and royal women, perhaps with the assistance of skilled commoner females who worked in the courtyard of elite residences. As mentioned earlier, the initial separation and cleaning of cotton fibers undoubtedly took place outside of palace courtyards but possibly not too far outside. At the Terminal Classic Puuc site of K'axil Kiuic – located in a prime cotton-growing area – George Bey (2003, 2004) notes the close proximity of small, modest residential platforms (where cotton-cleaners could have lived) to the palace complex of the Yaxche Group.

The recognition that female-gendered labor was intimately entangled with the spoils of war adds a new dimension to the saga of "axe," "star war," and "capture" events recorded hieroglyphically. Basically, whenever a seat of power suffered a setback in the realm of martial conflict, high-status females on the losing side could expect to spend increased time on the backstrap loom weaving textiles to fulfill a new tribute obligation or to ransom a captured husband, son, or more distant relative. Alternatively, the stockpile of already woven *mantas* that might have been used as gifts or to seal a political alliance could be seriously depleted by the repercussions of a military setback. As a last resort, personal or ancestral cloth might be used to fulfill a tributary obligation, but ceding one's inalienable possessions would send a signal of desperation both to the victors and to one's constituents. For females of the royal courts, two things could happen. Their warriors might be victorious; in which case, stacks of textiles might arrive at court, riming the ballcourt and bringing great wealth and magnifying dynastic legacy. An infusion of such wealth items would reduce the number of textiles that females needed to produce to conduct the ordinary business of the court. On the other hand, a military setback on the battlefield could seriously deplete the palace inventory of textiles and likely place greater labor demands on high-status females. From this perspective, the beautifully brocaded *huipiles* worn by Lady Xook on the sculptured masterpieces of Yaxchilán (Lintels 24, 25, and 26) can be understood to communicate several things. First, she likely was a weaver par excellence; second, her *mantas* were extremely valuable because of the fine brocade work; third, if any of them ever had to be used as ransom, they would be recognized as the materialization of her identity; and fourth, the fact that she wears such valuable pieces of worked cloth means that she does not expect to have to part with them to meet a tribute obligation. Her inalienable possessions were secure in no small part due to the successful military campaigns of her warring partner, Itzamnaaj Bahlam II, who between 681 and 732 C.E. took a record number of captives (Martin and Grube 2008[2000]:123–124).

Although royal Maya women probably seldom entered the battlefield, their labor in the transformation of cotton into highly valued cloth played a critical part in the political economy and was entangled intimately with the Classic Maya masculinist ethos of warfare. In reference to Colonial Yucatán, Farriss (1984:167) observes that men fed their family through agricultural labor, whereas women paid most of the taxes extracted by Spanish overlords through weaving and spinning, an observation echoed by Espejo-Ponce and Restall (1997:232). Whether men were fighting or farming, the burden of crafting the highly valued textiles that drove the political economy and ensured prosperity, or at least survival, seems to have fallen on the shoulders of Maya females in both the shallow and deeper history of Maya society.

Crafting Jadeite

Much has been written about the symbolic significance of the green color of jadeite, *yax* meaning "green" or "first" in most Mayan languages. Taube (2005:47) argues that "jade was esteemed for its beauty and preciousness and as a rarefied embodiment of life essence, not only as maize and life-giving water, but also as a physical manifestation of the breath spirit." For Taube (2005:31), jadeite earspools – particularly the long, tubular shaft – symbolized breadth and wind, the sacred *ik'* often shown as a "T" symbol in Maya iconography and conceived as the harbinger of rain. Earspools, pendants, beads, and plaques were fabricated from this hard, durable material that must have required hundreds if not thousands of hours to shape and carve, given the stone-working technology employed by Classic Maya artisans. Masterpieces of jadeite carving were buried with deceased royalty. Famous examples include the jadeite masks covering the face of the deceased seventh-century ruler of Palenque, K'inich Janahb Pakal, and that of Jasaw Chan K'awiil, eighth-century ruler of Tikal. An unnamed member of the Classic-period royal family of Altun Ha was buried in Tomb B–4/7 with a jadeite-sculpted deity, weighing 4.42 kilograms (Pendergast 1982:59). Although jadeite and other types of semiprecious greenstone are found with nonregal and even non-elite burials, the quantity of material and crafting intensivity is far greater in royal burials.

Although burial patterns indicate that jadeite ornaments often were interred with the person who wore them during her/his life, heirloom pieces of jadeite also are known. A prime example is the unprovenienced Dumbarton Oaks pectoral that features a Middle Preclassic Olmec "were-jaguar" carving on one face and an Early Classic Maya text and image of a seated figure on the other (see McAnany 2001:Figure 5). The durability of the raw material clearly lent itself to ancestral linkages as Joyce (2000b:13–15) and Taube (2005:47) both have noted, and many pieces likely remained within families for generations, if not centuries, as valued and inalienable possessions.

Like cloth, jadeite appears to have been transferred between courts in finished form rather than as raw boulders. Given the artisan ethos of the Classic Maya world, the tradition of supplying finished pieces of jadeite as tributary obligations may have been an acknowledgment of the value added to raw material through laborious and highly skilled craftsmanship (see Figure 7.7). In effect, the biography of a thing was instantiated by the entanglement of labor intensivity with raw material. With Mexica tribute demands also, semiprecious stone appears to have been transferred primarily as a crafted item (Berdan 1996:126; Gasco and Voorhies 1989:59). In this light, the unworked jadeite boulders found in Terminal Classic Bayal-phase caches at Seibal – the largest weighing more than 8 kilograms – is particularly intriguing (Willey 1978:100). Located on the upper Pasión River, which drains the Alta Verapaz, Seibal was well situated to supply the western half of the lowlands with valuable products from the southern highlands, such as quetzal feathers and jadeite as well as the more pedestrian obsidian. The textual record pertinent to this seat of power, however, indicates a conflictive and sometimes humiliating relationship with the Petexbatún region immediately to the west, and so it is not surprising that Seibal does not emerge as a place with a large supply of jadeite until it undergoes a renaissance during the Terminal Classic period, at which point the Petexbatún sites had already been eclipsed.

Even more pertinent to the discussion at hand is the evidence of jadeite-working at the Classic-period site of Cancuen located strategically near the headwaters of the western Petén drainages (Demarest et al. 2004). More than 77 kilograms of worked jadeite (including a 9-kilogram boulder) have been recovered from a modest residential area that appears to have been involved in producing rough-outs or blanks for earspools, beads, and so forth (Kovacevich 2007). Little in the way of finished jadeite artifacts were recovered either from the workshop areas or from associated mortuary contexts, a fact that suggests that the jade workers did not have access to finished jadeite and were involved only in early-stage reduction of large boulders. Although evidence of the final finishing of jadeite artifacts was recovered from nearby elite architectural contexts (Kovacevich 2007), the intensity of production in elite contexts appears to have been much lower. Possibly, at Cancuen, jadeite boulders were reduced and roughed out by commoners and then transferred via trade networks or channels of gifting downriver and overland to ruling families and allied seats of power where final crafting took place.

Even though we do not have many specific clues as to the gender of the lapidary crafters, Clark and Houston (1998:43) suggest that they were male and base their conclusion on the gender ascribed to such artisans in Colonial-period Maya dictionaries. The majority of figural images cut into jade appear to be have been male, and the frequent adornment of worked jadeite with glyphic texts and complex iconography indicates that, as with textile production, the crafters themselves were high-ranking individuals, at least those who performed finishing work. In a manner analogous to textiles, items of worked jadeite involved in tributary transfers, as shown in Classic Maya imagery, could have been crafted in response to a tribute demand, taken from a store of jadeite items in a royal treasury (shelf life is not an issue here) or, in dire circumstances, removed from the personal effects – some of which would have been inherited – of high-status family members at a vanquished capital. Whichever situation prevailed – and perhaps there were other arrangements not considered here – there is no getting around the fact that jadeite could not be locally procured by most courts and would have been acquired through trade or other connections with royal courts, such as Copán, Quirgua, and Cancuen, situated more proximate to the geological source.

Diving for *Spondylus* and Plucking Quetzal Feathers

Like jadeite, *Spondylus* shells and quetzal feathers are not locally available in the lowlands and thus would have been acquired somehow before being transferred as part of a tributary obligation. In this regard, sites such as Cancuen that occupy a gateway to the Alta Verapaz (habitat of quetzal birds) and a corridor to the Pacific (a source of *Spondylus* shells) were in a highly advantageous position. Even though those who dived for the shells may have lived far away from the Maya lowlands, long and attenuated trading chains must have existed in order to bring the shells across the Guatemalan highlands and into the Maya lowlands.

On a tributary vessel from Tikal (Figure 9.1), three of the four standing white-caped emissaries wear a string of *Spondylus* shells around their neck, as do the figures in the Bonampak murals. In both cases, the shells appear to be unworked except for perforation holes drilled in order to string the shells. As mentioned earlier, the fact that *Spondylus* shells were not as easily acquired as *Strombus* shells obviously increased their value, and their archaeological distribution is weighted toward elite contexts, particularly tomb burials (Andrews IV 1969:25–26; Moholy-Nagy 1985:Table 10.3). Often conceived as linked symbolically with death and the Underworld, Moholy-Nagy (1985:152) reports a pattern of nine (or multiples of nine) unmodified or scarcely altered *Spondylus* shells positioned around the skeletons of three royal Tikal burials, specifically Burials 23, 196, and 116. In all cases, a final *Spondylus* shell was placed in the region of the head. At Tikal, *Spondylus* also was cut and shaped into items of personal adornment and crafted into small, flat figurines (nicknamed Charlie Chaplins), the latter placed in Early Classic caches (Moholy-Nagy 1985:147, 154). So, the crafting and wearing of *Spondylus* occurred at royal courts, but, clearly, the shell was perceived as a symbolically important burial accoutrement. The symbolic value placed on *Spondylus* was shared with Moche royality who reigned during a coeval time over the north coast of Peru. The well-known Lord of Sipan, for instance, was interred with several *Spondylus* shells.

Long, iridescent green quetzal feathers generally project from headdress or turban elements worn by Classic Maya royalty. In the Tikal tributary scene (Figure 9.1), each of the seven, cloaked lords wear two quetzal feathers in their turbans. One of the figures ascending the steps – dressed only in a loincloth – carries a large bundle of quetzal feathers. Since the color green held special significance (iconic of growth, fertility, and the rain that produces such luxuriance), quetzal feathers were highly valued and the length of a tail feather added to its value. As described earlier, the birds were caught in a trap that removed their tail feathers but allowed them to live and grow a new set of feathers. Only this type of sustainable harvesting saved the quetzal from encountering the same fate – extinction – that befell many Polynesian birds with bright plumage, killed to make the brilliant feathered cloaks of *ali'i nui.*

Little crafting was involved with quetzal feathers other than wrapping the quill ends together, their value residing in their size, brilliant color, and scarcity. Feathers that were incorporated into textiles – either by spinning into a delicate thread or applying directly to a warp under tension (see Morris and Karasik 2003:Figures 3.1 and 3.8 for contemporary Tzotzil examples) – appear to have been shorter feathers of variable colors from different species.

FINAL THOUGHTS ON ANCESTRAL MAYA PRACTICES OF STATE FINANCE

Beyond the elegant drapery of the palace precinct and the flowery speech of Maya royalty, there existed predatory rules of engagement for martial conflict and its aftermath. In some respects, the strategy of state finance suggested for Classic Maya kingdoms resembles that known to have existed within the Mexica empire. Specifically, tribute was levied against a conquered province with more regard for the needs of the royal court than for the local availability of demanded goods and desired luxury items (Berdan 1996:129). Mexica rulers shied away from direct bureaucratic control of conquered provinces, preferring instead to enfranchise conquered elites into the imperium and to bully provinces into submission through threat of military action. Similar practices of domination and wealth enhancement could have existed in the Maya region. In other respects, there were vast differences between the Classic Maya and the Postclassic Mexica, most notably in the size and imperial structure of the latter. Although captive taking also was a goal of Mexica warfare (as sixteenth-century Spaniards were surprised and horrified to learn), it does seem that many captives taken by Mexica warriors were sacrificed rather than held for tribute ransom. Among the Mexica, the leverage used to pry tribute out of conquered kingdoms was the threat of a punitive military campaign rather than the humiliation of a captive ruler.

State financing through "appropriation on demand," operationally linked to warfare, fueled explosive growth among Classic Maya royal courts and their sustaining populations. The seventh and eighth centuries represent the period during which maximum growth occurred by every conceivable measure: population size, number of royal courts, number of recorded martial events, and so forth. Given ongoing hostilities and revenge for hostilities that must have occupied the energies of Late Classic Maya rulers, it is possible that this mode of state finance – tribute ransom – bankrupted the southern lowlands by the ninth century. As Tuchman (1978:83, 199) notes in reference to the Hundred Years War between France and England, "medieval armies had no means of achieving a decisive result" but rather aimed at "seizure of dynastic rule at the top by inflicting enough damage to bring about downfall of the opponent." Webster (2002:343–347) refers to this more broadly as a failure of kings and kingship (laced with degradation of the agrarian landscape). The environmental doomsday scenario has been brought into question of late; archaeozoological as well as sediment data (Emery 2004:81, 91; Dunning and Beach 2000:197) have failed to deliver evidence of an apocalyptic landscape (see also Freidel 2007; Freidel and Shaw 2000; McAnany and Gallareta Negrón 2009). Assuredly, the Late Classic was a time during which all forms of production were operating at a high level of intensity in a manner that was comparable to the Roman economy of the first two centuries C.E. where state finance in the form of taxes and rents has been implicated in explosive population growth and agricultural intensification (Greene 1986:14–15; Hopkins 1983:xv–xxi).

Classic-period rulers in the southern lowlands used flowery prose to refer to a political practice in which success in military engagements brought great wealth to their kingdom with minimal investment in bureaucracy. In this regard, the access-pattern analysis by Liendo Stuardo (2003), introduced in Chapter 6, is particularly interesting because he is able to show that the spatial geometry and room accessibility of Terminal Classic royal courts in northern Yucatán was radically different from that of southern lowland sites. A complex, multinodal access pattern with many control points funneled traffic into a few, highly restricted rooms, whereas the temporally sequential (although overlapping) northern sites exhibit shallow access patterns with fewer nodes of control. Liendo Stuardo (2003:194) interprets this difference as "evidencing the growth of a formal bureaucracy associated with the state." In other words, the architecture of the northern capitals might indicate a change in the manner in which states were financed that likely was accompanied by a change in the construal of rulership, as many have discussed for the Classic–Postclassic transition. Judging from the painted murals in the upper and lower Temple of the Jaguar at Chichén Itzá (Coggin and Shane 1984:157–165), the importance of martial engagement did not diminish during the Terminal Classic, but the linkage between warfare and tribute ransom may have been altered in favor of a more bureaucratized manner of state financing. In light of this possibility, tribute ransom should not be perceived as a static, timeless quality of Maya state financing but rather as a strategy that was employed for a limited time.

Although the goal of this chapter has been to amplify politico-economic information from Classic Maya sources where little was thought to exist and to bring shape and definition to Classic Maya tribute systems, the intent is not to suggest that material transfers across space could not have happened in any other way. Within each Maya kingdom, ordinary people as well as elites would have incurred an obligation to provide services and goods to the royal court, if incorporated into one. These obligations – while attested ethnohistorically among indigenous *hidalgos* of northern Yucatán (Morley 1941:236–243) – are difficult to recover from Classic-period sources but would have resulted in considerable up-the-line movement of goods. In Chapter 8, the flourishing trading networks and marketplaces that existed for royalty, elites, and commoners are discussed, and the importance of this mode of transfer should not be underestimated. Also, true gifting undoubtedly occurred between royal courts as alliances were forged, conflicts resolved peacefully, and marriages arranged. Likely, very generous amounts of high-quality luxury goods were exchanged in the course of court diplomacy. A quotable example comes from the early Colonial period and the so-called Treaty of Maní, which resolved a long-standing territorial conflict among the royal houses of Xiu, Cocom, and Cupul. Following a lavish feast held in 1556, each participating ruler (called a Halach Uinic in Postclassic Yucatán) was given five *bakal* (400 piece lots) of cacao, five cotton *mantas* (of four breadths each), a string of red beads as long as an arm, and one *hunkal* (unit of 20) pieces of jadeite (Morley 1941:159; Roys 1943:186). Using measures that are easier to understand today, these gifts translate into 2,000 cacao beans, 30 to 40 yards of cloth, a string of either red coral or *Spondylus* beads over 2 feet in length, and 20 pieces of worked jadeite. Regal generosity materialized in the practice of diplomacy.

10

Skeining the Threads

The title of this final chapter conveys the hope that, in the end, the contours of ancestral Maya economic forms might take the shape of an orderly coil of thread. The entangled mass of the preceding chapters – like the chaos left by a kitten's play with yarn – disentangled and rewound into a usable form. But recall that skeins are twisted and coiled like the double helix of DNA. The overall effect is one of organization but upon closer inspection there is much crisscrossing and doubling back of threads. The structure of a skein is recursive, redundant, and continually on the edge of disorganization should improper tension be applied – very much, in fact, like human society. Although structurally complex, a skein is but the starting point for projects to come. This sense of "skein" is what I mean to impart with the title of this chapter. To my mind, the previous nine chapters do not represent the final word but rather initial words regarding social and ritual practices of ancestral Maya economies. This study can be approached as a skein of thread ready to be utilized as warp or weft on a weaving loom. Much work has gone into its production but even more work will need to take place before narratives of ancestral Maya society achieve the texture and interlock of a finely woven fabric.

The metaphor of entangled threads is invoked to convey the notion that this study embraces an ontological – rather than a strict epistemological – approach to understanding the past (as per Henare et al. 2007a). Rather than seeking to artificially partition economic practices from other realms of life or examining how one thing impacts another, this study has embraced the messiness of reality and the relational meshing of ritual, social, political, and economic practices. An effort has been made to study the entanglements among topics traditionally sequestered into separate analytical corrals – landscape, households, gendered labor, monumental construction, royal courts, artisanship, trade, and state finance. In the process, and as the reader no doubt has detected, the word "economy" has appeared rather infrequently. Was the absence of this term due to its profound fundamentality or its irrelevance? Economic studies have a venerable history within archaeology, particularly among mid-twentieth-century British archaeologists, one of whom declared it fairly easy to infer and ranked it first in a climax of four degrees of increasingly difficult inference (Hawkes 1954:161). Elsewhere (McAnany and Pool 2008), I have written of the irony of this statement and the fact that Mesoamerican economies, in general, have defied easy understanding. But in a field where so much about past societies seems beyond our grasp, should we discard one of our venerable touchstones? As discussed in Chapter 1, the study of economy within anthropology, as a whole, also sits upon an uneasy past that goes beyond the impact of Marxist studies and the formalist/substantivist debates. John Clark (2007) – an archaeologist with a history of scholarship heavily vested in economic studies – goes so far as to suggest that the term "economy" itself may be far too entangled with formal economics and events unique to the Western Renaissance/mercantile–capitalism experience to be relevant to the deeper past. Certainly, within Chapter 7 in which I critically examine archaeological approaches to crafting, it is clear that our analytical frame has been overly shaped by pioneer theoreticians of capitalism, such as Adam Smith and Thorstein Veblen.

Rather than wrestle with the baby/bath water dilemma, perhaps the best way forward is simply to pose this question: How can we best skein the threads of our understanding of ancestral Maya practices so as to weave narratives of the past that approach a realistic and integrative understanding of past livelihoods, relations with landscape, gendered identity, social difference, artisan ethos, and state finance? Here, this goal has been approached by shifting the harsh, raking light of analytical perspective from economy per se and toward social/ritual practice and its constitutive fields of operation in reference to an animated landscape, notions of value, gendered labor, schemes of power, the royal body, the politics of tribute extraction, and so forth. After all, the economy is not some monolithic thing that casts a shadow across people, it is the things that people do and do repetitively – crafting, farming, hunting, sweeping, grinding maize, hauling stone for pyramid construction, transporting goods on a *cacaste* backframe, weaving fine *mantas* as gifts or tribute obligations, and bartering at a marketplace. Through the lens of practice theory, the past hopefully has been enlivened and projected in a manner that begins to approximate the deeply ritualized – and fundamentally agentive – experience of life that is indicated by archaeological remains. By engaging with the full spectrum of available information (archaeological, epigraphic, historical, and ethnographic), transformations of practice within Maya society have been highlighted. Changes in gendered identity and female involvement with weaving and maize grinding, for instance, have been studied through an examination of the materiality of these practices across the space–time continuum in a manner that seeks to avoid essentialization of gendered identity but acknowledges the strong linkages among pedagogy, identity, and practice.

In every topic pursued in this work – be it tribute ransom or the residue of a swept patio surface – the profound engagement of ancestral Maya actors with materiality has loomed large. Here, a relational approach also has provided space for considering not only social relations that shape and are shaped by larger social fields but also the role of things in instantiating relations among persons. Positionally, this study has reckoned with things (and their metaphysical significance to human lives) as more than passive objects to be manipulated by active human agency. This approach aligns with *thing* theorists such as Gell (1998), Henare and colleagues (2007b), Latour (1999, 2005), and Miller (2005), as well as Mesoamerican art historian Pasztory (2005). In an uncanny way, these approaches – most of which advocate a new cosmology of either science or art history – converge with indigenous cosmologies of Mesoamerica in which things instantiate vital forces and the causal interaction between humans and things is bidirectional. In a remarkable twist, what was once conceived in terms of *alterity* is now understandable by a refocus of study methods and perspective. Perhaps more profound than it appears, this shift is argued by Henare and colleagues

(2007a:8) to be a fundamental change from an epistemological to an ontological approach to understanding (and unsettling the current understanding of) the relations between people and things.

Of course, an issue that remains fundamental to this study and others is whether or not this perspectival shift actually helps in the task of skeining the threads and weaving a better narrative of Maya pasts. From the perspective of archaeology – which essentially is a chronicle of human engagement with the material world – an ontological approach has great resonance. If *things* are understood to be active players in figuring relational worlds of the past and present, then the "past residues" that form the core of our study materials take on enhanced significance and meaning. Indeed, it is the liveliness and dynamism of this engagement that has so preoccupied *thing* theorist Bruno Latour (1999:197) who asks why humans "so incessantly recruit and socialize nonhumans." Although Latour focuses on science studies, his non-Cartesian approach resonates with traditional Mesoamerican cosmologies in which things are perceived as animate beings, possessing agency and, oftentimes, dangerous powers. Chapter 3 addressed the animated state of Maya landscapes as well as meteorological forces and the manner in which the collective of humans and landscape resulted in a rich constellation of ritual practices framed, at least in part, within the metaphor of debt repayment. In a related study of ecology and Maya ritual practice, Scarborough (1998:155) observes that Maya studies will be greatly impoverished if more time is not spent integrating what often are seen as completely different research orientations (i.e., ritual practice, ecological ethos, and environmental reconstruction). This study responds to the call for a more integrated and cognitive approach to our interpretation of ancestral Maya landscape.

Likewise, the constructs of gendered labor and social identity – primary topics of Chapters 4 and 7 – do not exist in an abstract state but rather are given movement and reality by the materiality that results from constitutive action. Thus, swept debris, ground maize, a pine-needle carpet lain at the base of a domestic altar, a hoed field of maize, a well-fashioned pottery vessel, or an exemplary stone eccentric provide, in Latour's terms, both the means to and ends of a social fabric (1999:197). Our changing relationship with things and the value that we ascribe to them – how we make them and how they then remake us – is the message of Chapter 5 in which we considered how social relations were fundamentally and forever altered by the construction of monumental architecture. Predictably and yet still remarkably, a pyramidal construction of earth and stone can transform the social landscape in a unidirectional manner and decisively thwart attempts to defeat social hierarchy.

Social difference in ancestral Maya society, likewise, appears to have been created and maintained through the establishment of distinct sets of collective relationships between humans and things. Royal courts were inhabited by socially differentiated royal bodies who drank from calligraphically adorned bowls and cups, feasted diacritically, wore luxurious clothing, lived in elaborate stone houses adorned with sacred texts and icons, and were entombed after death in monumental mortuary facilities (Chapter 6). Such *social speciation* could not have been naturalized without being materialized. Perhaps the most powerful example of the bidirectional dynamism between people and things occurred in the realm of Classic Maya martial conflict in which human messenger emissaries, in effect, stood for the desired and demanded tribute that represented the spoils of war (Chapter 9). In this case, a human took on the properties of a thing – a tribute bundle. Yet another layer of complexity can be added to this inversion when one considers the central role of textiles in tribute presentation scenes. Indicative of female-gendered labor, textiles were entangled profoundly in political strife as well as alliance. In this way, a fabricated item – constitutive of elite female identity – came to exert tremendous influence within political negotiation.

An example of the power of things to lead interpretation is provided in Chapter 8 in which accumulating evidence of the presence of marketplaces at ancestral Maya political centers is discussed. The chain of relational inference – from marketplace to administered production and exchange – is a source of considerable resistance to many who hesitate to admit the reality of marketplace. Reasoning from a regional study of the biography of things to marketplace exchange as has been done by Hirth (2000:189–194) may be a way of confirming the reality of marketplace without the controversy that surrounds identification of a physical locale.

This study of ancestral Maya economies has been seated firmly within a material world. This positionality allows us to entertain the notion that the threads of social practice discussed in foregoing chapters were not separate spheres of action but rather part of a weft that tied humans together and persons with things, particularly things perceived to embody supernatural forces. As much economic practice involves making, hauling, trading, and using/consuming things, this consideration is an important part of moving beyond skeining the threads. Just as ancestral Maya economies were shaped by iterative practice, so we are called continually to weave narratives of the past that realistically entwine its many relevant threads.

References Cited

Abrams, E.M. 1994 *How the Maya Built Their World: Energetics and Ancient Architecture.* University of Texas Press, Austin.

Ackerman, K. 1993 Introduction. In *Incidents of Travel in Central America, Chiapas, and Yucatan*, pp. 1–9. Smithsonian Institution, Washington and London.

Adams, A. E. and J. E. Brady 2005 Ethnographic Notes on Maya Q'eqchi' Cave Rites: Implications for Archaeological Interpretation. In *In the Maw of the Earth Monster: Mesoamerican Ritual Cave Use*, edited by J.E. Brady and K.M. Prufer, pp. 301–327. University of Texas Press, Austin.

Adams, R.E.W. 1999 *Río Azul: An Ancient Maya City.* University of Oklahoma Press, Norman.

Aimers, J.J. and P.M. Rice 2006 Astronomy, Ritual, and the Interpretation of Maya "E – Group" Architectural Assemblages. *Ancient Mesoamerica* **17**(1):79–96.

Aimers, J.J., T. Powis and J. Awe 2000 Formative Period Round Structures of the Upper Belize Valley. *Latin American Antiquity* **11**:71–86.

Alexander, R.T. 2005 Isla Cilvituk and the Difficulties of Colonization in Southwestern Campeche. In *The Postclassic to Spanish-Era Transition in Mesoamerica*, edited by S.M. Kepecs and R.T. Alexander, pp. 161–183. University of New Mexico Press, Albuquerque.

Ambrosino, J. N. 2003 The Function of a Maya Palace at Yaxuna: A Contextual Approach. In *Maya Palaces and Elite Residences: An Interdisciplinary Approach*, edited by J.J. Christie, pp. 253–273. University of Texas Press, Austin.

Ames, K. M. 1995 Chiefly Power and Household Production on the Northwest Coast. In *Foundations of Social Inequality*, edited by T.D. Price and G.M. Feinman, pp. 155–187. Plenum Press, New York.

Anawalt, P.R. 1981 *Indian Clothing Before Cortés: Mesoamerican Clothing from the Codices.* University of Oklahoma Press, Norman.

Anderson, B. R. O. G. 1972 The Idea of Power in Javanese Culture. In *Culture and Politics in Indonesia*, edited by C. Holt, pp. 1–70. Cornell University Press, Ithaca and London.

Andrews, A. P. 1983 *Maya Salt Production and Trade*. University of Arizona Press, Tucson.

Andrews, A. P. and S. B. Mock 2002 New Perspectives on the Salt Trade. In *Ancient Maya Political Economies*, edited by D. A. Freidel and M. A. Masson, pp. 307–334. AltaMira Press, Walnut Creek, CA.

Andrews IV, E. W. 1969 *The Archaeological Use and Distribution of Mollusca in the Maya Lowlands*. Publication 34, Middle American Research Institute. Tulane University, New Orleans.

Andrews V, E. W. and W. L. Fash (editors) 2005 *Copán: The History of an Ancient Maya Kingdom*. School of American Research Advanced Seminar Series, Santa Fe.

Andrews V, E. W., J. L. Johnson, W. F. Doonan, G. E. Everson, K. E. Sampeck and H. E. Starratt 2003 A Multipurpose Structure in the Late Classic Palace at Copan. In *Maya Palaces and Elite Residences: An Interdisciplinary Approach*, edited by J. J. Christie, pp. 69–97. University of Texas Press, Austin.

Annis, S. 1987 *God and Production in a Guatemalan Town*. University of Texas Press, Austin.

Anschuetz, K. F., R. H. Wilshusen and C. Scheick 2001 An Archaeology of Landscapes: Perspectives and Directions. *Journal of Archaeological Research* **9**(2):157–211.

Aoyama, K. 1999 *Ancient Maya State, Urbanism, Exchange, and Craft Specialization: Chipped Stone Evidence from the Copán Valley and the La Entrada Region*. University of Pittsburgh Memoirs in Latin American Archaeology, Volume 12. University of Pittsburgh, Pittsburgh.

2007 Elite Artists and Craft Producers in Classic Maya Society: Lithic Evidence from Aguateca, Guatemala. *Latin American Antiquity* **18**(1): 3–26.

Appadurai, A. 1986 Introduction: Commodities and the Politics of Value. In *The Social Life of Things: Commodities in Cultural Perspective*, edited by A. Appadurai, pp. 3–63. Cambridge University Press, Cambridge.

Ardren, T. 2008 Studies of Gender in the Prehispanic Americas. *Journal of Archaeological Research* **16**:1–35.

Ardren, T. and D. R. Hixson 2006 The Unusual Sculptures of Telantunich, Yucatán: Phalli and the Concept of Masculinity among the Ancient Maya. *Cambridge Archaeological Journal* **16**(1):7–25.

Arnold, D. E. 1971 Ethnomineralogy of Ticul, Yucatán, Potters: Etics and Emics. *American Antiquity* **36**(1):20–40.

1985 *Ceramic Theory and Cultural Process*. Cambridge University Press, Cambridge.

2000 Does the Standardization of Ceramic Pastes Really Mean Specialization? *Journal of Archaeological Method and Theory* **7**(4): 333–375.

2005 Pots as Symbols: The Potter's Gremio in Ticul, Yucatán, Mexico. Paper presented at the American Anthropological Association, Washington, DC, November 30–December 4.

Arnold, P. P. 2001 *Eating Landscape: Aztec and European Occupation of Tlalocan.* University Press of Colorado, Boulder.

Arnould, E. J., C. Folkman Curasi and L. L. Price 2004 Inalienable Wealth in North American Households. In *Value and Valuables: From the Sacred to the Symbolic,* edited by C. Werner and D. Bell, pp. 209–230. AltaMira Press, Walnut Creek, CA.

Ashmore, W. 2002 Encountering Maya Women. In *Ancient Maya Women,* edited by T. Ardren, pp. 229–245. AltaMira Press, Walnut Creek, CA.

2004a Ancient Maya Landscapes. In *Continuities and Changes in Maya Archaeology: Perspectives at the Millennium,* edited by C. Golden and G. Borgstede, pp. 97–111. Routledge, New York.

2004b Social Archaeologies of Landscape. In *A Companion to Social Archaeology,* edited by L. Meskell and R. W. Preucel, pp. 255–271. Blackwell, Malden, MA.

Ashmore, W. and A. B. Knapp (editors) 1999 *Archaeologies of Landscape: Contemporary Perspectives.* Blackwell, Malden, MA.

Atran, S. and E. Ucan Ek 1999 Classification of Useful Plants by the Northern Petén Maya (Itzaj). In *Reconstructing Ancient Maya Diet,* edited by C. D. White, pp. 19–59. University of Utah Press, Salt Lake City.

Awe, J. J. 1992 *Dawn in the Land Between the Rivers: Formative Occupation at Cahal Pech, Belize and its Implications for Preclassic Development in the Maya Lowlands.* Ph.D. dissertation, University of London, Institute of Archaeology.

Baer, P. and W. R. Merrifield 1971 *Two Studies on the Lacandones of Mexico.* Summer Institute of Linguistics of the University of Oklahoma, Norman, OK.

Bailey, D. W. 1998 On Being Famous Through Time and Across Space. In *The Archaeology of Value: Essays on Prestige and the Processes of Valuation,* edited by D. W. Bailey, pp. 1–9. BAR International Series 730, Oxford.

Baines, J. and N. Yoffee 1988 Order, Legitimacy, and Wealth in Ancient Egypt and Mesopotamia. In *Archaic States,* edited by G. M. Feinman and J. Marcus, pp. 199–260. School of American Research, Santa Fe.

2000 Order, Legitimacy, and Wealth: Setting the Terms. In *Order, Legitimacy, and Wealth in Ancient State,* edited by J. Richards and M. van Buren, pp. 13–17. Cambridge University Press, Cambridge.

Bakhtin, M. 1984 *Rabelais and His World.* Indiana University Press, Bloomington.

Balée, W. and C. L. Erickson (editors) 2006 *Time and Complexity in Historical Ecology: Studies in the Neotropical Lowlands.* Columbia University Press, New York.

Ball, J. W. 1993 Pottery, Potters, Palaces, and Polities: Some Socio-economic and Political Implications of Late Classic Maya Ceramic Industries. In *Lowland Maya Civilization in the Eighth Century A.D.,* edited by J.A. Sabloff and J.S. Henderson, pp. 243–272. Dumbarton Oaks Research Library and Collection, Washington, DC.

Ball, J.W. and J.T. Taschek 2007 Sometimes a "Stove" Is "Just a Stove": A Context-based Reconsideration of Three-prong "Incense Burners" from the Western Belize Valley. *Latin American Antiquity* **18**(4):451–470.

Barrera Vásquez, A.D. 1995 *Diccionario Maya*. Editorial Porrúa, S.A., México DF.

Bartlett, M.L. 2004a The Potter's Choice of Clays and Crafting Technologies. In *K'axob: Ritual, Work, and Family in an Ancient Maya Village*, edited by P.A. McAnany, pp. 143–167. Monumenta Archaeologica 22, Cotsen Institute of Archaeology at UCLA, Los Angeles.

2004b Ornaments of Bone and Semiprecious Stone. In *K'axob: Ritual, Work and Family in an Ancient Maya Village*, edited by P.A. McAnany, pp. 353–364. Monumenta Archaeologica 22, Cotsen Institute of Archaeology at UCLA, Los Angeles.

2004c Artifacts of Fired Clay. In *K'axob: Ritual, Work and Family in an Ancient Maya Village*, edited by P.A. McAnany, pp. 263–277. Monumenta Archaeologica 22, Cotsen Institute of Archaeology at UCLA, Los Angeles.

Bartlett, M.L. and P.A. McAnany 2000 "Crafting" Communities: The Materialization of Formative Maya Identities. In *The Archaeology of Communities: A New World Perspective*, edited by M.-A. Canuto and J. Yaeger, pp. 102–122. Routledge, London.

Bartlett, M.L., H. Neff and P.A. McAnany 2000 Differentiation of Clay Resources on a Limestone Plain: The Analysis of Clay Utilization during the Maya Formative at K'axob, Belize. *Geoarchaeology* **15**(2):95–133.

Bawaya, M. 2006 Living Among the Maya: Past and Present. *Science* **313**:1876–1877.

Beach, T., N. Dunning, S. Luzzadder-Beach, D.E. Cook and J.C. Lohse 2006 Impacts of the Ancient Maya on Soils and Soil Erosion in the Central Maya Lowlands. *Catena* **65**:166–178.

Beach, T., S. Luzzadder-Beach, N. Dunning, J. Hageman and J.C. Lohse 2002 Upland Agriculture in the Maya Lowlands: Ancient Maya Soil Conservation in Northwestern Belize. *Geographical Review* **92**:372–397.

Beals, R.L. 1970 Gifting, Reciprocity, Savings, and Credit in Peasant Oaxaca. *Southwestern Journal of Anthropology* **26**:231–241.

Beaubien, H.F. and M. Beaudry-Corbett 2002 Artifacts Made from Plant Materials. In *Before the Volcano Erupted: The Ancient Cerén Village in Central America*, edited by P. Sheets, pp. 159–168. University of Texas Press, Austin.

Beaudry-Corbett, M. and S. McCafferty 2002 Spindle Whorls: Household Specialization at Ceren. In *Ancient Maya Women*, edited by T. Ardren, pp. 52–67. Altamira Press, Walnut Creek, CA.

Becker, M.J. 1971 *The Identification of a Second Plaza Plan at Tikal, Guatemala, and Its Implications for Ancient Maya Social Complexity*. Ph.D. dissertation, Department of Anthropology, University of Pennsylvania.

1973 Archaeological Evidence for Occupational Specialization Among the Classic Period Maya at Tikal, Guatemala. *American Antiquity* **38**:396–406.

1992 Burials as Caches; Caches as Burials: A New Interpretation of the Meaning of Ritual Deposits Among the Classic Period Lowland Maya. In *New Theories on the Ancient Maya*, edited by E. C. Danien and R. J. Sharer, pp. 185–196. The University Museum, University of Pennsylvania, Philadelphia.

Bell, C. B. 1992 *Ritual Theory, Ritual Practice.* Oxford University Press, New York.

Bell, E. E. 2002 Engendering a Dynasty: A Royal Woman in the Margarita Tomb, Copan. In *Ancient Maya Women*, edited by T. Ardren, pp. 89–104. AltaMira Press, Walnut Creek, CA.

Berdan, F. F. 1996 The Tributary Provinces. In *Aztec Imperial Strategies*, edited by F. F. Berdan, R. E. Blanton, E. H. Boone, M. G. Hodge, M. E. Smith and E. Umberger, pp. 115–135. Dumbarton Oaks Research Library and Collection, Washington, DC.

Berkes, F. 1999 *Sacred Ecology: Traditional Ecological Knowledge and Resource Management.* Taylor & Francis, Philadelphia.

Berry, K. and P. A. McAnany 2007 Reckoning with the Wetlands and Their Role in Ancient Maya Society. In *The Political Economy of Ancient Mesoamerica: Transformations During the Formative and Classic Periods*, edited by V. L. Scarborough and J. E. Clark, pp. 149–162. University of New Mexico, Albuquerque.

Bey III, G. J. 2003 Las Excavaciones en el Grupo Yaxché durante el 2003: Resumen y Conclusiones. In *Investigaciones Arqueológicas en Las Ruinas de Kiuic y La Zona Labná-Kiuic, Distrito de Bolonchén, Yucatán, México: Temporada de Campo 2003*, edited by T. Gallareta Negrón, G. J. Bey III and W. M. Ringle, pp. 7–4 to 7–8. Informe técnico al Consejo de Arqueología del Instituto Nacional de Antropología e Historia, Mérida, Yucatán, México.

2004 Kiuic: Continuación del Estudio del Grupo Yaxché. In *Investigaciones Arqueológicas en Las Ruinas de Kiuic y La Zona Labná-Kiuic, Distrito de Bolonchén, Yucatán, México: Temporada de Campo 2004*, edited by T. Gallareta Negrón, G. J. Bey III and W. M. Ringle, pp. 5–9 to 5–10. Informe técnico al Consejo de Arqueología del Instituto Nacional de Antropología e Historia, Mérida, Yucatán, México.

Bilsky, L. J. (editor) 1980 *Historical Ecology: Essays on Environment and Social Change.* Kennikat Press, Port Washington, NY.

Binford, M. W., M. Brenner, T. J. Whitmore, A. Higuera-Gundy and E. S. Deevey 1987 Ecosystems, Paleoecology and Human Disturbance in Subtropical and Tropical America. *Quaternary Science Review* **6**:115–128.

Blanton, R. E. 1994 *Houses and Households: A Comparative Study.* Plenum Press, New York.

Blanton, R.E., G.M. Feinman, S.A. Kowalewski and P.N. Peregrine 1996 A Dual-Processual Theory for the Evolution of Mesoamerican Civilization. *Current Anthropology* **37**(1):1–86.

Blanton, R.E., S.A. Kowalewski, G.M. Feinman and J. Appel 1981 *Ancient Mesoamerica: A Comparison of Change in Three Regions.* Cambridge University Press, Cambridge.

Bloch, M. 1986 *From Blessing to Violence.* Cambridge University Press, Cambridge.

1989 *Ritual, History and Power: Selected Papers in Anthropology.* Athlone, London.

Bohannon, P. 1955 Some Principles of Exchange and Investment Among the Tiv. *American Anthropologist* **57**:60–70.

Bolles, J.S. 1977 *Las Monjas: A Major Pre-Mexican Architectural Complex at Chichén Itzá.* University of Oklahoma Press, Norman.

Boone, E.H. 1994 *The Aztec World.* St. Remy Press and Smithsonian Books, Montreal and Washington, DC.

Boremanse, D. 1993 The Faith of the Real People: The Lacandon of the Chiapas Rain Forest. In *South and Meso-America Native Spirituality: From the Cult of the Feathered Serpent to the Theology of Liberation,* edited by G.H. Gossen and M. León Portilla, pp. 324–351. Crossroad, New York.

Boucher, S. and L. Quiñones 2007 Entre mercados, ferias y festines: los murales de la Sub 1–4 de Chiik Nahb, Calakmul. *Mayab* **19**:27–50.

Bourdieu, P. 1977 *Outline of a Theory of Practice.* Cambridge University Press, Cambridge.

1990 *The Logic of Practice.* Stanford University Press, Stanford, CA.

1993 *The Field of Cultural Production: Essays on Art and Literature.* Columbia University Press, New York.

2005 *The Social Structures of the Economy.* Polity Press, Cambridge, UK, and Malden, MA.

Bradley, R. 1998 *The Significance of Monuments: On the Shaping of Human Experience in Neolithic and Bronze Age Europe.* Routledge, London and New York.

2000 *An Archaeology of Natural Places.* Routledge, London and New York.

2005 *Ritual and Domestic Life in Prehistoric Europe.* Routledge, London.

Brady, J.E. 1989 *An Investigation of Maya Ritual Cave Use with Special Reference to Naj Tunich, Peten, Guatemala.* Ph.D. dissertation, Department of Anthropology, University of California, Los Angeles.

1997 Settlement Configuration and Cosmology: The Role of Caves at Dos Pilas. *American Anthropologist* **99**(3):602–618.

2006 The Impact of Ritual on Ancient Maya Economy. In *Stone Houses and Earth Lords: Maya Ritual and Religion in the Cave Context,* edited by K.M. Prufer and J.E. Brady, pp. 115–134. University Press of Colorado, Boulder.

Brady, J.E. and K.M. Prufer (editors) 2005 *In the Maw of the Earth Monster: Mesoamerican Ritual Cave Use.* University of Texas Press, Austin.

Branaman, A. 1997 Goffman's Social Theory. In *The Goffman Reader*, edited by C. Lemert and A. Branaman, pp. xiv–lxxxii. Blackwell, Malden, MA.

Braswell, G.E. 2001 Post-Classic Maya Courts of the Guatemalan Highlands: Archaeological and Ethnohistorical Approaches. In *Royal Courts of the Ancient Maya, Volume 2: Data and Case Studies*, edited by T. Inomata and S.D. Houston, pp. 308–334. Westview Press, Boulder, CO.

Braswell, G.E. and M.D. Glascock 2002 The Emergence of Market Economies in the Ancient Maya World: Obsidian Exchange in Terminal Classic Yucatán, Mexico. In *Geochemical Evidence for Long-Distance Exchange*, edited by M.D. Glascock, pp. 33–52. Bergin and Garvey, Westport, CT.

Breglia, L. 2006 *Monumental Ambivalence: The Politics of Heritage*. University of Texas Press, Austin.

Brenner, M., B. Leyden and M.W. Binford 1990 Recent Sedimentary Histories of Shallow Lakes in the Guatemalan Savannas. *Journal of Paleolimnology* **4**(3):239–252.

Bricker, V.R. 1973 *Ritual Humor in Highland Chiapas*. University of Texas Press, Austin.

Brown, C.T. 2006 Water Sources at Mayapan, Yucatán, Mexico. In *Precolumbian Water Management: Ideology, Ritual, and Power*, edited by L.J. Lucero and B.W. Fash, pp. 171–185. University of Arizona Press, Tucson.

Brown, L.A. 2001 Feasting on the Periphery: The Production of Ritual Feasting and Village Festivals at the Cerén Site, El Salvador. In *Feasts: Archaeological and Ethnographic Perspectives on Food, Politics, and Power*, edited by M. Dietler and B. Hayden, pp. 368–390. Smithsonian Institution Press, Washington, DC.

2004 Dangerous Places and Wild Spaces: Creating Meaning with Materials and Space at Contemporary Maya Shrines on el Duende Mountain. *Journal of Archaeological Method and Theory* **11**(1):31–58.

2005 Planting the Bones: Hunting Ceremonialism at Contemporary and Nineteenth-Century Shrines in the Guatemalan Highlands. *Latin American Antiquity* **16**(2):131–146.

Brück, J. 2001 Monuments, Power, and Personhood in the British Neolithic. *Journal of the Royal Anthropological Institute* **7**:649–667.

Brumfiel, E.M. 1991 Weaving and Cooking: Women's Production in Aztec Mexico. In *Engendering Archaeology*, edited by J. M. Gero and M.W. Conkey, pp. 224–251. Blackwell, Oxford.

2003 It's a Material World: History, Artifacts, and Anthropology. *Annual Review of Anthropology* **32**:205–223.

Brumfiel, E. and T.K. Earle 1987 Specialization, Exchange, and Complex Societies: An Introduction. In *Specialization, Exchange, and Complex Societies*, edited by E. Brumfiel and T.K. Earle, pp. 1–9. Cambridge University Press, Cambridge.

Burger, R.L. 1992 *Chavin and the Origins of Andean Civilization*. Thames & Hudson, London.

Burkhart, L.M. 1997 Mexica Women on the Home Front: Housework and Religion in Aztec Mexico. In *Indian Women of Early Mexico*, edited by

S. Schroeder, S. Wood and R. Haskett, pp. 25–54. University of Oklahoma Press, Norman.

Cancian, F. 1965 *Economics and Prestige in a Maya Community: The Religious Cargo System in Zinacantan*. Stanford University Press, Stanford, CA.

Carlson, R. and F. Eachus 1977 The Kekchi Spirit World. In *Cognitive Studies of Southern Mesoamerica*, edited by H. L. Neuenswander and D. E. Arnold, pp. 38–65. SIL Museum of Anthropology Publication 3. Summer Institute of Linguistics, Dallas.

Carmack, R. M. 1988 *Harvest of Violence: The Maya Indians and the Guatemalan Crisis*. University of Oklahoma Press, Norman.

Carrasco, D. 1995 Cosmic Jaws: We Eat the Gods and the Gods Eat Us. *Journal of the American Academy of Religion* **63**(3):429–463.

Carrasco, P. 1967 Don Juan Cortés, Cacique de Santa Cruz Quiché. *Estudios de Cultura Maya* **6**:251–266.

Carrasco Vargas, R. and M. Colón González 2005 El Reino de Kaan y la Antiqua Ciudad Maya de Calakmul. *Arqueología Mexicana* **13**(75): 40–47.

Casas, Bartolomé de las 1877 *Historia de las Indias* [Book 2, Chapter 20], México.

1909 *Apologética historia sumaria cuanto a las cualidades, disposición, descripción, cielo y suelo destas terras*. Nueva Biblioteca de Autores Españoles, volumen 13. Serrano y Ganz, Madrid.

Castañada, Q. E. 1996 *In the Museum of Maya Culture: Touring Chichén Itzá*. University of Minnesota Press, Minneapolis.

Cecil, L. G. 2004 Inductively Coupled Plasma Emission Spectroscopy and Postclassic Petén Slipped Pottery: An Examination of Pottery Wares, Social Identity and Trade. *Archaeometry* **46**(3):385–404.

Chadwick, J. 1976 *The Mycenaean World*. Cambridge University Press, Cambridge.

Chapman, R. 2003 *Archaeologies of Complexity*. Routledge, London.

Chase, A. F. and D. Z. Chase 1987 Putting Together the Pieces: Maya Pottery of Central Belize and Central Peten, Guatemala. In *Maya Ceramics: Papers from the 1985 Maya Ceramic Conference*, edited by P. M. Rice and R. J. Sharer, pp. 47–72. BAR International Series 345 (i), Oxford.

1996 More than Kin and King: Centralized Political Organization among the Late Classic Maya. *Current Anthropology* **37**(5):803–810.

1998a Scale and Intensity in Classic Period Maya Agriculture: Terracing and Settlement of the "Garden City" of Caracol. *Culture and Agriculture* **20**:60–77.

1998b The Architectural Context of Caches, Burials, and Other Ritual Activities for the Classic Period Maya (as reflected at Caracol, Belize). In *Function and Meaning in Classic Maya Architecture*, edited by S. D. Houston, pp. 299–332. Dumbarton Oaks Research Library and Collection, Washington, DC.

2001a The Royal Court of Caracol, Belize: Its Palaces and People. In *Royal Courts of the Ancient Maya, Volume 2: Data and Case Studies*, edited by T. Inomata and S.D. Houston, pp. 102–137. Westview Press, Boulder, CO.

2001b Ancient Maya Causeways and Site Organization at Caracol, Belize. *Ancient Mesoamerica* **12**(2):273–281.

Chase, A.F., D.Z. Chase, E. Zorn and W.G. Teeter 2008 Textiles and the Maya Archaeological Record: Gender, Power, and Status in Classic Period Caracol, Belize. *Ancient Mesoamerica* **19**(1):127–142.

Chayanov, A.V. 1966 *The Theory of the Peasant Economy.* Richard D. Irwin, Homewood, IL.

Childe, V.G. 1950 The Urban Revolution. *Town Planning Review* **21**(1):3–17.

Christenson, A.J. 2001 *Art and Society in a Highland Maya Community: The Altarpiece of Santiago Atitlán.* University of Texas Press, Austin.

2007 *Popol Vuh: The Sacred Book of the Maya.* University of Oklahoma Press, Norman.

Christie, J.J. (editor) 2003 *Maya Palaces and Elite Residences: An Interdisciplinary Approach.* University of Texas Press, Austin.

Clark, J.E. 1987 Politics, Prismatic Blades, and Mesoamerican Civilization. In *The Organization of Core Technology*, edited by J.K. Johnson and C.A. Morrow, pp. 259–284. Westview Press, Boulder, CO, and London.

1989 Obsidian: The Primary Mesoamerican Sources. In *La Obsidiana en Mesoamérica*, edited by M. Gaxiola G. and J.E. Clark, pp. 299–319. Instituto Nacional de Antropologia e Historia, Mexico.

1995 Craft Specialization as an Archaeological Category. In *Research in Economic Anthropology, Volume 16*, edited by B.L. Isaac, pp. 267–294. JAI Press, Greenwich, CT.

1997 The Arts of Government in Early Mesoamerica. *Annual Review of Anthropology* **26**:211–234.

2003a A Review of Twentieth-Century Mesoamerican Obsidian Studies. In *Mesoamerican Lithic Technology: Experimentation and Interpretation*, edited by K.G. Hirth, pp. 15–54. University of Utah Press, Salt Lake City.

2003b Craftsmanship and Craft Specialization. In *Mesoamerican Lithic Technology: Experimentation and Interpretation*, edited by K.G. Hirth, pp. 220–223. University of Utah Press, Salt Lake City.

2007 In Craft Specialization's Penumbra: Things, Persons, Action, Value, and Surplus. In *Rethinking Craft Specialization in Complex Societies: Archaeological Analysis of the Social Meaning of Production*, edited by Z.X. Hruby and R.K. Flad, pp. 20–35. Archaeological Papers of the American Anthropological Association No. 17, Arlington, VA.

Clark, J.E. and M. Blake 1994 The Power of Prestige: Competitive Generosity and the Emergence of Rank Societies in Lowland Mesoamerica. In *Factional Competition and Political Development in the New World*, edited by E.M. Brumfiel and J.W. Fox, pp. 17–30. Cambridge University Press, Cambridge.

Clark, J.E. and D. Cheetham 2002 Mesoamerica's Tribal Foundations. In *The Archaeology of Tribal Societies*, edited by W.A. Parkinson, pp. 278–339.

International Monographs in Prehistory, Archaeological Series 15, Ann Arbor, MI.

Clark, J.E. and R.D. Hansen 2001 The Architecture of Early Kingship: Comparative Perspectives on the Origins of the Maya Royal Court. In *Royal Courts of the Ancient Maya, Volume 2*, edited by T. Inomata and S.D. Houston, pp. 1–45. Westview Press, Boulder, CO.

Clark, J.E., R.D. Hansen and T. Pérez Suárez 2000 La Zona Maya en el Preclásico. In *Historia Antiqua de México Volume 1: El México Antiquo, sus Áreas Culturales, los Orígenes y el Horizonte Preclásico*, edited by L. Manzanilla and L. López Lujan, pp. 437–510. Instituto de Investigaciones Antropológicas, Instituto Nacional de Antropología e Historia, México DF.

Clark, J.E. and S.D. Houston 1998 Craft Specialization, Gender, and Personhood Among the Post-Conquest Maya of Yucatan, Mexico. In *Craft and Social Identity*, edited by C.L. Costin and R.P. Wright, pp. 31–46. Archaeological Papers of the American Anthropological Association No. 8, Washington, DC.

Clark, J.E. and W.J. Parry 1990 Craft Specialization and Cultural Complexity. In *Research in Economic Anthropology, Volume 12*, edited by B.L. Isaac, pp. 289–346. JAI Press, Greenwich, CT.

Clark, J.E. and M.E. Pye (editors) 2000 *Olmec Art and Archaeology in Mesoamerica.* National Gallery of Art, Washington, DC. Distributed by Yale University Press, New Haven, CT.

Clutton-Brock, J. and N. Hammond 1994 Hot Dogs: Comestible Canids in Preclassic Maya Culture at Cuello, Belize. *Journal of Archaeological Science* **21**:819–826.

Codex Tro-Cortesianus (Codex Madrid) 1967 *Introduction and Summary by F. Anders.* Akademische Druck-u, Graz, Austria.

Coe, M.D. 1956 The Funerary Temple Among the Classic Maya. *Southwestern Journal of Anthropology* **12**:387–394.

1978 *Lords of the Underworld: Masterpieces of Classic Maya Ceramics.* The Art Museum, Princeton University, Princeton University Press, Princeton, NJ.

1992 *Breaking the Maya Code.* Thames & Hudson, New York.

Coe, M.D. and J. Kerr 1998 *The Art of the Maya Scribe.* Harry N. Abrams, New York.

Coe, M.D. and M. Van Stone 2001 *Reading the Maya Glyphs.* Thames & Hudson, London.

Coe, S.D. 1994 *America's First Cuisines.* University of Texas Press, Austin.

Coe, S.D. and M.D. Coe 1996 *The True History of Chocolate.* Thames & Hudson, London.

Coe, W.R. 1988 *Tikal: A Handbook of the Ancient Maya Ruins.* 2nd ed. Asociacion Tikal, Guatemala.

Coggins, C.C. 1975 *Painting and Drawing Styles at Tikal: An Historical and Iconographic Reconstruction.* Ph.D. dissertation, Department of Fine Arts, Harvard University.

Coggins, C. C. and O. C. Shane, III (editors) 1984 *Cenote of Sacrifice: Maya Treasures from the Sacred Well at Chichen Itza.* University of Texas Press, Austin.

Colas, P.R. 2003 K'inich and King: Naming Self and Person among Classic Maya Rulers. *Ancient Mesoamerica* **14**(2):269–283.

Comaroff, J. 1985 *Body of Power, Spirit of Resistance: The Culture and History of a South African People.* University of Chicago Press, Chicago.

Conkey, M.W. and J.M. Gero 1991 Tensions, Pluralities, and Engendering Archaeology: An Introduction to Women and Prehistory. In *Engendering Archaeology: Women and Prehistory,* edited by J. M. Gero and M.W. Conkey, pp. 3–30. Blackwell, Oxford.

Connerton, P. 1989 *How Societies Remember.* Cambridge University Press, Cambridge.

Cook, G.W. 2000 *Renewing the Maya World: Expressive Culture in a Highland Town.* University of Texas Press, Austin.

Cosgrove, D.E. 1993 *The Palladian Landscape: Geographical Change and Its Cultural Representations in Sixteenth-Century Italy.* Pennsylvania State University Press, University Park.

Costin, C.L. 1991 Craft Specialization: Issues in Defining, Documenting, and Explaining the Organization of Production. In *Archaeological Method and Theory, Volume 3,* edited by M.B. Schiffer, pp. 1–56. University of Arizona Press, Tucson.

1998 Introduction: Craft and Social Identity. In *Craft and Social Identity,* edited by C. L. Costin and R. P. Wright, pp. 3–16. Archaeological Papers of the American Anthropological Association No. 8, Washington, DC.

2004 Craft Economies of Ancient Andean States. In *Archaeological Perspectives on Political Economies,* edited by G. M. Feinman and L. M. Nicholas, pp. 189–221. University of Utah Press, Salt Lake City.

Cowgill, G.L. 2004 Origins and Development of Urbanism: Archaeological Perspectives. *Annual Review of Anthropology* **33**:525–549.

Coyston, S., C. D. White and H. P. Schwarcz 1999 Dietary Carbonate Analysis of Bone and Enamel for Two Sites in Belize. In *Reconstructing Ancient Maya Diet,* edited by C. D. White, pp. 221–243. University of Utah Press, Salt Lake City.

Crane, C.J. 1996 Archaeobotanical and Palynological Research at a Late Preclassic Maya Community, Cerros, Belize. In *The Managed Mosaic: Ancient Maya Agriculture and Resource Use,* edited by S. Fedick, pp. 262–277. University of Utah Press, Salt Lake City.

Crown, P.L. 2007 Learning about Learning. In *Archaeological Anthropology: Perspectives on Method and Theory,* edited by J. M. Skibo, M.W. Graves and M. T. Stark, pp. 198–217. University of Arizona Press, Tucson.

Crumley, C.L. (editor) 1994 *Historical Ecology: Cultural Knowledge and Changing Landscapes.* School of American Research Press, Santa Fe, NM.

Crumley, C.L., A.E. van Deventer and J.J. Fletcher (editors) 2001 *New Directions in Anthropology and Environment: Intersections.* AltaMira Press, Walnut Creek, CA.

Cucina, A. and V. Tiesler 2003 Dental Caries and Antemortem Tooth Loss in the Northern Peten Area, Mexico: A Biocultural Perspective on Social Status Differences among the Classic Maya. *American Journal of Physical Anthropology* **122**:1–10.

Culbert, T.P. 1993 *The Ceramics of Tikal: Vessels from the Burials, Caches and Problematical Deposits, Tikal Report No. 25, Part A.* University Museum Monographs 81, The University Museum, University of Pennsylvania, Philadelphia.

Cyphers, A. 1996 Reconstructing Olmec Life at San Lorenzo. In *Olmec Art of Ancient Mexico,* edited by E.P. Benson and B. de la Fuente, pp. 61–71. National Gallery of Art, Washington, DC. Distributed by Harry N. Abrams, New York.

Dacus, C. 2005 *Weaving the Past: An Examination of Bones Buried with an Elite Maya Woman.* Unpublished Masters Thesis, Department of Art History, Southern Methodist University.

Dahlin, B.H. 2003 Chunchucmil: A Complex Economy in Northwest Yucatan. *Mexicon* **25**:129–138.

Dahlin, B.H. and T. Ardren 2002 Modes of Exchange and Regional Patterns: Chunchucmil, Yucatan, Mexico. In *Ancient Maya Political Economies,* edited by M. Masson and D.A. Freidel, pp. 249–284. AltaMira Press, Walnut Creek, CA.

Dahlin, B.H., C.T. Jensen, R.E. Terry, D.R. Wright and T. Beach 2007 In Search of an Ancient Maya Market. *Latin American Antiquity* **18**(4): 363–384.

D'Altroy, T.N. and T.K. Earle 1985 Staple Finance, Wealth Finance, and Storage in the Inka Political Economy. *Current Anthropology* **26**(2):187–206.

Danforth, M.E. 1997 Late Classic Maya Health Patterns: Evidence from Enamel Microdefects. In *Bones of the Maya,* edited by S.L. Whittington and D. Reed, pp. 127–137. Smithsonian Institution Press, Washington, DC.

1999 Coming up Short: Status and Nutrition among the Ancient Maya of the Southern Lowlands. In *Reconstructing Ancient Maya Diet,* edited by C.D. White, pp. 103–117. University of Utah Press, Salt Lake City.

Davis, N.Z. 1975 *Society and Culture in Early Modern France.* Stanford University Press, Stanford, CA.

de Certeau, M. 1984 *The Practice of Everyday Life.* University of California Press, Berkeley.

Demarest, A.A. 2004 *Ancient Maya: The Rise and Fall of a Rainforest Civilization.* Cambridge University Press, Cambridge.

Demarest, A.A. and G.W. Conrad (editors) 1992 *Ideology and Pre-Columbian Civilizations.* School of American Research Press, Santa Fe, NM.

Demarest, A.A., T. Barrientos Q., B. Kovacevich, M. Callaghan, B. Woodfill and L.F. Luin 2004 *Proyecto Arqueológico Cancuén: Informe Temporada 2003.* Submitted to Ministerio de Cultura y Deportes, Instituto de Antropologia e Historia, Guatemala City.

Demarest, A.A., K. Morgan, C. Wolley and H. Escobedo 2003 The Political Acquisition of Sacred Geography. In *Maya Palaces and Elite Residences: An*

Interdisciplinary Approach, edited by J.J. Christie, pp. 120–153. University of Texas Press, Austin.

DeMarrais, E., L.J. Castillo and T. Earle 1996 Ideology, Materialization, and Power Strategies. *Current Anthropology* **37**:15–31.

Devereaux, L. 1987 Gender Difference and Relations of Inequality in Zinacantan. In *Dealing with Inequality: Analyzing Gender Relations in Melanesia and Beyond*, edited by M. Strathern, pp. 89–111. Cambridge University Press, Cambridge.

Diakonoff, I.M. 1969 *Ancient Mesopotamia Socio-economic History*. Nauka Publishing. House, Moscow.

Diamond, J. 2005 *Collapse: How Societies Choose to Fail or Succeed*. Viking, Penguin Group, New York.

Dietler, M. 2001 Theorizing the Feast: Rituals of Consumption, Commensal Politics, and Power in African Contexts. In *Feasts: Archaeological and Ethnographic Perspectives on Food, Politics, and Power*, edited by M. Dietler and B. Hayden, pp. 65–114. Smithsonian Institution Press, Washington, DC, and London.

Dietler, M. and B. Hayden 2001 Digesting the Feast: Good to Eat, Good to Drink, Good to Think. In *Feasts: Archaeological and Ethnographic Perspectives on Food, Politics, and Power*, edited by M. Dietler and B. Hayden, pp. 1–20. Smithsonian Institution Press, Washington, DC.

Dietler, M. and I. Herbich 1989 Tich Matek: The Technology of Luo Pottery Production and the Definition of Ceramic Style. *World Archaeology* **21**(1):148–164.

1998 *Habitus*, Techniques, Style: An Integrated Approach to the Social Understanding of Material Culture and Boundaries. In *The Archaeology of Social Boundaries*, edited by M.T. Stark, pp. 232–269. Smithsonian Institution Press, Washington, DC.

2001 Feasts and Labor Mobilization: Dissecting a Fundamental Economic Practice. In *Feasts: Archaeological and Ethnographic Perspectives on Food, Politics, and Power*, edited by M. Dietler and B. Hayden, pp. 240–264. Smithsonian Institution Press, Washington, DC.

Dirks, N.B. 1991 Ritual and Resistance: Subversion as a Social Fact. In *Contesting Power: Resistance and Everyday Social Relations in South Asia*, edited by D. Haynes and G. Prakash, pp. 213–238. University of California Press, Berkeley.

Dobres, M.A. 2000 *Technology and Social Agency: Outlining a Practice Framework for Archaeology*. Blackwell, Oxford.

Dobres, M.A. and J.E. Robb 2000 Agency in Archaeology: Paradigm or Platitude? In *Agency in Archaeology*, edited by M.A. Dobres and J.E. Robb, pp. 3–17. Routledge, London.

Douglas, M. 1972 *Natural Symbols: Explorations in Cosmology*. Pantheon Books, New York.

Douglas, M. and B. Isherwood 1996 *The World of Goods: Towards an Anthropology of Consumption*. Routledge, London and New York.

Dreiss, M.L. and D.O. Brown 1989 Obsidian Exchange Patterns in Belize. In *Prehistoric Maya Economies of Belize*, edited by P.A. McAnany and

B. L. Isaac, pp. 57–90. Research in Economic Anthropology, Supplement 4, JAI Press, Greenwich, CT.

Drennan, R. D. 1984 Long-Distance Movement of Goods in the Mesoamerican Formative and Classic. *American Antiquity* **49**(1):27–43.

Dunning, N. and T. Beach 2000 Stability and Instability in Prehispanic Maya Landscapes. In *Imperfect Balance: Landscape Transformations in the Precolumbian Americas,* edited by D. L. Lentz, pp. 170–202. Columbia University Press, New York.

2004 Noxious or Nurturing Nature? Maya Civilization in Environmental Context. In *Continuities and Changes in Maya Archaeology: Perspectives at the Millennium,* edited by C. Golden and G. Borgstede, pp. 125–141. Routledge, New York.

Dunning, N., T. Beach, P. Farrell and S. Luzzadder-Beach 1998 Prehispanic Agrosystems and Adaptive Regions in the Maya Lowlands. *Culture and Agriculture* **20**(2/3):87–101.

Dunning, N. P., T. Beach and S. Luzzader-Beach 2006 Environmental Variability among Bajos in the Southern Maya Lowlands and Its Implications for Ancient Maya Civilization and Archaeology. In *Precolumbian Water Management: Ideology, Ritual, and Power,* edited by L. J. Lucero and B. W. Fash, pp. 81–99. University of Arizona Press, Tucson.

Dunning, N., J. G. Jones, T. Beach and S. Luzzadder-Beach 2003 Physiography, Habitats, and Landscapes of the Three Rivers Region. In *Heterarchy, Political Economy, and the Ancient Maya: The Three Rivers Region of the East-Central Yucatán Peninsula,* edited by V. L. Scarborough, F. Valdez, Jr. and N. Dunning, pp. 14–24. University of Arizona Press, Tucson.

Dunning, N., S. Luzzadder-Beach, T. Beach, J. G. Jones, V. L. Scarborough and T. P. Culbert 2002 Arising from the Bajos: The Evolution of a Neotropical Landscape and the Rise of Maya Civilization. *Annals of the Association of American Geographers* **92**(2):267–283.

Durkheim, E. 1961[1915] *The Elementary Forms of the Religious Life.* Translated from French by J. W. Swain. Collier Books, New York.

Earle, D. M. 1986 The Metaphor of the Day in Quiche: Notes on the Nature of Everyday Life. In *Symbol and Meaning Beyond the Closed Community: Essays in Mesoamerican Ideas,* edited by G. H. Gossen, pp. 155–172. Institute for Mesoamerican Studies, The University at Albany, State University of New York, Albany.

Earle, T. K. 1977 A Reappraisal of Redistribution: Complex Hawaiian Chiefdoms. In *Exchange Systems in Prehistory,* edited by T. K. Earle and J. E. Ericson, pp. 213–29. Academic Press, New York.

1981 Comment on P. Rice, Evolution of Specialized Pottery Production: A Trial Model. *Current Anthropology* **22**(3):230–231.

Ebersole, J. 2001 *Ground and Polished Stone Artifacts of K'axob, Belize, Central America.* Independent Work for Distinction, Boston University. Manuscript on file with author.

Ebert, J. I. 1992 *Distributional Archaeology.* University of New Mexico Press, Albuquerque.

Edmondson, M. S. 1982 *The Ancient Future of the Itza, the Book of Chilam Balam of Tizimin.* University of Texas Press, Austin.

Eerkens, J. W. 2000 Practice Makes Within 5% of Perfect: Visual Perception, Motor Skills, and Memory in Artifact Variation. *Current Anthropology* **41**(4):663–668.

Egan, J. A. 2004 Keeping-for-Giving and Giving-for-Keeping: Value, Hierarchy, and the Inalienable in Yap. In *Value and Valuables: From the Sacred to the Symbolic,* edited by C. Werner and D. Bell, pp. 21–48. AltaMira Press, Walnut Creek, CA.

Eliade, M. 1954 *The Myth of the Eternal Return.* Translated from French by W. R. Trask. Pantheon Books, New York.

Emery, K. F. 2003 The Noble Beast: Status and Differential Access to Animals in the Maya World. *World Archaeology* **34**(3):498–515.

2004 Environments of the Maya Collapse: A Zooarchaeological Perspective from the Petexbatún. In *Maya Zooarchaeology: New Directions in Method and Theory,* edited by K. F. Emery, pp. 81–95. Monograph 51, Cotsen Institute of Archaeology at UCLA, Los Angeles.

Emery, K. F. and K. Aoyama 2005 La Elaboración de Herramientas de Hueso en los Grupos Domésticos de la Elite Maya de Aguateca, Guatemala. In *XVII Simposio de Investigaciones Arqueológicas en Guatemala, 2004,* edited by J. P. Laporte, B. Arroyo and H. E. Mejía, Chap. 77, pp. 1–18. Instituto de Antropología e Historia, Guatemala.

2007 Bone, Shell, and Lithic Evidence for Crafting in Elite Maya Households at Aguateca, Guatemala. *Ancient Mesoamerica* **18**(1):69–89.

Ensminger, J. (editor) 2002 *Theory in Economic Anthropology.* AltaMira Press, Walnut Creek, CA.

Espejo-Ponce, M. and M. Restall 1997 Work, Marriage, and Status: Maya Women of Colonial Yucatan. In *Indian Women of Early Mexico,* edited by S. Schroeder, S. Wood and R. Haskett, pp. 231–252. University of Oklahoma Press, Norman.

Estrada Belli, F. and P. M. Rice 2006 Lightening Sky, Rain, and the Maize God: The Ideology of Preclassic Maya Rulers at Cival, Peten, Guatemala. *Ancient Mesoamerica* **17**(1):57–78.

Evans, R. K. 1978 Early Craft Specialization: An Example from the Balkan Chalcolithic. In *Social Archaeology: Beyond Subsistence and Dating,* edited by C. L. Redman, M. J. Berman, E. V. Curtin, W. T. Langhorne, Jr., N. M. Versaggi and J. C. Wanser, pp. 113–129. Academic Press, New York.

Evans, S. T. and J. Pillsbury (editors) 2004 *Palaces of the Ancient New World.* Dumbarton Oaks Research Library and Collection, Washington, DC.

Farriss, N. M. 1983 Indians in Colonial Yucatan: Three Perspectives. In *Spaniards and Indians in Southeastern Mesoamerica,* edited by M. J. MacLeod and R. Wasserstrom, pp. 1–39. University of Nebraska Press, Lincoln.

1984 *Maya Society Under Colonial Rule: The Collective Enterprise of Survival.* Princeton University Press, Princeton, NJ.

Fash, B. W. and W. L. Fash 2007 The Roles of Ballgames in Mesoamerican Ritual Economy. In *Mesoamerican Ritual Economy: Archaeological and*

Ethnological Perspectives, edited by E.C. Wells and K.L. Davis-Salazar, pp. 267–284. University Press of Colorado, Boulder.

Fash, W.L. 1991 *Scribes, Warriors and Kings*. Thames & Hudson, London.

Fauvet-Berthelot, M.-F. 1986 *Ethnoprehistoire de la maison Maya (Guatemala 1250–1525)*. Collection Etudes Mésoaméricaines I-13, Mexico City.

Fedick, S.E. (editor) 1996 *The Managed Mosaic: Ancient Maya Agriculture and Resource Use*. University of Utah Press, Salt Lake City.

Feeley-Harnik, G. 1985 Issues in Divine Kingship. *Annual Review of Anthropology* **14**:273–313.

Feinman, G.M. and J. Marcus (editors) 1998 *Archaic States*. School of American Research, Santa Fe, NM.

Feinman, G.M. and L.M. Nichols 1995 Household Craft Specialization and Shell Ornament Manufacture in Ejutla, Mexico. *Expedition* **37**(2): 14–25.

Feldman, L.H. 1985 *A Tumpline Economy: Production and Distribution Systems in Sixteenth-Century Eastern Guatemala*. Labyrinthos, Culver City, CA.

Fernandez Tejero, I. 1997 El Ppolom, mercaderillo o regatón. *Arqueología Mexicana* **29**:46–53.

Few, M. 2002 *Women Who Lead Evil Lives*. University of Texas Press, Austin.

Firth, R.W. 1983 Magnitude and Values in Kula Exchange. In *The Kula: New Perspectives in Massim Exchange*, edited by J. Leach and E. Leach, pp. 89–102. Cambridge University Press, Cambridge.

Fischer, E.F. 1999 Cultural Logic and Maya Identity: Rethinking Constructivism and Essentialism. *Current Anthropology* **40**:473–499.

2001 *Cultural Logics and Gobal Economies: Maya Identity in Thought and Practice*. University of Texas Press, Austin.

Fischer, E.F. and R. McKenna Brown (editors) 1996 *Maya Cultural Activism in Guatemala*. University of Texas Press, Austin.

Fitzsimmons, J.L. 1998 Classic Maya Mortuary Anniversaries at Piedras Negras, Guatemala. *Ancient Mesoamerica* **9**:271–278.

Fitzsimmons, J.L.(editor) 2010 *Between the Living and the Dead in Mesoamerica*. University of Arizona Press, Tucson.

Fogelin, L. 2007 The Archaeology of Religious Ritual. *Annual Review of Anthropology* **36**:55–71.

Foias, A.E. 2002 At the Crossroads: The Economic Basis of Political Power in the Petexbatun Region. In *Ancient Maya Political Economies*, edited by M. Masson and D.A. Freidel, pp. 223–248. AltaMira Press, Walnut Creek, CA.

2004 The Past and Future of Maya Ceramic Studies. In *Continuities and Change in Maya Archaeology: Perspectives at the Millennium*, edited by C.W. Golden and G. Borgstede, pp. 143–176. Routledge, New York.

Folan, W.J., J.D. Gunn and M. del R. Domínguez Carrasco 2001 Triadic Temples, Central Plazas and Dynastic Palaces: A Diachronic Analysis of the Royal Court Complex, Calakmul, Campeche, Mexico. In *Royal Courts of the Ancient Maya, Volume 2: Data and Case Studies*, edited by T. Inomata and S.D. Houston, pp. 223–265. Westview Press, Boulder, CO.

Foshag, W.F. 1984 *Mineralogical Studies on Guatemalan Jade.* Smithsonian Institution Publication 4307, Washington, DC.

Foster, B.R. 1981 A New Look at the Sumerian Temple State. *Journal of the Economic History and Society of the Orient* **24**(3):225–241.

Foucault, M. 1979 *Discipline and Punish.* Vintage Books, New York.

Freidel, D.A. 1979 Culture Areas and Interaction Spheres: Contrasting Approaches to the Emergence of Civilization in the Maya Lowlands. *American Antiquity* **44**:36–54.

1981 The Political Economics of Residential Dispersion Among the Lowland Maya. In *Lowland Maya Settlement Patterns,* edited by W. Ashmore, pp. 371–382. University of New Mexico Press, Albuquerque.

1986a The Monumental Architecture. In *Archaeology at Cerros, Belize, Central America,* edited by R. Robertson and D.A. Freidel, pp. 1–22. Southern Methodist University Press, Dallas.

1986b Maya Warfare: An Example of Peer Polity Interaction. In *Peer Polity Interaction and Socio-political Change,* edited by C. Renfrew and J. F. Cherry, pp. 93–108. Cambridge University Press, Cambridge.

2007 Betraying the Maya: Who Does the Violence in Apocalypto Really Hurt? *Archaeology* May/June:36–41.

Freidel, D.A. and J. Shaw 2000 The Lowland Maya Civilization: Historical Consciousness and Environment. In *The Way the Wind Blows: Climate, History, and Human Action,* edited by R.J. McIntosh, J.A. Tainter and S.K. McIntosh, pp. 271–300. Columbia University Press, New York.

Freidel, D., L. Schele and J. Parker 1993 *Maya Cosmos: Three Thousand Years on the Shaman's Path.* William Morrow, New York.

Fry, R.E. 1979 The Economics of Pottery at Tikal, Guatemala: Models of Exchange for Serving Vessels. *American Antiquity* **44**(3):494–512.

1980 Models of Exchange for Major Shape Classes of Lowland Maya Pottery. In *Models and Methods in Regional Exchange,* edited by R.E. Fry, pp. 3–18. SAA Papers No. 1. Society for American Archaeology, Washington, DC.

Gallareta Negrón, T. (editor) 2005 *Proyecto Arqueologico Xocnaceh: Segunda Temporada de Campo. Informe Técnico al Consejo de Arqueología del Instituto Nacional de Antropología e Historia.* Mérida, Centro INAH Yucatán, México.

Garber, J. 2001 Ground Stone Tools. In *The Archaeology of Ancient Mexico and Central America: An Encyclopedia,* edited by E.S.T. and D.L. Webster, pp. 300–303. Garland, New York and London.

García L., G. 1981 Conservación del material procedente del Cenote Sagrado de Chichén Itzá. In *Memoria del Congreso Interno, 1979,* pp. 255–259. Centro Regional del Sureste, Instituto Nacional de Antropología e Historia, Mexico City.

García Moll, G. 2004 Shield Jaguar and Structure 23 at Yaxchilan. In *Courtly Art of the Ancient Maya,* edited by M. Miller and S. Martin, pp. 268–270. Thames & Hudson, Fine Arts Museum of San Francisco, San Francisco.

Gasco, J. 2005 The Consequence of Spanish Colonial Rule for the Indigenous Peoples of Chiapas, Mexico. In *The Postclassic to Spanish-Era Transition in Mesoamerica: Archaeological Perspectives*, edited by S. Kepecs and R.T. Alexander, pp. 77–96. University of New Mexico, Albuquerque.

Gasco, J. and B. Voorhies 1989 The Ultimate Tribute: The Role of the Soconusco as an Aztec Tributary. In *Ancient Trade and Tribute: Economies of the Soconusco Region of Mesoamerica*, edited by B. Voorhies, pp. 48–94. University of Utah Press, Salt Lake City.

Gates, B. 2008 How to Fix Capitalism. *Time* **172**(6):40–45.

Geertz, C. 1973 *The Interpretation of Cultures*. Basic Books, New York.

1979 From the Native's Point of View: On the Nature of Anthropological Understanding. In *Interpretive Social Science: A Reader*, edited by P. Rabinow and W.M. Sullivan, pp. 225–242. University of California Press, Berkeley.

1980 *Negara: The Theatre State in Nineteenth-Century Bali*. Princeton University Press, Princeton, NJ.

Gell, A. 1998 *Art and Agency: An Anthropological Theory*. Clarendon Press, Oxford.

Gero, J.M. 1991 Genderlithics: Women's Roles in Stone Tool Production. In *Engendering Archaeology: Women and Prehistory*, edited by J.M. Gero and M.W. Conkey, pp. 163–193. Blackwell, Oxford.

1992 Feasts and Females: Gender Ideology and Political Meals in the Andes. *Norwegian Archaeological Review* **25**(1):15–30.

2000 Troubled Travels in Agency and Feminism. In *Agency in Archaeology*, edited by M.A. Dobres and J.E. Robb, pp. 34–39. Routledge, London and New York.

Gerry, J.P. 1997 Bone Isotope Ratios and their Bearing on Elite Privilege among the Classic Maya. *Geoarchaeology* **12**(1):41–69.

Gerry, J.P. and H.W. Krueger 1997 Regional Diversity in Classic Maya Diets. In *Bones of the Maya: Studies of Ancient Skeletons*, edited by S.L. Whittington and D.M. Reed, pp. 196–207. Smithsonian Institution Press, Washington, DC.

Giddens, A. 1979 *Central Problems in Social Theory: Action, Structure, and Contradiction in Social Analysis*. Macmillan, London.

1981 *A Contemporary Critique of Historical Materialism, Volume 1: Power, Property and the State*. University of California Press, Berkeley and Los Angeles.

1984 *The Constitution of Society*. Polity Press, Cambridge.

Gillingham, J. 1978 *Richard the Lionheart*. Times Books, New York.

Gluckman, M. 1959 The Lozi of Barotseland in North-Western Rhodesia. In *Seven Tribes of British Central Africa*, edited by E. Colson and M. Gluckman, pp. 1–91. Manchester University Press, Manchester, UK.

Godelier, M. 1999 *The Enigma of the Gift*. Translated by N. Scott. University of Chicago Press, Chicago.

2004 What Mauss Did Not Say: Things You Give, Things You Sell, and Things That Must Be Kept. In *Values and Valuables: From the Sacred to the Symbolic*, edited by C. Werner and D. Bell, pp. 3–20. AltaMira Press, Walnut Creek, CA.

Goffman, E. 1974 *Frame Analysis: An Essay on the Organization of Experience.* Harvard University, Cambridge, MA.

Goldberg, P. and R. MacPhail 2006 *Practical and Theoretical Geoarchaeology.* Blackwell, Malden, MA.

Gomez-Pompa, A., J. Salvador Flores and M. Aliphat Fernandez 1990 The Sacred Cacao Groves of the Maya. *Latin American Antiquity* **1**:247–257.

Gonlin, N. and J.C. Lohse (editors) 2007 *Commoner Ritual and Ideology in Ancient Mesoamerica.* University Press of Colorado, Boulder.

González Cruz, A. and G. Fernández Martínez 1994 Inscripciones calendáricas encontradas en Palenque, Chiapas. *Arqueología Mexicana* **2**(8):60–62.

Goody, J. 1982 *Cooking, Cuisine, and Class: A Study in Comparative Sociology.* Cambridge University Press, Cambridge.

Gosner, K. 1997 Women, Rebellion, and the Moral Economy of Maya Peasants. In *Indian Women of Early Mexico*, edited by S. Schroeder, S. Wood and R. Haskett, pp. 217–230. University of Oklahoma Press, Norman.

Gossen, G.H. 1993 On the Human Condition and the Moral Order: A Testimony from the Chamula Tzotzil Maya of Chiapas, Mexico. In *South and Meso-American Native Spirituality: From the Cult of the Feathered Serpent to the Theology of Liberation*, edited by G.H. Gossen and M. Léon-Portilla, pp. 414–435. Crossroad, New York.

1994 From Olmecs to Zapatistas: A Once and Future History of Souls. *American Anthropologist* **96**:553–570.

Graham, E. 1998 Mission Archaeology. *Annual Review of Anthropology* **27**:25–62.

2002 Perspectives on Economy and Theory. In *Ancient Maya Political Economies*, edited by M.A. Masson and D.A. Freidel, pp. 398–418. AltaMira Press, Walnut Creek, CA.

2006 An Ethnicity to Know. In *Maya Ethnicity: The Construction of Ethnic Identity from Preclassic to Modern Times*, edited by F. Sachse, pp. 109–124. Acta Mesoamerica, Volume 19. Markt Schwaben, Verlag Anton Saurwein.

In press Close Encounters. In *Maya Worldviews at Conquest*, edited by L.G. Cecil and T.W. Pugh. University Press of Colorado, Boulder.

Graham, E. and D.M. Pendergast 1989 Excavations at the Marco Gonzalez Site, Ambergris Cay, Belize, 1986. *Journal of Field Archaeology* **16**:1–16.

Graham, E., D.M. Pendergast and G.D. Jones 1989 On the Fringes of Conquest: Maya-Spanish Contact in Colonial Belize. *Science* **246**:1254–1259.

Gramsci, A. 1971 *Selections from the Prison Notebooks of Antonio Gramsci.* Edited and translated by Q. Hoare and G.N. Smith. International Publishers, New York.

Greene, K. 1986 *The Archaeology of the Roman Economy.* University of California Press, Berkeley.

Grove, D.C. 2000 Faces of the Earth at Chalcatzingo, Mexico: Serpents, Caves, and Mountains in Middle Formative Period Iconography. In *Olmec Art and Archaeology in Mesoamerica*, edited by J.E. Clark and M.E. Pye, pp. 277–295. Distributed by Yale University Press, New Haven and London, National Gallery of Art, Washington, DC.

Gruzinski, S. 1989 *Man-Gods in the Mexican Highlands: Indian Power and Colonial Society, 1520–1800*. Translated from French by E. Corrigan. Stanford University Press, Stanford, CA.

Guiteras-Holmes, C. 1961 *Perils of the Soul: The World View of a Tzotzil Indian*. Free Press of Glencoe, New York.

Guzmán Medina, M.G.V. 2005 *Una Nueva Mirada Hacia los Mayas de Yucatán: Identidad, Cultura, y Poder*. Ediciones de la Universidad Autónoma de Yucatán, Mérida, Yucatán, México.

Hall, G.D., S.M. Tarka, Jr., W.J. Hurst, D. Stuart and R.E.W. Adams 1990 Cacao Residues in Ancient Maya Vessels from Rio Azul, Guatemala. *American Antiquity* **55**(1):138–143.

Halperin, C.T. 2008 Classic Maya Textile Production: Insights from Motul de San José, Peten, Guatemala. *Ancient Mesoamerica* **19**(1):111–125.

Halperin, R.H. 1994 *Cultural Economies: Past and Present*. University of Texas Press, Austin.

2007 The Political Economy of the Early Mesoamerican State: An Economic Ethnographer's View. In *The Political Economy of Ancient Mesoamerica*, edited by V.L. Scarborough and J.E. Clark, pp. 175–184. University of New Mexico Press, Albuquerque.

Hammond, N. 1978 The Myth of the Milpa: Agricultural Expansion in the Maya Lowlands. In *Pre-Hispanic Maya Agriculture*, edited by P.D. Harrison and B.L. Turner II, pp. 23–34. University of New Mexico Press, Albuquerque.

1991a Ceramic, Bone, Shell, and Ground Stone Artifacts. In *Cuello: An Early Maya Community in Belize*, edited by N. Hammond, pp. 176–191. Cambridge University Press, Cambridge.

(editor) 1991b *Cuello: An Early Maya Community in Belize*. Cambridge University Press, Cambridge.

2006 Early Symbolic Expression in the Maya Lowlands. *Mexicon* **28**: 26–28.

Hammond, N. and J. Cartwright Gerhardt 1991 Offertory Practices: Caches. In *Cuello: An Early Maya Community in Belize*, edited by N. Hammond, pp. 225–231. Cambridge University Press, Cambridge.

Hammond, N., A. Aspinall, S. Feather, J. Hazelden, T. Gazard and S. Agrell 1977 Maya Jade: Source Location and Analysis. In *Exchange Systems in Prehistory*, edited by T.K. Earle and J.E. Ericson, pp. 35–67. Academic Press, New York.

Handy, E.S.C. and M.K. Pukui 1972 *The Polynesian Family System in Ka'-u, Hawai'i*. Tuttle, Rutland, VT, and Tokyo.

Hanks, W.F. 1990 *Referential Practice: Language and Lived Space among the Maya*. University of Chicago Press, Chicago.

Hansen, R.D. 1998 Continuity and Disjunction: The Pre-Classic Antecedents of Classic Architecture. In *Form and Meaning in Classic Maya Architecture,* edited by S.D. Houston, pp. 49–122. Dumbarton Oaks Research Library and Collection, Washington, DC.

Hansen, R.D., S. Bozarth, J. Jacob, D. Wahl and T. Schreiner 2002 Climate and Environmental Variability in the Rise of Maya Civilization. *Ancient Mesoamerica* **13**:273–295.

Harris III, C.H. and L.R. Sadler 2003 *The Archaeologist Was a Spy: Sylvanus G. Morley and the Office of Naval Intelligence.* University of New Mexico Press, Albuquerque.

Harrison, P.D. 1970 *The Central Acropolis, Tikal, Guatemala: A Preliminary Study of the Functions and Its Structural Components During the Late Classic Period.* Ph.D. dissertation, University of Pennsylvania. University Microfilms, Ann Arbor, MI.

1993 Aspects of Water Management in the Southern Maya Lowlands. In *Economic Aspects of Water Management in the Prehispanic New World.* edited by V.L. Scarborough and B.L. Isaac, pp. 71–119. Research in Economic Anthropology Supplement 7. JAI Press, Greenwich, CT.

1999 *The Lords of Tikal: Rulers of an Ancient Maya City.* Thames & Hudson, London.

Harrison, P.D. and B.L. Turner II (editors) 1978 *Pre-Hispanic Maya Agriculture.* University of New Mexico Press, Albuquerque.

Harrison-Buck, E. 2004 Nourishing the Animus of Lived Space through Ritual Caching. In *K'axob: Ritual, Work, and Family in an Ancient Maya Village,* edited by P.A. McAnany, pp. 65–85. Monumenta Archaeologica 22, Cotsen Institute of Archaeology at UCLA, Los Angeles.

2007 *Materializing Identity Among the Terminal Classic Maya: Architecture and Ceramics in the Sibun Valley, Belize.* Unpublished Ph.D. dissertation, Boston University.

Harrison-Buck, E. and P.A. McAnany 2006 Terminal Classic Circular Shrines and Ceramic Material in the Sibun Valley, Belize: Evidence of Northern Yucatec Influence in the Eastern Maya Lowlands. In *Archaeological Investigations in the Eastern Maya Lowlands: Papers of the 2005 Belize Archaeology Symposium, Research Reports in Belizean Archaeology, Volume 3,* edited by J. Morris, S. Jones, J. Awe and C. Helmke, pp. 287–299. Belize Print, Belmopan, Belize.

Harrison-Buck, E., P.A. McAnany and R. Storey 2007 Empowered and Disempowered during the Late to Terminal Classic Transition: Maya Burial and Termination Rituals in the Sibun Valley, Belize. In *New Perspectives on Human Sacrifice and Ritual Body Treatments in Ancient Maya Society,* edited by V. Tiesler and A. Cucina, pp. 74–101. Springer Science + Business Media, New York.

Haviland, W.A. 1974 Occupational Specialization at Tikal, Guatemala: Stoneworking-Monument Carving. *American Antiquity* **39**:494–496.

1981 Dower Houses and Minor Centers at Tikal, Guatemala: An Investigation into the Identification of Valid Units in Settlement

Hierarchies. In *Lowland Maya Settlement Patterns*, edited by W. Ashmore, pp. 89–117. University of New Mexico Press, Albuquerque.

Hawkes, C. 1954 Archeological Theory and Method: Some Suggestions from the Old World. *American Anthropologist* **56**(2):155–168.

Hayden, B. 1995 Pathways to Power: Principles for Creating Socioeconomic Inequalities. In *Foundations of Social Inequality*, edited by T. D. Price and G. M. Feinman, pp. 15–86. Plenum Press, New York and London.

Healy, P. F., J. D. H. Lambert, J. T. Arnason and R. J. Hebda 1983 Caracol, Belize: Evidence of Ancient Maya Agricultural Terraces. *Journal of Field Archaeology* **10**:397–410.

Helms, M. W. 1993 *Craft and the Kingly Ideal: Art, Trade, and Power.* University of Texas Press, Austin.

1998 *Access to Origins: Affines, Ancestors, and Aristocrats.* University of Texas Press, Austin.

Henare, A., M. Holbraad and S. Wastell 2007a Introduction: Thinking Through Things. In *Thinking through Things: Theorising Artefacts Ethnographically*, edited by A. Henare, M. Holbraad, and S. Wastell, pp. 1–31. Routledge, London.

Henare, A., M. Holbraad and S. Wastell (editors) 2007b *Thinking through Things: Theorising Artefacts Ethnographically.* Routledge, London.

Hendon, J. A. 1996 Archaeological Approaches to the Organization of Domestic Labor: Household Practice and Domestic Relations. *Annual Review of Anthropology* **25**:45–61.

1997 Women's Work, Women's Space, and Women's Status Among the Classic-Period Maya Elite of the Copan Valley, Honduras. In *Women in Prehistory: North America and Mesoamerica*, edited by C. Claassen and R. Joyce, pp. 33–46. University of Pennsylvania Press, Philadelphia.

1999 Multiple Sources of Prestige and the Social Evaluation of Women in Prehispanic Mesoamerica. In *Material Symbols: Culture and Economy in Prehistory*, edited by J. E. Robb, pp. 257–276. Center for Archaeological Investigations, Southern Illinois University, Carbondale, Occasional Paper No. 26, Carbondale, IL.

2002 Household and State in Pre-Hispanic Maya Society: Gender, Identity, and Practice. In *Ancient Maya Gender Identity and Relations*, edited by L. S. Gustafson and A. M. Trevelyan, pp. 75–92. Bergin & Garvey, Westport, CT.

2003 Feasting at Home: Community and House Solidarity among the Maya of Southeastern Mesoamerica. In *The Archaeology and Politics of Food and Feasting in Early States and Empires*, edited by T. L. Bray, pp. 203–233. Kluwer Academic/Plenum Publishers, New York.

2004 Living and Working at Home: The Social Archaeology of Household Production and Social Relations. In *A Companion to Social Archaeology*, edited by L. Meskell and R. W. Preucel, pp. 272–286. Blackwell, Malden, MA.

2006 Textile Production as Craft in Mesoamerica. *Journal of Social Archaeology* **6**(3):354–378.

Herring, A. 2005 *Art and Writing in the Maya Cities, A.D. 600–800: A Poetics of Line.* Cambridge University Press, Cambridge.

Hester, T. R. and H. J. Shafer 1994 The Ancient Maya Craft Community at Colha, Belize, and Its External Relationships. In *Archaeological Views from the Countryside: Village Communities in Early Complex Societies*, edited by G. M. Schwartz and S. E. Falconer, pp. 48–63. Smithsonian Institution Press, Washington and London.

Hirth, K. G. 2000 *Ancient Urbanism at Xochicalco.* University of Utah Press, Salt Lake City.

Hodder, I. 1990 *The Domestication of Europe: Structure and Contingency in Neolithic Societies.* Blackwell, Oxford, UK, and Cambridge, MA.

1999 *The Archaeological Process: An Introduction.* Blackwell, Malden, MA.

2006 *Çatalhöyük: The Leopard's Tale.* Thames & Hudson Ltd, London.

Hodder, I. and S. Hutson 2003 *Reading the Past: Current Approaches to Interpretation in Archaeology.* 3rd ed. Cambridge University Press, Cambridge.

Hodell, D. A., M. Brenner and J. H. Curtis 2000 Climate Change in the North American Tropics and Subtropics Since the Last Ice Age. In *Imperfect Balance: Landscape Transformations in the Precolumbian Americas*, edited by D. L. Lentz, pp. 13–38. Columbia University Press, New York.

Holland, D., W. Lachiotte, Jr., D. Skinner and C. Cain 1998 *Identity and Agency in Cultural Worlds.* Harvard University Press, Cambridge, MA.

Holsbeke, M. and J. Montoya (editors) 2003 *"With Their Hands and Their Eyes": Maya Textiles, Mirrors of a Worldview.* Etnografisch Museum Antwerpen, Belgium, Antwerp.

Hopkins, K. 1983 Introduction. In *Trade in the Ancient Economy*, edited by P. Garnsey, K. Hopkins and C. R. Whittaker, pp. ix–xxv. University of California Press, Berkeley.

Houston, S. D. 1993 *Hieroglyphs and History at Dos Pilas: Dynastic Politics of the Classic Maya.* University of Texas Press, Austin.

1997 A King Worth a Hill of Beans. *Archaeology* **50**(3):40.

1998 Classic Maya Depictions of the Built Environment. In *Function and Meaning in Classic Maya Architecture*, edited by S. D. Houston, pp. 333–372. Dumbarton Oaks Research Library and Collection, Washington, DC.

2000 Into the Minds of Ancients: Advances in Maya Glyph Studies. *Journal of World Prehistory* **14**(2):121–201.

2006 Impersonation, Dance, and the Problem of Spectacle among the Classic Maya. In *Archaeology of Performance: Theaters of Power, Community, and Politics*, edited by T. Inomata and L. S. Coben, pp. 135–155. AltaMira Press, Lanham, MD.

2008 The Small Deaths of Maya Writing. In *The Disappearance of Writing Systems*, edited by J. Baines, J. Bennett and S. D. Houston, pp. 231–252. Equinox, London.

2009 A Splendid Predicament: Young Men in Classic Maya Society. *Archaeological Journal* **19**(2):149–178.

Houston, S.D. and H.L. Escobedo 1996 Descifrando la Politica Maya: Perspectivas Arqueologicas y Epigraficas sobre el concepto de los Estados Segmentarios. In *X Simposio de Investigaciones Arqueologicas en Guatemala*, edited by J. P. Laporte and H. Escobedo, pp. 463–481. Museo Nacional de Arqueologia y Ethnologia, Ministerio de Cultura y Deportes Guatemala, Guatemala.

Houston, S.D. and T. Inomata 2009 *The Classic Maya*. Cambridge University Press, New York.

Houston, S.D. and A. Lacadena Garcia-Gallo 2004 Maya Epigraphy at the Millennium: Personal Notes. In *Continuities and Changes in Maya Archaeology: Perspectives at the Millennium*, edited by C. Golden and G. Borgstede, pp. 115–123. Routledge, New York.

Houston, S.D. and P.A. McAnany 2003 Bodies and Blood: Critiquing Social Construction in Maya Archaeology. *Journal of Anthropological Archaeology* **22**:26–41.

Houston, S.D. and D. Stuart 1996 Of Gods, Glyphs, and Kings: Divinity and Rulership among the Classic Maya. *Antiquity* **70**:289–312.

2001 Peopling the Classic Maya Court. In *Royal Courts of the Ancient Maya, Volume 1: Theory, Comparison, and Synthesis*, edited by T. Inomata and S.D. Houston, pp. 54–83. Westview Press, Boulder, CO.

Houston, S.D., D. Stuart and K. Taube 1989 Folk Classification of Classic Maya Pottery. *American Anthropologist* **91**(3):720–726.

1992 Image and Text on the "Jauncy Vase." In *The Maya Vase Book, Volume 3*, edited by J. Kerr, pp. 499–512. Kerr Associates, New York.

2006 *The Memory of Bones: Body, Being, and Experience Among the Classic Maya*. University of Texas Press, Austin.

Houston, S. D., D. Stuart, C. Wolley and L. Wright n.d. A Death Monument: Dos Pilas Throne 1. Manuscript on file with author.

Houston, S.D., K. Taube, R. Matheny, D. Matheny, Z. Nelson, G. Ware and C. Mesick 2005 The Pool of the Rain God: An Early Stuccoed Altar at Aguacatal, Campeche, Mexico. *Mesoamerican Voices* **2**:37–62.

Hruby, Z.X. and R.K. Flad (editors) 2007 *Rethinking Craft Specialization in Complex Societies: Archaeological Analyses of the Social Meaning of Production*. Archaeological Papers of the American Anthropological Association No. 17, Arlington, VA.

http://www.law.arizona.edu/depts/iplp/advocacy/maya_belize. Maintained by the University of Arizona Indigenous Peoples Law and Policy Program. Accessed on 28 August 2008.

Hurst, W.J., S.M. Tarka, Jr., T.G. Powis, F. Valdez, Jr. and T.R. Hester 2002 Archaeology: Cacao Usage by the Earliest Maya Civilization. *Nature* **418**:289–290.

Hutson, S.R. 2000 Carnival and Contestation in the Aztec Marketplace. *Dialectical Anthropology* **25**:123–149.

Iceland, H.B. 1997 *The Preceramic Origins of the Maya: The Results of the Colha Preceramic Project in Northern Belize*. Ph.D. dissertation, University of Texas at Austin.

2005 The Preceramic to Early Middle Formative Transition in Northern Belize: Evidence for the Ethnic Identity of the Preceramic Inhabitants. In *New Perspectives on Formative Mesoamerican Cultures*, edited by T. G. Powis, pp. 15–26. BAR International Series 1377, Oxford, England.

Ingold, T. 2000 Making Culture and Weaving the World. In *Matter, Materiality, and Modern Culture*, edited by P. M. Graves-Brown, pp. 50–71. Routledge, London.

Inomata, T. 2001 The Power and Ideology of Artistic Creation. *Current Anthropology* **42**(3):321–349.

Inomata, T. and L.S. Coben (editors) 2006 *Archaeology of Performance*. AltaMira Press, Lanham, MD.

Inomata, T. and S.D. Houston 2001a Opening the Royal Maya Court. In *Royal Courts of the Ancient Maya, Volume 1: Theory, Comparison, and Synthesis*, edited by T. Inomata and S.D. Houston, pp. 3–23. Westview Press, Boulder, CO.

2001b *Royal Courts of the Ancient Maya, Volume 1: Theory, Comparison, and Synthesis*. Westview Press, Boulder, CO.

2001c *Royal Courts of the Ancient Maya, Volume 2: Data and Case Studies*. Westview Press, Boulder, CO.

Inomata, T. and L. Stiver 1998 Floor Assemblages from Burned Structures at Aguateca, Guatemala: A Study of Classic Maya Households. *Journal of Field Archaeology* **25**:431–452.

Inomata, T. and D. Triadan 2000 Craft Production by Classic Maya Elites in Domestic Settings: Data from Rapidly Abandoned Structures at Aguateca, Guatemala. *Mayab* **13**:57–66.

2003 Where Did the Elites Live? Identifying Elite Residences at Aguateca, Guatemala. In *Maya Palaces and Elite Residences: An Interdisciplinary Approach*, edited by J.J. Christie, pp. 154–183. University of Texas Press, Austin.

Insoll, T. 2004 *Archaeology, Ritual, Religion*. Routledge, New York.

(editor) 2007 *The Archaeology of Identities: A Reader*. Routledge, New York.

Isaac, B.L. 1986 Introduction. In *Economic Aspects of Prehispanic Highland Mexico, Research in Economic Anthropology Supplement* 2, edited by B.L. Isaac, pp. 1–19. JAI Press, Greenwich, CT.

1993 AMP, HH, & OD: Some Comments. In *Economic Aspects of Water Management in the Prehispanic New World*, edited by V. L. Scarborough and B.L. Isaac, pp. 429–471. *Research in Economic Anthropology Supplement* 7. JAI Press, Greenwich, CT.

2005 Karl Polanyi. In *A Handbook of Economic Anthropology*, edited by J. G. Carrier, pp. 14–25. Edward Elgar, Cheltenham, UK.

Isaza A., I.I. 2004 The Art of Shell Working and the Social Uses of Shell Ornaments. In *K'axob: Ritual, Work and Family in an Ancient Maya Village*, edited by P.A. McAnany, pp. 335–351. Monumenta Archaeologica 22, Cotsen Institute of Archaeology at UCLA, Los Angeles.

Ishihara, R. 2007 *Bridging the Chasm between Religion and Politics: Archaeological Investigations of the Grietas at the Late Classic Maya site of Aguateca, Peten, Guatemala*, Unpublished Ph.D. dissertation, Department of Anthropology, University of California, Riverside.

Islebe, G.A., H. Hooghiemstra, M. Brenner, J.H. Curtis and D.A. Hodell 1996 A Holocene Vegetation History from Lowland Guatemala. *The Holocene* **6**(3):265–271.

Jackson, S. and D. Stuart 2001 The Aj K'uhun Title: Deciphering a Classic Maya Term of Rank. *Ancient Mesoamerica* **12**:217–228.

Jameson, F. 1991 *Postmodernism or, the Cultural Logic of Late Capitalism.* Duke University Press, Durham, NC.

Janusek, J.W. 1999 Craft and Local Power: Embedded Specialization in Tiwanaku Cities. *Latin American Antiquity* **10**(2):107–131.

Johnson, J.K. 1991 Obsidian: A Technological Analysis. In *Cuello: An Early Maya Community in Belize,* edited by N. Hammond, pp. 169–173. Cambridge University Press, Cambridge.

Johnston, K.J. 2001 Broken Fingers: Classic Maya Scribe Capture and Polity Consolidation. *Antiquity* **75**:373–381.

2003 The Intensification of Pre-industrial Cereal Agriculture in the Tropics: Boserup, Cultivation Lengthening, and the Classic Maya. *Journal of Anthropological Archaeology* **22**(2):126–161.

Johnston, K.J. and N. Gonlin 1998 What Do Houses Mean? Approaches to the Analysis of Classic Maya Commoner Residences. In *Function and Meaning in Classic Maya Architecture,* edited by S.D. Houston, pp. 141–185. Dumbarton Oaks Research Library and Collection, Washington, DC.

Jones, C. 1996 *Excavations in the East Plaza of Tikal, Volume 1.* Tikal Report No. 16. The University Museum, University of Pennsylvania, Philadelphia.

Jones, G.D. 1989 *Maya Resistance to Spanish Rule: Time and Resistance on a Colonial Frontier.* University of New Mexico Press, Albuquerque.

1998 *The Conquest of the Last Maya Kingdom.* Stanford University Press, Stanford, CA.

Jones, J.G. 1994 Pollen Evidence for Early Settlement and Agriculture in Northern Belize. *Palynology* **18**:205–211.

1999 Analysis of Pollen from K'axob, Belize. In *Where the Water Meets the Land: 1998 Excavations in Wetland Fields and Along Transects at K'axob, Belize,* edited by P.A. McAnany, pp. 125–137. Submitted to the Department of Archaeology, Belmopan, Belize. On file Boston University, Department of Archaeology.

Josserand, J.K. 2002 Women in Classic Maya Hieroglyphic Texts. In *Ancient Maya Women,* edited by T. Ardren, pp. 114–151. AltaMira Press, Walnut Creek, CA.

Joyce, A.A. and E.T. Weller 2007 Commoner Rituals, Resistance, and the Classic-to-Postclassic Transition in Ancient Mesoamerica. In *Commoner Ritual and Ideology in Ancient Mesoamerica,* edited by N. Gonlin and J.C. Lohse, pp. 143–184. University Press of Colorado, Boulder.

Joyce, R. 1992 Images of Gender and Labor Organization in Classic Maya Society. In *Exploring Gender Through Archaeology: Selected Papers from the 1991 Boone Conference,* edited by C. Claassen, pp. 63–70. Prehistory Press, Madison, WI.

1993 Women's Work: Images of Production and Reproduction in Pre-Hispanic Southern Central America. *Current Anthropology* **34**(3): 255–274.

2000a *Gender and Power in Prehispanic Mesoamerica.* University of Texas Press, Austin.

2000b Heirlooms and Houses: Materiality and Social Memory. In *Beyond Kinship: Social and Material Reproduction in House Societies*, edited by R.A. Joyce and S.D. Gillespie, pp. 189–212. University of Pennsylvania Press, Philadelphia.

2002 Desiring Women: Classic Maya Sexualities. In *Ancient Maya Gender Identity and Relations*, edited by L.S. Gustafson and A.M. Trevelyan, pp. 329–344. Bergin & Garvey, Westport, CT.

2003 Archaeology and Nation Building: A View from Central America. In *The Politics of Archaeology and Identity in a Global Context*, edited by S. Kane, pp. 79–100. Archaeological Institute of America Colloquia and Conference Papers 7, Boston.

2004 Unintended Consequences: Monumentality as a Novel Experience in Formative Mesoamerica. *Journal of Archaeological Method and Theory* **11**(1):5–29.

2005 Archaeology of the Body. *Annual Review of Anthropology* **34**: 139–158.

Joyce, R.A. and S.D. Gillespie (editors) 2000 *Beyond Kinship: Social and Material Reproduction in House Societies.* University of Pennsylvania Press, Philadelphia.

Karttunen, F. 1983 *An Analytical Dictionary of Nahuatl.* University of Texas Press, Austin.

Kelly, J.D. and M. Kaplan 1990 History, Structure, and Ritual. *Annual Review of Anthropology* **19**:119–150.

Kepecs, S. 2005 Mayas, Spaniards, and Salt: World Systems Shifts in Sixteenth-Century Yucatán. In *The Postclassic to Spanish-Era Transition in Mesoamerica: Archaeological Perspectives*, edited by S. Kepecs and R.T. Alexander, pp. 117–137. University of New Mexico, Albuquerque.

Kepecs, S. and S. Boucher 1996 The Pre-Hispanic Cultivation of *Rejolladas* and Stone-Lands: New Evidence from Northeast Yucatán. In *The Managed Mosaic: Ancient Maya Agriculture and Resource Use*, edited by S.L. Fedick, pp. 69–91. University of Utah Press, Salt Lake City.

Kerr, J. (editor) 1989–2000 *Maya Vase Book.* 6 vols. Kerr Associates, New York. (Images available at http://research.famsi.org/kerrmaya.html.)

Killion, T.W. 1990 Cultivation Intensity and Residential Site Structure: An Ethnoarchaeological Examination of Peasant Agriculture in the Sierra de los Tuxtlas, Veracruz, Mexico. *Latin American Antiquity* **1**(3): 191–215.

King, E. and D. Potter 1994 Small Sites in Prehistoric Maya Socioeconomic Organization: A Perspective from Colha, Belize. In *Archaeological Views from the Countryside: Village Communities in Early Complex Societies*, edited by G.M. Schwartz and S.E. Falconer, pp. 64–90. Smithsonian Institution Press, Washington, DC, and London.

King, E.M. and L.C. Shaw 2003 A Heterarchical Approach to Site Variability: The Maax Na Archaeology Project. In *Heterarchy, Political Economy, and the Ancient Maya: The Three Rivers Region of the East-Central Yucatán Peninsula*, edited by V.L. Scarborough, F. Valdez, Jr. and N. Dunning, pp. 64–76. University of Arizona Press, Tucson.

Kluckholn, C. 1962 The Conceptual Structure of Middle American Studies. In *The Maya and Their Neighbors*, edited by C. L. Hay, pp. 41–51 (originally published in 1940). Appleton-Century, New York.

Knecht, R.J. 1994 *Renaissance Warrior and Patron: The Reign of Francis I.* Cambridge University Press, Cambridge.

Kopytoff, I. 1986 The Cultural Biography of Things: Commoditization as Process. In *The Social Life of Things*, edited by A. Appadurai, pp. 64–91. Cambridge University Press, Cambridge.

Kovacevich, B. 2007 Ritual, Crafting, and Agency at the Classic Maya Kingdom of Cancuen. In *Mesoamerican Ritual Economy: Archaeological and Ethnological Perspectives*, edited by E. C. Wells and K. L. Davis-Salazar, pp. 67–114. University Press of Colorado, Boulder.

Kowalski, J.K. 2003 Evidence for the Functions and Meanings of Some Northern Maya Palaces. In *Maya Palaces and Elite Residences: An Interdisciplinary Approach*, edited by J.J. Christie, pp. 204–252. University of Texas Press, Austin.

Krochock, R.J. 2002 Women in the Hieroglyphic Inscriptions of Chichén Itzá. In *Ancient Maya Women*, edited by T. Ardren, pp. 152–170. AltaMira Press, Walnut Creek, CA.

Kroshus Medina, L. 2003 Commoditizing Culture: Tourism and Maya Identity. *Annals of Tourism Research* **30**(2):353–368.

Kunen, J. L. 2004 *Ancient Maya Life in the Far West Bajo: Social and Environmental Change in the Wetlands of Belize.* Anthropological Papers of the University of Arizona No. 69. University of Arizona Press, Tucson.

La Lone, D. E. 1982 The Inca as a Nonmarket Economy: Supply on Command versus Supply and Demand. In *Contexts for Prehistoric Exchange*, edited by J. E. Ericson and T. K. Earle, pp. 291–316. Academic Press, New York.

Laporte, J.P. 1989 *Alternativas del Clasico Temprano in la Relacion Tikal-Teotihuacan: Grupo 6C-XVI, Tikal, Peten, Guatemala.* Ph.D. dissertation, Universidad Nacional Autónoma de Mexico.

Laporte, J. P. and J. E. Chocón 2007 ¿Será un Palacio? No! ¿Será un Acrópolis? No! Un Conjunto de Función Desconcertante en el Centro de Pueblito, Petén. In *XXI Simposío de Investigacíones Arqueológicas en Guatemala*, edited by J. P. Laporte, B. Arroyo, and H. Mejia, pp. 696–712. Museo de Arqueología y Etnología Guatemala.

Laporte, J. P. and V. Fialko C. 1990 New Perspectives on Old Problems: Dynastic References for the Early Classic at Tikal. In *Vision and Revision in Maya Studies*, edited by F. S. Clancy and P. D. Harrison, pp. 33–66. University of New Mexico Press, Albuquerque.

Latour, B. 1999 *Pandora's Hope: Essays on the Reality of Science.* Harvard University Press, Cambridge, MA.

2005 *Reassembling the Social: An Introduction to Actor-Network Theory*. Oxford University Press, Oxford.

LeCount, L.J. 2001 Like Water for Chocolate: Feasting and Political Ritual Among the Late Classic Maya at Xunantunich, Belize. *American Anthropologist* **103**(4):935–953.

Le Fort, G. and R. Wald 1995 Large numbers on Naranjo Stela 32. *Mexicon* **17**:112–114.

Lemonnier, P. 1986 The Study of Material Culture Today: Toward an Anthropology of Technical Systems. *Journal of Anthropological Archaeology* 5:147–186.

Lentz, D.L. 1991 Maya Diets of the Rich and Poor: Paleoethnobotanical Evidence from Copan. *Latin American Antiquity* **2**(3):269–287.

1999 Plant Resources of the Ancient Maya. In *Reconstructing Ancient Maya Diet*, edited by C.D. White, pp. 3–18. University of Utah Press, Salt Lake City.

Lenz, H. 1961 *Mexican Indian Papermaking: Its History and Survival*. Rafael Loéra y Chávez Editorial Libros, SA, México DF.

Lévi-Strauss, C. 1982 *The Way of the Masks*. Translated from French by S. Modelski. University of Washington Press, Seattle.

Levitt, S.D. and S.J. Dubner 2005 *Freakonomics: A Rogue Economist Explores the Hidden Side of Everything*. William Morrow, New York.

Lewis, B.S. 1996 The Role of Attached and Independent Specialization in the Development of Sociopolitical Complexity. In *Research in Economic Anthropology, Volume 17*, edited by B.L. Isaac, pp. 357–388. JAI Press, Greenwich, CT.

2003 Environmental Heterogeneity and Occupational Specialization: An Examination of Lithic Tool Production in the Three Rivers Region of the Northeastern Petén. In *Heterarchy, Political Economy, and the Ancient Maya: The Three Rivers Region of the East-Central Yucatán Peninsula*, edited by V.L. Scarborough, F. Valdez, Jr. and N. Dunning, pp. 122–135. University of Arizona Press, Tucson.

Leyden, B.W., M. Brenner, T. Whitmore, J.H. Curtis, D.R. Piperno and B.H. Dahlin 1996 A Record of Long- and Short-Term Climatic Variation from Northwest Yucatán: Cenote San José Chulchacá. In *The Managed Mosaic: Ancient Maya Agriculture and Resource Use*, edited by S.L. Fedick, pp. 30–50. University of Utah Press, Salt Lake City.

Liendo Stuardo, R. 2002 *The Organization of Agricultural Production at a Classic Maya Center: Settlement Patterns in the Palenque Region, Chiapas, Mexico*. Instituto Nacional de Antropología e Historia/University of Pittsburgh, México/Pittsburgh.

2003 Access Patterns in Maya Royal Precincts. In *Maya Palaces and Elite Residences: An Interdisciplinary Approach*, edited by J.J. Christie, pp. 184–203. University of Texas Press, Austin.

Little, W.E. 2008 Weaving Ritual and the Production of Commemorative Cloth in Highland Guatemala. In *Dimensions of Ritual Economy, Research in*

Economic Anthropology, Volume 27, edited by E. C. Wells and P. A. McAnany, pp. 121–148. JAI Press, Emerald Group Publishing, Bingley, UK.

Lipp, F.J. 1991 *The Mixe of Oaxaca: Religion, Ritual, and Healing.* University of Texas Press, Austin.

Lohse, J. C. and N. Gonlin 2007 Preface. In *Commoner Ritual and Ideology in Ancient Mesoamerica*, edited by N. Gonlin and J. C. Lohse, pp. xvii–xxxix. University Press of Colorado, Boulder.

Lohse, J. C., J. Awe, C. Griffith, R.M. Rosenswig and F. Valdez, Jr. 2006 Preceramic Occupations in Belize: Updating the Paleoindian and Archaic Record. *Latin American Antiquity* **17**(2):209–226.

Long, N. and B. R. Roberts (editors) 1978 *Peasant Cooperation and Capitalist Expansion in Central Peru.* Latin American Monographs No. 46, Institute of Latin American Studies, The University of Texas at Austin, Austin.

Looper, M. G. 2003 *Lightning Warrior: Maya Art and Kingship at Quirigua.* University of Texas Press, Austin.

Looper, M. G. and T. Tolles 2000 *Gifts of the Moon: Huipil Designs of the Ancient Maya.* Museum of Man, San Diego.

López Austin, A. 1988 *The Human Body and Ideology: Concepts of the Ancient Nahuas, Volumes 1 and 2.* Translated by T. and B. Ortiz de Montellano. University of Utah Press, Salt Lake City.

López Varela, S. L. 1996 *The K'axob Formative Ceramics: The Search for Regional Integration through a Reappraisal of Ceramic Analysis and Classification in Northern Belize.* Ph.D. dissertation, University of London.

López Varela, S., P. A. McAnany and K. Berry 2001 Ceramic Technology at Late Classic K'axob, Belize. *Journal of Field Archaeology* **28**(1 & 2):177–191.

Loughmiller-Newman, J. A. 2008 Canons of Maya Painting: A Spatial Analysis of Classic Period Polychromes. *Ancient Mesoamerica* **19**(1):29–42.

Love, M.W. 1999 Ideology, Material Culture, and Daily Practice in Pre-Classic Mesoamerica: A Pacific Coast Perspective. In *Social Patterns in Pre-Classic Mesoamerica*, edited by D.C. Grove and R.A. Joyce, pp. 127–153. Dumbarton Oaks Research Library and Collection, Washington, DC.

Lowenthal, D. 1985 *The Past Is a Foreign Country.* Cambridge University Press, Cambridge.

Lucero, L.J. 1999 Water Control and Maya Politics in the Southern Maya Lowlands. In *Complex Politics in the Ancient Tropical World*, edited by E.A. Bacus and L.J. Lucero, pp. 35–49. Archaeological Papers of the American Anthropological Association No. 9, Arlington, VA.

2006 The Political and Sacred Power of Water in Classic Maya Society. In *Precolumbian Water Management: Ideology, Ritual, and Power*, edited by L.J. Lucero and B.W. Fash, pp. 116–128. University of Arizona Press, Tucson.

2007 Classic Maya Temples, Politics, and the Voice of the People. *Latin American Antiquity* **18**(4):407–427.

Lucero, L.J. and B.W. Fash (editors) 2006 *Precolumbian Water Management: Ideology, Ritual, and Power.* University of Arizona Press, Tucson.

Lucero, L.J. and S.A. Gibbs 2007 The Creation and Sacrifice of Witches in Classic Maya Society. In *New Perspectives on Human Sacrifice and Ritual Body Treatments in Ancient Maya Society*, edited by V. Tiesler and A. Cucina, pp. 45–73. Springer Science + Media, New York.

Luke, C. 2008 Carving Luxury: Late Classic White Stone Vase Traditions in Mesoamerica. In *New Approaches to Old Stones: Recent Studies of Ground Stone Artifacts*, edited by Y.M. Rowan and J.R. Ebeling, pp. 298–319. Equinox Publishing, London.

Luke, C. and R.H. Tykot 2007 Celebrating Place Through Luxury Craft Production: Trevesia and Ulua Style Marble Vases. *Ancient Mesoamerica* **18**(2):315–328.

MacKinnon, J.J. and S. M. Kepecs 1989 Prehispanic Saltmaking in Belize: New Evidence. *American Antiquity* **54**(3):522–533.

MacLeod, B. and A. Stone 1995 The Hieroglyphic Inscriptions of Naj Tunich. In *Images from the Underworld: Naj Tunich and the Tradition of Maya Cave Painting*, edited by A. Stone, pp. 155–184. University of Texas Press, Austin.

MacLeod, M.J. 1973 *Spanish Central America: A Socioeconomic History, 1520–1720*. University of California Press, Berkeley, Los Angeles, and London.

Magennis, A. L. 1999 Dietary Change at the Lowland Maya Site of Kichpanha, Belize. In *Reconstructing Ancient Maya Diet*, edited by C. D. White, pp. 133–150. University of Utah Press, Salt Lake City.

Maler, T. 1970–1976 *Researches in the Central Portion of the Usumatsintla Valley: Report of Explorations for the Museum, 1898–1900*. 2 vols. Kraus Reprint of the 1901–1903 ed. published by the Peabody Museum, Cambridge, Mass., as Vol. 2 of the Memoirs of the Peabody Museum of American Archaeology and Ethnology, Harvard University, New York.

Malinowski, B. 1961[1922] *Argonauts of the Western Pacific*. E. P. Dutton & Co., New York.

1934 Stone Implements in Eastern New Guinea. In *Essays Presented to C. G. Seligman*, edited by E. Evans-Pritchard, R.W. Firth, B. Malinowski and I. Schapera, pp. 189–196. Kegan Paul, Trench, Tribner & Co., London.

Manz, B. 2004 *Paradise in Ashes: A Guatemalan Journey of Courage, Terror, and Hope*. University of California Press, Berkeley.

Manzanilla, L. and L. Barba 1990 The Study of Activities in Classic Households: Two Case Studies from Coba and Teotihuacan. *Ancient Mesoamerica* **1**(1):41–49.

Marcus, J. 1983 On the Nature of the Mesoamerican City. In *Prehistoric Settlement Patterns: Essays in Honor of Gordon R. Willey*, edited by E. Z. Vogt and R.M. Leventhal, pp. 195–242. University of New Mexico Press, Albuquerque.

Márquez Morfín, L., P. O. Hernández Espinosa and C. Serrano Sánchez 2004 La Edad de Pakal en el Contexto Demográfico de la Sociedad de Palenque durante el Clásico Tardío. In *Janaab' Pakal de Palenque: Vida y Muerte de un Governante Maya*, edited by V. Tiesler and A. Cucina, pp. 153–185. Universidad Nacional Autónoma de México and Universidad Autónoma de Yucatán, México DF, and Mérida, Yucatán.

Martin, S. 2006 Cacao in Ancient Maya Religion: First Fruit from the Maize Tree and Other Tales from the Underworld. In *Chocolate in Mesoamerica: A Cultural History of Cacao*, edited by C. McNeil, pp. 154–183. University of Florida Press, Gainesville.

2007a Un informe provisional sobre los murales de la Estructura 1 de la Acrópolis de Chiik Nahb. Ms. Archivo del Proyecto Arqueológico Calakmul.

2007b Hieroglyphs and the Painted Pyramid: Research on the Murals of Calakmul Structure Sub 1–4. Paper presented at the 31st Maya Meeting at Texas, March 9–14, 2007. University of Texas, Austin.

Martin, S. and N. Grube 2008 [2000] *Chronicle of the Maya Kings and Queens: Deciphering the Dynasties of the Ancient Maya.* 1st and 2nd eds. Thames & Hudson, London.

Masson, M.A. 2000 *In the Realm of Nachan Kan: Postclassic Maya Archaeology at Laguna de On, Belize.* University Press of Colorado, Boulder.

2004 Contribution of Fishing and Hunting to Subsistence and Symbolic Expression. In *K'axob: Ritual, Work, and Family in an Ancient Maya Village*, edited by P.A. McAnany, pp. 382–397. Monumenta Archaeologica 22, Cotsen Institute of Archaeology at UCLA, Los Angeles.

Masson, M.A. and D.A. Freidel (editors) 2002 *Ancient Maya Political Economies.* AltaMira Press, Walnut Creek, CA.

Masson, M. and C. Peraza Lopez Forthcoming *Kukulkan's Realm: The Postclassic Maya City of Mayapán.* University Press of Colorado, Boulder.

Masson, M.A. and R.M. Rosenswig 2005 Production Characteristics of Postclassic Maya Pottery from Caye Coco, Northern Belize. *Latin American Antiquity* **16**(4):355–384.

Masson, M.A., T.S. Hare and C. Peraza L. 2006 Postclassic Maya Society Regenerated at Mayapan. In *After Collapse: The Regeneration of Complex Societies*, edited by G.M. Schwartz and J.J. Nichols, pp. 188–207. University of Arizona Press, Tucson.

Mauss, M. 1967 *The Gift: Forms and Functions of Exchange in Archaic Societies.* Translated by T.I. Cunnison. Norton, New York.

McAnany, P.A. 1986 *Lithic Technology and Exchange Among Wetland Farmers of the Eastern Maya Lowlands.* Ph.D. dissertation, University of New Mexico, Albuquerque. University Microfilms, Ann Arbor, MI.

1990 Water Storage in the Puuc Region of the Northern Maya Lowlands: A Key to Population Estimates and Architectural Variability. In *Precolumbian Population History in the Maya Lowlands*, edited by T.P. Culbert and D.S. Rice, pp. 263–284. University of New Mexico Press, Albuquerque.

1993 Resources, Specialization, and Exchange in the Maya Lowlands. In *The American Southwest and Mesoamerica: Systems of Prehistoric Exchange*, edited by J.E. Ericson and T.G. Baugh, pp. 213–245. Plenum Press, New York.

1995 *Living with the Ancestors: Kinship and Kingship in Ancient Maya Society.* University of Texas Press, Austin.

1998 Ancestors and the Classic Maya Built Environment. In *Function and Meaning in Classic Maya Architecture*, edited by S. D. Houston, pp. 271–298. Dumbarton Oaks Research Library and Collection, Washington, DC.

2001 Cosmology and the Institutionalization of Hierarchy in the Maya Region. In *Leaders to Rulers*, edited by J. Haas, pp. 125–148. Plenum Publishers, New York.

2004a Situating K'axob within Formative Period Lowland Maya Archaeology. In *K'axob: Ritual, Work, and Family in an Ancient Maya Village*, edited by P. A. McAnany, pp. 1–12. Cotsen Institute of Archaeology at UCLA, Los Angeles.

2004b Appropriative Economies: Labor Obligations and Luxury Goods in Ancient Maya Society. In *Archaeological Perspectives on Political Economies*, edited by G. M. Feinman and L. M. Nicholas, pp. 145–165. University of Utah Press, Salt Lake City.

2004c Obsidian Blades and Source Areas. In *K'axob: Ritual, Work and Family in an Ancient Maya Village*, edited by P. A. McAnany, pp. 307–315. Monumenta Archaeologica 22, Cotsen Institute of Archaeology at UCLA, Los Angeles.

2006 Habitus and Hierarchy: The Double Helix of Preclassic Maya Ethnicity. In *Maya Ethnicity: The Construction of Ethnic Identity from the Preclassic to Modern Times. Acta Americana*, edited by F. Sachse, pp. 9–18. Verlag Anton Saurwein, Markt Schwaben.

2007a A View from Mesoamerica. *Cambridge Archaeological Journal* **17**(2): 217–220.

2007b Culture Heroes and Feathered Serpents: The Contribution of Gordon R. Willey to the Study of Ideology. In *Gordon R. Willey and American Archaeology: Contemporary Perspectives*, edited by J. A. Sabloff and W. L. Fash, pp. 209–231. University of Oklahoma Press, Norman.

2008a Shaping Social Difference: Political and Ritual Economy of Classic Maya Royal Courts. In *Dimensions of Ritual Economy, Research in Economic Anthropology, Volume 27*, edited by E. C. Wells and P. A. McAnany, pp. 219–247. JAI Press, Emerald Group Publishing, Bingley, UK.

2010 Towards a Hermeneutics of Death: Commentary on Seven Essays. In *Between the Living and the Dead in Mesoamerica*, edited by J. L. Fitzsimmons. University of Arizona Press, Tucson, in press.

McAnany, P. A. and J. P. Ebersole 2004 Ground and Polished Stone Tools. In *K'axob: Ritual, Work, and Family in an Ancient Maya Village*, edited by P. A. McAnany, pp. 317–330. Monumenta Archaeologica 22, Cotsen Institute of Archaeology at UCLA, Los Angeles.

McAnany, P. A. and T. Gallareta Negrón 2009 Bellicose Rulers and Climatological Peril? Retrofitting 21st Century Woes on 8th Century Maya Society. In *Questioning Collapse: Human Resilience, Ecological Vulnerability, and the Aftermath of Empire*, edited by P. A. McAnany and N. Yoffee, pp. 142–175. Cambridge University Press, New York.

McAnany, P. A. and I. Hodder 2009 Thinking about Stratigraphic Sequence in Social Terms. *Archaeological Dialogues* **16**(1):1–22.

McAnany, P. A. and S. L. López Varela 1999 Re-Creating the Formative Maya Village of K'axob: Chronology, Ceramic Complexes, and Ancestors in Architectural Context. *Ancient Mesoamerica* **10**:147–168.

McAnany, P. A. and S. Murata 2006a Mystery at Mile 12: Explaining the Earthen Mounds in the Mangrove Swamp. Paper presented at the 2006 Belize Archaeology Symposium, July 5, Belize City, Belize.

2006b From Chocolate Pots to Maya Gold: Belizean Cacao Farmers through the Ages. In *Chocolate in Mesoamerica: A Cultural History of Cacao*, edited by C. McNeil, pp. 429–450. University of Florida Press, Gainesville.

2007 America's First Connoisseurs of Chocolate. *Food and Foodways* **15**(1–2):7–30.

McAnany, P. A. and S. Plank 2001 Perspectives on Actors, Gender Roles, and Architecture at Classic Maya Courts and Households. In *Royal Courts of the Ancient Maya, Volume 1: Theory, Comparison, and Synthesis*, edited by T. Inomata and S. D. Houston, pp. 84–129. Westview Press, Boulder, CO.

McAnany, P. A. and C. A. Pool 2008 Rational Exuberance. Mesoamerican Economies and Landscapes in the Research of Robert S. Santley. *Journal of Anthropological Research* **64**:323–340.

McAnany, P. A. and E. C. Wells 2008 Toward a Theory of Ritual Economy. In *Dimensions of Ritual Economy, Research in Economic Anthropology, Volume 27*, edited by E. C. Wells and P. A. McAnany, pp. 1–16. JAI Press, Emerald Group Publishing, Bingley, UK.

McAnany, P. A., K. A. Berry and B. Thomas 2002 Wetlands, Rivers, and Caves: Agricultural and Ritual Practice in Two Lowland Maya Landscape. In *Perspectives on Ancient Maya Rural Complexity*, edited by G. Iannone and S. V. Connell, pp. 71–81. Cotsen Institute of Archaeology at UCLA, Los Angeles.

McAnany, P. A., E. Harrison-Buck and S. Murata 2005 Desire and Political Influence: The Archaeology of the Sibun River Valley. In *Archaeological Investigations in the Eastern Maya Lowlands: Papers of the 2004 Belize Archaeology Symposium*, edited by J. Awe, J. Morris, S. Jones and C. Helmke, pp. 313–327. Research Reports in Belizean Archaeology, Volume 2. Print Belize, Belmopan, Belize.

McAnany, P. A., B. S. Thomas, S. Morandi, P. A. Peterson and E. Harrison 2002 Praise the Ahaw and Pass the Kakaw: Xibun Maya and the Political Economy of Cacao. In *Ancient Maya Political Economies*, edited by M. A. Masson and D. A. Freidel, pp. 123–139. AltaMira Press, Walnut Creek, CA.

McBryde, F. W. 1971 *Cultural and Historical Geography of Southwest Guatemala*. Greenwood Press, Westport, CT.

McCafferty, G. G. and S. D. McCafferty 1999 The Metamorphosis of Xochiquetzal. In *Manifesting Power: Gender and the Interpretation of Power in Archaeology*, edited by T. L. Sweely, pp. 103–125. Routledge, London.

McCafferty, S. D. and G. G. McCafferty 2000 Textile Production in Postclassic Cholula, Mexico. *Ancient Mesoamerica* **11**:39–54.

McKillop, H. 1995 Underwater Archaeology, Salt Production, and Coastal Maya Trade at Stingray Lagoon, Belize. *Latin American Antiquity* **6**(3):214–228.

1996 Ancient Maya Trading Ports and the Integration of Long-Distance and Regional Economies: Wild Cane Cay in South-Coastal Belize. *Ancient Mesoamerica* **7**:49–62.

2002 *Salt: White Gold of the Ancient Maya.* University Press of Florida, Gainesville.

Menard, C. and M. Shirley (editors) 2005 *Handbook of New Institutional Economics.* Edward Elgar, Cheltenham, UK.

Meskell, L. (editor) 2005 *Archaeologies of Materiality.* Blackwell, Malden, MA.

Meskell, L. M. and R. A. Joyce 2003 *Embodied Lives: Figuring Ancient Maya and Egyptian Experience.* Routledge, London.

Miksicek, C. H. 1991 The Natural and Cultural Landscape of Preclassic Cuello. In *Cuello: An Early Maya Community in Belize,* edited by N. Hammond, pp. 70–84. Cambridge University Press, Cambridge.

Milbrath, S. and C. Peraza Lope 2003 Revisiting Mayapan: Mexico's Last Maya Capital. *Ancient Mesoamerica* **14**:1–46.

Miller, D. 2005 Materiality: An Introduction. In *Materiality,* edited by D. Miller, pp. 1–50. Duke University Press, Durham, NC.

Miller, M. 1997 Imaging Maya Art. *Archaeology* **50**(3):34–40.

2001 Life at Court: The View from Bonampak. In *Royal Courts of the Ancient Maya, Volume 1: Data and Case Studies,* edited by T. Inomata and S. D. Houston, pp. 201–222. Westview Press, Boulder, CO.

Miller, M. and S. Martin 2004 *Courtly Art of the Ancient Maya.* Thames & Hudson, Fine Arts Museum of San Francisco.

Miller, V. E. 1988 The Role of Gender in Precolumbian Art and Architecture: Introduction. In *The Role of Gender in Precolumbian Art and Architecture,* edited by V. E. Miller, pp. vii–xii. University Press of America, Lanham, MD.

Mills, B. J. 2004 The Establishment and Defeat of Hierarchy: Inalienable Possessions and the History of Collective Prestige Structures in the Pueblo Southwest. *American Anthropologist* **106**(2):238–251.

Minc, L. D. 2006 Monitoring Regional Market Systems in Prehistory: Models, Methods, and Metrics. *Journal of Anthropological Archaeology* **25**(1): 82–116.

Mintz, S. W. 1985 *Sweetness and Power: The Place of Sugar in Modern History.* Penguin Group, New York.

Mitchell, W. E. 1988 The Defeat of Hierarchy: Gambling as Exchange in a Sepik Society. *American Ethnologist* **15**(4):638–657.

Mithen, S. 1998 The Supernatural Beings of Prehistory and the External Storage of Religious Ideas. In *Cognition and Material Culture: The Archaeology of Symbolic Storage,* edited by C. Renfrew and C. Scarre, pp. 97–106. McDonald Institute Monographs, Cambridge.

Mock, S. B. 2004 Maya Traders on the North Central Belize Coast. In *Archaeological Investigations in the Eastern Maya Lowlands: Papers of the 2003*

Belize Archaeology Symposium, edited by J. Awe, J. Morris and S. Jones, pp. 359–370. Institute of Archaeology, National Institute of Culture and History, Print Belize, Belmopan, Belize.

(editor) 1998 *The Sowing and the Dawning: Termination, Dedication, and Transformation in the Archaeological Record of Mesoamerica*. University of New Mexico Press, Albuquerque.

Moholy-Nagy, H. 1985 The Social and Ceremonial Uses of Marine Molluscs at Tikal. In *Prehistoric Lowland Maya Environment and Subsistence Economy*, edited by M. D. Pohl, pp. 147–158. Peabody Museum of Archaeology and Ethnology, Harvard University, Cambridge, MA.

1990 Misidentification of Mesoamerican Lithic Workshops. *Latin American Antiquity* **1**:268–279.

1997 Middens, Construction Fill, and Offerings: Evidence for the Organization of Classic Period Craft Production at Tikal, Guatemala. *Journal of Field Archaeology* **24**(3):293–313.

Monaghan, J. 1995 *The Covenants with Earth and Rain: Exchange, Sacrifice, and Revelation in Mixtec Society*. University of Oklahoma Press, Norman and London.

1996 Fiesta Finance in Mesoamerica and the Origins of a Gift Exchange System. *Journal of the Royal Anthropological Institute* **2**:499–516.

1998 Dedication: Ritual or Production? In *The Sowing and the Dawning: Termination, Dedication, and Transformation in the Archaeological and Ethnographic Record of Mesoamerica*, edited by S. B. Mock, pp. 47–52. University of New Mexico Press, Albuquerque.

2000 Theology and History in the Study of Mesoamerican Religions. In *Handbook of Middle American Indians, Supplement 6, Ethnology*. University of Texas Press, Austin.

Montejo, V. D. 1987 *Testimony: Death of a Guatemalan Village*. Curbstone Press, Willamantic, CT.

2002 The Multiplicity of Mayan Voices: Mayan Leadership and the Politics of Self-Representation. In *Indigenous Movements, Self-Representation, and the State in Latin America*, edited by K. B. Warren and J. E. Jackson, pp. 123–148. University of Texas Press, Austin.

2005 *Maya Intellectual Renaissance: Identity, Representation, and Leadership*. University of Texas Press, Austin.

Moore, J. D. 1996 *Architecture and Power in the Ancient Andes: The Archaeology of Public Buildings*. Cambridge University Press, Cambridge.

2004 The Social Basis of Sacred Spaces in the Prehispanic Andes: Ritual Landscapes of the Dead in Chimú and Inka Societies. *Journal of Archaeological Method and Theory* **11**(1):83–124.

Morehart, C. T., D. L. Lentz and K. M. Prufer 2005 Wood of the Gods: The Ritual Use of Pine (*Pinus* Spp.) by the Ancient Lowland Maya. *Latin American Antiquity* **16**(3):255–274.

Morley, S. G. 1941 The Xiu Chronicle. Part I: The History of the Xiu. Unpublished manuscript, Tozzer Library. Harvard University, Cambridge, MA.

Morris, W.F. and C. Karasik 2003 Chiapas Textiles: The Art of Ancient Dreams. In *"With Their Hands and Their Eyes": Maya Textiles, Mirrors of a Worldview*, edited by M. Holsbeke and J. Montoya, pp. 72–91. Etnografisch Museum Antwerpen, Antwerp, Belgium.

Munn, N.D. 1983 Gawan Kula: Spatiotemporal Control and the Symbolism of Influence. In *The Kula: New Perspectives on Massim Exchange*, edited by J.W. Leach and E. Leach, pp. 277–308. Cambridge University Press, Cambridge.

1986 *The Fame of Gawa: A Symbolic Study of Value Transformation in a Massim (Papua New Guinea) Society*. Cambridge University Press, Cambridge.

Murata, S. 2010 *Crafting Pottery and Cooking Salt: The Archaeology of a Production Landscape on the Lowland Maya Caribbean Seaboard*. Unpublished Ph.D. dissertation, Department of Archaeology, Boston University.

Nash, J. 1970 *In the Eyes of the Ancestors: Belief and Behavior in a Maya Community*. Yale University Press, New Haven and London.

Nations, J.D. 2006 *The Maya Tropical Forest: People, Parks, and Ancient Cities*. University of Texas Press, Austin.

Nations, J.D. and R.B. Nigh 1980 The Evolutionary Potential of Lacandon Maya Sustained-Yield Tropical Forest Agriculture. *Journal of Anthropological Research* **36**(1):1–30.

Neff, L.S. 2002 Gender Divisions of Labor and Lowland Terrace Agriculture. In *Ancient Maya Women*, edited by T. Ardren, pp. 31–51. AltaMira, Walnut Creek, CA.

Netting, R.M. 1965 Household Organization and Intensive Cultivation: The Kofyar Case. *Africa* **35**:422–429.

1993 *Smallholders, Householders: Farm Families and the Ecology of Intensive, Sustainable Agriculture*. Stanford University Press, Stanford, CA.

Nichols, D.L., E.M. Brumfiel, H. Neff, M. Hodge, T.H. Charlton and M.D. Glascock 2002 Neutrons, Markets, Cities, and Empires: A 1000-Year Perspective on Ceramic Production and Distribution in the Postclassic Basin of Mexico. *Journal of Anthropological Archaeology* **21**:25–82.

Nielsen, J. 2006 The Queen's Mirrors: Interpreting the Iconography of Two Teotihuacan Style Mirrors from the Early Classic Margarita Tomb at Copan. *The PARI Journal* **6**(4):1–8.

Oppenheim, A.L. 1964[1977] *Ancient Mesopotamia: Portrait of a Dead Civilization*. Revised ed. University of Chicago, Chicago.

Orlove, B.S. and G. Custred (editors) 1980 *Land and Power in Latin America*. Holmes & Meier Publishers, New York and London.

Ortiz, P. and M. del Carmen Rodgríguez 2000 The Sacred Hill of El Manatí: Preliminary Discussion of the Site's Ritual Paraphernalia. In *Olmec Art and Archaeology in Mesoamerica*, edited by J.E. Clark and M.E. Pye, pp. 75–93. Distributed by Yale University Press, New Haven and London, National Gallery of Art, Washington, DC.

Ortner, S. 1994 Theory in Anthropology Since the Sixties. In *Culture/Power/History: A Reader in Contemporary Social Theory*, edited by N.B. Dirks, G. Eley and S.B. Ortner, pp. 372–411. Princeton University Press, Princeton, NJ.

2006 *Anthropology and Social Theory: Culture, Power, and the Acting Subject.* Duke University Press, Durham, NC.

Palka, J.W. 2005 *Unconquered Lacandon Maya: Ethnohistory and Archaeology of Indigenous Culture Change.* University Press of Florida, Gainesville.

Palka, J., D. Stuart and S.D. Houston n.d. A Coming of Age Ceremony? Dos Pilas Panel 19. Manuscript on file with author.

Parks, S. 2009 *Archaeological Ethics and the Struggle for Community Legitimacy in the Maya Archaeoscape.* Unpublished Ph.D. dissertation. Department of Archaeology, Boston University.

Parks, S. and P.A. McAnany 2007 Reclaiming Maya Ancestry. In *Look Close, See Far: A Cultural Portrait of the Maya*, edited by B.T. Martin, pp. 17–26. George Braziller, New York.

Parsons, M.H. 1975 The Distribution of Late Postclassic Spindle Whorls in the Valley of Mexico. *American Antiquity* **40**:207–215.

Pasztory, E. 2005 *Thinking with Things: Toward a New Vision of Art.* University of Texas Press, Austin.

Pauketat, T.R. 2001 Practice and History in Archaeology. *Anthropological Theory* (**1**):73–98.

Peacock, J.L. 2001 *The Anthropological Lens: Harsh Light, Soft Focus.* Cambridge University Press, Cambridge.

Pendergast, D.M. 1974 *Excavations at Actun Pobilche, Belize.* Royal Ontario Museum Monograph 1, Toronto.

1981 Lamanai, Belize: Summary of Excavation Results, 1974–1980. *Journal of Field Archaeology* **8**(1):29–53.

1982 *Excavations at Altun Ha, Belize, 1964–1970, Volume* 2. Royal Ontario Museum, Toronto.

1990 *Excavations at Altun Ha, Belize, 1964–1970, Volume 3.* Royal Ontario Museum, Toronto.

1993 Worlds in Collision: The Maya/Spanish Encounter in Sixteenth and Seventeenth Century Belize. *Proceedings of the British Academy* **81**:105–143.

Perera, V. and R.D. Bruce 1982 *Los Ultimos Señores de Palenque: Los Lacandones Herederos de los Mayas.* Editorial Argos Vergara, Barcelona.

Perez Romero, J.A. 1988 *Algunas Consideraciones sobre Cacao en el Norte de la Peninsula de Yucatán.* Tesis de Licenciatura en Ciencias Antropologicas, Universidad Autónoma de Yucatán, Mérida.

Peterson, P.A. 2006 *Ancient Maya Ritual Cave Use in the Sibun Valley, Belize.* Ph.D. dissertation, Boston University.

Petroshyn, J.T. 2005 A Lacandon Religious Ritual in the Cave of the God Tsibana' at the Holy Lake of Mensabok in the Rainforest of Chiapas. In *In the Maw of the Earth Monster: Mesoamerican Ritual Cave Use,* edited by J.E. Brady and K.M. Prufer, pp. 328–341. University of Texas Press, Austin.

Phillips, D.A. 1979 Material Culture and Trade of the Postclassic Maya. Ph.D. dissertation, University of Arizona, Tucson.

Pillsbury, J. 1996 The Thorny Oyster and the Origins of Empire: Implications of Recently Uncovered *Spondylus* Imagery from Chan Chan, Peru. *Latin American Antiquity* 7(4):313–340.

Piña Chan, R. 1978 Commerce in the Yucatan Peninsula: The Conquest and Colonial Period. In *Mesoamerican Communication Routes and Cultural Contacts*, edited by T.A. Lee and C. Navarrete, pp. 37–48. New World Archaeological Foundation, Brigham Young University, Provo, UT.

Piperno, D.R. and D.M. Pearsall 1998 *The Origins of Agriculture in the Lowland Neotropics*. Academic Press, San Diego.

Plank, S.E. 2004 *Maya Dwellings in Hieroglyphs and Archaeology: An Integrative Approach to Ancient Architecture and Spatial Cognition*. BAR International Series 1324, Oxford.

Plattner, S. 1989 Markets and Marketplaces. In *Economic Anthropology*, edited by S. Plattner, pp. 171–208. Stanford University Press, Stanford, CA.

Plunket, P. (editor) 2002 *Domestic Ritual in Ancient Mesoamerica*. Monograph 46, Cotsen Institute of Archaeology, Los Angeles.

Pohl, J.M.D. 2003 Ritual Ideology and Commerce in the Southern Mexican Highlands. In *The Postclassic Mesoamerican World*, edited by M.E. Smith and F.F. Berdan, pp. 172–177. University of Utah Press, Salt Lake City.

Pohl, M.D., K.O. Pope, J.G. Jones, J.S. Jacob, D.R. Piperno, S.D. deFrance, D.L. Lentz, J.A. Gifford, M.E. Danforth and J.K. Josserand 1996 Early Agriculture in the Maya Lowlands. *Latin American Antiquity* 7(4):355–372.

Polanyi, K. 1957 The Economy as Instituted Process. In *Trade and Market in the Early Empires*, edited by K. Polanyi, C. Arensberg and H.W. Pearson, pp. 243–270. Free Press, New York.

1960 On the Comparative Treatment of Economic Institutions in Antiquity with Illustrations from Athens, Mycenae and Alalakh. In *City Invincible: A Symposium on Urbanization and Cultural Development in the Ancient Near East*, edited by C.H. Kraeling and R.M. Adams, pp. 329–350. University of Chicago Press, Chicago.

Pollock, H.E.D. 1962 Introduction. In *Mayapan, Yucatan, Mexico*, edited by H.E.D. Pollock, R. Roys, T. Proskouriakoff and A.L. Smith, pp. 1–18. Carnegie Institution of Washington Publication No. 619, Washington, DC.

Pollock, H.E.D., R. Roys, T. Proskouriakoff and A.L. Smith (editors) 1962 *Mayapan, Yucatan, Mexico*. Carnegie Institution of Washington, Publication 619, Washington, DC.

Potter, D.R. and E.M. King 1995 A Heterarchical Approach to Lowland Maya Socioeconomies. In *Heterarchy and the Analysis of Complex Societies*, edited by R.M. Ehrenreich, C.L. Crumley and J.E. Levy, pp. 17–32. Archaeological Papers of the American Anthropological Association No. 6, American Archaeological Association, Arlington, VA.

Proskouriakoff, T. 1963 *An Album of Maya Architecture*. University of Oklahoma Press, Norman, OK.

Proskouriakoff, T. and C.R. Temple 1955 A Residential Quadrangle: Structures R–85 to R–90. *Current Reports, Carnegie Institute of Washington* 29:289–362. Department of Anthropology, Washington, DC.

Prufer, K.M. 2002 *Communities, Caves, and Ritual Specialists: A Study of Sacred Space in the Maya Mountains of Southern Belize.* Ph.D. dissertation, Southern Illinois University, Carbondale.

Puleston, D.E. 1983 *The Settlement Survey of Tikal.* Tikal Report No. 13, University Museum Monograph 48. The University Museum, University of Pennsylvania, Philadelphia.

Puleston, D.E. and O.S. Puleston 1971 An Ecological Approach to the Origins of Maya Civilization. *Archaeology* **24**:330–337.

Pyburn, K.A. 1998 Smallholders in the Maya Lowlands: Homage to a Garden Variety Ethnographer. *Human Ecology* **26**(2):267–286.

1999 Repudiating Witchcraft. In *Manifesting Power: Gender and the Interpretation of Power in Archaeology*, edited by T.L. Sweely, pp. 190–197. Routledge, London.

Quezada, S. 1985 Encomienda, cabildo, y gubernatura indígena en Yucatán, 1541–1583. *Historia Mexicana* **34**(4):662–684.

Rappaport, R.A. 1984 [1968] *Pigs for the Ancestors.* 1st and 2nd ed. Yale University Press, New Haven and London.

Rathje, W.L. 2002 The Nouveau Elite Potlatch: One Scenario for the Monumental Rise of Early Civilizations. In *Ancient Maya Political Economies,* edited by M. Masson and D.A. Freidel, pp. 31–40. AltaMira Press, Walnut Creek, CA.

Reents-Budet, D.J. 1994 *Painting the Maya Universe: Royal Ceramics of the Classic Period.* Duke University Press, Durham and London.

1998 Elite Maya Pottery and Artisans as Social Indicators. In *Craft and Social Identity,* edited by C.L. Costin and R.P. Wright, pp. 71–89. Archaeological Papers of the American Anthropological Association No. 8, American Anthropological Association, Washington, DC.

2000 Feasting Among the Classic Maya: Evidence from the Pictorial Ceramics. In *The Maya Vase Book, Volume 6,* edited by J. Kerr, pp. 1022–1037. Kerr Associates, New York.

2001 Classic Maya Concepts of the Royal Court: An Analysis of Renderings on Pictorical Ceramics. In *Royal Courts of the Ancient Maya, Volume 1: Theory, Comparison, and Synthesis,* edited by T. Inomata and S.D. Houston, pp. 195–231. Westview Press, Boulder, CO.

Reents-Budet, D., R.L. Bishop, J.T. Taschek and J.W. Ball 2000 Out of the Palace Dumps: Ceramic Production and Use at Buenavista del Cayo. *Ancient Mesoamerica* **11**:99–121.

Reina, R.E. and R.M. Hill 1978 *The Traditional Pottery of Guatemala.* University of Texas Press, Austin.

Reina, R.E. and J. Monaghan 1981 The Ways of the Maya: Salt Production in Sacapulas, Guatemala. *Expedition* **23**(3):13–33.

Reiter, R.R. (editor) 1975 *Toward an Anthropology of Women.* Monthly Review Press, New York and London.

Renfrew, C. 1972 *The Emergence of Civilization: The Cyclades and the Aegean in the Third Millennium B.C.* Methuen & Co., London.

Restall, M.B. 1992 *The World of the Cah: Postconquest Yucatec Society*. Ph.D. dissertation, University of California, Los Angeles. University Microfilms International, Ann Arbor, MI.

Restall, M. 1997 *The Maya World: Yucatec Culture and Society, 1550–1850*. Stanford University Press, Stanford, CA.

Restall, M. and J.F. Chuchiak, IV 2002 A Reevaluation of the Authenticity of Fray Diego de Landa's Relación de las cosas de Yucatán. *Ethnohistory* **49**(3):651–669.

Reynolds, V. and R. Tanner 1995 *The Social Ecology of Religion*. Oxford University Press, Oxford.

Rice, D.S. 1993 Eighth-Century Physical Geography, Environment, and Natural Resources in the Maya Lowlands. In *Lowland Maya Society in the Eighth Century A.D.*, edited by J.A. Sabloff and J.S. Henderson, pp. 11–63. Dumbarton Oaks Research Library and Collection, Washington, DC.

Rice, D.S. and P.M. Rice 2005 Sixteenth- and Seventeenth-Century Maya Political Geography in Central Petén, Guatemala. In *The Postclassic to Spanish-Era Transition in Mesoamerica: Archaeological Perspectives*, edited by S. Kepecs and R.T. Alexander, pp. 139–160. University of New Mexico, Albuquerque.

Rice, P.M. 1987a Lowland Maya Pottery Production in the Late Classic Period. In *Maya Ceramics: Papers from the 1985 Maya Ceramics Conference*, edited by P.M. Rice and R.J. Sharer, pp. 525–543. BAR International Series (ii), Oxford.

1987b *Pottery Analysis: A Sourcebook*. University of Chicago Press, Chicago.

1987c Economic Change in the Lowland Maya Late Classic Period. In *Specialization, Exchange, and Complex Societies*, edited by E.M. Brumfiel and T.K. Earle, pp. 76–85. Cambridge University Press, Cambridge.

1991 Specialization, Standardization, and Diversity: A Retrospective. In *The Ceramic Legacy of Anna O. Shepard*, edited by R. Bishop and F. Lange, pp. 257–279. University Press of Colorado, Boulder, CO.

2004 *Maya Political Science: Time, Astronomy, and the Cosmos*. University of Texas Press, Austin.

Richards, J. and M. van Buren (editors) 2000 *Order, Legitimacy, and Wealth in Ancient States*. Cambridge University Press, Cambridge.

Ricketson, O.G., Jr. and E.B. Ricketson 1937 *Uaxactun, Guatemala Group E – 1926–1931. Part I: The Excavations* and *Part II. The Artifacts*. Carnegie Institution of Washington Publ. 477, Washington, DC.

Ricoeur, P. 1984 *Time and Narrative, Volume 1*. Translated by K. McLaughlin and D. Pellauer. University of Chicago Press, Chicago.

1985 *Time and Narrative, Volume 2*. Translated by K. McLaughlin and D. Pellauer. University of Chicago Press, Chicago.

Ringle, W.M. 1999 Pre-Classic Cityscapes: Ritual Politics among the Early Lowland Maya. In *Social Patterns in Pre-Classic Mesoamerica*, edited by D.C. Grove and R.A. Joyce, pp. 183–223. Dumbarton Oaks Research Library and Collection, Washington, DC.

Ringle, W.M., T. Gallareta Negrón and G.J. Bey III 1998 The Return of Quetzalcoatl: Evidence for the Spread of a World Religion during the Epiclassic Period. *Ancient Mesoamerica* **9**:183–232.

Robb, J.E. 1999 Secret Agents: Culture, Economy, and Social Reproduction. In *Material Symbols: Culture and Economy in Prehistory*, edited by J.E. Robb, pp. 3–15. Occasional Paper No. 26, Center for Archaeological Investigations, Southern Illinois University, Carbondale.

Robin, C. 2002 Gender and Maya Farming: Chan No'ohol. In *Ancient Maya Women*, edited by T. Ardren, pp. 12–30. AltaMira Press, Walnut Creek, CA.

2003 New Directions in Classic Maya Household Archaeology. *Journal of Archaeological Research* **11**:307–356.

2006 Gender, Farming, and Long-Term Change. *Current Anthropology* **47**(3):409–433.

Rosenmeier, M.F., D.A. Hodell, M. Brenner, J.H. Curtis and T.P. Guilderson 2002 A 4,000-Year Lacustrine Record of Environmental Change in the Southern Maya Lowlands, Petén, Guatemala. *Quaternary Research* **57**:183–190.

Rossignol, J. and L. Wandsnider (editors) 1992 *Space, Time, and Archaeological Landscapes*. Plenum Press, New York.

Rowlands, M. 1993 The Role of Memory in the Transmission of Culture. *World Archaeology* **25**(2):141–151.

Roys, R.L. 1939 *The Titles of Ebtun*. Carnegie Institution of Washington, Publication No. 505, Washington, DC.

1943 *The Indian Background of Colonial Yucatan*. Carnegie Institution of Washington Publication 548, Washington, DC.

1957 *The Political Geography of the Yucatan Maya*. Carnegie Institution of Washington Publication 613, Washington, DC.

Sabloff, J.A. 2005 The Maya and the Aztecs. In *Technology in World History, Volume 4: Traditional Cultures*, edited by W.B. Carlson, pp. 64–91. Oxford University Press, Oxford.

2007 It Depends on How We Look at Things: New Perspectives on the Postclassic Period in the Northern Maya Lowlands. *Proceedings of the American Philosophical Society* **151**(1):11–26.

Sabloff, J.A. and W.L. Rathje 1975 The Rise of a Maya Merchant Class. *Scientific American* **233**:72–82.

Sachse, F. and A.J. Christenson 2005 Tulan and the Other Side of the Sea: Unraveling a Metaphorical Concept from Colonial Guatemalan Highland Sources. Available at http://www.mesoweb.com/articles/tulan/tulan.html.

Sahagún, B. de 1950–1982 *Florentine Codex: General History of the Things of New Spain*. Translated by A.J.O. Anderson and C.E. Dibble. School of American Research/University of Utah, Santa Fe, NM, and Salt Lake City.

1997 *Primeros Memoriales. Paleography of Nahuatl Text*. Translated by T.D. Sullivan. University of Oklahoma Press, Norman.

Sahlins, M.D. 1972 *Stone Age Economics*. Aldine-Atherton, Chicago.

1981 *Historical Metaphors and Mythical Realities: Structure in the Early History of the Sandwich Islands Kingdom.* University of Michigan Press, Ann Arbor.

1985 *Islands of History.* University of Chicago Press, Chicago.

1994 Cosmologies of Capitalism: The Trans-Pacific Sector of "The World System." In *Culture/Power/History: A Reader in Contemporary Social Theory,* edited by N.B. Dirks, G. Eley and S.B. Ortner, pp. 412–455. Princeton University Press, Princeton, NJ.

Sanders, W.T. and R.S. Santley 1983 A Tale of Three of Cities: Energetics and Urbanization in Pre-Hispanic Central Mexico. In *Prehistoric Settlement Patterns: Essays in Honor of Gordon R. Willey,* edited by E.Z. Vogt and R.M. Leventhal, pp. 243–291. University of New Mexico Press and Peabody Museum of Archaeology and Ethnology, Harvard University, Albuquerque and Cambridge.

Sandstrom, A.R. 1991 *Corn Is Our Blood: Culture and Ethnic Identity in a Contemporary Aztec Indian Village.* University of Oklahoma Press, Norman and London.

2005 The Cave-Pyramid Complex among the Contemporary Nahua of Northern Veracruz. In *In the Maw of the Earth Monster: Mesoamerican Ritual Cave Use,* edited by J.E. Brady and K.M. Prufer, pp. 35–68. University of Texas Press, Austin.

Sandstrom, A.R. and P.E. Sandstrom 1986 *Traditional Papermaking and Paper Cult Figures of Mexico.* University of Oklahoma Press, Norman.

Sanford, V. 2003 *Buried Secrets: Truth and Human Rights in Guatemala.* Palgrave Macmillan, New York.

Santley, R.S. 2007 *The Prehistory of the Tuxtlas.* University of New Mexico Press, Albuquerque.

Saturno, W., K. Taube and D. Stuart 2005 *The Murals of San Bartolo, El Petén, Guatemala, Part 1: The North Wall.* Ancient American No. 7, Center for Ancient American Studies, Barnardsville, NC.

Scarborough, V.L. 1998 Ecology and Ritual: Water Management and the Maya. *Latin American Antiquity* **9**(2):135–159.

2003 *The Flow of Power: Ancient Water Systems and Landscapes.* SAR Press, Santa Fe, NM.

Scarborough, V.L. and F. Valdez, Jr. 2003 The Engineered Environment and Political Economy of the Three Rivers Region. In *Heterarchy, Political Economy, and the Ancient Maya: The Three Rivers Region of the East-Central Yucatán Peninsula,* edited by V.L. Scarborough, F. Valdez, Jr. and N. Dunning, pp. 3–13. University of Arizona Press, Tucson.

Schechner, R. and W. Appel (editors) 1989 *By Means of Performance: Intercultural Studies of Theatre and Ritual.* Cambridge University Press, Cambridge.

Schele, L. 1997 *Hidden Faces of the Maya.* Impetus Comunicación S.A. de C.V., México, D.F.

Schele, L. and D. Freidel 1990 *A Forest of Kings: The Untold Story of the Ancient Maya.* William Morrow, New York.

Schele, L. and P. Mathews 1998 *The Code of Kings: The Language of Seven Sacred Maya Temples and Tombs.* Scribner, New York.

Schele, L. and M.E. Miller 1986 *Blood of Kings, Dynasty and Ritual in Maya Art*. George Braziller and the Kimball Art Museum – Fort Worth, New York.

Scholes, F.V. and E.B. Adams 1938 *Don Diego Quijada: Alcalde Mayor de Yucatan, 1561–1565*. 2 vols. Antigua Libreria Robredo, de Jose Porrua e Hijos, Mexico.

Schroeder, S. 1997 Introduction. In *Indian Women of Early Mexico*, edited by S. Schroeder, S. Wood and R. Haskett, pp. 3–22. University of Oklahoma Press, Norman.

Seidemann, R.M. and H. McKillop 2007 Dental Indicators of Diet and Health for the Postclassic Coastal Maya on Wild Cane Cay, Belize. *Ancient Mesoamerica* **18**(2):303–313.

Service, E.R. 1975 *Origins of the State and Civilization*. Norton, New York.

Shafer, H.J. and T.R. Hester 1991 Lithic Craft Specialization and Product Distribution at the Maya site of Colha, Belize. *World Archaeology* **23**(1):79–97.

Shanks, M. 2001 Culture/Archaeology: The Dispersion of a Discipline and Its Objects. In *Archaeological Theory Today*, edited by I. Hodder, pp. 284–305. Polity Press, Cambridge.

Sharer, R.J. 2003 Tikal and the Copan Dynastic Founding. In *Tikal: Dynasties, Foreigners, and Affairs of State*, edited by J.A. Sabloff, pp. 319–353. School of American Research Press and James Currey, Santa Fe, NM, and Oxford.

Sharer, R.J. and L.P. Traxler 2006 *The Ancient Maya*. 6th ed., revised from earlier editions by Sylvanus G. Morley (1946) and George W. Brainerd (1956). Stanford University Press, Stanford, CA.

Shaw, L.C. 1999 Social and Ecological Aspects of Preclassic Maya Meat Consumption at Colha, Belize. In *Reconstructing Ancient Maya Diet*, edited by C.D. White, pp. 83–100. University of Utah Press, Salt Lake City.

Sheets, P. (editor) 2002 *Before the Volcano Erupted: The Ancient Cerén Village in Central America*. University of Texas Press, Austin.

Shimada, I. (editor) 2007 *Craft Production in Complex Societies: Multicraft and Producer Perspectives*. University of Utah Press, Salt Lake City.

Sidrys, R. 1977 Mass-Distance Measures for the Maya Obsidian Trade. In *Exchange Systems in Prehistory*, edited by T.K. Earle and J.E. Ericson, pp. 91–107. Academic Press, New York.

Silverblatt, I. 1987 *Moon, Sun and Witches: Gender Ideologies and Class in Inca and Colonial Peru*. Princeton University Press, Princeton, NJ.

Sinopoli, C. 1988 The Organization of Craft Production at Vijayanagara, South India. *American Anthropologist* **90**:580–597.

1998 Identity and Social Action among South Indian Craft Producers of the Vijayanagara Period. In *Craft and Social Identity*, edited by C.L. Costin and R.P. Wright, pp. 161–172. Archaeological Papers of the American Anthropological Association No. 8, American Anthropological Association, Washington, DC.

2003 *The Political Economy of Craft Production: Crafting Empire in South India, c. 1350–1650*. Cambridge University Press, New York.

Smith, A. 1991[1776] *The Wealth of Nations*. Alfred A. Knopf, New York.

Smith, A.L. 1982 Major Architecture and Caches. In *Excavations at Seibal, Department of Peten, Guatemala*, edited by G.R. Willey. Memoirs of the Peabody Museum of Archaeology and Ethnology, Volume 15. Harvard University, Cambridge, MA.

Smith, A.T. 2003 *The Political Landscape: Constellations of Authority in Early Complex Polities*. University of California Press, Berkeley.

Smith, C.A. (editor) 1990 *Guatemalan Indians and the State, 1540–1988*. University of Texas Press, Austin.

Smith, M.E. 2004 The Archaeology of Ancient State Economies. *Annual Review of Anthropology* **33**:73–102.

Smith, M.E. and F.F. Berdan 2003a Postclassic Mesoamerica. In *The Postclassic Mesoamerican World*, edited by M.E. Smith and F.F. Berdan, pp. 3–13. University of Utah Press, Salt Lake City.

(editors) 2003b *The Postclassic Mesoamerican World*. University of Utah Press, Salt Lake City.

Smith, M.E. and K. Schreiber 2005 New World States and Empires: Economic and Social Organization. *Journal of Archaeological Research* **13**(3):189–229.

2006 New World States and Empires: Politics, Religion, and Urbanism. *Journal of Archaeological Research* **14**(1):1–52.

Smyth, M.P. 1996 Storage and the Political Economy: A View from Mesoamerica. In *Research in Economic Anthropology, Volume 17*, edited by B. L. Isaac, pp. 335–355. JAI Press, Greenwich, CT.

Spielmann, K.A. 2002 Feasting, Craft Specialization, and the Ritual Mode of Production in Small-Scale Societies. *American Anthropologist* **104**(1):195–207.

2008 Crafting the Sacred: Ritual Places and Paraphernalia in Small-scale Societies. In *Dimensions of Ritual Economy, Research in Economic Anthropology, Volume 27*, edited by E.C. Wells and P.A. McAnany, pp. 37–72. JAI Press, Emerald Group Publishing, Bingley, UK.

Stanchly, N. 2003 Sibun Valley Fauna from Excavations and Caves. In *Between the Gorge and the Estuary: Archaeological Investigations of the 2001 Season of the Xibun Archaeological Research Project*, edited by P.A. McAnany and B. Thomas, pp. 297–337. Available from http://www.bu.edu/tricia.

Stanish, C. 2004 The Evolution of Chiefdoms: An Economic Anthropology Model. In *Archaeological Perspectives on Political Economies*, edited by G.M. Feinman and L.M. Nicholas, pp. 7–24. University of Utah Press, Salt Lake City.

Steinberg, M.K. 2002 The Globalization of a Ceremonial Tree: The Case of Cacao (*Theobroma cacao*) Among the Mopan Maya. *Economic Botany* **56**(1):58–65.

Stephens, J.L. 1993 *Incidents of Travel in Central America, Chiapas, and Yucatan*. Smithsonian Institution Press, Washington, DC, and London.

Steward, J.H. 1955 *Theory of Culture Change*. University of Illinois Press, Urbana.

Stone, A. 1989 Disconnection, Foreign Insignia and Political Expansion: Teotihuacan and the Warrior Stelae of Piedras Negras. In *Mesoamerica After the Decline of Teotihuacan, AD 700–900*, edited by R.A. Diehl and J.C. Berlo, pp. 153–172. Dumbarton Oaks Research Library and Collection, Washington, DC.

1995 *Images from the Underworld: Naj Tunich and the Tradition of Maya Cave Painting*. University of Texas Press, Austin.

Stone, E.C. 1987 *Nippur Neighborhoods*. Studies in Ancient Oriental Civilization No. 44, The Oriental Institute of the University of Chicago, Chicago.

Storey, R. 1999 Late Classic Nutrition and Skeletal Indicators at Copán, Honduras. In *Reconstructing Ancient Maya Diet*, edited by C.D. White, pp. 169–179. University of Utah Press, Salt Lake City.

2004 Ancestors: Bioarchaeology of the Human Remains of K'axob. In *K'axob: Ritual, Work, and Family in an Ancient Maya Village*, edited by P.A. McAnany, pp. 109–138. Monumenta Archaeologica 22, Cotsen Institute of Archaeology at UCLA, Los Angeles.

Stout, D. 2002 Skill and Cognition in Stone Tool Production: An Ethnographic Case Study from Irian Jaya. *Current Anthropology* **43**(5):693–722.

Stuart, D. 1988 The Río Azul Cacao Pot: Epigraphic Observations on the Function of a Maya Ceramic Vessel. *Antiquity* **62**:153–157.

1989 Hieroglyphs on Maya Vessels. In *The Maya Vase Book, Volume 1*, edited by J. Kerr, pp. 149–160. Kerr Associates, New York.

1997 The Hills Are Alive: Sacred Mountains in the Maya Cosmos. *Symbols* (Spring):13–17.

1998 "The Fire Enters His House": Architecture and Ritual in Classic Maya Texts. In *Function and Meaning in Classic Maya Architecture*, edited by S.D. Houston, pp. 373–425. Dumbarton Oaks Research Library and Collection, Washington, DC.

2000 The Arrival of Strangers: Teotihuacan and Tollan in Classic Maya History. In *Mesoamerica's Classic Heritage*, edited by D. Carrasco, L. Jones and S. Session, pp. 465–513. University of Colorado Press, Boulder.

Stuart, D. and S. Houston 1994 *Classic Maya Place Names*. Dumbarton Oaks Research Library and Collection, Washington, DC.

Sullivan, T.D. 1982 Tlazolteotl-Ixcuina: The Great Spinner and Weaver. In *The Art and Iconography of Late Post-Classic Central Mexico*, edited by E.H. Boone, pp. 7–35. Dumbarton Oaks Research Library and Collection, Washington, DC.

Sweely, T.L. 1999 Gender, Space, People, and Power at Cerén, El Salvador. In *Manifesting Power: Gender and the Interpretation of Power in Archaeology*, edited by T.L. Sweely, pp. 155–171. Routledge, London.

Taschek, J.T. 1994 *The Artifacts of Dzibilchaltun, Yucatan, Mexico: Shell, Polished Stone, Bone, Wood, and Ceramics*. Middle American Research Institute Publication 50, Tulane University, New Orleans.

Tate, C.E. 1992 *Yaxchilan: The Design of a Maya Ceremonial City*. University of Texas Press, Austin.

1999 Writing on the Face of the Moon: Women's Products, Archetypes, and Power in Ancient Maya Civilization. In *Manifesting Power: Gender and the Interpretation of Power in Archaeology*, edited by T. L. Sweely, pp. 81–102. Routledge, London.

Taube, K. 1985 The Classic Maya Maize God: A Reappraisal. In *Fifth Palenque Round Table, 1983*, edited by M. G. Robertson and V. M. Fields, pp. 171–181. The Pre-Columbian Art Research Institute, San Francisco.

1989 The Maize Tamale in Classic Maya Diet, Epigraphy, and Art. *American Antiquity* **54**:31–51.

1993 *Aztec and Maya Myths.* British Museum Press, London, and University of Texas, Austin, TX.

1998 The Jade Hearth: Centrality, Rulership, and the Classic Maya Temple. In *Function and Meaning in Classic Maya Architecture*, edited by S. D. Houston, pp. 427–478. Dumbarton Oaks Research Library and Collection, Washington, DC.

2000 The Turquoise Hearth: Fire, Self-Sacrifice, and the Central Mexican Cult of War. In *Mesoamerica's Classic Heritage*, edited by D. Carrasco, L. Jones and S. Sessions, pp. 269–340. University Press of Colorado, Boulder.

2003 Ancient and Contemporary Maya Conceptions About Field and Forest. In *The Lowland Maya Area: Three Millennia at the Human-Wildland Interface*, edited by A. Gómez-Pompa, M. F. Allen, S. E. Fedick and J.J. Jiménez-Osornio, pp. 461–492. Ford Products Press, New York.

2004 Flower Mountain: Concepts of Life, Beauty, and Paradise among the Classic Maya. *RES: Anthropology and Aesthetics* **45**:69–98.

2005 The Symbolism of Jade in Classic Maya Religion. *Ancient Mesoamerica* **16**:23–50.

Tedlock, B. 1982 *Time and the Highland Maya.* University of New Mexico Press, Albuquerque.

Tedlock, B. and D. Tedlock 1985 Text and Textile: Language and Technology in the Arts of the Quiché Maya. *Journal of Anthropological Research* **41**:121–46.

Tedlock, D. 1985 *Popol Vuh: The Mayan Book of the Dawn of Life.* Simon & Schuster, New York.

2002 How to Drink Chocolate from a Skull at a Wedding Banquet. *RES* **42**(Autumn):166–179.

2003 *Rabinal Achi: A Mayan Drama of War and Sacrifice.* Oxford University Press, Oxford.

Teeter, W. G. 2004 Animal Utilization in a Growing City. In *Maya Zooarchaeology: New Directions in Method and Theory*, edited by K. F. Emery, pp. 177–191. Monograph 51, Cotsen Institute of Archaeology at UCLA, Los Angeles.

Thomas, B. S. 2005 *Maya Settlement and Political Hierarchy in the Sibun River Valley, Belize, Central America.* Unpublished Ph.D. dissertation, Department of Archaeology, Boston University.

Thomas, J. 1998 Some Problems with the Notion of External Symbolic Storage, and the Case of Neolithic Material Culture in Britain. In *Cognition and Material Culture: The Archaeology of Symbolic Storage*, edited by C. Renfrew and C. Scarre, pp. 149–156. McDonald Institute Monographs, Cambridge.

2001 Archaeologies of Place and Landscape. In *Archaeological Theory Today*, edited by I. Hodder, pp. 165–186. Polity Press, Cambridge.

Thomas, N. 1991 *Entangled Objects: Exchange, Material Culture, and Colonialism in the Pacific*. Harvard University Press, Cambridge, MA.

1996 *Out of Time: History and Evolution in Anthropological Discourse*, 2nd ed. University of Michigan Press, Ann Arbor.

Thompson, J. E. S. 1930 *Ethnology of the Mayas of Southern and Central British Honduras*. Field Museum of Natural History Anthropological Series XVII, No. 2, Chicago.

1956 Notes on the Use of Cacao in Middle America. *Notes on Middle American Archaeology and Ethnology* **128**:95–116.

1964 Trade Relations between the Maya Highlands and the Lowlands. *Estudios de Cultura Maya* **4**:13–48.

Thompson, R. H. 1958 *Modern Yucatecan Maya Pottery Making*. Memoirs of the Society for American Archaeology No. 15, Society for American Archaeology, Salt Lake City.

Tiesler, V. and A. Cucina (editors) 2004 *Janaab' Pakal de Palenque: Vida y Muerte de un Governante Maya*. Universidad Nacional Autónoma de México and Universidad Autónoma de Yucatán, México, D.F. and Mérida, Yucatán.

Tilley, C. 1994 *A Phenomenology of Landscape: Places, Paths, and Monuments*. Berg, Oxford and Providence, RI.

Titmus, G. L. and J. C. Woods 2003 The Maya Eccentric: Evidence for the Use of the Indirect Percussion Technique in Mesoamerica from Preliminary Experiments Concerning Their Manufacture. In *Mesoamerican Lithic Technology: Experimentation and Interpretation*, edited by K. G. Hirth, pp. 132–146. University of Utah Press, Salt Lake City.

Touraine, A. 1977 *The Self-Production of Society*. University of Chicago Press, Chicago.

Tourtellot, G., F. Estrada Belli, J.J. Rose and N. Hammond 2003 Late Classic Maya Heterarchy, Hierarchy, and Landscape at La Milpa, Belize. In *Heterarchy, Political Economy, and the Ancient Maya: The Three Rivers Region of the East-Central Yucatán Peninsula*, edited by V. L. Scarborough, F. Valdez, Jr. and N. Dunning, pp. 37–51. University of Arizona Press, Tucson.

Tozzer, A. M. 1907 *A Comparative Study of the Mayas and the Lacandones*. The Macmillan Company, New York.

(translator) 1941 *Landa's Relacion de las Cosas de Yucatan*. Papers of the Peabody Museum of American Archaeology and Ethnology Volume XVIII. Harvard University, Cambridge, MA.

Trevelyan, A. M. and H. W. Forbes 2002 The Gendered Architecture of Uxmal. In *Ancient Maya Gender: Identity and Relations*, edited by L. S. Gustafson and A. M. Trevelyan, pp. 93–140. Bergin & Garvey, Westport, CT.

Trigger, B. G. 1989 *A History of Archaeological Thought.* Cambridge University Press, Cambridge.

2003 *Understanding Early Civilizations: A Comparative Study.* Cambridge University Press, Cambridge and New York.

Tringham, R. 1996 But Gordon, Where Are the People? Some Comments on the Topic of Craft Specialization and Social Evolution. In *Craft Specialization and Social Evolution: In Memory of V. Gordon Childe,* edited by B. Wailes, pp. 233–239. The University Museum of Archaeology and Anthropology, University of Pennsylvania, Philadelphia.

Tuchman, B. W. 1978 *A Distant Mirror: The Calamitous 14th Century.* Knopf, New York.

Turner, B. L., II 1983 *Once Beneath the Forest: Prehistoric Terracing in the Rio Bec Region of the Maya Lowlands.* Dellplain Latin American Studies, No. 13. Westview Press, Boulder, CO.

Turner, T. R. 1980 The Social Skin. In *Not Work Alone: A Cross-Cultural View of Activities Superfluous to Survival,* edited by J. Cherfas and R. Lewin, pp. 112–140. Sage Publications, Beverly Hills, CA.

Turner, V. W. 1969 *The Ritual Process: Structure and Anti-Structure.* Aldine, Chicago.

Tykot, R. H. 2002 Contribution of Stable Isotope Analysis to Understanding Dietary Variation among the Maya. *American Chemical Society* 2002: 214–230.

Urton, G. 1997 *The Social Life of Numbers: A Quechua Ontology of Numbers and Philosophy of Arithmetic.* University of Texas Press, Austin.

2003 *Signs of the Inka Khipu: Binary Coding in the Andean Knotted-String Records.* University of Texas Press, Austin.

Vail, G. 2002 *The Madrid Codex: A Maya Hieroglyphic Book,* Version 1.0. Web site and database at http://www.doarks.org/codex.

Vail, G. and A. Stone 2002 Representations of Women in Postclassic and Colonial Maya Literature and Art. In *Ancient Maya Women,* edited by T. Ardren, pp. 203–228. AltaMira Press, Walnut Creek, CA.

Valdés, J. A. 1986 Uaxactun: Recientes Investigaciones. *Mexicon* **7**(6): 126–128.

2001 Palaces and Thrones Tied to the Destiny of Royal Courts in the Maya Lowlands. In *Royal Courts of the Ancient Maya, Volume 2: Data and Case Studies,* edited by T. Inomata and S. D. Houston, pp. 138–164. Westview Press, Boulder, CO.

Valdés, J. A. and F. Fahsen 1995 The Reigning Dynasty of Uaxactun during the Early Classic: The Rulers and the Ruled. *Ancient Mesoamerica* **6**:197–219.

Veblen, T. 1934 [1899] *The Theory of the Leisure Class: An Economic Study of Institutions.* Random House, New York.

Vogt, E. Z. 1964 Ancient Maya Concepts in Contemporary Zinacantan Religion. In *Actes de VI Congrés International des Sciences Anthropologiques et Ethnologiques, Volume 2,* pp. 497–502. Museé de l'Homme, Paris.

1976 *Tortillas for the Gods: A Symbolic Analysis of Zinacanteco Rituals.* Harvard University Press, Cambridge, MA.

Vogt, E. Z. and D. Stuart 2005 Some Notes on Ritual Caves among the Ancient and Modern Maya. In *In the Maw of the Earth Monster: Mesoamerican Ritual Cave Use,* edited by J. E. Brady and K. M. Prufer, pp. 155–185. University of Texas Press, Austin.

Vokes, H.E. and E.H. Vokes 1983 *Distribution of Shallow-Water Marine Mollusca, Yucatan Peninsula, Mexico.* Mesoamerican Ecology Institute Monograph 1. Middle American Research Institute Publication 54, Tulane University, New Orleans.

Wainwright, J. 2008 *Decolonizing Development: Colonial Power and the Maya.* Blackwell, Malden, MA.

Warren, K. B. 1998 *Indigenous Movements and Their Critics: Pan-Maya Activism in Guatemala.* Princeton University Press, Princeton, NJ.

2002 Voting Against Indigenous Rights in Guatemala: Lessons from the 1999 Referendum. In *Indigenous Movements, Self-Representation, and the State in Latin America,* edited by K. B. Warren and J. E. Jackson, pp. 149–180. University of Texas Press, Austin.

Watanabe, J. M. 2004 Some Models in a Muddle: Lineage and House in Classic Maya Social Organization. *Ancient Mesoamerica* **15**(1):159–166.

Wauchope, R. 1938 *Modern Maya Houses: A Study of Their Archaeological Significance.* Carnegie Institution of Washington, Washington, DC.

Webster, D. 2000 The Not So Peaceful Civilization: A Review of Maya War. *Journal of World Prehistory* **14**(1):65–117.

2002 *The Fall of the Ancient Maya: Solving the Mystery of the Maya Collapse.* Thames & Hudson, London.

Weiner, A. B. 1992 *Inalienable Possessions: The Paradox of Keeping-While-Giving.* University of California Press, Berkeley.

Weiss-Krejci, E. 2004 Mortuary Representation of the Noble House. *Journal of Social Archaeology* **4**(3):368–404.

Wells, E. C. 2004 Investigating Activity Patterns in Prehispanic Plazas: Weak Acid-Extraction ICP-AES Analysis of Anthrosols at Classic Period El Coyote, Northwestern Honduras. *Archaeometry* **46**(1):67–84.

2006 Recent Trends in Theorizing Prehispanic Mesoamerican Economies. *Journal of Archaeological Research* **14**(4):265–312.

2007 Faenas, Ferias, and Fiestas: Ritual Finance in Ancient and Modern Honduras. In *Mesoamerican Ritual Economy: Archaeological and Ethnological Perspectives,* edited by E. C. Wells and K. L. Davis-Salazar, pp. 29–65. University Press of Colorado, Boulder.

Wells, E. C. and K. L. Davis-Salazar 2008 Environmental Worldview and Ritual Economy Among the Honduran Lenca. In *Dimensions of Ritual Economy, Research in Economic Anthropology, Volume 27,* edited by E. C. Wells and P. A. McAnany, pp. 189–217. JAI Press, Emerald Group Publishing, Bingley, UK.

Wells, E.C. and K.L. Davis-Salazar (editors) 2007 *Mesoamerican Ritual Economy: Archaeological and Ethnological Perspectives.* University Press of Colorado, Boulder.

Wells, E.C. and P.A. McAnany (editors) 2008 *Dimensions of Ritual Economy, Research in Economic Anthropology, Volume* 27. JAI Press, Emerald Group Publishing, Bingley, UK.

Welsh, W.B.M. 1988 *An Analysis of Classic Lowland Maya Burials.* British Archaeological Reports, Oxford.

West, G. 2002 Ceramic Exchange in the Late Classic and Postclassic Maya Lowlands: A Diachronic Approach. In *Ancient Maya Political Economies,* edited by M.A. Masson and D.A. Freidel, pp. 140–196. AltaMira Press, Walnut Creek, CA.

White, C.D., D.M. Pendergast, F.J. Longstaffe and K.R. Law 2001 Social Complexity and Food Systems at Altun Ha, Belize: The Isotopic Evidence. *Latin American Antiquity* **12**(4):371–393.

White, C.D., M.D. Pohl, H.P. Schwarcz and F.J. Longstaffe 2004 Feast, Field, and Forest: Deer and Dog Diets at Lagartero, Tikal, and Copán. In *Maya Zooarchaeology: New Directions in Method and Theory,* edited by K.F. Emery, pp. 141–158. Monograph 51, Cotsen Institute of Archaeology at UCLA, Los Angeles.

Wilk, R.R. 1983 Little House in the Jungle: The Causes of Variation in House Size among Modern Kekchi Maya. *Journal of Anthropological Archaeology* **2**:99–116.

1991 The Household in Anthropology: Panacea or Problem. *Reviews in Anthropology* **20**(1):1–12.

1996 *Economies and Cultures: Foundations of Economic Anthropology.* Westview Press, Boulder, CO.

Wilk, R.R. and W. Ashmore (editors) 1988 *Household and Community in the Mesoamerican Past.* University of New Mexico Press, Albuquerque.

Wilk, R.R. and R.M. Netting 1984 Households: Changing Forms and Functions. In *Households: Comparative and Historical Studies of the Domestic Group,* edited by R.M. Netting, R.R. Wilk and E.J. Arnould, pp. 1–28. University of California Press, Berkeley.

Wilk, R.R. and W.L. Rathje 1982 Household Archaeology. *American Behavioral Scientist* **25**(6):617–639.

Willey, G.R. 1965 Chapter VIII. Artifacts. In *Prehistoric Maya Settlements in the Belize Valley,* edited by G.R. Willey, W.R. Bullard, Jr., J.B. Glass and J.C. Gifford, pp. 391–522. Papers of the Peabody Museum of Archaeology and Ethnology, Volume LIV. Harvard University, Cambridge, MA.

1978 Number 1. Artifacts. In *Excavations at Seibal, Department of Peten, Guatemala,* edited by G. R. Willey, pp. 1–189. Peabody Museum of Archeology and Ethnology, Harvard University, Cambridge, MA.

1982 Foreword. *American Behavioral Scientist* **25**(6):613–616.

Wilson, R. 1995 *Maya Resurgence in Guatemala: Q'eqchi' Experiences.* University of Oklahoma Press, Norman.

Wisdom, C. 1940 *The Chorti Indians of Guatemala*. University of Chicago Press, Chicago.

Wolf, E.R. 1957 Closed Corporate Peasant Communities in Mesoamerica and Central Java. *Southwestern Journal of Anthropology* **13**(1):1–18.

1966 *Peasants*. Prentice-Hall, Englewood Cliffs, NJ.

1982 *Europe and the People Without History*. University of California Press, Berkeley.

1990 Distinguished Lecture: Facing Power – Old Insights, New Questions. *American Anthropologist* **92**:586–596.

Wright, L.E. 2005 Identifying Immigrants to Tikal, Guatemala: Defining Local Variability in Strontium Isotope Ratios of Human Teeth Enamel. *Journal of Archaeological Science* **32**(4):555–566.

Wright, R.P. 1998 Crafting Social Identity in Ur III Southern Mesopotamia. In *Craft and Social Identity*, edited by C.L. Costin and R.P. Wright, pp. 57–69. Archaeological Papers of the American Anthropological Association No. 8, Washington, DC.

Wurtzburg, S.J. 1991 *Sayil: Investigations of Urbanism and Economic Organization at an Ancient Maya City*. Ph.D. dissertation, Department of Anthropology, State University of New York, Albany. University Microfilms, Ann Arbor, MI.

Wylie, A. 1993 A Proliferation of New Archaeologies: "Beyond Objectivism and Relativism." In *Archaeological Theory: Who Sets the Agenda?* edited by N. Yoffee and A. Sherratt, pp. 20–26. Cambridge University Press, Cambridge.

Yaeger, J. and G. Borgstede 2004 Professional Archaeology and the Modern Maya: A Historical Sketch. In *Continuities and Changes in Maya Archaeology: Perspectives at the Millennium*, edited by C. Golden and G. Borgstede, pp. 259–285. Routledge, New York.

Yoffee, N. 1995 Political Economy in Early Mesopotamian States. *Annual Review of Anthropology* **24**:281–311.

2005 *Myths of the Archaic State: Evolution of the Earliest Cities, States, and Civilizations*. Cambridge University Press, Cambridge.

Young, A.M. 1994 *The Chocolate Tree: A Natural History of Cacao*. Smithsonian Institution Press, Washington and London.

Zvelebil, M. 2002a Demography and Dispersal of Early Farming: Populations at the Mesolithic-Neolithic Transition: Linguistic and Genetic Implications. In *Examining the Farming/Language Dispersal Hypothesis*, edited by P. Bellwood and C. Renfrew, pp. 379–394. McDonald Institute for Archaeological Research, University of Cambridge, Cambridge.

2002b Indo-Europeans Dispersals and the Agricultural Transition in Northern Europe: Culture, Genes, and Language. In *The Roots of Peoples and Languages of Northern Eurasia IV*, edited by K. Julku, pp. 318–343. Societas Historiae Fenno-Ugricae, Oulu, Finland.

2004 Who Were We 6000 Years Ago? In Search of Prehistoric Identities. In *Traces of Ancestry: Studies in Honor of Colin Renfrew*, edited by M. Jones, pp. 41–60. McDonald Institute for Archaeological Research, University of Cambridge, Cambridge.

Index